FIFIELD, Russell Hunt. **Americans in Southeast Asia; the roots of commitment.** T. Y. Crowell, 1973. 417p map tab bibl 72-7570. 10.00. ISBN 0-690-08692-X. C.I.P.

Reflects Fifield's rich background of study and research on post-World War II politics and diplomacy of Southeast Asia. Major emphasis is placed on the nine years, 1945–54. The latter year, he observes, marks the "watershed" of U.S. involvement. With ample facts and balanced judgment, he shows how five years of neglect were followed by a spurt of activity following the Communist takeover of China and its entry into the Korean War. The "watershed" was the signing of the Southeast Asia Treaty Organization with New Zealand, Australia, the Philippines, Thailand, Pakistan, France, and England. The object was to contain Communist China. The post-1954 period is treated less comprehensively — 200 pages for the 9 years, but only 86 for the next 18. Its compass is restricted to "two major themes in U.S. policy . . . : the Second Indochinese War and the emphasis on development." The former gets 60 pages which provide a succinct well-balanced account. The treatment of U.S. commitment in development in 18 pages is less than adequate. It under-reflects U.S. official involvement and overlooks completely current private investment, non-governmental technical assistance, and other American activities which are certainly part

Continued

FIFIELD

of the U.S. commitment. Although the volume leaves room for a more definitive study of the period since 1954, it does meet a vital need for undergraduates, the general reader, and the specialist. The documentation, bibliography, and index are all more than adequate.

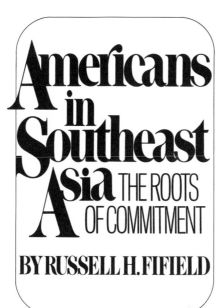

Americans in Southeast Asia

THE ROOTS OF COMMITMENT

BY RUSSELL H. FIFIELD

Americans in Southeast Asia

THE ROOTS OF COMMITMENT

BY RUSSELL H. FIFIELD

Thomas Y. Crowell Company
New York · Established 1834

Copyright acknowledgments appear on page 363

Designed by Jill Schwartz

MANUFACTURED IN THE UNITED STATES OF AMERICA

ISBN 0-690-08692-X

1 2 3 4 5 6 7 8 9 10

Fifield, Russell Hunt, date
    Americans in Southeast Asia.

    Bibliography: p.
1.   Asia, Southeastern—Foreign relations—United States.
2.   United States—Foreign relations—Asia, Southeastern.
I.   Title.

DS518.8.F47   327.73'059   72–7570

ISBN 0–690–08692–X

To
John K. Fairbank
For his contributions to the
advancement of Asian studies

CONTENTS

PREFACE

United States policy in Southeast Asia since the end of World War II has raised complex questions that confront the decision-makers of today and perplex the diplomatic historians of the period. What were the roots of American commitment? What was the watershed? What was the aftermath? What relevance does the past have for the present? In the realm of speculation, were there lost opportunities in Washington? What have been the responses of Southeast Asians to U.S. policy?

Although the involvement of the United States in Southeast Asia is relatively brief and Americans do not have the advantage of perspective based on long years of experience it is possible to fix landmarks and identify trends along the way. Only forty-three years removed the arrival of U.S. forces in the Philippines during the Spanish-American War from the outbreak of the Pacific War in 1941, and only thirteen years separated Pearl Harbor from the Manila Treaty of 1954. If we continue to set these critical points in portions of time—to "periodize"—eleven years later came the Second Indochinese War. In the brief period of twenty years, 1945–65, the United States moved from relative disengagement with an emphasis on decolonization in Southeast Asia to major engagement with a stress on international security. The roots of commitment, it can be argued, ended with the watershed of 1954.

For the student there is a real dividend in the process of analyzing events over a period of years and trying to distinguish the important trends from the inconsequential and the constants from the variables. A discerned pattern of events can give more meaning to the past and possibly more hope for the future.

The U.S. role in Southeast Asia over the years cannot be isolated from major forces and developments in the international system at the global level. They exert profound influence, especially in a strategic and transitional region of the world. By his fifteenth birthday a child born in Southeast Asia in 1939 would have lived through the disintegration of European colonial empires, the rise and fall of Japan's Greater East Asia, the emergence of numerous independent states, the Communist victory in mainland China, the First Indochinese War, and the growing involvement of the United States in the affairs of his part of the globe.

In this book, Southeast Asia is defined to include the region from Burma to the Philippines and Indonesia. Mainland Southeast Asia embraces Burma, Thailand, Cambodia, Laos, and divided Vietnam. Insular Southeast Asia covers Malaysia, Singapore, the Philippines, Indonesia, Portuguese Timor, and Brunei. The widespread use of the term is relatively new but the Southeast Asia Command of Admiral Lord Louis Mountbatten, the subsequent development of area programs in several universities, and the regional activities of Southeast Asians themselves have helped to establish the concept of Southeast Asia. Except when employed in a historical context, East Asia and, if appropriate, the Pacific are used instead of the obsolete expression Far East. And the names of cities like Kompong Som (Sihanoukville) or large geographical areas like West Irian in Indonesia, as of the date of the preface, are similarly given.

Particularly important is the terminology—the Second Indochinese War. Anthony Eden (the Earl of Avon), Bernard B. Fall, and Joseph Buttinger even before the overthrow of Norodom Sihanouk approached this usage in their writings. The First Indochinese War, 1946–54, was fought by Ho Chi Minh essentially against the French, and the Second Indochinese War, dating from 1965, was waged by Ho Chi Minh and his successors largely against the Americans and South Vietnamese.

The title of this book is derived from a classic work by Tyler Dennett first published in 1922—*Americans in Eastern Asia: A Critical Study of the Policy of the United States with Reference to China, Japan and Korea in the 19th Century*. Quite fittingly Dennett had relatively little to write about Southeast Asia although he did not ignore the region. The title *Americans in Southeast Asia: The Roots of Commitment* reflects a relatively new and vivid phase in the diplomatic history of the United States.

I have acquired information from interviews and correspondence over an extended period of time, from direct observation in Southeast Asia off and on for over twenty years, and from available primary and extensive secondary documentation. Altogether seventeen volumes of Pentagon Papers (Government Printing Office, Senator Gravel, and *The New York Times* editions) have been used. Many personal viewpoints expressed by Americans are woven into the fabric of the study. Presidents Truman and Eisenhower answered one specific question. In interviews and correspondence, I have sought and been able to reach almost all of the assistant secretaries of state for East Asian and Pacific Affairs of the United States or their equivalent since 1945 and at least three fourths of the American ambassadors serving in Southeast Asia since then. Particular emphasis has been placed on the viewpoints of Americans both in and out of Washington in various walks of life who have had long experience with the region. Many professors have also contributed to my understanding while a substantial number of foreign leaders in Europe, Asia, and Australia over the years have given their viewpoints in correspondence or interviews.

I would like to express my deep appreciation to all those who helped in the research and to the reviewers of the manuscript who helped give it direction. Some of my colleagues and all of my graduate students suffered in some way while this book was being written. Robert L. Youngblood and Ronald K. Edgerton worked diligently checking the data, and Donna Park, Shirley S. Cielinski, and Judith Kormos proved capable of reading the author's calligraphy and producing a typewritten manuscript.

The Twentieth Century Fund generously aided in financing research for this work. Travel in Southeast Asia was facilitated at an earlier time by The University of Michigan's Horace H. Rackham School of Graduate Studies.

Charts 1 and 4 in chapter 6 are taken from Admiral U. S. G. Sharp and General W. C. Westmoreland, *Report on the War in Vietnam (As of 30 June 1968),* Government Printing Office, Washington, Released 1969, pp. 197 and III. Chart 2 is from the Directorate for Information Operations, Department of Defense, March 22, 1972, and Chart 3 from the *Report to the Ambassador* from the Director of the United States Agency for International Development, Vietnam, 1970, Submitted January 1, 1971, p. 4. The map of Southeast Asia is adapted from my earlier book entitled *Southeast Asia in United States Policy*, published by Praeger for the Council on Foreign Relations in 1963, pp. 12–13. Permissions to quote are cited before the bibliography.

R. H. F.

Readfield Depot, Maine
September 1972

From *Southeast Asia in United States Policy* by Russell H. Fifield.
Published 1963 by Praeger Publishers, New York, for Council on
Foreign Relations. Reprinted by permission.

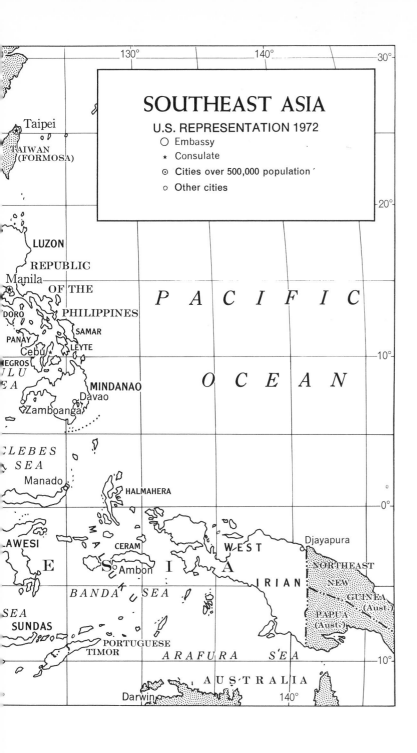

SOUTHEAST ASIA

U.S. REPRESENTATION 1972

○ Embassy
★ Consulate
⊙ Cities over 500,000 population
○ Other cities

Taipei
TAIWAN
(FORMOSA)

LUZON

REPUBLIC
Manila
OF THE
DORO
PHILIPPINES
PANAY
SAMAR
Cebu
LEYTE
NEGROS
MINDANAO
JLU
Davao
EA
Zamboanga

PACIFIC

OCEAN

CLEBES
SEA
Manado
HALMAHERA

AWESI
CERAM
WEST
Djayapura
E
S
Ambon
I
A
NORTHEAST
IRIAN
NEW
BANDA
SEA
GUINEA
(Aust.)
SEA
PAPUA
SUNDAS
(Aust.)
PORTUGUESE
TIMOR
ARAFURA
SEA

AUSTRALIA
Darwin
140°

| THE EARLY PERIOD

At the end of World War II the United States faced a Southeast Asia whose future was certain to be influenced by the events of the global conflict. A new international system was emerging but no one could be sure of its exact contours or of its durability. In Southeast Asia as a whole, Americans in the decades before Pearl Harbor—traders, missionaries, and diplomats—were not numerous and their role was generally limited.

The basic antecedents for U.S. policy in the region were first, the significant Philippine experience; second, the course of quiet relations with Thailand, the only independent country of Southeast Asia, and with the chief European colonial powers of Great Britain, France, and the Netherlands; and finally, in a category by itself, the climactic but relatively brief Japanese interlude. American blueprints for the future of Southeast Asia were considered during the Pacific War but they were influenced by the vicissitudes of the conflict and reflected different estimates of the postwar situation. Significantly President Franklin D. Roosevelt reserved for himself the question of French Indochina.

The purpose of Part One is to consider the antecedents of American policy as a prologue to the era that followed World War II. It would be hard to define any overall U.S. policy during the prewar decades. In fact, the area at the time was simply another geographical expression devoid of its present political significance. Washington, neither in its personnel and organization at home nor in its total representation overseas, gave Southeast Asia much emphasis.

Colonialism with its political, economic, social, and psychological imprint was long dominant in the area, first under Western sovereignties and then under Japanese auspices. Even Thailand and to a greater extent the Commonwealth of the Philippines could not escape the colonial impact. The blueprints of the United States for peace after the defeat of Japan quite naturally were concerned with colonial problems.

Two of America's three wars in Southeast Asia, it should be noted, were fought before V-J Day, 1945. The Spanish-American War and the Pacific War were both formally declared and both waged until Washington achieved a victory. In these respects they did not establish precedents for the future in East Asia.

1 ANTECEDENTS FOR AMERICAN POLICY (TO THE PACIFIC WAR)

THE PHILIPPINE EXPERIENCE

As a colonial power in Southeast Asia, the United States was a reluctant sovereign.[1] The Senate, in 1899, barely approved by the required two thirds vote the Treaty of Paris with Spain, which included the outright acquisition of the Philippines, Puerto Rico, and Guam. It was also necessary a few days later for the Vice-President to exercise his constitutional right to cast a deciding vote, thus defeating a resolution calling for the independence of the Philippines at some future date. In 1916 the Clarke amendment providing for the independence of the archipelago in two to four years passed the Senate and barely failed in the House of Representatives. In 1924, the Fairfield bill, calling for independence in twenty years, made progress on Capitol Hill but still failed to pass.

Although Philippine leaders like Manuel Quezon and Sergio Osmeña asked for "immediate, absolute, and complete independence," they were well aware of the pitfalls of premature freedom. Public statements and private viewpoints were often contradictory. On the one hand, Quezon exclaimed in 1926 that he preferred "a government run like hell by Filipinos to one run like heaven by Americans"[2] while on the other, he quietly helped to sabotage the Fairfield bill and at various times considered dominion or comparable status. The independence issue provided the cement of the Nacionalista Party which dominated the politics of the archipelago until the Japanese occupation. Philippine-American relations reached their low point almost at their very beginning in the revolution against the United States from 1899 to 1902. From then, Philippine nationalism was essentially channeled by its leaders, more often than not in response to basically enlightened U.S. colonial policy, toward cooperation between Washington and Manila.

The American Impact. "Damn the Americans. Why don't they tyrannize us more?"[3] These reported words of Quezon are indicative of the U.S. impact on the islands after the suppression of Emilio Aguinaldo's Philippine Republic. In retrospect, the American imprint on the archipelago during the relatively brief colonial rule is pronounced but cannot be isolated from the impact of centuries of Spanish rule or even from that of the short interlude of the Japanese occupation. The American community itself was never large—8,700 in 1939—and unlike the Spanish, the Americans seldom married Filipinos.

The United States introduced self-government in the archipelago, at first cautiously, then boldly. After local and provincial elections were held, a National Assembly was elected in 1907. Nine years later the appointed Philippine Commission was replaced by an elective Philippine Senate, thus giving the Filipinos full control of the legislative branch of government. Under Francis Burton Harrison, President Woodrow Wilson's governor general from 1913 to 1921, "Filipinization" of the civil service occurred at a rapid pace and a Philippine cabinet took over much of the direction of the country.[4] Although Governor General Leonard Wood, a Republican who served from 1921 to 1927, precipitated a cabinet crisis by restricting the role of the Filipinos, his high standards of honesty and efficiency helped prepare the people for eventual independence.

Popular education is one of the basic aspects of the United States heritage. In many respects the origins of the Peace Corps are found in the role of the American teachers in the Philippines.[5] Some of them were veterans of the wars against the Spanish and Filipinos around the turn of the century, soldiers who were detailed to teaching in the archipelago, while others, both men and then women, later took the long voyage across the Pacific from the United States. The work of the "Thomasites" and subsequent "Bewley's Beauties," "Bordner's Birds," and the "Boilermakers" is a part of the American heritage in the Philippines. Mass, free, secular education in the barrios and cities of the islands led to a marked increase in literacy—from 20 per cent of the population in 1899 to 50 per cent in 1935. A free press flourished in the country.

Health services received major American attention; sanitation had been neglected under the Spanish regime. A public health service was instituted by the Americans, and campaigns were waged against smallpox and cholera. The population of the islands doubled in only twenty years, a tribute in large measure to the American effort. Significantly the Philippine budget for health and education in terms of the proportion of total expenses surpassed in 1931 by almost three times that of the Netherlands East Indies, and was higher than that of French Indochina or the British Federated Malay States.

Although Washington developed a modern civil service, it was soon run mainly by Filipinos since the insular government was considered temporary. Attention was certainly given public works but probably not to the extent found in other dependencies of Southeast Asia. The United States separated church and state in the Philippines and revised the legal system inherited from Spain.

In marked contrast to the stress on self-rule and eventual sovereignty, American policy was in large measure conducive to the economic dependence of the islands. The Underwood Tariff in 1913 provided for reciprocal free trade, which stimulated the production and export of products like sugar, hemp, and coconut oil to the American market. This weakened the development of native manufacturing and increased the imports of consumer goods from the United States. By 1930, the year that Senate hearings in Washington led to the report of the Hawes-Cutting bill on independence, 79 per cent of the exports from the Philippines went to the United States and 63 per cent of Philippine imports came from the metropolitan power. An uneven and unbalanced economy was stimulated.

At the same time the United States, it should be noted, tried to encourage self-reliance. It was difficult under U.S. legislation relating to corporations and land for foreign capital, whether or not American, to create cartels or develop large plantations on the islands. In a significant policy Washington prevented the mass importation of Chinese coolies. As a general rule, private initiative and enterprise were encouraged.

During the colonial period the United States did not effect a major land reform for the *tao* or peasant apart from the purchase for the public domain of the valuable estates of the Catholic friars. There was no concerted attack on poverty in the rural or urban Philippines. If a land reform program in the islands comparable to that in Japan during the American occupation had been carried out—the contrast between U.S. policy on agrarian reform in the two countries is startling—the subsequent history of the Philippines would have been quite different. This omission in American policy may be one of the most significant aspects of U.S. rule in the islands.

It is ironic that the Philippines proved indefensible under the American flag, except for the short period of liberation from the Japanese, but is now well defended by the United States. In 1926, for instance, one third of the American navy was based in the Pacific; the Asiatic Fleet was small, chiefly composed of destroyers and submarines; no major naval base existed in the Philippines; and about 5,000 American ground troops were stationed there. The United States during the colonial period did not effectively build up the capacity of the Filipinos for self-defense. The Scouts constituted a regular army of only 7,000 and the Constabulary, a national police of 6,000. In contrast to other colonial powers in Southeast Asia, the United States, not the local government, bore all the military expenses. Theodore Roosevelt, changing his mind as early as 1907, called the Philippines "our heel of Achilles" and urged its independence. The Washington disarmament conference of 1921–22, producing a settlement which limited naval construction and restricted fortifications in the Pacific, left the Philippines vulnerable. As Japanese power and ambition grew, American and Philippine leaders showed greater concern over the defense of the islands, but no effective steps were taken to change the balance of power in the Western Pacific.

Despite suggestions that would have altered the territorial integrity of the Philippines, Washington continued to think in terms of the archipelago as a whole. The Moslems of Mindanao and Sulu and the pagan peoples of northern Luzon presented special problems of pacification and integration. They came to prefer American rule to that of the Christian Filipino. Nevertheless, the Bacon bill of 1926, which provided for the U.S. retention of Mindanao and Sulu when the Philippines received independence, made no headway and Secretary of War Patrick J. Hurley considered only briefly in late 1931 an independence proposal that would except the Mountain Province, Sulu, and Mindanao. When independence came to the Philippines there were no Netherlands New Guineas to impair relationships between the former metropolitan and colonial countries.

The search of the modern Filipino for a distinct self-identity has evolved from the imposition of Hispanic and American culture upon his Malay background. What is the nature of his culture? José Rizal, who was executed by the Spanish in 1896 and who subsequently became the national hero of the Philippines, was concerned with the cultural integration of his people as a nation. The synthesis of Malay and Spanish culture was further altered after his death by the American impact. Many Filipinos believe the most permanent aspect of the Spanish heritage may be the Roman Catholicism of about 80 per cent of the people. In contrast, they argue that the most permanent aspect of the American influence may be materialism, an outlook on life they admit is hard to define but is abundantly in evidence.

The Road to Independence. A combination of events speeded the establishment of a timetable for the achievement of sovereignty. Although the Jones Act of 1916 had promised independence no date was set, and in 1919 the first mission from Manila to Washington was not successful. Philippine nationalism, however, continued to exist and exert pressure for independence. The Great Depression beginning in 1929 produced pressure groups in the United States who wanted to sever economic ties with the Philippines. The Japanese invasion of Manchuria in September 1931 strengthened the conviction of many Americans that the United States should disengage entirely from the Western Pacific.

In December 1931 a Philippine legislative mission led by Sergio Osmeña and Manuel Roxas left Manila for Washington where Congress during a lame duck session late the following year passed the Hare-Hawes-Cutting bill for Philippine independence. President Herbert Hoover vetoed it in January 1933, but Congress quickly overrode him. Quezon came to oppose the measure on grounds of inadequacy while Osmeña and Roxas backed it as the best possible. Actually Quezon was more concerned over the political future of his two rivals than over the Hare-Hawes-Cutting Act. Through adroit political manipulation he removed Roxas as speaker of the House of Representatives and Osmeña as vice-president of the Senate, caused the legislature to reject the Hare-Hawes-Cutting Act, and then headed himself a new independence mission to Washington. In March 1934 Congress approved the Tydings-McDuffie bill, essentially identical to the previous independence act except that it did not provide for U.S. army bases. President Franklin D. Roosevelt signed it, and in May, with the blessing of Quezon as well as of Osmeña and Roxas the Philippine legislature accepted it.

The arguments in 1899 about the annexation of the Philippines and in the early 1930s about independence bear comparison, because they highlight major issues. In the spirited and acrimonious debate in the Senate in 1899 the Republicans, except for a minority of New England senators, backed President William McKinley in his call for annexation. In general the Democrats and the Populists opposed the Treaty of Paris but the support of William Jennings Bryan, the national leader of the Democratic Party, was a key factor in its approval. *Imperialism* was the emotional word of the day with the imperialists (usually Republicans) battling the anti-imperialists (usually Democrats).[6] Imperialists talked in terms of strategic gains, of national prestige, and of other powers taking over the Philippines if the United States failed to act, as well as of economic advantage and of the civilizing mission of America. Anti-imperialists stressed that the acquisition of overseas territory inhabited by people of an alien culture without democratic institutions was a torpedo to the isolationist policy of the United States, a violation of the American principles of self-government, and an infringement on the Monroe Doctrine.

The opposition in the early 1930s to quick independence was best expressed by President Hoover in his veto message of the Hare-Hawes-Cutting bill. Although Hoover was personally opposed to colonies, he indicated in his message that the Philippines should acquire independence only after a transition period of fifteen years as a minimum characterized by graduated autonomy and concluded by a plebiscite. He considered the legislation before him a threat to freedom for both Americans and Filipinos. The advocates of quick Philippine independence amid the Great Depression were pressure groups in the United States opposed to the agricultural imports of sugar, cordage, and coconut oil from the archipelago and opposed to the immigration of Filipinos to the United States on economic and social grounds. In another area of contention, some Americans argued no Japanese threat to the Philippines existed; and some asserted, even if it did, the U.S. policy should be to withdraw to Hawaii. But basic to the argument in the United States for quick independence was the bipartisan opposition to colonialism.

The Philippine-American war, in the wake of the defeat of Spain in 1898, is relevant partly because it aroused opposition, often highly emotional and vocal, in the United States. Harvard's award of an honorary LL.D. to President McKinley was probably a casualty of the dissent; opposition on the Board of Overseers was sufficient to cause the President to omit Cambridge from his June travel plans. McKinley was damned on moral grounds for the killing of Filipino guerrillas and the suppression of Aguinaldo's republic; on legal grounds for waging war without approval by Congress; and on racial and political grounds because white Americans were denying brown Filipinos self-government. Echoes of some of the arguments in another Southeast Asian context were to be heard in America in the late 1960s and early 1970s.

When the timetable for Philippine independence was established by the Tydings-McDuffie Act of 1934 a watershed was reached in the history of Southeast Asia. The significance of the Tydings-McDuffie Act was not immediately recognized either in the region or on the world stage. It was generally viewed as an isolated act of decolonization, not as a precedent. The vast British, French, and Dutch empires appeared well entrenched while the Japanese had just enlarged their empire in Asia, the Italians were preparing to expand their own in Africa, and the Germans were looking toward *Lebensraum* in Europe.

As the Philippines progressed along the road to independence—a constitutional convention, national elections under the new constitution, and the inauguration of the Commonwealth on November 15, 1935, as a prelude to independence on July 4, 1946—European response was limited but generally critical. There were apprehensions in London, Paris, and The Hague about the ambitions of Japan and concern over the impact of Philippine developments on Asian nationalism. Winston Churchill, as early as December 1932, urged the United States to keep the Philippines and stressed the aspects of obligation to its people and of international responsibility.[7] Moscow considered the projected independence a fraud perpetrated by the Americans against the Filipinos.

On the other hand, the Japanese welcomed the planned termination of American sovereignty in the islands, and tried on occasion to strengthen the stature of the president of the Commonwealth and weaken that of the American high commissioner. Indonesian nationalists were especially pleased with the progress of the Philippines toward sovereignty. Quezon visited the Netherlands East Indies in September 1934 and counseled the nationalists on the wisdom of talking their way to independence. The Chinese in Nanking were sympathetic to the aspirations of the Filipinos but in view of Japanese expansionism did not like the timing. As for the overseas Chinese in the Philippines, they had been generally protected by the Americans and were fearful of Philippine discrimination.

The Tydings-McDuffie Act of 1934 symbolized the determination of the United States to leave Southeast Asia. After the Commonwealth period the links with the Philippines would, basically, be those between two sovereign states. American naval bases in the islands would be subject to negotiations with the acquisition of sovereignty, but if the Pacific War had not intervened, there might not have been any bases. No defense pact, it should be added, was planned between the two countries. A 100 per cent tariff would apply after independence, and the Tydings-Kocialkowski Act of August 1939 accomplished very little with the great problems of economic readjustment in the islands. On the international stage, even during the Commonwealth period before independence, Quezon played the role of a chief executive; his trip around the world in 1936–37 raised questions of precedence, flags, and salutes.

The Japanese Threat. The expected course of Philippine-American relations was drastically altered by Japanese expansionism. In the complex relationships between Tokyo and Washington the Philippines became a hostage in the Western Pacific. After Japan emerged as a great power following the Russo-Japanese War of 1904–05 the interests of the Western powers in the Far East (as it was then widely called) were greatly affected and readjustments were necessary. Japan recognized America's position in the Philippines in the Taft-Katsura and Root-Takahira agreements of 1905 and 1908. Winston Churchill, however, indicated in 1932 that U.S. withdrawal from the Philippines would increase the possibilities of war by helping to upset the balance of power in the Far East.

The Japanese had begun to enter the archipelago in numbers with the approval of the American colonial regime shortly after the United States acquired the islands. By 1931 they numbered 16,000, and the largest concentration was in Davao where they monopolized the abacá industry. They were also active in the lumber business and in deep-sea fishing. By the end of the decade 30,000 Japanese were living in the Philippines, investments had risen to over $32 million, and Tokyo's exports had increased to $13 million a year. Although political infiltration was significant among the Japanese minority it never made deep inroads among the Filipinos.

Before the inauguration of the Commonwealth, President Quezon made General Douglas MacArthur his military adviser and in June 1936 elevated him to the grand rank of Field Marshal. In the same month MacArthur in a report on the defense of the Philippines proposed the expenditure of $80 million over the ten-year period before independence for a small air force of hit-and-run light bombers, a small naval squadron of hit-and-run torpedo boats, a standing, semi-guerrilla army of 19,000, and a citizen reserve of 400,000. The Filipinos themselves would defend the Philippines. The previous March, the U.S. army and navy members of the Joint Planning Committee, Joint Board of the Army and Navy, had significantly disagreed on War Plan *Orange* which involved the defense of the Philippines in a war with Japan.[8] The army omitted from the plan provision for reinforcements to the islands while the navy favored an increase in army and naval forces for the period of the Commonwealth. Both expected the Japanese to conquer the Philippines once war broke out. In Manila, the implementation of MacArthur's defense plans for the islands was slow and difficult, for the Filipinos had practically no military tradition. Quezon himself, motivated by events in Europe, moved from full support to a reduction in financial assistance in the latter part of 1939.

Against this background Japan was rapidly augmenting its power and expanding its influence in East Asia and the Pacific. On July 7, 1937, the Marco Polo bridge incident led to the outbreak of full-scale undeclared war between the Chinese and Japanese, a conflict that would not end until the conclusion of World War II in August 1945. Relations between Japan and the United States continued to deteriorate over China policy. Washington's opposition to Tokyo's pressure on the French in Indochina and the Dutch in the East Indies opened new areas of conflict. In July 1941, as tension escalated between Japan and the United States, Roosevelt appointed MacArthur as commanding general, United States Armed Forces in the Far East.

By the middle of the summer, Washington began to respond to Mac-Arthur's urging for a quick buildup in the Philippines. Continuing reinforcements in troops, ships, and planes enabled him in late November to get his mission expanded by his superiors to the defense of the entire Philippines. The Japanese, apprehensive over the American buildup, decided in the event of war to attack the archipelago at the outset.

Ten hours after the Nipponese assaulted Pearl Harbor on December 7 they bombed Clark Field in Luzon. On December 22 they landed their main forces at Lingayen Gulf; on January 2, 1942, they entered Manila; and on May 6 they received the surrender of "The Rock" or Corregidor. In the fighting the Filipinos had stood with the Americans, most of them willingly. During March MacArthur and Quezon, both critical of the U.S. sacrifice of the archipelago, reached Australia from Corregidor. In Japanese eyes the Commonwealth was dead; in American eyes it would rise again like the Phoenix and be transformd into the Republic of the Philippines.

Quezon was to head a government-in-exile in the United States until his death in August 1944, before the liberation of his country. But during his last days in the islands he proposed to President Roosevelt on February 8, 1942, from Corregidor, an armistice, immediate independence, and the neutralization of the Philippines. It was rejected on February 9 in a message drafted by Secretary of War Henry L. Stimson and signed by President Roosevelt. When Quezon received the reply he at first dictated his resignation, then reconsidered, and never again proposed surrender. Even if the United States had accepted Quezon's proposal, the Japanese would not have agreed, for they had their own plans for the future of the Philippines.

The neutralization of the islands was not a new proposal. The Hare-Hawes-Cutting Act of 1933 had requested the President upon the independence of the Philippines to undertake negotiations with foreign states for the purpose of making a treaty of perpetual neutralization. The Tydings-McDuffie Act of 1934 contained a similar provision. The Filipinos never revealed any sustained concern about the matter but it was occasionally discussed among them. Various Japanese reactions at different times indicated that Tokyo wavered on the subject. In discussions with Washington in the months before Pearl Harbor, Tokyo suggested as part of a general settlement a joint guarantee of the independence of the islands in exchange for American assurances of no discrimination in business and immigration against the Japanese in the archipelago. The United States indicated that neutralization was a subject that should await the independence of the islands in 1946.

The Philippines could probably not have avoided military involvement in World War II. With the outbreak of hostilities between Japan and the United States the stakes were maximum and no holds were barred. Even if Tokyo and Washington in the period of the Commonwealth had worked out a gentleman's agreement not to fight in the Philippines, Japan would probably not have dared bypass the islands in its drive toward the rest of Southeast Asia. The American military position in the Western Pacific was not strong in late 1941 and Japan was determined to drive the United States from East Asia.

In retrospect, American policy towards the Philippines during the 1930s was paradoxical. When President Hoover exclaimed: "How long must we keep the Islands in order to do our duty to them?" he reflected a basic viewpoint.[9] The fulfillment of duty, however, was subject to various interpretations and modified by selfish interests.[10] The United States had a legal and moral commitment to the defense of the Philippines until July 4, 1946; the threat of imperial Japan was real, not academic; but Washington did not take the military steps to support the commitment until it was too late. The administration of President Roosevelt was basically internationalist in outlook while Congress in the 1930s was strongly oriented toward isolationism. Roosevelt, for instance, wanted to make Guam a key naval base; Congress refused to provide funds for the project in early 1939. In the War and Navy Departments the army was eager to reduce the defense perimeter in the Pacific while the navy desired a greater offensive capability. The Roosevelt administration in prewar years was unwilling to advance the date for Philippine independence; the Congress was not willing to delay it. Subject to conflicting attitudes in Washington, the Commonwealth of the Philippines, even under a dynamic, popular, and powerful leader like Manuel Quezon, reaped the whirlwind.

RELATIONS WITH THAILAND

Apart from the Philippines, the only country in Southeast Asia with which the United States had direct relations during the period of Western colonization was Thailand.* Although the United States did not act to preserve Thai independence when Bangkok was pressured by the British from Burma and Malaya and by the French from Cambodia and Laos, it was the first foreign power to establish a legation in Thailand and the first to sign a treaty granting the kingdom judicial and fiscal autonomy. As in the Philippines, the United States was ahead of other powers.

Thai-American relations prior to Japan's attack on Pearl Harbor were generally cordial. They were marked by a minimum of controversy partly because they were not extensive and the U.S. impact was generally mar-

*The name Thailand is used in place of Siam, an older designation of the kingdom.

ginal. The earliest contacts were made by American merchants probably as a by-product of trade with Batavia in the Netherlands East Indies, Hong Kong in China, and later Singapore. Next were the Protestant missionaries who began to arrive in the 1830s. Although they did not succeed in making many converts from Theravada Buddhism they were very effective in education and public health and often served as advisers to the Thai monarchs. Last to appear in Thailand were American consular and diplomatic representatives, a small number of special missions preceding them. The impact of the traders, missionaries, and officials varied over the decades and was affected by events in Thailand and the world.[11]

Edmund Roberts negotiated in 1833 the first American treaty with the kingdom, making Thailand the first Asian nation with which Washington had a treaty relationship. On a special mission he was well received in Bangkok and made a good impression on the Thai. His commercial treaty was comparable to that of his British predecessor Henry Burney in 1826. In practice, however, the tonnage duties were too high, and in 1849 Joseph Balestier, consul at Singapore, was designated a special envoy to negotiate a new pact with Thailand. He did not succeed largely because he lost his temper in discussions.

Townsend Harris was later requested by Washington to seek treaty revision with Bangkok while en route to Japan as consul general. He was told to point out to the Thai the difference between American and British foreign policy. The United States had no territorial ambitions while Great Britain had recently fought Burma and was a close neighbor to Thailand. The treaty of 1856 between Washington and Bangkok reflected the terms of the treaty of 1855 between London and Bangkok. Once more the United States was able to reap benefits won by Great Britain in Thailand. Washington gained in the treaty the rights of extra-territoriality and acquired the benefits of fixed Thai tariffs. A U.S. consulate could be established and Americans could have religious freedom in the kingdom.

During the negotiations in 1856 the Thai, fearful of Great Britain, wanted an alliance with or even a protectorate under the United States. Harris reported that the Thai ministers "were most anxious to be taken under the protection of the United States. They plainly told me that if I would make a treaty of alliance they would give us all we could ask, even to a monopoly of the trade."[12] Townsend Harris gave the Thai no encouragement, and they had to wait until 1954 for an alliance with Washington. He was no Commodore Matthew C. Perry, who believed the United States should extend its "national friendship and protection" to Thailand, Cochin China, Cambodia, parts of Sumatra and Borneo, and other islands in the eastern archipelago. Indeed, in the words of Tyler Dennett, "Perry appears to have been the first American in official position to view not merely the commercial but also the political problems of Asia and the Pacific as a unity."[13]

Thai-American relations were enlivened on February 14, 1861, by an offer of King Mongkut to President James Buchanan to provide some elephants for the United States if Washington would furnish the transportation. President Abraham Lincoln judiciously replied on February 3, 1862, that "our political jurisdiction . . . does not reach a latitude so low as to favor the multiplication of the elephant."[14] Late in the next decade General Ulysses S. Grant, former President of the United States, visited Bangkok on a world tour and was received as a state guest by King Chulalongkorn. Grant urged the Thai to send students to America for higher education. In 1882 the United States raised its consulate in Bangkok to the status of a legation and two years later the first mission of Thai officials visited Washington.

The monarchs of Thailand came to employ foreign advisers from several countries as one way of maintaining the independence of the kingdom. It is significant that the advisers in the foreign office were Americans. From 1902 until 1949, except during World War II, Americans, often professors from the Harvard Law School, served as foreign advisers in Bangkok.[15] Their influence at times was considerable on the foreign policy of the kingdom and noticeable in official American attitudes toward the Thai.

Bangkok entered World War I in July 1917 as one of the Allied and Associated Powers. As a consequence, Thailand attended the Paris Peace Conference and became a member of the League of Nations. Bangkok, it should be stressed, was the only official voice from Southeast Asia in world councils.

Taking advantage of its role in World War I, Thailand stepped up its efforts to end the unequal treaties. President Woodrow Wilson was sympathetic at the Paris Peace Conference to Thai aspirations and wanted to take action, but, apart from the Central Powers being forced to relinquish their unequal treaty rights, the victorious allies took no concrete steps. In December 1920 Wilson carried out his pledge: the United States gave up extraterritoriality (with minor provision for Bangkok to improve further its legal codes) and restored tariff autonomy to Thailand (effective when all other treaty powers would take similar steps). Two years later a treaty of extradition was signed.

Francis B. Sayre, son-in-law of President Wilson and a professor at the Harvard Law School, served as foreign affairs adviser in Bangkok. He was asked by the Thai government toward the end of his term, in

1924, to undertake a mission in Europe to end the remaining unequal treaties. With the American pact of 1920 as a model, he successfully negotiated with France, Great Britain, the Netherlands, Italy, Spain, Portugal, Belgium, Denmark, Norway, and Sweden.[16] By March 1927 Thailand had virtually won fiscal and judicial autonomy from all the Western powers. In November 1937 the United States in a new treaty removed the minor provision on extraterritoriality of the 1920 pact. As other countries took comparable action, a humiliating period in Thai history came to a complete close.

After the Revolution of 1932 in which the absolute monarchy was ended, relations between Bangkok and Washington were minimal until World War II. There were relatively few U.S. citizens in the kingdom; missionary influence had greatly declined over the years; American advisers now had less impact than previously. Trade was not extensive; indeed, its two most significant periods came shortly before the Civil War and after World War II.

Nipponese Inroads. Japan's inroads in Southeast Asia introduced a new dimension in Thai politics and foreign policy. As far back as February 1933, Bangkok had been the only member of the League of Nations to abstain from the Assembly vote against Japan for its role in Manchuria. Washington observed with concern the growth of Japanese influence, politically, economically, and culturally, in Thailand. Tokyo's "mediation" in the hostilities between Bangkok and Vichy France of 1940–41 led to the cession of territory in Laos and Cambodia in May 1941 to Thailand and strengthened the hand of the Japanese. The United States consistently urged Bangkok not to alter the status quo by force, but to no avail. American export controls and airplane sequestration greatly irked the Thai.

Washington doubted if Bangkok would resist a Japanese invasion and questioned the ability of the allies to help Thailand in the event of one. Great Britain wanted to have the best possible defense position for the approaches to Malaya but did not desire to be the technical aggressor by moving into southern Thailand. The United States did not want to find itself defending a colonial aggressor in Southeast Asia. Under the circumstances Japan would have scored a diplomatic victory if it could have maneuvered Great Britain into military measures against Thailand.

Against this background President Roosevelt in July 1941 secretly suggested the neutralization of Thailand and Indochina.[17] Under the plan the United States, Japan, Great Britain, the Netherlands, and China would neutralize and guarantee Thailand and Indochina, giving them a status somewhat like that of Switzerland. If Japan withdrew all its forces from Indochina and promised no intervention in Thailand, Tokyo would be able to get raw materials from those areas. Significantly President Roosevelt did not inform the Thai of his effort. Great Britain supported the proposal but Japan was evasive. On August 6 and 7 both London and Washington publicly warned Tokyo not to move against Thailand. Roosevelt failed to deter or delay a Nipponese occupation of Southeast Asia through neutralization of two key areas, but he established precedents for some future day.

Meanwhile Thailand secretly sought a guarantee for its neutrality from the United States and Great Britain without the knowledge of Japan. On June 12, 1940, Bangkok had signed treaties of nonaggression with France and Great Britain and a treaty of general friendship and cooperation with Japan. With the buildup of Nipponese forces in southern Indochina in the summer of 1941, the Thai were eager for a more effective counterweight than the treaty of 1940 with Great Britain. The fall of France, it should be added, had prevented ratification of the nonaggression pact between Bangkok and Paris.

In the middle of July Prime Minister Pibul Songgram told the U.S. Minister that he wanted American aid in the cause of Thai independence, indicating he would look to his "friends," Washington and London, in this difficult period. Despite this appeal and subsequent ones and despite American desire to encourage Thai resistance to Japan the United States only assured Thailand that it would be placed in the same category as China for American aid if Japanese aggression occurred. By December 6, however, Washington was leaning toward a loan to Bangkok and the kingdom was clearly on the President's mind, but the next day Japan attacked Hawaii as well as Thailand. London took no steps that significantly strengthened the Thai capacity to fight Japan although the British had increased their naval and air forces at Singapore. After resisting the invaders for a few hours Bangkok agreed on December 8 to the peaceful passage of Japanese forces through Thai territory.

RELATIONS WITH
EUROPEAN COLONIAL POWERS

As all Southeast Asia except Thailand and the Philippines was a part of the colonial empires of Great Britain, France, the Netherlands, and Portugal, U.S. relations with the countries of the region were conducted with the metropolitan governments either in London, Paris, The Hague, and Lisbon or with the authorities of the colonial regimes in Southeast Asia.[18] Portugal's empire in the area having been reduced to Portuguese Timor, Washington had very little dealings with Lisbon on Southeast Asia.

Although the United States was opposed in principle to colonialism and looked forward to the eventual liberation of colonies, it made no effort before World War II to upset the status quo in colonial Southeast Asia except, of course, for its own decisions in the Philippines. A policy of deference to Great Britain, France, and the Netherlands was followed whenever their colonial empires in the region were concerned. The United States had no desire to interfere in the internal affairs of the European possessions or in the relations between them, while the European powers would have firmly resisted any U.S. attempt at interference. The policy of deference was the only feasible one given the attitudes of Washington and of London, Paris, and The Hague.

Early U.S. Experience. The United States only had a little experience in Southeast Asia before the Europeans consolidated their holdings, especially in the islands, or established their empires, particularly on the mainland. American trade with the pepper coast of Sumatra started shortly after 1790, and within thirty years American merchants had almost a monopoly. After the natives of Quallah Battoo on the northwest coast of Sumatra attacked the pepper ship "Friendship" of Salem in 1830, the U.S. frigate "Potomac" visited the coastal area and punished them. There was no United Nations Security Council to challenge the diplomacy of pepper! The American trade with Batavia on Java was important because of its bearing on the East Indies and because of its bearing on China and Japan. The United States, for instance, learned much about Japan in the early 1800s through various Dutch sources and through some Americans who sailed to Nagasaki in the employ of the Dutch. American trade with Batavia declined in the 1820s as a result of better trade regulations in Singapore. Nevertheless, Java remained significant in U.S. commerce with Canton in China, for the route from the Cape across the Indian Ocean ran through the Sunda Strait and the merchants needed supplies after the long voyage. Manila was another outpost of Canton for the American merchant. The Spanish placed no special obstacles to U.S. trade, which began in the 1790s but never reached significant dimensions. The United States concluded an "engagement" with Sulu for trade and the protection of citizens in 1842 and a "convention" with Borneo (Brunei) in 1850 for peace, friendship, and commerce.

Apart from Thailand, American relations with the other countries on mainland Southeast Asia in the precolonial period were sporadic and almost casual. The first Burmese diplomatic mission came to the United States in 1857; Eugenio Kincaid, an American missionary, financed by King Mindon, delivered to President Franklin Pierce a royal letter calling for friendship and trade. President James Buchanan sent a reply, dated

May 19, 1857, in which he pointedly noted that "as we have no interest, the promotion of which so far as can be foreseen, would render it necessary to desire that Your Majesty's sovereignty should be diminished or in any way put in jeopardy, we trust that peace and good will may be perpetual between us."[19] Since Burma had recently been defeated by Britain in 1852, the President's statement indirectly contrasted American and British policy. Burma would disappear, in fact, as a sovereign state as a consequence of the Third Anglo-Burmese War in 1885. Kincaid was only one of the American missionaries who went to Burma in the 1800s. During that century American trade was limited but it crested just before the Civil War.

In later years, Herbert Hoover as a young engineer was involved in the development of the Bawdwin lead and silver mines, and drillers from the United States were active in the creation of the oil industry.

Cochin China (now southern Vietnam) attracted for some time more interest in Washington. Captain John White, a Yankee trader, visited Saigon in 1820; he was probably the first American in Vietnam. Edmund Roberts, in 1832, attempted to negotiate a trade agreement. He contacted local officials on the coast but never got to the sovereign, for Roberts indicated he was not willing to perform the kowtow. He left for Thailand, but a few years later upon instructions from the United States, he made another attempt to parley with Cochin China. This effort also failed, largely due to his ill health, and he sailed to Macao where he died in 1836. Washington did not lose interest, for Joseph Balestier was instructed in 1849 to negotiate a treaty not only with Thailand but also with Cochin China, Borneo, and other East Indian areas.

In the 1880s the United States tried to mediate the conflict between France and China over Annam. France, who had taken over Cochin China in 1862 and 1867, was challenging China's claim to suzerainty over Annam. With war on the horizon, in 1883 the U.S. Minister to China, John Russell Young, took an active role in mediation efforts. China requested the good offices of the President of the United States; Washington indicated in July it was willing to assist if both France and China wanted its help; but France declined. Although fighting broke out in December, a similar Chinese request to Washington was made in July 1884 with the same results. In the Franco-Chinese War of 1884–85 the best the United States could do was to serve as a medium of communications on occasion between Paris and Peking.

In the late 1920s Saigon and the American Pacific Coast were linked by a regular steamship service, and American commerce expanded in Indochina. In addition to traders, a few tourists from the United States visited the area, encouraged by travel brochures. In the 1930s Washington maintained for all Indochina only a consul and a vice-consul in Saigon.

European colonialism reached its zenith in Southeast Asia when Malaya, a part of Borneo, and Burma came under the rule of London (the governor of the Straits Settlements was high commissioner for the Malay States and Brunei and agent for Sarawak and North Borneo, while Burma had its own governor); when Annam with Cochin China and Tonkin, Cambodia, and Laos fell under the domination of Paris (the governor general of Indochina represented the federalization of the colonial territories); and when the East Indies were consolidated under the aegis of The Hague (the governor general of the Netherlands East Indies was the symbol of the territorial unity of the archipelago). The Philippines, of course, for several centuries was under a Spanish governor general and then for a short period was under an American. The imperial facade appeared more durable than subsequent events would indicate.

Southeast Asia as largely colonial territory did not escape involvement in the global conflicts of the first half of the twentieth century. In World War I all the region except the Netherlands East Indies was eventually belligerent territory. In 1914 Great Britain and France were at war with Germany; they were followed by Portugal, the United States, and Thailand. Yet the war was not fought on the soil of Southeast Asia and the people of the area escaped destruction. A large number of Vietnamese, however, went to France where they were exposed to French values and culture. Upon returning home, their ideas influenced the future of Indochina. Apart from the Thai claims at the Paris Peace Conference, Southeast Asia was not a subject of discussion by the Allied and Associated Powers. Ho Chi Minh was unsuccessful in his efforts to secure freedom in stages for his people. His appeal, for instance, to Secretary of State Robert Lansing was unheeded. The status of none of the colonial dependencies was altered by World War I and the Paris Peace Conference.

Southeast Asia and Pearl Harbor. In contrast to its role in World War I, the region was very much involved in the origins and development of the Asian phase of World War II. As Japan threatened the European dependencies in Southeast Asia before Pearl Harbor, the Dutch, British, and French under varying circumstances tried to resist the pressure. Japan's interests in the Netherlands East Indies were primarily economic and in French Indochina, largely military. In Burma Tokyo was eager for the British to close the Burma Road. The United States was involved in the moves and countermoves bearing on Japan and the European dependencies in Southeast Asia.

On April 15, 1940, before Hitler's invasion of the Netherlands, Japan indicated to The Hague that it would be deeply concerned if the European war had repercussions for the status quo of the East Indies. The United States interpreted the Japanese statement as a warning that Tokyo, in the event of the German invasion of the Netherlands, might well seek a special position in the Netherlands East Indies or even the protective custody of the islands. Secretary of State Cordell Hull asserted on April 17 that any change in the status quo of the archipelago except by "peaceful processes would be prejudicial" to the peace, stability, and security not only of the East Indies but also of the entire Pacific.[20] The Hague stressed it would refuse an offer of protection from any country and would resist intervention from any source.

After the invasion and conquest of the Netherlands in May 1940 by Nazi Germany Japan began to stress its grievances against the Dutch in the Netherlands East Indies. Tokyo wanted more exports of key raw materials from the islands, especially supplies of petroleum; more opportunities for Japanese enterprise; and the freedom of its nationals to enter the East Indies. In 1940 and 1941 economic negotiations between the Japanese and Dutch in Batavia did not go well, and on July 25, 1941, the Japanese foreign minister indicated to the American Ambassador in Tokyo the "unsatisfactory result" of the discussions. The Dutch were convinced if they agreed to all the Nipponese requests the East Indies would become a Japanese colony while Tokyo believed the Dutch put harsh obstacles to Japanese trade, enterprise, and immigrants.

Washington, which was sympathetic to the Dutch, noted that in 1937 only 11.6 per cent by value of the trade with the Netherlands East Indies was with Japan while 15.8 per cent was with the United States. President Roosevelt indicated publicly on July 24 that he had allowed petroleum shipments from the United States to Japan despite strong domestic opposition in order to prevent the Japanese from probably trying to get supplies of petroleum by force in the Netherlands East Indies. On the same day he told the Japanese Ambassador that if Tokyo forcefully tried to get petroleum shipments from the East Indies the Dutch would fight; they would be supported by the British and war would ensue with Japan against the Netherlands and Great Britain. As a result of "our own policy of assisting Great Britain," the President noted, "an exceedingly serious situation would immediately result."[21] Roosevelt's complete oil embargo on Japan and freezing of its assets in America had clear-cut implications for the Netherlands East Indies.

After the fall of France in 1940, Tokyo put considerable pressure on London to close the Burma Road. The Japanese wanted to shut all land transportation avenues from Southeast Asia to Chiang Kai-shek in Chungking. Great Britain announced on July 17 it would close the

Burma Road, as of the next day, for three months to arms, gasoline, trucks, and railroad materials for Free China. On July 16 Hull announced the United States had a "legitimate interest" in keeping "arteries of commerce" open in the entire world. Washington, though aware of world realities, was not sympathetic to the British step. It sought to maintain a separate and independent policy. The Burma Road, over the opposition of Japan, was reopened October 18.

The United States under President Roosevelt was greatly concerned over Japanese military inroads in Indochina. Washington, however, did relatively little to stop them;[22] protests not backed by force were generally ineffective. In June 1940, shortly before the French armistice with Germany, U.S. Undersecretary of State Sumner Welles indicated to the French Ambassador in Washington that should Japan attack Indochina the American government would not militarily oppose the act.[23] Secretary Hull asserted on September 16 that U.S. policy in Southeast Asia was to encourage Indochina and other countries threatened by Japan to delay, to parley, and to withstand to the last moment Tokyo's demands. He did not believe the Nipponese would presently dare to chance a military attack.

On June 19, after the French government had fled Paris and was on its knees, Japan sent an ultimatum to General Georges Catroux, Governor General of Indochina, directed in effect toward joint control of the Tonkinese-Chinese border in the interests of Tokyo. The Japanese were especially concerned over a railroad, important in carrying supplies to Free China, which ran from Haiphong to Kunming in Yunnan. Before giving his approval, Catroux tried unsuccessfully to get American or British aid. The United States, in fact, had forbidden the delivery of modern antiaircraft artillery and modern fighter aircraft to Indochina. And Great Britain, in June 1939 in Anglo-French talks, had indicated it could not send any reinforcements from Malaya. Since Catroux gave in to the Japanese demands without instructions from the French government, he was relieved of his post on June 25 and subsequently replaced by Admiral Jean Decoux.

After the Japanese presented further demands on August 2 the Admiral asked them to negotiate with the Vichy government. A few days before Vichy's accord with Tokyo on August 30, Welles told the French Ambassador the United States was not able to aid Indochina but understood the difficulties facing France and could not reproach it if certain military facilities were granted to Japan. The Vichy-Tokyo agreement of August 30 involved French acceptance of Tokyo's preëminent position in East Asia and Japanese recognition of French sovereignty over Indochina. It also gave Japan in principle certain military rights in Tonkin, though the details of the accord had to be worked out on the spot. The military discussions between the French commander in Tonkin and the Japanese began on September 5 but the negotiations dragged on for a while. On September 15 the French made a request to the American naval commander in the Philippines for a demonstration by Washington in the Gulf of Tonkin. The United States took no military action, and the Japanese continued their military pressure. According to the agreement of September 22 Tokyo could use three airfields in Tonkin; a maximum of 25,000 Japanese at one time could have transit rights in Indochina; and the occupation force in Tonkin was set at 6,000. Four days later Washington stopped the export of scrap iron and steel to Nippon. Japan signed a treaty of alliance with Germany and Italy on September 27 bringing into formal existence the Rome-Berlin-Tokyo axis.

Japan stepped up its pressure on Indochina in 1941, this time especially for airfields in Cochin China. On July 19, when Vichy was about to yield, Admiral William D. Leahy, the American Ambassador, orally gave a message from Roosevelt to Marshal Henri Pétain urging that the decision be delayed as long as possible. Washington believed Vichy would have to yield to Tokyo but delay was in American interests. There was vigorous internal debate among FDR's advisers on the degree of U.S. pressure on Japan. On July 24 Roosevelt specifically proposed to the Japanese Ambassador the neutralization of Indochina.[24] The freezing of Nipponese assets in the United States on July 26 and the stopping of all petroleum exports to Japan were ordered before a Nipponese reply. The Tokyo-Vichy agreement of July 29 provided for the joint Franco-Japanese defense of Indochina and gave Japan de facto control of all key port facilities and airfields in the dependency. The United States viewed the agreement as a threat to the Philippines and Thailand, to "vital trade routes," and to general American interests in East Asia.

In the final negotiations between Washington and Tokyo before Pearl Harbor, Indochina was once more a subject of concern. On November 26 Hull gave Japan an outline of a proposed basis of agreement which included negotiations for an accord among the United States, Japan, the Netherlands, China, Great Britain, and Thailand to respect the territorial integrity of French Indochina and to give each of the participants equal treatment in commerce there. Tokyo would withdraw all military and police forces. In President Roosevelt's personal appeal to the Emperor of Japan on December 6, as war seemed inevitable, the United States criticized Japanese troop movements in Indochina and suggested the Nipponese evacuation of the territory for a nonaggression assurance. On December 7, the day of Pearl Harbor, Tokyo, in notifying Washington of its termination of negotiations, condemned the U.S. proposal on Indochina and pointedly noted the absence of France from it.

Japan's expansion in Southeast Asia was a major development on the road to war with the United States. Pearl Harbor was only an occasion; its objective was to protect Tokyo's move south. American economic sanctions along with those of the Dutch and British really hurt Japan. If they could not be raised, the alternatives for Tokyo were to relinquish its New Order in Greater East Asia or to fight the Americans, British, and Dutch. Such were the stakes! Washington was keenly aware of the dilemma facing Tokyo—thanks to "Magic" or code breaking—but President Roosevelt was not willing to compromise. Herbert Feis has well pointed out FDR's final ordeal:

> During the last few days of somber waiting the President faced three entwined questions. First: should he promise the British and Dutch that the United States would join them if Japanese forces attacked their territories or crossed certain bounds? Second: should he so warn Japan—openly or secretly? Third: should he inform Congress about the fast-coming crisis and the action he proposed to take?
> The President, at one time or another, was on the point of doing each or all of these things. After listening, to Hull most especially, he did none of them. . . . It was best, he concluded, to wait until the event itself dramatized the danger and marked the response.[25]

Despite the controversy surrounding the underlying causes of the war between the United States and Japan and the circumstances of the attack on Pearl Harbor, certain facts stand out. It seems likely that China, not Southeast Asia, was the basic area of contention; that Ambassador Joseph C. Grew's "green light" cable of September 12, 1940, to Washington urging support for the British Empire and preservation of the status quo in the Pacific with a "show of force" was not seminal at the time; and that the U.S. response to Japanese inroads in Indochina in 1940–41 was far more related to overall American-Japanese relations in the world context and to Southeast Asia as a whole than to any intrinsic value of Indochina to the United States.

A Look Around. At the outbreak of the Pacific War, Washington's representation in the region was not extensive. In the Philippines there was an office of the high commissioner as well as a consulate in Manila; in Thailand, a legation in Bangkok; in French Indochina representation was modest, a consulate in Saigon; in the Netherlands East Indies there were a consulate general in Batavia and consulates in Medan and Surabaya; in British territories, a consulate general in Rangoon, Burma, another in Singapore, and a consulate in Penang. In Washington the Division of Far Eastern Affairs of the Department of State focused on the independent countries of Thailand, Japan, and China. It also worked with the Office of Philippine Affairs. The Division of European Affairs embraced the European territories and possessions in the Far East.

United States representation in the European colonial areas reflected the limited political and economic interests of Washington. Relatively few Americans lived in the countries at the time and only a handful of U.S. citizens traveled there. The vast distances of the Pacific and Indian Oceans had not yet been reduced by extensive air travel. American investments in the European colonial territories, even in the petroleum of the East Indies, were not large while trade was limited except for certain imports like natural rubber and tin from the Netherlands East Indies and British Malaya. As the Philippines was a fairly well defined archipelago, its proximity to British North Borneo and the Netherlands East Indies raised few border problems to perplex American officials. Although the United States had a stake in ocean shipping its concern over air routes in Southeast Asia was chiefly a matter of the future. American interests, limited though they were before Pearl Harbor, were subjected on December 7 to the ordeal of a long and bloody struggle.

2 THE PACIFIC WAR
(DECEMBER 1941-V-J DAY, 1945)

THE JAPANESE INTERLUDE

The Japanese conquest of Southeast Asia was effected through a series of land-sea-air operations that brought the entire region under the rule of one power for the first time in history.[1] Within a few months after Pearl Harbor the Japanese reached the boundaries of Australia in the southeast and of India in the northwest. Although the military position of the Western powers was weak, the war plans of Tokyo were well conceived and executed. With no more than 400,000 troops and with relatively minor losses Japan accomplished its military objectives.

Indochina was a key to the Nipponese conquest of Southeast Asia. The acquisition of footholds in northern Indochina in 1940 and southern Indochina in 1941 enabled Japan to move into Thailand, which facilitated the conquest of Burma and Malaya. The capture of Singapore by land gave Tokyo a great naval base. The Nipponese position in Indochina on the west shore of the South China Sea removed any threat from that direction to Japan's invasion of the Philippines for which Taiwan or Formosa was the key staging area. From the Philippines and Malaya the Netherlands East Indies could be invaded and its petroleum resources secured for the Japanese navy.

In November 1942 Tokyo established by imperial ordinance the Greater East Asia Ministry.[2] After Hitler's triumph in Western Europe the Japanese had proclaimed, in August 1940, the New Order in Greater East Asia and after Pearl Harbor they had named the Asian phase of

World War II the Greater East Asia War. The new ministry was divided into a general and three regional bureaus, one each for China, Manchuria, and the Nan Yo or Southern Seas (Southeast Asia). Although the organization of the Nan Yo reflected military and political expediency, it is interesting to observe how the entire region was structured by one power for the first time in history.

Thailand occupied a special status, for it had quickly joined the New Order in Greater East Asia and had declared war on the United States and Great Britain. Indochina also had a special status since Japan maintained the facade of French rule until March 1945. The rest of Southeast Asia, reflecting outright conquest, was divided for purposes of administration into the Philippines, Burma, Malaya and Sumatra, and Java and Madura, each of the four domains under the military officer who occupied it. Borneo with the Celebes and other Indonesian islands east of a line from the Makassar Strait to Bali remained under a naval command. The Japanese linking of Malaya and Sumatra reflected the historic, economic, and strategic ties of the two areas divided by the Strait of Malacca. The strategic headquarters of the Nan Yo was Singapore, renamed Shonan or Light of the South.

The blueprint of the Coprosperity Sphere of Greater East Asia had a goal of self-sufficiency and called for the concentration of industrial power in Japan with the rest of the empire providing raw materials and markets. The Bank for the Development of the Southern Areas was created, and a five-year plan was adopted in 1942. Some of Japan's projects involved the redistribution of labor in Southeast Asia, with considerable individual hardship. In October 1943 Tokyo completed the Thailand-Burma Railway made famous in later years by the novel and motion picture *Bridge on the River Kwai*. The Japanese did not succeed, however, in their efforts to link the railroads of west and east Sumatra. As allied attacks increasingly interrupted the shipping of Greater East Asia, Tokyo was forced to stress economic decentralization in the Coprosperity Sphere.

Japan placed considerable emphasis on cultural propaganda despite the limitations imposed by the war. Vehicles were goodwill missions, cultural societies, exchanges of students, scientific meetings, and the dispatch of Japanese language instructors. The Nipponese stressed many of the themes widely exploited later by the Communists in Southeast Asia such as the liberation of the Asiatics from the exploitation of American and British imperialists and the creation of peace and prosperity in the region. A solidarity conference of Japan and the allegedly independent countries of Greater East Asia—China, Manchukuo, Thailand, Burma, and the Philippines—was held in Tokyo in the fall of 1943. Their Joint Declaration of November 5 resembles some of the Communist propaganda today.

The Philippines. Japan's New Order in the Philippines found the people generally uncooperative and basically friendly to the Americans.[3] On January 23, 1942, a number of Filipino politicians organized themselves as a provisional Council of State to work with the Japanese military administration. An executive commission of the Council under Chairman Jorge B. Vargas represented the limits of Philippine authority at the time. In May 1943 Premier Hideki Tojo visited Manila and announced that the Philippines would soon receive the "honor of independence" as Japan had previously promised. After consideration of various individuals the Japanese selected José Laurel as the architect of the new republic. He was appointed chairman of the Preparatory Committee for Philippine Independence, and was the most influential voice in the drafting of the constitution, and became president of the Republic of the Philippines on October 14. With a U.S. invasion of the islands imminent, Tokyo pressured Laurel the following September into declaring war on the United States and Great Britain. As the American forces under General MacArthur advanced, the Laurel cabinet moved in December 1944 to Baguio. Subsequently Laurel himself went to Taiwan and then to Japan, where, after Tokyo's surrender, he formally decreed the end of his government. It will still be some time before Laurel's place in Philippine history will be established. Was he puppet or patriot or a combination of both? The Japanese considered his regime the most recalcitrant in the Nan Yo.

Outside the political arena, Tokyo, apart from reaching certain immediate goals of exploitation, was not successful in implementing its economic objectives in the Philippines. Dr. Royama Masamichi and a commission of scholars had made a challenging report directed at planning the future economic growth of the islands. They sought a shift in emphasis in education—more experts or technicians in business administration, agriculture, and light industry. Less stress in the life of the Filipino should be placed on politics; the legal profession should be deemphasized. In the Coprosperity Sphere the Japanese wanted the Philippines to supply sugar along with Java and Taiwan and to increase rice production while Indochina met the deficits in the early stages. In a classified agreement probably made by Laurel Tokyo gained special privileges in the economy of the islands with respect to natural resources and utilities.

The failure of the Japanese in long-range economic goals was matched by failure in their cultural program. The Filipinos were cynical of Asian brotherhood as exemplified by Tokyo and questioned the cultural leadership of Nippon. The New Order in Greater East Asia, of course, did not last long enough for the Japanese to capitalize on time.

The Philippine government-in-exile in Washington watched carefully the course of events in the occupied nation. Quezon was relatively tolerant of the Laurel regime partly because he probably expected to work with some of its leaders after the war. American officials varied in their evaluation, some essentially agreeing with Quezon and others like Secretary of the Interior Harold Ickes eager to execute collaborators. Philippine guerrillas operating against the Japanese in growing numbers in the islands were hostile to Laurel and his government. Many of the guerrillas were supported by American arms and aid, although the Communist-led Hukbalahaps, or Huks, were a notable exception.

As President Quezon's term of office was due to expire in 1943 the question arose about the procedure of prolonging it. He favored an executive order by President Roosevelt but Osmeña, Quezon's vice-president, believed an act of Congress was necessary. Roosevelt, himself sensitive to criticism of longevity in office, agreed with Osmeña's approach, and Congress passed the measure which kept Quezon in office.

Motivated by a desire to get ahead of the Japanese, Manuel Quezon in September requested immediate independence for the Philippines, and Senator Millard Tydings with Roosevelt's approval introduced a bill to that effect. Secretary Stimson, helped by his supporters, was able to convince American leaders, and Quezon himself, that immediate independence for the Philippines in the midst of the war was not desirable. In June 1944 Congress authorized the President, if he desired, to advance the date of sovereignty. Quezon's death in August elevated Osmeña to the presidency of the Commonwealth.

On October 20, Osmeña, a few steps behind General MacArthur, waded ashore at the Visayan island of Leyte. MacArthur's words are famous: "I have returned." Quezon, had he lived, might well have tried to match them. At the Honolulu Conference of July 1944 the General in opposition to the navy had persuaded Roosevelt that the Philippines rather than Taiwan should be seized from the Japanese on the way to Tokyo. MacArthur left the conference, however, convinced that the man the President selected as candidate for vice-president in 1944 would enter the White House. Such, he believed, was FDR's state of health.

As the Philippines was being liberated from the Japanese, MacArthur placed more and more territory under the civil authority of President Osmeña and the Commonwealth. On February 27, 1945, the General in a ceremony in Manila returned full constitutional authority to the Philippines. Osmeña, however, was dependent upon what aid the U.S. army in the Commonwealth could give him. And the army was occupied in defeating the Japanese in the islands and in preparing for the eventual struggle against the Nipponese homeland.

One of the greatest problems facing Osmeña was the handling of the collaborators. MacArthur, Stimson, and Roosevelt believed this matter should be under the jurisdiction of the restored Commonwealth. A significant number of collaborators were imprisoned by MacArthur's forces and Osmeña was under pressure from Truman and Ickes to investigate and try the individuals. The Commonwealth President set up people's courts to handle cases, but it soon became evident that he did not have the facilities to make such a procedure operational. MacArthur himself in April pushed into the limelight Manuel Roxas, a person whom he liked and with whom he could work. In the thinking of the General the anti-Japanese activities of Roxas during the occupation outweighed his role in the republic of José Laurel. With the blessing of MacArthur Roxas started his campaign for the presidency in the next elections, a factor which caused Osmeña's cabinet to indicate that Manila wanted independence on schedule rather than a postponement.

Osmeña returned to the United States early in 1945 to get aid for the relief and reconstruction of the Philippines. After some delay he was finally able to see President Roosevelt. The long conversation between them encouraged Osmeña but the death of the American President a few days later changed the situation. Osmeña was then able to see President Harry S. Truman three times in April and May. Although not well informed on the situation in the Philippines and advised to the contrary by Ickes, Truman wanted to expedite the independence of the islands. Roosevelt had told Osmeña on April 5 that he hoped to grant independence by autumn. Truman promised Osmeña help in rehabilitation but the Philippine leader returned to Manila without a settlement of trade and rehabilitation problems. The surrender of Japan found the Philippines devastated by war and on the verge of independence in an unknown world.

Thailand. Bangkok's experience with the New Order in Greater East Asia varied in many respects from that of the Philippines. Apart from a few hours in December 1941 Japan did not have to fight the Thai, and Tokyo surrendered in August 1945 before the allies entered Thailand. Thus the kingdom escaped the devastation the Philippines experienced when the Japanese invaded the islands and especially when they were defeated there. As an ally of Nippon, Thailand did not technically undergo occupation but the Japanese military presence was nevertheless evident.

In general the Thai people were not sympathetic to the Japanese, and the opposition to them grew as the war continued and Tokyo's New Order began to crumble. The deterioration of economic conditions through the effects of the war and the Thai handling of the currency with resulting inflation contributed to the opposition.

Thailand and Japan signed a formal alliance on December 21, 1941.

In a secret protocol Bangkok agreed to assist Tokyo in the war against the United States and Great Britain and Tokyo agreed to help Bangkok get certain territories from the United Kingdom. Thailand honored the agreement by declaring war on both the United States and Great Britain on January 25, 1942. At the official level relations were cordial between the Thai and Japanese governments until 1944. During an Imperial Conference on May 31, 1943, Tokyo formally decided the time had come to turn over to Thailand the four Malay States Great Britain had taken in 1909 and two Shan States in Burma. Premier Tojo visited Bangkok in July, and a treaty on the transfer of the territories was signed on August 20.

American relations with Thailand during the Pacific War had some similarities to those with the Philippines.[4] Washington considered the Thai government of Premier Pibul Songgram an instrument of the Japanese after their occupation of Thailand. It worked closely with the Thai Minister in Washington, Seni Pramoj, and his "Free Thai"; and it came to support the "underground" in Thailand headed by Pridi Panomyong (*Ruth* was his code name) who became in the summer of 1944 the sole regent of the kingdom. Indeed, if Japan had not surrendered when it did, a Thai government led by Pridi in cooperation with allied invasion forces conceivably could have declared war on the Japanese.

Minister Seni Pramoj in January 1942 had refused to deliver to the United States the Thai declaration of war; he took the position his legation was independent of the government of Pibul Songgram. The Minister became the driving force of a Free Thai organization of Thai nationals in America, especially students. Having informed Secretary Hull that Bangkok's declaration of war did not represent the will of the people, he urged Washington to assist in the liberation of the kingdom.

The United States, supported by China, refused to consider the Thai declaration valid, and early in 1942 took concrete steps to help the Free Thai movement in America. (A smaller one was set up in Great Britain.) Thirty-nine Thai student volunteers were trained near Washington under the direction of the Department of State and the Office of Strategic Services (OSS). In the spring of 1943 a Thai contingent left the United States for southern China to infiltrate Thailand. Liaison between the underground of Pridi in Bangkok and the Free Thai from Washington was eventually established. Valuable intelligence was forthcoming, some downed allied fliers and allied prisoners of war were eventually freed, and toward the end of the conflict, American officers from the OSS were sent into the kingdom and arms and supplies provided the underground. In fact, on April 21, 1945, the Joint Chiefs of Staff formally authorized OSS aid to the Thai resistance forces consistent with the requirements of other theaters and the resources of the American commanding general in

India and Burma. Qualified cooperation with the British Special Forces and their Thai student volunteers occurred. A Thai guerrilla force of some size was created.

Three days after the fall of Tojo on July 21, 1944, the Pibul cabinet collapsed in Bangkok. It was replaced by one headed by Major Khuang Aphaiwongse with Pridi in a powerful role. By the surrender of Japan in August 1945, Thai leadership had already shifted and was in a better position to cope with the victors of World War II.

Burma. The people of Burma, like those of the Philippines, suffered from both conquest by the Japanese and their subsequent defeat on Burmese soil. The United Kingdom rather than the United States, however, was the Western power most deeply involved. Although Great Britain had separated Burma from the Indian Empire in 1937 and was taking cautious steps toward self-government the British found little support especially from the dominant people of Burma, the Burmans, in the losing battle against the Japanese invaders. On August 1, 1943, Tokyo granted "independence" to the country under a regime led by Dr. Ba Maw as *Adipadi*.[5] The new government aligned itself with Japan and immediately declared war on Great Britain and the United States. In late 1944 Tokyo used Burma as a base for an invasion of the Indian state of Manipur.

In the defeat of the Japanese in Burma (Rangoon fell May 3, 1945) Detachment 101 of OSS had armed, trained, and directed the Kachins (Kachin Rangers) against the enemy and gained valuable experience in guerrilla warfare. Washington also trained in India some of the Chinese who fought the Japanese. Brigadier General Frank D. Merrill and Colonel Philip G. Cochran became known for their "marauders" and air commandos. American engineers guided the construction of the Ledo Road, later called Stilwell Road, from Assam in India through northern Burma to the Burma Road leading to Free China. Washington, however, had relatively little to do with the Burmans and their relations with the British and Japanese, for the U.S. wartime role in Burma stressed the opening of transportation links with Free China. It was Aung San among the Burmans who played a key role in fighting the Japanese. After training in Nippon he served as minister for national defense in the cabinet of Dr. Ba Maw, but in February 1945, he turned against the Japanese and led his Burma Defense Army in revolt.

Indochina. Like Thailand, Indochina was not freed by the allies from Japanese rule. The facade of French control maintained by Tokyo until late in the war served its interests. After all, it had a free military hand and was master of the economic resources of the area. On March 9, 1945, however, Japan, in view of developments in the war including reports of a possible U.S. invasion, took over the administration of

French Indochina making Governor General Jean Decoux a prisoner, disarming wherever possible French forces, and restricting French civilians.[6] The Japanese allowed Emperor Bao Dai to proclaim on March 11 the independence of Annam, and he was permitted to unite Tonkin with it. Not until August 8, however, was he allowed to add Cochin China to his Vietnam. King Norodom Sihanouk of Cambodia proclaimed the independence of his country on March 12 and King Sisavang Vong of Luang Prabang took a similar step April 18. The Vietnamese, Cambodian, and Laotian monarchs, nevertheless, were aware of the limits of their rule under the Japanese.

President Roosevelt watched developments in Indochina with genuine interest. He had informed Secretary Hull on October 16, 1944, that he believed the United States should do nothing at that time about resistance groups in Indochina. On November 3 American field commanders in Asia were instructed to give no support to the accrediting of a French military mission to the Southeast Asia Command of Admiral Lord Louis Mountbatten.

Although the Japanese coup against the French the following March was successful due in measure to the inefficiency of the underground movement of the French, some of their troops were able to escape the Nipponese snare, retreat to favorable terrain, and eventually reach China. General G. Sabattier, key commander of these troops in Tonkin, urged General Claire L. Chennault, commander of the Fourteenth Air Force in nearby Yunnan, to furnish American aid. The latter, having sent a few liaison officers who made a quick survey of needs, apparently followed up with some air strikes against the Japanese and some supply drops to the French, although he later indicated that orders from the War Department in Washington to theater headquarters forbade aid to the French forces.[7] General Albert C. Wedemeyer at the theater level subsequently said Roosevelt personally told him in early March not to provide any help whatsoever to the French cause and Secretary Stimson later the same day suggested he mention the matter to General George C. Marshall.[8]

After Tokyo's coup on March 9 Paris put intense pressure on Washington for military and other aid to French resistance forces in Indochina. General Charles de Gaulle himself, head of the Provisional French Government, told the American Ambassador on March 13:

> If the public here comes to realize that you are against us in Indochina there will be terrific disappointment and nobody knows to what that will lead. We do not want to become Communist; we do not want to fall into the Russian orbit, but I hope that you do not push us into it.[9]

On March 16 the Department of State in a memorandum for the President called attention to General de Gaulle's position and recommended (in view of the possibility that France and Great Britain might try to blame the United States for the weakness of French resistance forces in Indochina) that the Department issue a proposed statement wherein Washington would commit itself to help them all it could consistent with the operations now occurring in the Pacific and with plans already made. The next day FDR directed that the proposed statement not be issued at the present time.

Admiral William D. Leahy apparently did get Roosevelt's approval around March 19 to authorize U.S. help to the French resistance forces, but assistance was not to interfere with the Sino-American war effort against the Japanese. Apart from some earlier aid, "an appreciable number of [U.S.] missions" from March 29 to April 13, it was officially stated in Washington on April 19, were "flown into Indo-China at direct request of the French in addition to other air forces operations into Indo-China."[10]

President Truman supported the continuation of qualified aid. General de Gaulle, however, thought the American assistance to the French resistance forces was very little and very late. Paris was also unhappy over the refusal of the United States on April 20 to enter into a civil affairs agreement on Indochina.

Malaya and British Borneo. Japanese policy in occupied Malaya was more consistent than in French Indochina. In Tokyo's plans Malaya was to be an integral part of the Japanese Empire. The area was divided into eight provinces; the institution of the Malay sultans was preserved though the government organization set up by the British was terminated. Sumatra in 1944 was administratively separated from Malaya and again tied to Indonesia. Across the South China Sea, Sarawak, Brunei, and North Borneo were also administered by the Japanese. Tokyo surrendered before Malaya and British Borneo could be liberated from the Nipponese with the exception of Brunei, Miri, and Seria, which they lost in June 1945. The United States had no decisive role in developments involving Malaya and British Borneo.

Indonesia. In this huge archipelago Japan's policy shifted very much with the fortunes of war. At first Tokyo was not interested in the territorial integrity of the islands let alone independence for them. Economic exploitation and a minimum of political concessions were the order of the day. The threefold division of Indonesian territory for administrative purposes reflected a concept of the islands as a geographical expression. In the postwar period Nippon was eager to have full control of the petroleum production as well as other resources of Indonesia.

Influenced by military reverses, Japan in September 1944 made a public promise of independence at some time but did not define the area to be included nor the nature of statehood. In fact, Java was the focus of attention, then Sumatra, and afterwards the eastern islands. With the military situation further deteriorating Japan decided on July 17, 1945, to give independence as soon as possible to all Indonesia and to take early steps to implement the decision. The Indonesian nationalists proclaimed independence on August 17, not long after hearing of the Japanese surrender. The Nipponese military leaders in Indonesia could probably have prevented the step if they had made a concerted effort. As it was, they created a situation which added greatly to the problems of the Western forces when they finally arrived.

The leaders of the independence struggle in the islands, Sukarno and Hatta being outstanding examples of the nationalist intelligentsia, thus rose to postwar prominence through the assistance of the Japanese in the later phase of the Pacific War. Moslem groups, long encouraged by the Nipponese, youth organizations flourishing under their auspices, and local defense leaders backed by the men from Tokyo, though the pattern was not black and white, contributed to the power base of Sukarno and his colleagues before August 17. If Japan had not surrendered when it did and if the allies had had to invade Java, the Nipponese might well have had active Indonesian support in the cause of independence from Dutch nationalism.[11]

The United States played no decisive role in the developments. General MacArthur in the Southwest Pacific had leapfrogged on Indonesian territory, Netherlands New Guinea and Morotai in the northern Moluccas, on his way to the Philippines. The objective had been not the liberation of Indonesia but the long-range preparation for an attack on Japan. After the American military return to the Philippines, Australian forces under MacArthur's command occupied Tarakan and Balikpapan in Dutch Borneo and Brunei, Miri, and Seria in British Borneo.

Further Dimensions. The Greater East Asia War or the Asian phase of World War II brought out the contrast in alliance diplomacy. Japan's position was relatively simple since its Asian colleagues were really satellites and its distant European allies had their own theaters of war. But for the allied powers it was different. In the 1930s the United States was not willing to cooperate effectively with Great Britain and France in stopping Japanese expansion. The British, French, and Dutch had never worked out, before World War II, a coordinated defense plan for Southeast Asia. When the Japanese struck at Pearl Harbor, France and the Netherlands had already been overrun by Hitler, and Great Britain was still recovering from Dunkirk. Nevertheless, the Americans, British, Dutch, and Australians under the command of Field Marshal Sir Archibald Wavell (known as ABDACOM) put up a military effort in Southeast Asia against overwhelming Japanese odds.

In planning for the expulsion of Japan from the region President Roosevelt and Prime Minister Churchill at the Quebec Conference in August 1943 approved the creation of a Southeast Asia Command (SEAC).[12] The British Chiefs of Staff had proposed the establishment of the Command under a British supreme allied commander with an American deputy. In the SEAC theater of operations would be Indochina, a suggestion the American Joint Chiefs accepted. On August 21, however, the Combined Chiefs of Staff approved a theater which did not include Indochina but left it in the China theater under Chiang Kai-shek whose chief of staff was General Joseph W. Stilwell. There was much discussion in Quebec over the command aspects of the China and SEAC theaters in Southeast Asia. On August 23 at a summit meeting Roosevelt asked if Thailand was in the SEAC theater. Admiral Leahy replied in the affirmative but indicated Indochina was staying in the China theater at this time.

As far as Southeast Asia itself was concerned, Burma, Thailand, Malaya, Singapore, and Sumatra were placed under the new Southeast Asia Command at Quebec and General Douglas MacArthur had at the time the rest of Southeast Asia under his Southwest Pacific Area (SWPA) except for Indochina which remained, as already indicated, with the China theater of operations.[13] Admiral Lord Louis Mountbatten was named the supreme allied commander of SEAC with General Stilwell in China the deputy commander. The Combined Chiefs of Staff had "general jurisdiction over strategy" in the SEAC theater.

The collapse of Japan's New Order in Greater East Asia was widely welcomed by the people of Southeast Asia. The destruction of war varied depending upon the resistance to the invasion of the Japanese and upon the circumstances of their defeat or surrender. Manila, for instance, shared with Warsaw the reputation of being the most damaged capital city of World War II. Japanese inhumanity in many instances in Southeast Asia could not be easily forgotten. It also became clear that Asia for the Asiatics really meant Asia for the Japanese.

Nippon was not able effectively to channel the rising nationalism of Southeast Asia in the direction of Tokyo. At the same time Japan was a catalyst of major proportions in promoting this very nationalism. Tokyo succeeded in easily overthrowing the imperial structure of the West in the Nan Yo and in creating conditions where the status quo ante bellum could never be restored. The planting of a number of time bombs by the Nipponese required the most adept defusing by the Western victors if explosions were to be avoided.

Japan's experience in Southeast Asia illustrates how a country cannot build a New Order and fight a major war at the same time. Historians one day will reevaluate the Japanese role in the Nan Yo. Tokyo's mobilization of youth and its "revolutionary legacy" will be particularly examined. Indeed, the process has already begun.[14] But only if the New Order in Greater East Asia with its Coprosperity Sphere had lasted several decades could its permanent features have emerged.

AMERICAN BLUEPRINTS FOR PEACE

The United States did considerable planning for peace after it entered World War II. Southeast Asia was not an area of major consideration like Japan or Germany but some parts of the region were given particular attention. President Roosevelt had his own ideas; the State Department formulated proposals; a number of summit conferences had Southeast Asia as one of the subjects of discussion; and the planning and drafting of the United Nations Charter involved provisions that could be applied to the region. Much of the planning revolved around winning the war but the nature of the subsequent peace could not be ignored.

FDR. Roosevelt was interested in Southeast Asia although he did not possess a deep knowledge of it. Some of his comments were casual and superficial; his critics thought him a dilettante or a dreamer. Yet he had a grasp of the fundamental emerging forces in the area, like the rising tide of nationalism with the corresponding recession of imperialism. This grasp probably reflected his overall view of the outlook for colonial peoples. He was very sympathetic to Cordell Hull's draft Declaration by the United Nations on National Independence in March 1943. In Southeast Asia the President accepted the domino theory when it came to one country winning independence from a European power. Apart from the Philippines whose future as an independent state had already been decided, Roosevelt also was very much interested in the future of French Indochina and somewhat less interested in that of the Netherlands East Indies. He showed only limited interest in Thailand and practically none per se in Burma and Malaya. He, however, did urge Churchill to give the Burmese a stake in a United Nations victory by promising to liberalize their postwar status.

In a proposed memorandum for President Truman on April 21, 1945, the Division of Far Eastern Affairs of the Department of State summarized the late President Roosevelt's views as follows:

> President Roosevelt recognized the future increasing importance to the United States of Southeast Asia. He saw the necessity of aiding the 150,000,000 people there to achieve improved social, economic and political standards. He realized that dynamic forces

leading towards self-government are growing in Asia; that the United States—as a great democracy—cannot and must not try to retard this development but rather act in harmony with it; and that social, economic or political instability in the area may threaten the peace and stability of the Far East and indeed the world.[15]

To Roosevelt the road to independence in the Philippines was an example to be emulated in Southeast Asia. Over and over again he referred to this point. He reportedly offered Charles de Gaulle some Filipino advisers to assist the French in liberalizing their policy in Indochina. He even thought of a Philippine role in a future trusteeship for the area. The Philippines went to meetings of the Pacific War Council, signed the Declaration by United Nations in 1942, and attended the San Francisco conference and became a charter member of the United Nations Organization in 1945. Yet Roosevelt was not especially interested in the Filipinos and often indicated confusion about them. Secretary Stimson once complained he was "all mixed up" about the islands.

FDR distinguished between good and bad colonial rulers in Southeast Asia; the French represented the bad and the Dutch, the good. Partly as a result of his close personal ties with the royal family of the Netherlands (he liked Wilhelmina and Juliana and disliked de Gaulle) and his deep sympathy and admiration for the Dutch (he did not admire the French) he believed he could influence the Netherlands to pursue a liberal colonial policy in the East Indies, one that would lead in stages to increasing self-government and eventual independence. In fact, Roosevelt asserted in 1944 that in long talks with Queen Wilhelmina "she agreed that the policy we have in the Philippines would be the pattern she would follow in the Dutch East Indies, after the war."[16] The President foresaw the return of the Dutch to the archipelago and he significantly did not urge an international trusteeship for the islands.

Roosevelt considered Thailand enemy-occupied territory but not an enemy of the United States. He personally approved a policy of viewing the Thai government of Pibul Songgram in Bangkok as a puppet of the Japanese occupation, of continuing to recognize the Thai Minister in Washington, and of helping the Free Thai movement. Roosevelt supported a statement by Chiang Kai-shek calling for an independent Thailand and he wanted the British to assert unequivocally that they had no territorial ambitions in the kingdom.

The future of Indochina was the subject of the President's deep concern in numerous conversations at home and abroad. The United States early in the war had given pledges to the Vichy government and to the Free French of General de Gaulle supporting the preservation of the

French Empire. It is true that the pledges mainly came at a time when Washington was concerned lest more components of the Empire succumb to the pressure of the axis and when problems of the postwar world seemed far away. Colonial resistance and American sympathy were obviously related. Roosevelt indicated in March 1943 that he thought the pledges did not extend to Indochina but Undersecretary of State Sumner Welles reminded him of the contrary. The Vichy French and the Free French despite their many differences fully agreed on the objective of preserving the French Empire.

During a meeting of the Joint Chiefs of Staff at the White House on January 7, 1943, the President expressed grave doubts about the restoration of Indochina to France after the war, and at Casablanca the same month he told his son Elliott that the people of Indochina had been so "flagrantly downtrodden" that they had concluded: "Anything must be better than to live under French colonial rule!"[17] FDR believed French exploitation of Indochina was one of the causes of the Pacific War. At the White House on March 27 Roosevelt suggested to Anthony Eden, the British Foreign Secretary, that Indochina should be placed under an international trusteeship in preparation for independence.[18] The President expressed a similar viewpoint at a meeting of the Pacific War Council. Secretary Hull carried with him to the Moscow conference of foreign ministers in October a request from the President that the subject be presented to the Russians. FDR had previously mentioned it to Soviet Foreign Minister Vyacheslav Molotov in June 1942. Hull observed in his memoirs that the chief executive "entertained strong views on independence for French Indo-China."[19] At the Cairo Conference in November 1943 Roosevelt discussed the trusteeship proposal with Chiang Kai-shek, suggesting a "definite period of time, perhaps 20 to 30 years" before independence.[20] The President later asserted that Chiang Kai-shek had assured him "China had no designs on Indochina."[21]* According to Stilwell, FDR believed a commission of three, an American, a Briton, and a

*Roosevelt claimed he asked Chiang Kai-shek at Cairo if China wanted Indochina and the answer was a flat no. Nevertheless, Vice-President Henry Wallace was instructed the next year to inform Chiang Kai-shek of the President's interest in China's getting the area. The Generalissimo apparently had not changed his mind when Wallace saw him in June. Was Roosevelt actually serious about this solution to postwar Indochina? It certainly stood in contrast to his belief in independence for the territory. If he ever was serious about this option, it was possibly related to his desire to keep China in the war against Japan.

Although Chiang Kai-shek asserted he did not want Indochina he did not think it should be restored to France. Chungking, tacitly at least during the war, favored independence advocates. At the same time the warlords in Yunnan and Kwangsi who were essentially independent from Chungking looked upon Indochina as an arena of possible postwar economic concessions. The French for their part thought that Chiang Kai-shek wanted to annex or dominate northern Indochina.

Chinese, should head the trusteeship.[22]* The President also reportedly mentioned the subject to Egyptian and Turkish representatives at Cairo. At the Tehran Conference, November 27–December 1, Roosevelt and Stalin agreed that Indochina should not go back to France and that a trusteeship was desirable.[23] Later the President told Edward R. Stettinius, Jr., Undersecretary of State, that the line-up for a trusteeship was three to one—Roosevelt, Stalin, and Chiang Kai-shek against Churchill.[24]

In 1944 Roosevelt continued his efforts to prevent the restoration of Indochina to the French. In January he told Lord Halifax, the British Ambassador, that for over a year he had favored an international trusteeship for the area. He indicated later in the month to Hull that he had the support of Stalin and Chiang but that the British apparently feared for their possessions and those of the Dutch.

On February 17 the Department of State in a memorandum to the President asserted it was operating on the assumption, subject to his approval and "without prejudice" to the ultimate status of Indochina, that French armed forces would be used "to at least some extent" in military action in the area and that French nationals who know Indochina could be usefully employed in its administration.[25] Roosevelt orally replied to Stettinius that no French troops should be used, the operations should be Anglo-American, and an international trusteeship should follow them.[26] At the Second Quebec Conference in September he and Churchill reached no agreement on French participation in liberating Indochina. In fact, the subject was not even raised despite Roosevelt's previously expressed desire to discuss the question of the area orally with Churchill.†

*An interesting exchange of viewpoints occurred before the Cairo Conference involving the question of whether the Vietnamese considered the Chinese hereditary enemies. The Free French on October 20 in their desire to get U.S. support for French military participation in the liberation of Indochina and also to exclude the Chinese stressed in Washington that this was the case. John Carter Vincent, Assistant Chief of the State Department's Division of Far Eastern Affairs, on November 2 seriously questioned the assertion, and Acting Secretary of State Stettinius six days later in a memorandum to Roosevelt asserted the Department did not agree with the French viewpoint. Roosevelt himself on November 9 supported the conclusion of the State Department on the subject. (For documentation, see *Foreign Relations of the United States, 1943, China,* Government Printing Office, Washington, 1957, pp. 882–87.)

†At the Second Quebec Conference Admiral Ernest J. King of the United States indicated that the best use of available British forces was to retake Singapore and help the Dutch recover the East Indies. Churchill himself pointedly indicated in February a few months before the Conference that if the British played a subsidiary role under the Americans in military operations in the Pacific serious political questions about the future of "our Malayan possessions" and the "East Indian Archipelago" would be raised. He was thinking of trusteeship.

On October 10 Secretary Hull addressed a memorandum to the President about various matters the British had raised in connection with French participation in the liberation of Indochina. Three days later the Secretary, in support of a request from General William J. Donovan, OSS Director, wrote the President:

> Subject to your approval, the Department will reply to General Donovan that it has no objection to furnishing supplies and equipment to resistance groups, both French and native, actually within Indochina, nor to American collaboration with the French Military Mission at Chungking or other French officers or officials in furtherance of the contemplated operations or any other military operations in Indochina for the defeat of Japan.[27]

Roosevelt informed Hull on October 16 that the United States at the time should not only "do nothing in regard to resistance groups" but also "in any other way in relation to Indochina."[28]

Undersecretary Stettinius on November 2 sent the President a memorandum on recent developments involving the area. It stressed the British sympathy for the French and the probability of an Anglo-Dutch accord on the future of Southeast Asia with the French being brought in and with the danger of Americans losing out in policy matters. Roosevelt quickly reacted. The very next day he informed Stettinius that "we have made no final decisions on the future of Indo-China. This should be made clear. . . . It should [also] be made clear to all our people that the United States expects to be consulted with regard to any future of Southeast Asia."[29]

General Wedemeyer on November 15 reported that the French, Dutch, and British were making an intense effort to recover the position they had held in the Far East before the war. He asked for guidance on American policy toward Indochina, since it was in the China theater by decision of the Combined Chiefs of Staff.[30] The next day Roosevelt told Patrick J. Hurley, U.S. Ambassador to China, to keep him informed of French, Dutch, and British activities in Southeast Asia and to tell Wedemeyer that U.S. policy on Indochina could not be formulated before discussions at a future Combined Chiefs of Staff conference.

Two strong instructions expressing the will of the President were sent from Washington on November 21. The Joint Chiefs of Staff at his request told the commanding generals of American forces in China, Burma, and India: "This Government had made no final decisions on the future of Indo-China, and it expects to be consulted in advance with regard to any arrangements applicable to the future of southeast Asia."[31] After noting reports that Great Britain and the Netherlands might have agreed concerning the future of the region and might have included or planned to include France, Acting Secretary Stettinius told the American Ambassador to Great Britain along with representatives to the Dutch and French: "The President desires that it be made clear to all appropriate officers of the Government that we expect to be consulted on any arrangements as to the future of Southeast Asia."[32]

Actually Anglo-American discussions on Indochina involving the Department of State and the Joint Chiefs had been under way for some time. Secretary Stettinius on December 27 called Roosevelt's attention to increased British urging of American approval of a French military mission to the Southeast Asia Command and of military participation by France in the liberation of Indochina. The British believed Washington had not yet decided its policy on the area. The President replied on January 1, 1945: "I still do not want to get mixed up in any Indochina decision. It is a matter for post-war. By the same token, I do not want to get mixed up in any military effort toward the liberation of Indochina from the Japanese."[33]

The Yalta Conference of Roosevelt, Stalin, and Churchill, February 4–11, afforded another forum for the President's ideas on Indochina. Although not well briefed on the subject he vaguely told his advisers on February 4 he had no objection to any U.S. action in Indochina providing it did not entail alignments with the French. In a historic conversation with Stalin on February 8 Roosevelt again revealed his desire for a trusteeship for Indochina. He had already recalled to the Russian leader the U.S. experience in the Philippines. The President indicated the British wanted Indochina to go back to France, for they feared the implications for Burma of a trusteeship. Stalin noted that Great Britain had lost Burma once by depending upon Indochina; he did not believe the United Kingdom was "a sure country to protect this area," and observed that Indochina was "a very important area."[34] Roosevelt noted that General de Gaulle had asked for ships to carry French forces to Indochina. When Stalin inquired where he would get the troops Roosevelt replied that de Gaulle had said he would find the troops when the American President found the ships. Up to now, Roosevelt indicated, he had found no ships. The Department of State later revealed on May 18 it knew of no Yalta decision on Indochina.

The President never expressed in detail his plans for an international trusteeship. It is possible that at Yalta he was thinking of participation that would include Indochinese, French, Philippine, Chinese, American, and Russian representatives. Churchill, however, was adamant on the entire trusteeship proposal. During his return home on the American cruiser "Quincy" the President was notably bitter at the British for their attitude.

This feeling did not prevent him on March 15 from discussing with Charles Taussig, an adviser on Caribbean affairs, the concept of trusteeship and the future of Indochina. Referring in general to Yalta, Roosevelt said he "had had a successful time."[35] In response to a question from Taussig the President stressed that "French Indo-China and New Caledonia should be taken from France and put under a trusteeship," but after a moment of hesitation he noted—"well if we can get the proper pledge from France to assume for herself the obligations of a trustee, then I would agree to France retaining these colonies with the proviso that independence was the ultimate goal."[36] The President said he would not settle for self-government or dominion status and that "that is to be the policy."[37]

When the Japanese took over the direct administration of Indochina from the French in March, Roosevelt was concerned about the implications for the postwar future of the area. General Chennault believed the United States favored seeing the French forced out of Indochina so that "the problem of postwar separation from their colony would be easier."[38] Roosevelt himself had informed Wedemeyer in early March that he "was going to do everything possible to give the people in that area their independence."[39] The President at lunch brought up the subject of French Indochina which remained a major topic of conversation. He was opposed to colonialism anywhere in the world and specifically wanted to prevent the restoration of Indochina to the French. The General was instructed to carefully watch British and French political activities and to back the Anglo-French only as needed in direct operations against the Japanese foe.[40]

Hurley, on March 24, told the President that the French, Dutch, and British were cooperating to prevent a trusteeship for Indochina and that the British would attempt, using American lend-lease supplies and, if possible, manpower, to occupy the area. According to Hurley, Roosevelt spoke of the coming conference at San Francisco where a trusteeship system would be established in a United Nations Organization.[41]

While Hurley and Wedemeyer were both in Washington Churchill contacted the President about the difficulties that had arisen between Wedemeyer and Mountbatten over theater command in Indochina and suggested that the President and the Prime Minister tell the Combined Chiefs of Staff to make arrangements for full exchange of information on matters of mutual concern. Roosevelt replied on March 22 that he understood both military leaders were independently conducting air operations and intelligence missions in Indochina. To remedy this unfortunate situation, the President suggested that he and Churchill agree that all Anglo-American-Chinese military operations in the area be coordinated by Wedemeyer as chief of staff to Chiang. Roosevelt's death threw the problem into the hands of President Truman.

In retrospect the evolution of the trusteeship concept for Indochina reflected the President's style of operation. As far as can be determined, the concept was never "staffed out," in an expression of Chester L. Cooper, or incorporated into a working official document of the White House. Roosevelt preferred guidance in conversations to a definitive written directive. FDR liked to keep his options open just as long as possible and not to make hasty decisions. Lord Halifax observed that the President employed conversation as other people utilized the first draft of a paper. Ideas could be tried out—accepted, changed, or dropped. W. Averell Harriman, moreover, has indicated that the chief executive was reluctant to take the Department of State into his confidence on the trusteeship proposal, for he considered department officials pro-French. Roosevelt may not have reached a final hard decision on the future of French Indochina. It is certainly difficult to argue that a definite policy existed. Clearly, military strategy—the focusing of the American war effort toward defeating Japan in its homeland (with its implications for Southeast Asia)—must not be minimized. Nevertheless, the personal diplomacy of the President and his style of operation cannot be ignored in any analysis of the situation. If his trusteeship concept had been implemented, possibly two bloody and costly wars might have been avoided.

State. Postwar planning for Southeast Asia in the Department of State was linked with proposals for Japan and areas under its control.[42] The War and Navy Departments prepared the basic memorandum "Preliminary Political and Policy Questions Bearing on Civil Affairs Planning for the Far East and Pacific Areas"[43] and transmitted it for replies to the Department of State on February 18, 1944. It asked specific questions about "liberated" territories such as Dutch and French possessions and "neutral" countries such as Portugal and Thailand in Southeast Asia. It noted that the United States and the United Kingdom had agreed that for their own liberated territories the government concerned would prepare the necessary directives for Civil Affairs Administration. The replies to most of the questions of the memorandum were prepared by the Inter-Divisional Area Committee on the Far East of the Department of State and approved as the position of the Department.

For Southeast Asia the pattern of reply was not so uniform as for Japan. Pointed questions had been asked about Thailand, and the Department indicated as late as May 15 they were still being studied. Likewise pointed questions about Indochina revealed the fact that the matter was in the hands of the President.

In the case of the Netherlands East Indies the Department on February 28 gave a careful reply indicative of thinking on the postwar future of the islands. Since Sumatra was under the Southeast Asia Command, the British and the Dutch would have to do the civil affairs planning, but for the rest of the Netherlands East Indies, the Americans and the Dutch bore the responsibility. The Department of State assumed that the Netherlands would resume the exercise of sovereignty as soon as the situation permitted in the judgment of the supreme commander of the Allied Expeditionary Forces. Crucially, no commitments would be made that would prejudice Washington's right to bring up, before or after the Dutch resumed control, general proposals of rightful interest to the United States and other countries who backed the principles of the Atlantic Charter of 1941 and the Moscow declaration on general security of 1943, as well as specific proposals of mutual interest to the peoples of the Netherlands Empire and the United States.[44] On December 10 an agreement was signed by General MacArthur as commander in chief of the Southwest Pacific Area and H. J. Van Mook as lieutenant governor general of the Netherlands East Indies on principles governing civil administration. The sovereignty of the Dutch was expressly not affected by the agreement and they would assume full civil administration of reoccupied areas even in combat zones just as quickly as possible.

The Joint Chiefs of Staff in a significant communication to the Secretary of State on May 14, 1944, presented their assumptions in planning for civil affairs during the period of military occupation in various areas of Southeast Asia.[45] The administration of civil affairs in the Philippines was an American responsibility (the United States, if it wanted, could make an arrangement with the Commonwealth of the Philippines). The administration in Burma, Malaya, and Thailand was not an American responsibility unless U.S. forces were to be employed, whereupon the extent of U.S. civil affairs administration was a matter of recommendation by the American commander concerned to the Joint Chiefs. In Sumatra the same provision applied, and during any U.S. participation Dutch administrators would be used in combat zones to the extent the military situation allowed, with the entire administration being Dutch "as soon as military expediency permits." In the rest of the Netherlands East Indies the administration of civil affairs was an American responsibility except where other allied forces might assume operational responsibility for certain territory as a consequence of strategic developments (the basic role of the Dutch being cited as in the case of Sumatra). The administration in Sarawak, Brunei, and North Borneo was primarily a British responsibility. Finally, in Portuguese Timor administration was initially American but would be Portuguese as soon as military expediency permitted.

In view of military events the State Department suggested to the War

Department on November 9 the creation of what came to be the State-War-Navy Coordinating Committee (SWNCC) to deal with emerging problems of a political-military nature.

A far-reaching memorandum on colonial Southeast Asia was prepared in the Department of State and forwarded to Roosevelt by Hull on September 8, 1944. According to the latter, the President "warmly approved" the viewpoints[46] which included "early, dramatic, and concerted announcements" by the colonial powers of "specific dates when independence or complete (dominion) self-government will be accorded" and "a pledge to establish a regional commission." The announcements would be strengthened if each colonial power "would pledge a formal declaration of trusteeship under an international organization for the period of tutelage."[47] Such viewpoints were not appreciated by the European sovereigns, but Hull was convinced "we were taking long-range views, and that a lasting peace in the Pacific was of greater ultimate benefit to Britain, France, and the Netherlands—as well as to the whole world—than the possible immediate benefits of holding on to colonies."[48]

A lively dispute within the Department of State erupted the next year —right after Roosevelt's death—over U.S. policy toward Indochina.[49] On April 13, 1945, the State-War-Navy Coordinating Committee agreed that the State Department should take up the "prompt clarification" of American policy toward Indochina by reference of the question to President Truman in the light of several factors. It was clear from the discussion that the question was of "lively military interest" and that differences of viewpoint in the Department of State had already existed.

In the battle of memoranda between April 20 and May 9 the Division of European Affairs and the Division of Far Eastern Affairs could not agree on a memorandum for the President embracing observations and recommendations. Both divisions did not advocate under the circumstances the trusteeship formula for Indochina and both supported the return of France to the area. But European Affairs in contrast to Far Eastern Affairs did not insist that France give assurances for a fully self-governing Indochina in the forseeable future. The Division of Far Eastern Affairs on April 21 so modified the memorandum of the Division of European Affairs of the previous day that Assistant Secretary James C. Dunn reported to Undersecretary Joseph C. Grew on April 23 that Indochina policy should be allowed to drift rather than have it based on the viewpoints of Far Eastern Affairs. (Dunn had approved the original version of European Affairs.) Although a compromise memorandum to President Truman with a draft cable to the American embassy in Paris on May 9 was prepared, neither memorandum nor cable was sent. And for a while at least American policy toward Indochina was left to drift.

In a policy paper of June 22 the Department of State estimated conditions in Asia and the Pacific when the war ended and cited policies Washington planned to follow in the new international environment. This remarkable paper represented "the considered views of the Department of State as a whole" and was sent to Secretary of War Stimson less than two months before Japan surrendered.[50]

The sections on French Indochina, Thailand, and Malaya and British Borneo estimated well the future situation, but the one on the Netherlands East Indies did not. Burma and the Philippines were not covered. French policy and to a lesser extent Dutch policy were well forecast but not British (probably the estimate was based on a continuation of Churchill in power).

Significantly it was repeated in almost identical words (once more in the last weeks of the Pacific War) that in French Indochina, the Netherlands East Indies, Malaya and British Borneo, and by inference Burma, it was "the general policy of the United States to favor a policy which would allow colonial peoples an opportunity to prepare themselves for increased participation in their own government with eventual self-government as the goal."[51] In Indochina, however, there was no reference to trusteeship, and French sovereignty was expressly recognized. The statement that Washington was following a noninterference policy in British possessions applied to Malaya, British Borneo, and by inference Burma, and nonintervention was the chosen course of action in the Netherlands East Indies.

Indicative of troubles to come was the statement:

> The United States Government may properly continue to state the political principle which it has frequently announced, that dependent peoples should be given the opportunity, if necessary after an adequate period of preparation, to achieve an increased measure of self-government, *but it should avoid any course of action which would seriously impair the unity of the major United Nations.*[52]

At the same time U.S. interests and those of the European allies, it was asserted, would be best served if the Far East ceased to be an area of "colonial rivalry and conflict" both between the Great Powers and between them and the Asian peoples. Independence or dominion status once more was a goal. Yet the realistic dilemma of the future was specifically pointed up close to the end of the policy paper—how "to harmonize support of France in Europe with support of a greater measure of self-government in Indo-China."[53] So much for planning in Washington for the future; events of the day would shape to a large extent actual U.S. policy.

Summits. Despite specific references to Indochina, Southeast Asia at summit conferences was usually not a major topic of discussion. It was considered when a general review of the war was held and when military command structure or certain proposed operations were on the agenda. Planning for the liberation of Burma, for example, aroused lively discussion.

Before the United States entered the war Roosevelt and Churchill issued the Atlantic Charter on August 14, 1941. It stated that the United States and Great Britain sought "no aggrandizement, territorial or other," desired to "see no territorial changes that do not accord with the freely expressed wishes of the peoples concerned," and respected "the right of all peoples to choose the form of government under which they will live."[54] The Far East including Indochina was much discussed at the meeting of the leaders, and the President issued a warning to Japan on August 17. After Pearl Harbor the Declaration by United Nations, January 1, 1942, reaffirmed the principles of the Atlantic Charter and established the mightiest alliance of powers in history. Prime Minister Churchill, however, later stressed that the Charter applied to Europe and not to the British Empire.

At the Casablanca Conference of Roosevelt and Churchill in January 1943 the Combined Chiefs of Staff met frequently for ten days and reported at intervals to the President and to the Prime Minister. The entire war "theater by theater throughout the world" was surveyed and plans were made for campaigns in 1943. At Quebec in August Roosevelt and Churchill gave special attention to Southeast Asia. The creation of the Southeast Asia Command under Admiral Lord Louis Mountbatten reflected the planning of the Combined Chiefs of Staff and of the President and Prime Minister to defeat Japan and to aid China. The Moscow Conference of the foreign ministers of the United States, the United Kingdom, and the Soviet Union in October focused on Europe and on the organization of peace in the postwar world.

The only time Roosevelt, Churchill, and Chiang met was at the Cairo Conference in November. They produced a statement on December 1 centering on the defeat of Japan and the future of its empire. Although it was clear Japan would lose its conquests in Southeast Asia and elsewhere, the "Three Great Allies" stated that they "covet no gain for themselves and have no thought of territorial expansion."[55]

Roosevelt and Churchill left Egypt for Iran, where they met with Stalin in Tehran. Here the emphasis was on Europe and the defeat of Hitler. Stalin was informed of allied plans to land in Western Europe and agreed to launch a major offensive on the eastern front in connection with the landing. At Yalta, the last summit conference of Roosevelt,

Churchill, and Stalin, a future world organization including the subject of "territorial trusteeship" was discussed in some detail.* Europe and Germany again received considerable attention, and a formal agreement was concluded for the Soviet Union's entrance into the war against Japan.

By the time of the Potsdam Conference of Truman, Stalin, and Churchill (and his successor as Prime Minister, Clement Attlee), July 17–August 2, 1945, President Truman had had to face a number of decisions on Southeast Asia, some of which were postponed until the Combined Chiefs of Staff were to meet. On April 11 Churchill had contacted Roosevelt in response to his communication of March 22 about the friction between Wedemeyer and Mountbatten. Wedemeyer, on his return from Washington to China, had visited Mountbatten and believed an agreement had been reached whereby Mountbatten would conduct operations in Indochina only if approved by Wedemeyer.

Churchill indicated on April 11 that the agreement simply involved the exchange of information. Basic to Churchill's thinking was his conviction that in view of the Japanese takeover of Indochina and the resistance of French patriots the United States and Great Britain should help the French "by all the means in our power" and associate with them in operations in Indochina, while France should participate in Anglo-American councils on the area.[56] President Truman replied on April 14, virtually hours after assuming office, that his understanding was that Mountbatten should conduct no military operations in Indochina unless approved by Chiang (whose chief of staff was Wedemeyer).

In May open discord arose between Mountbatten and Wedemeyer when the former said he would fly twenty-six sorties in support of French guerrillas in the area and, despite an exchange of messages, did not wait for the approval of Wedemeyer or Chiang. On May 28 Ambassador Hurley cabled Washington outlining his March 24 conversation with President Roosevelt on Indochina. Hurley said that Roosevelt gave verbal directions but no written directive on U.S. political policy in the area. Accusing Mountbatten of using lend-lease supplies and other U.S. aid in Indochina to restore French imperialism, Hurley asked Washington for a definite American policy on the area as well as on Hong Kong or as an alternative, that he be directed to follow the policy of Roosevelt.[57]† Wedemeyer in a communication to General Marshall on May 31 supported Hurley's conviction that the British were increasing their polit-

*At the Dumbarton Oaks Conversations in 1944 on a future United Nations Organization differences between London and Washington had prevented any meaningful discussion on the colonial question.

†President Roosevelt believed Great Britain should return Hong Kong to China, who should then make it a free port.

ical and economic operations in Indochina as a way of recovering their position in Southeast Asia.

Actually any trusteeship for Indochina was dead. The Department of State had indicated the final determination of U.S. policy in the area depended upon discussions with France, and the Secretary of State asserted he did not want discussions started before or during the San Francisco Conference on International Organization (April 25–June 26), at the earliest. At the Conference on or before May 8 Stettinius assured the worried French that the record was entirely clear of any official U.S. statement questioning even by implication their sovereignty over Indochina.

On June 7 the Department of State finally replied to Hurley's cables of May 28 and again on June 6 requesting guidance on American policy in the Indochina area. President Truman wanted him to know that "no basic change" in U.S. policy had occurred and that a trusteeship for the territory was precluded unless with the consent of France which seemed unlikely. "Nevertheless," the Department asserted, "it is the President's intention at some appropriate time to ask that the French Government give some positive indication of its intentions in regard to the establishment of civil liberties and increasing measures of self-government in Indochina before formulating further declarations of policy in this respect."[58] To Hurley, of course, the answer seemed like double-talk.

Further developments confirmed the American shift. General Charles de Gaulle, for instance, quotes President Truman as assuring him shortly after the defeat of Japan that "my government offers no opposition to the return of the French Army and authority in Indochina."[59] And on August 29 the President told Madame Chiang Kai-shek that as far as he was concerned there had been no discussion about a trusteeship for Indochina. Moreover, he indicated he was satisfied with de Gaulle's statement that he favored independence for Indochina and quick steps toward achieving it![60]

What really happened to the trusteeship concept, such as it was, after the death of FDR? It is doubtful that there was a formal decision in the White House to drop Roosevelt's concept. Rather, no person in the highest circles of the government pushed the trusteeship idea. Indeed, President Truman himself probably did not know about it when he assumed office.

Considerable stress was placed after Roosevelt's death on a statement issued by Secretary Stettinius on April 3 with FDR's approval asserting that as a consequence of the Yalta discussions the United States believed the trusteeship structure after the war should permit, *inter alia*, the placing under it of territories that might voluntarily be put under trusteeship.

Given the context and given the Secretary's subsequent interpretation, Indochina was viewed in this category. In contrast, it has been argued that Roosevelt's views on trusteeship for Indochina were misrepresented to President Truman after the former's death. FDR's conversations in March with Charles Taussig, Ambassador Hurley, and General Wedemeyer, it is contended, were not given enough emphasis.

One aspect of this shift in American policy was Truman's greater interest—when compared with Roosevelt—in the desire of the War and Navy Departments to attain certain Japanese islands in the Pacific for use as American bases. American advocacy of trusteeship for outright European colonial possessions in Southeast Asia would have weakened the arguments of the military in Washington. President Truman was a genuine opponent of colonialism but he was definitely interested in the acquisition of American bases in the Pacific.

Major decisions on Southeast Asia were made at Potsdam by the British and the Americans. On July 17 a memorandum by the U.S. Chiefs of Staff focused on a proposed significant alteration in the boundaries of Mountbatten's Southeast Asia Command. Adding Borneo, the Celebes, and Java (with the area to the east an Australian Command under the British Chiefs of Staff) and including Indochina south of the fifteenth parallel, SEAC would then embrace an area of British Empire responsibility with the Dutch, Portuguese, and perhaps later the French. The initial operational concern of the Americans in the area, it was pointed out, had substantially declined as they increasingly concentrated on Japan.* (In fact, no U.S. combat forces had been in what came to be Mountbatten's enlarged command since June.) The Chiefs observed that the division of Indochina at the fifteenth parallel was primarily a subject for the approval of Chiang. It is significant that the proposed boundaries of SEAC would place the Americans in a much weaker position in postwar Southeast Asia. Also important is the U.S. suggestion concerning the division of Indochina between Mountbatten's and Chiang's commands.

A July 18 memorandum by the British Chiefs of Staff expressed a desire for their American colleagues to support them in asking the Presi-

---

*At the Malta meeting of Roosevelt and Churchill in February prior to their conference with Stalin at Yalta it was particularly evident that the focus of the British and Americans was diverging in the war against Japan. The Combined Chiefs of Staff directed Mountbatten after Burmese liberation to drive the Japanese out of Malaya and free the Strait of Malacca. American forces in the China-Burma area were considered at the time a reserve for the Chinese, the U.S. military effort being essentially directed toward supporting China and defeating metropolitan Japan. After the Yalta Conference American commanders in the Pacific were told that Washington planned to turn over responsibility for operations in the Netherlands East Indies and New Guinea to the British.

dent of the United States and the Prime Minister of Great Britain to urge Chiang to agree to a transfer in Indochina. At a session of the Combined Chiefs of Staff the same day the memorandum of the British was considered. General Marshall asked them for their reaction to dividing Indochina, and Admiral Ernest J. King asserted the fifteenth parallel was arbitrary and might be altered for operational needs. The British agreed to study the proposal, and their memorandum of July 22 indicated the division between the Chinese theater and SEAC should be as a result of the "run of communications in Indo-China" at the sixteenth parallel.[61] The next day the American Joint Chiefs considered a memorandum on an Anglo-American approach to Chiang. Secretary Stimson noted in his diary that the British and French had refused to discuss a trusteeship for Indochina or Hong Kong.

On July 24 a tripartite military meeting was held. The British discussed the recent defeat of the Japanese in Burma (although some of the enemy remained in the country). It was indicated that Mountbatten now planned to move on to Thailand and to take Singapore and Malaya, with the reopening of the Strait of Malacca a major objective.

At a meeting of the Combined Chiefs of Staff the same day Marshall urged Mountbatten to take over his new area of command "at the earliest possible moment."[62] When Marshall asked about his reaction to the proposed division of Indochina, the latter replied that his initial reaction was favorable, but that he believed the French might not like it.

In a report to the President of the United States and the Prime Minister of Great Britain, also on July 24, the Combined Chiefs of Staff formally defined the new area of SEAC. They noted the division of Indochina and asserted that at a later date it might be desirable to place all or a part of it north of the sixteenth parallel under SEAC. Chiang would be approached by the United States and Great Britain for his approval of the current division, Mountbatten would take over the new area of his command "as soon as practicable" after August 15, and the French and Dutch would be informed of Anglo-American intentions in any operations directly affecting their territories in the Far East.[63] The President and the Prime Minister approved the report, and asked Chiang for his agreement to the Indochina division.

Right up to the surrender of Japan the French, Dutch, and Portuguese were eager to have a role in the recapture of their territories in Southeast Asia. General de Gaulle realized the importance of French military participation, "French blood shed on the soil of Indochina," in any peace settlement with Japan.[64] Furthermore, he expressed his zeal in no uncertain terms—"extreme desire" and "capital importance"—in a message to President Truman on May 15 urging French participation with American forces in the operations against Tokyo.[65] The American chief executive indicated that French military and naval assistance in the Pacific should have the objective of defeating metropolitan Japan and that such help as might be provided by France or other allies and synchronized with planned operations or those under way would be welcomed. Truman believed that since military considerations were involved it was up to General MacArthur to judge the merits of the proposed aid. The matter dragged. At the meeting of the Combined Chiefs on July 24 during the Potsdam Conference Marshall mentioned a French offer of two divisions to fight Japan and said the Combined Chiefs believed the best location for them was probably Indochina. Although Mountbatten agreed, Paris was watching the calendar.*

The concern of the Dutch over their military participation was especially marked in the summer. On July 13 they indicated to the United States their need for facilities to transport Dutch troops to Australia to train for the eventual occupation of the Netherlands East Indies. They stressed that if only American and Australian forces moved into the islands the Netherlands would lose face in the eyes of the natives. Despite Washington's emphasis on the unconditional surrender of Japan with the likely surrender of Nipponese forces in the East Indies, the Dutch wanted to participate in the liberation of the islands, even if it were bloodless.

The Unique Case of Portuguese Timor. America was under special obligations to help Lisbon regain Portuguese Timor. In a tripartite agreement of the United States, Portugal, and Great Britain on November 28, 1944, several months before Roosevelt's death, Washington gained facilities for the building, use, and control of an air base on Santa Maria in the Azores and in essence Portuguese forces would participate in military operations to expel Japan from Portuguese Timor. The only territory of Lisbon overrun during World War II was its part of Timor, and Premier Antonio de Oliveira Salazar was deeply interested in regaining the area. American delays in 1945 as regards Timor caused considerable concern in Lisbon circles. Australia did not want to provide facilities for training Portuguese troops on its soil. The United States, however, was taking steps in the summer to meet Portuguese requests, and the Combined

---

*Another blow to French pride was losing the dispute with Chungking over the surrender of the Japanese in Indochina. The French wanted to receive the surrender and did not favor Chinese forces in the territory. They also urged the Chinese to use the some 5,000 French and Vietnamese troops in the Kunming area in the occupation, but Chungking would only agree to allow their return under the Supreme Commander of the China Theater or his representative. Washington was sympathetic to the Chinese, favoring French representation at the surrender, but London, having its own difficulties with Chiang Kai-shek over the surrender of Hong Kong, better understood the French feelings.

Chiefs on July 24 in their report to the American President and the British Prime Minister noted the progress.[66]*

United Nations Charter. The UN Charter drafted at San Francisco in 1945 before the end of World War II included provisions which directly related to colonialism. President Wilson in the fifth of his famous Fourteen Points had urged that colonies be ruled in the interests of the inhabitants. He strongly advocated self-determination and played an important role in the provision for mandates in the Covenant of the League of Nations. In the drafting of the Charter of the United Nations the United States gave full support to Chapters XI, XII, and XIII relating to dependent peoples. Ralph J. Bunche, a distinguished United Nations official, characterized the role as one of "initiative and constructive leadership."[67]

At Yalta Roosevelt, Churchill, and Stalin had agreed on certain aspects of territorial trusteeship. It would only apply to mandates of the League of Nations, lands taken from current enemy countries, and any territory voluntarily placed under trusteeship. As regards the last category, Bunche realistically observed in October 1946: "It cannot be truthfully said that there is any imminent threat of a deluge of offers of this type."[68]

No dependencies of Southeast Asia were placed under Chapters XII and XIII of the Charter providing for trusteeship. However, the colonial rulers of all of them were subject to Chapter XI, "Declaration Regarding Non-Self-Governing Territories." They were obligated to promote self-government, to ensure just treatment, and to transmit periodically to the Secretary General information on educational, social, and economic conditions in the territories. Toward the reporting, the British and Portuguese, the French and Dutch, varied in their attitudes.

By the time Japan surrendered, U.S. planning and action in Southeast Asia had greatly reduced the options open to Washington, at least in the immediate postwar period. This development was no accident; it was the result of deliberate decision as regards British possessions, French Indochina, and the Netherlands East Indies. Only in the Philippines did V-J Day find the United States willing and able to play a decisive role. Although Washington was the chief architect of Tokyo's defeat in the Pacific War, American leadership was not prepared to shoulder the burdens of Southeast Asia. American public opinion would probably have been opposed if it had been U.S. forces in Indochina and Indonesia who had been forced to cope with the problems confronting Admiral Lord Louis Mountbatten.

*The entire island of Timor was not included in Mountbatten's new SEAC boundaries.

‖ UNEXPECTED TRANSITION

Changes in American policy toward Southeast Asia from the formal surrender of Japan in September 1945 to the opening of the Geneva Conference on Indochina in May 1954 were profound and reflected major
world developments, particularly in the Northeast and Southeast Asian
scenes. In only nine years the United States drastically shifted its policy
in the face of great events. This unexpected transition from a deemphasis
in Southeast Asia toward major security commitments in the area was
gradual, late 1949 and early 1950 being a signpost. Even apart from the
notion of commitments, the trend of the American impact was upward
though uneven in Southeast Asia. Malaya and British Borneo, for
instance, were still dependencies of the United Kingdom and subject to
British priorities.

The purpose of Part Two is to describe and analyze the major themes
of American policy in the nine-year transition starting from V-J Day,
1945. First in focus is a consideration of the United States and Southeast
Asian nationalism, a significant subject in the early postwar years. Attention is then directed to the rise of Communist China and its implications
for American policy in Southeast Asia. Here the significance of the
Korean War, the Japanese peace settlement, and the First Indochinese
War is brought into the analysis. All are part and parcel of the unexpected transition in American policy.

3 THE UNITED STATES AND SOUTHEAST ASIAN NATIONALISM (V-J DAY–EARLY 1950)

From the end of World War II in 1945 to early 1950 the United States had to cope with rising nationalism in Southeast Asia. The Cold War was rising to prominence but the significance of the fall of mainland China to the Communists could not be fully assessed. A contest flourished in Washington between those officials who viewed Southeast Asia largely in terms of its relationship to the future of Great Britain, France, and the Netherlands in Western Europe and those who viewed Southeast Asia substantially in terms of the emerging independent states of the region with a new, complex relationship to the United States. In this conflict of interests and priorities the "Old Europe" school more often prevailed but the "New Asia" school never capitulated. Although American opposition to colonialism was deep-rooted and sincere it was not always easy to express in clear-cut policy. In the Philippines the United States carried out its promise to grant independence in 1946 and in Thailand it waged a successful diplomatic battle with Great Britain to preserve genuine independence. In Burma, Washington was essentially an observer as London gave the country its independence. But in Indonesia and Indochina the conflicts of American interests were longstanding and pronounced.

During this period Southeast Asia's nationalism and its relevance to the Western colonial powers were to a large extent a focus of U.S. concern. The development of the Cold War and the growing power of the Chinese Communists added a new and major dimension. Yet, American policy toward colonialism in Southeast Asia was somewhat ambivalent even before these developments. President Truman's general approach placed more emphasis on security than that of President Roosevelt, as some of the former's critics on Indonesia and Indochina, like Sumner Welles, stressed in 1946. Colonial wars, as they were often called, waged by the Dutch and French in Southeast Asia were upsetting in Washington and they countered U.S. policy in the Philippines and Thailand as well as eventual British policy in Burma.

EARLY POSTWAR ENVIRONMENT

The World. One of the most significant years of the twentieth century was 1945, the year World War II ended and a new global order began to emerge. The transition from the old to the new was not sudden, for the entrance of the United States into the war meant the eventual doom of the Rome-Berlin-Tokyo axis, probably one member after the other. Furthermore, the new world had many of the characteristics of the old, especially with the development of the Cold War. Still, only twenty-one years, 1918 to 1939, separated the two global conflicts of the first half of the twentieth century, and the avoidance of a third world war for a much longer period already is significant.

The polarization of power between two superpowers, the United States and the Soviet Union, was a major characteristic of the postwar international environment. The concept is subject to qualifications, especially in its time dimensions, but it remains substantially valid.[1] When World War II began in September 1939 seven great powers occupied the center of the stage—Germany, Italy, France, and Great Britain in Europe; Japan in Asia; the Soviet Union in Eurasia; and the United States in North America. In succession France, Italy, Germany, and Japan were defeated. Great Britain was severely weakened and unable to regain its prewar stature. Although the Soviet Union suffered badly in loss of life and property its military position at the end of the war and its power potential enabled it to emerge as one of the superpowers. The United States was the only major belligerent of the conflict to escape any devastation of its homeland and through the buildup of its power potential emerged as the strongest state ever to appear on the face of the earth. The Soviet Union and the United States represented the poles of power in the new international order.

This polarization was reinforced by the acquisition of nuclear weapons and later thermonuclear arms by both states. Washington exploded its first atomic bomb in July 1945 and Moscow in September 1949. American monopoly of atomic weapons was altered to a superior stockpile of them. As both superpowers developed their nuclear arsenals and delivery capabilities in the 1950s and 1960s, mutual deterrence became a fact of life in their relations. Indeed, it is possible that a third world war involving them was prevented because of their nuclear armament.

The distribution of world power in the early postwar environment was reflected in the United Nations. The veto in the Security Council was given to its five permanent members: the United States, the Soviet Union, Great Britain, France, and China. Clearly the disparity in power between the first two and the other three was profound. The Soviet Union frequently resorted to the veto, for the United States in the early years of the United Nations had solid support from the majority of the other members both in the Security Council and the General Assembly.

The rapid decline of colonialism was another major characteristic of the postwar world.[2] Germany lost its overseas empire through surrender in World War I and Italy and Japan through defeat in its successor. Although the British, French, Dutch, and Belgians emerged on the winning side in 1945 and sought at the time to maintain their overseas empires they were handicapped by the consequences of the war at home and in their possessions. The Spanish and Portuguese were not belligerents in the conflict, the former under Generalissimo Francisco Franco subsequently accepting the decline of colonialism and the latter under Salazar resolutely refusing to adjust to the new order. Even before the war the United States was relinquishing its overseas possessions through steps or plans that led to independence, commonwealth status, or statehood.

The achievement of decolonization (here narrowly interpreted as the actual termination of a state of dependency) was faster than anticipated after V-J Day and speedier in Asia than in Africa.* By the time it was over except for Portuguese possessions and various scattered dependencies independence had come to countries varying in size and population from India (1,176,000 square miles and 498,680,000 people as of 1966) to Nauru in the Pacific (8 square miles and 6,056 people as of 1966). In fact, the emergence of microstates presented serious problems of membership and relationship for the United Nations.

*Apart from the actual termination of dependency like the formal independence of the Philippines or the joining of Sarawak with Malaya in Malaysia, decolonization, it is clear, was a process involving political, economic, psychological, and other dimensions. In some countries decolonization was evolutionary in character and in others revolutionary. In the perspective of time it may be called an era.[3]

The loss of colonial empire forced the metropolitan powers to adjust to new conditions at home and in the world. The degree of adjustment by the former mother countries was related to the importance of the lost possessions and to the type of settlement when worked out with them. The old question of whether colonies were worth their cost to maintain can never be definitively answered since so many variables were involved, but many metropolitan powers are more prosperous in the postcolonial period than they were in the colonial era. For some of them the solution to the loss of empire lay in regional economic cooperation.

Related to the polarization of power and the decline of colonialism in the postwar world was another major characteristic of the international environment, the emergence of power vacuums. With a distribution of power among several states of roughly comparable strength and with a large part of the world their colonial territory, power vacuums were less apt to occur. The eclipse of German power created a vacuum in Europe, and Japanese power, a vacuum in East Asia, while the decline of British and French power had profound effects in various parts of the world. Decolonization, furthermore, replaced the power of the metropolitan countries, weak though it widely was after the war, with that of weaker, newly independent fledglings.

Although subject to variation in time and extent power vacuums emerged particularly in Central Europe, the Middle East, Southeast Asia, and Northeast Asia. The Soviet Union and the United States as superpowers filled in all or part of the vacuums but even their capabilities were limited. As a consequence certain power vacuums became areas of intense international competition, at times threatening the peace of the world. The evidence indicates that power flows into a vacuum often intensifying the instability of an area. The management of power in such a situation is a matter of supreme concern for world peace. Only the continent of Antarctica has been substantially internationalized—but Antarctica is permanently inhabited largely by emperor penguins who have no imperial ambitions.

The Cold War was another major characteristic of the postwar environment. Although the terminology is unfortunate—cold war and war in its traditional meaning are quite different—force was applied in relations between the two superpowers. This force involved political, diplomatic, economic, psychological, and even military pressure on a world scale but stopped just short of open war, as in the Berlin airlift crisis and the Cuban missile crisis. In the actual fighting of the Korean War and Second Indochinese War, Moscow and Washington supported opposite sides, the latter with large numbers of combat forces. Indeed, if the element of global struggle between two major alignments with deep commitment and high stakes is accepted as the basis of comparison, World War I, World War II, and the Cold War represent a continuum.*

The Cold War began very shortly after the defeat of the axis—1945, 1946, 1947 are given as dates by different analysts. Its conclusion is even more debatable, for various aspects in varying degrees continued for some time. No formal declaration of war and no unconditional surrender provide convenient dates for future students to memorize. Rise and decline are better words to characterize the time dimensions of the conflict.[5]

Even more controversial is the argument on the causes of the Cold War.[6] W. Averell Harriman, U.S. Ambassador to the Soviet Union, 1943–46, wrote in 1951: "The postwar difficulties stem from the fact that Stalin did not carry out his commitments and from the fact that the Soviet Union has failed to live up to the Charter of the United Nations. . . . The one great thing accomplished by our constant efforts during and since the war to reach a settlement with the Soviet Union is that we have firmly established our moral position before the world."[7] The United States and its allies officially waged the Cold War in response to the aggression of the Soviet Union and its friends.

In marked contrast, the extreme revisionists argue that with Roosevelt's death, with the defeat of the axis, and with the American monopoly of the atomic bomb Truman ended the policy of cooperation with Moscow and substituted one of blind and fanatic anticommunism. This new policy forced Stalin to secure his borders especially in Eastern Europe and precipitated the Cold War.

All American wars have been subjected to the analysis of revisionists but despite the publicity and the argument revisionism has not usually carried the day. The Cold War represented a complex pattern of offense and defense, of action and counteraction, of thrust and parry. Each side was convinced the other constituted a threat and was an aggressor. Although the United States is certainly not blameless in the Cold War its basic role will probably be vindicated in history. Professor Arthur Schlesinger, Jr., for instance, has placed stress in his able analysis of the roots of the conflict on "the intransigence of Leninist ideology, the sinister dynamics of a totalitarian society and the madness of Stalin."[8]

Southeast Asia. The early postwar environment in Southeast Asia was affected by and in turn contributed to the prevailing world situation.[9] As a conquered and occupied area during the war, only parts of it being liberated toward the end, Southeast Asia's problems of relief and rehabilita-

---

*Louis J. Halle has pointed out that "since the end of the eighteenth century four great wars have been fought to maintain or restore the European balance of power. The fourth was the Cold War."[4]

tion were staggering. Destruction of property, decline in production of basic commodities, trade dislocation first with countries outside Southeast Asia and then within it, the impairment or breakdown of transportation facilities, the crippling effects of inflation, the dislocation of the labor market, the exhaustion of stocks, the stagnation of the cities and the setback to rural development, the isolation from the technology of the West—these and others were contributing factors.

But the cost of the war in human values may have been greater. Individual struggle for existence was intensified, although the traditional subsistence economy of the vast majority of the people should not be minimized. The struggle for a living under wartime conditions contributed to the decline of law and order in Southeast Asia. The availability of arms and weapons in many parts of the area as a consequence of the fighting encouraged this decline. Tactics of trying to outwit the Japanese in civil life or in guerrilla operations could be used against postwar authorities whether foreign or indigenous. What was patriotic in wartime might be corruption or even treason in peacetime. Health conditions had deteriorated and disease was rampant. The shortage in expertise in education, industry, and government was pronounced.

Political chaos reigned in some areas of Southeast Asia for a time after Japan surrendered. In other parts it was not complete political chaos but a state hovering near that. Civil disorder was a major characteristic. Bandits, smugglers, and revolutionaries of various persuasions, religious, separatist, and Communist, were active. Instability was prevalent, for the political future of Southeast Asia was uncertain. Exiles and puppets were caught in the vortex of victory for some and defeat for others. Puppets were not sure in the collapse of Japan's New Order whether they could make their claim stick that they served as genuine buffers between the Japanese and the people. Exiles could not be certain of the attitude toward them at home. Nationalists in Southeast Asia of various backgrounds and persuasions sought to capitalize on the collapse of Japan. Minorities within the body politic like the Chinese and Indians were concerned over their political future. National unification and social integration, long range in nature, would not be easy. One fact of life was clear: the Japanese were out. But, and this is a large but, who for the forseeable future would take their place?

The British, French, and Dutch expected their return to Southeast Asia would last for some time. The enlargement of Mountbatten's Southeast Asia Command at Potsdam, the composition and disposition of forces under him, and the sudden surrender of Japan in August strengthened London for a while. British-commanded forces arrived in various parts of the region, the chief exceptions being the Philippines under

MacArthur's command and Indochina north of the sixteenth parallel under Chiang's command. Insofar as possible the British, it will be later stressed, facilitated the return of the Dutch to the East Indies and especially the French to southern Indochina. Nor did the European colonial powers upon their return to Southeast Asia anticipate in 1945 any serious obstacles from outside Asians. The Chinese Nationalists were exhausted from the long war with Japan; the Chinese Communists were located far from the borders of Southeast Asia; and both were quarreling, with civil war a real possibility. Japan's power was eclipsed, and the Soviet Union, both a European and an Asian power, was much more concerned with events in Europe than in Asia.

With the collapse of Japan the problems of SEAC shifted from those of fighting a war to administering former enemy territory. Economic and political considerations came to the forefront. Mountbatten had suggested that soon after the conflict a governor-general or possibly a special commissioner for Southeast Asia should be appointed although he had not carefully considered his functions. In March 1946 Lord Killearn arrived as special commissioner and in May Malcolm MacDonald as governor general of Malaya and British Borneo. A British defense committee in Southeast Asia was created consisting in effect of the supreme commander, governor general, and special commissioner. Lord Killearn's Economic Organization provided a framework for relief and rehabilitation—food was a major consideration—not only in British territories but also in some other dependencies of Southeast Asia. It became one of the early benchmarks on the long, winding, pothole road of regionalism.

The Western colonial powers underestimated the force of nationalism in Southeast Asia. It originated in the hearts, the emotions, of a small number of Western-educated leaders living or having lived in the capital cities of the dependencies. This is, of course, a generalization, but it does contain an array of common denominators. Nationalism is emotional rather than rational; Sukarno, for instance, was a living monument of Indonesian nationalism. The early Southeast Asian leaders were usually educated in Western schools at home or abroad where they studied the historical development of nationalism in the West. Moreover, nationalism generally arose in urban rather than rural Southeast Asia. The capital cities like Batavia, Rangoon, and Saigon were the centers of colonial activities which the emerging nationalist elite observed and increasingly disliked.

Nationalism in Southeast Asia thrived, nourished by the defeat of the Western colonial powers at the hands of the Japanese, by the actions intentional and unintentional of the Nipponese conquerors, and by postwar colonial policies, especially of the Dutch and French. It became the

strongest force in Southeast Asia. When the Communists under Ho Chi
Minh captured the nationalism of most of the Vietnamese in the long
war against the French, they erected a foundation whose international
consequences are profound.

United States Objectives: World, Northeast Asia, Southeast Asia.
American objectives in the world at the end of World War II were well
articulated.[10] In addition to global, the United States had regional and
country goals. Events in the early postwar years, however, changed some
of the objectives or at least altered priorities. The development of the
Cold War was a major consideration. Furthermore, the ability of a state,
even the mightiest in history in mid-1945, to control the direction of
world events has been exaggerated. And even the most powerful leaders
are subject to restraints in the international system.

In global terms the United States sought a world order based on the
sovereign equality of states but recognizing inequality in power and influence. Within this system Washington wanted to maintain world peace
and international security through its own unilateral contributions,
through the concept of the cooperation of the Great Powers—the Soviet
Union, Great Britain, China, France, and itself—and through the collective security of the United Nations. In economic relations the United
States sought to advance international economic stability through cooperative national effort. In the immediate future Washington wanted, on the
one hand, a settlement with the major enemy states that would eliminate
renewed threats to the peace, that would create an environment where
economic freedom and political democracy could develop, and that
would enable them eventually to play a peaceful role in the world community. On the other hand, it wanted the reconstruction of the liberated
states—minor enemy countries in effect being classified here—as independent members of the world community under democratic governments.

The global objectives of Washington in 1945 reflected a "sincerely calculated risk" that wartime cooperation among the leaders of the alliance
could become the foundation of postwar international security.[11] Roosevelt, however, toward the end of his life, was becoming disillusioned
about Stalin's keeping his promises. And the American Joint Chiefs of
Staff in 1944 believed the greatest chance of eventual war after the present conflict was between the Soviet Union and Great Britain. Yet in
1946 the impasse over the future of Germany between Moscow and
Washington became a fact of international life and an Anglo-American
alignment was under way. With the benefit of hindsight it is clear that a
major premise of Roosevelt's peacetime planning during the war—the
solidarity of the Great Powers—was not valid, at least for some time, if

indeed ever. In addition, Washington overestimated the postwar strength of France and Nationalist China in the international community.

The strategic concept of containment of the Soviet Union by the United States, reflecting the polarization of power and arising from the Cold War, crystallized by early 1947.[12] In an international environment where the monolithic aspect of international communism under Stalin's leadership essentially seemed a reality and where the anti-Communist forces of the Free World were fundamentally disposed to follow the leadership of Washington, the United States moved from emphasis on political adjustment through conferences and discussions to the building of "situations of strength" from which to negotiate. At home the rapid demobilization of American armed forces as a consequence of public opinion had weakened the voice of Washington in discussions with Moscow, but President Truman as the Cold War intensified was able to start rebuilding the military power of the country. In the economic field reconversion from World War II had been speedy but did not markedly weaken the economic power of the nation. The political influence of Washington, of course, was affected by developments in its military and economic positions. The world, however, had just witnessed an example of the total military, economic, and political power potential of the United States.

President Truman took concrete steps toward containment of the Soviet Union, many of them later becoming applicable to Southeast Asia. The Truman Doctrine of March 1947 under which assistance was given to Greece and Turkey asserted that "it must be the policy of the United States to support free peoples who are resisting attempted subjugation by armed minorities or by outside pressures."[13] The Marshall Plan for American aid in the economic recovery of Europe was suggested by Secretary of State Marshall in an address at Harvard in June and subsequently implemented. Influenced by the Communist takeover in Czechoslovakia late in February 1948 and supported by the Vandenberg Resolution in June on American association with regional collective defense arrangements, the United States signed the North Atlantic Treaty of April 1949 and subsequently became the key member of the North Atlantic Treaty Organization (NATO). Military assistance was made possible under the Mutual Defense Assistance Act of October to various nations, some of whom, like Greece and Turkey, were already receiving it. In his inaugural address of January 1949 President Truman had asked for a program of aid to the underdeveloped countries. Point Four, as it came to be called, involved U.S. technical assistance. Among the multiple motivations of the proposal was a desire to extend the strategy of containment to areas emerging from colonialism.

As distinguished from global objectives, the United States had goals in East Asia: in Japan, Korea, and China in Northeast Asia and in the peninsular and insular region called Southeast Asia. During the early postwar years these goals were affected by the shift in American global objectives but basic changes did not occur in some areas until the rise of Communist China and the outbreak of the Korean War. As Southeast Asia proved not immune to developments in Northeast Asia, attention must be given to the latter.

A memorandum of April 18, 1944, prepared in the Office of Far Eastern Affairs for the use of the Secretary in discussion with individuals outside the Department indicated State Department thought on the Far East. "After the people who have come under the domination of Japan's armed forces are liberated," it stated, "our task will be that of making the Pacific and eastern Asia safe—safe for the United States, safe for our Allies, safe for all peace-loving peoples."[14] The cooperation of the United States, the Soviet Union, the British Commonwealth, and China was considered the key in maintaining the future peace of the area.

After V-J Day the United States clearly realized that no unified policy by the major powers was possible in East Asia and that the situation in the vast area was not conducive to an East Asian policy as contrasted to a separate Japanese, Korean, Chinese, and possibly Southeast Asian policy. In other words, with the defeat of Japan, the common foe, the interests and policies of the major powers were so diverse and the problems and difficulties of the countries of East Asia so varied that the United States, in effect, was forced to act to a large extent on its own and at least in Northeast Asia on a country-to-country basis. (China, it should be recalled, was considered a major power.) The United States containment policy of the Soviet Union was more quickly and easily applied to Europe than to East Asia. When it came to the latter there were marked variations from application in Europe.

The United States wanted China after V-J Day to be the chief "stabilizing factor" in East Asia. A stable, united, strong China under a government representing the will of the people would fill the vacuum created by the eclipse of Japanese power. Needed for peace and security in East Asia, such a China, working closely with the United States, would be the major power around which Washington could build its policy in the vast reaches of the area. At the same time the United States—even as stated in official documentation back in February 1945—did not want Chinese "domination" or Chinese "political control" over such nearby areas as Korea in Northeast Asia or Indochina, Thailand, and Burma in Southeast Asia. Roosevelt took a personal interest in the future of China and was largely responsible for its receiving veto power in the Security Council. Churchill did not share this evaluation of the country. The China the

United States wanted after World War II fitted into the historic pattern of Sino-American friendship and met American political and strategic needs in East Asia.

The major stumbling block after V-J Day to Chinese political unity was the profound difference between the Nationalists of Chiang Kai-shek and the Communists of Mao Tse-tung. In an effort first designed to halt the fighting and later altered to create a government of national unity— all aimed at a "strong, united, and democratic China"—President Truman sent General Marshall on a special mission to the war-torn country. The Marshall Mission, December 1945–January 1947, for a while stopped fighting between the Nationalists and Communists through the institution of truce teams in contested areas and an executive head-quarters in Peking—called by some observers a miracle—but it failed to reconcile the basic political and military differences among the Chinese. No person could have made a more dedicated effort than General Marshall, though in retrospect his mission was probably impossible from the beginning. He left China blaming the extremists of both sides for his fail-ure. Even before Marshall's departure fighting had erupted in different parts of the country. The full resumption of the civil war found the United States unwilling and unable under the circumstances to make a major effort to save the government of Chiang on the mainland. Although differences in Russian and American policy toward the Chinese became pronounced in 1946 and 1947, Washington's early effort toward containment of the Soviet Union was not focused on China.[15] Indeed, President Truman and Secretary of State Dean Acheson became fearful lest American domestic opposition to China policy weaken U.S. support for Western Europe.

In contrast to the role the United States in 1945 wanted China to play in East Asia, Japan would be placed under American occupation, its military machine would be obliterated, and its political, cultural, and economic institutions would be reformed with the goal of creating a democratic Japan purified of aggressive intentions and playing the role of a Switzerland in East Asia. General Douglas MacArthur became Supreme Commander for the Allied Powers in Japan and governed with a minimum of influence from either the Allied Council in Tokyo or the Far Eastern Commission in Washington. History may record that the General's greatest contribution was his handling of the American occupation of Nippon. When the occupation ended the new Japan would replace China, now Communist, as the chief focus of American hopes in East Asia. And, as the containment policy developed, first toward the Soviet Union and then the Sino-Soviet bloc, the United States placed greater emphasis on Japan's role in it.

Korea would probably never have received major attention in American policy had it not been for the Korean War of 1950–53. At Cairo the United States along with Great Britain and China in 1943 had asserted that the country "in due course" should be "free and independent." The Soviet Union later agreed to the Cairo statement. Responsibility for receiving the surrender of Japanese forces in Korea was divided between the United States in the area south of the thirty-eighth parallel and the Soviet Union in the territory north of it. Despite negotiations, Moscow and Washington could not agree on the formation of a Korean government for the whole country, and the occupying powers took steps that led to rival Korean regimes with each superpower helping its protégé. The impasse on Korea, becoming firm in 1946, became a living example of the Cold War in East Asia until June 1950.

American goals for Southeast Asia in the early period after the war were more integrated than those for Northeast Asia. The course of events in the latter area and its ramifications for the former were not foreseen. Since all Southeast Asia except Thailand was colonial the American attitude toward colonialism provided a common denominator. Washington liked to stress that the Philippines, about to become independent, was a beacon for Southeast Asia. The beacon, however, was often dim. As the containment policy of the United States developed, American policy makers were more torn than before between the priorities of local self-government and international security in the region. Although the two were definitely related, situations could arise where the time differential was important.

The American support of self-government, limited though it proved to be, was more than just an ideal. It was asserted by realists or idealists (depending on the expert) that nationalism strengthened by the war had reached or was reaching sufficient dimensions that the colonial powers would have to give it an outlet in self-determination and self-government, or face instability and even armed revolt. In the latter situation the dependencies would become anti-Western and threaten world peace, especially if the Communists tried to take advantage of conditions. They might also develop an "anti-Western Pan-Asiatic" front. As the Cold War developed, the Communist aspect received increased attention in Washington. But how could it best be handled?

In retrospect, the United States did not appear to foresee the degree of instability that might characterize the road to self-government. Nor was the degree of instability that might result after the achievement of self-government in Southeast Asia widely realized. American officials at the time, it is clear, did not have much expertise in the area, apart from the Philippines and to a lesser extent Thailand. Common problems existed but each country was unique, and a number of key questions could not be easily answered in 1945. Just what would be the long-range effect of Japan's occupation in Southeast Asia? How strong was nationalism in various countries? What directions would it ultimately take?

Although the United States reiterated that it favored self-government for those who were prepared for it, Washington sought its achievement through evolutionary and peaceful means. Colonial rule did have certain material benefits and these might be better preserved through cooperation between the former ruler and the former subjects. The peaceful political settlement of differences between Southeast Asian nationalists and colonial powers was urged. In effect, the object but not the method of the American Revolution was favored as a long-run solution. Self-government was generally interpreted in Washington in the early postwar period as independence, at least in terms of the Canadian or Australian relationship with Great Britain or its equivalent. Nationalism would reach an intensity, it was argued, where hardly any status short of the Canadian model would be feasible.

Self-government was also widely interpreted as democracy. It was believed that self-governing peoples were not only likely to settle internal troubles by peaceful methods but also would cooperate with the United States and assist the cause of world peace.* This interpretation, of course, was disputed and could turn out to be wishful thinking. As for American political policies and economic programs in East Asia, it was stated by one official in October 1946 that they were geared toward promoting self-government.[17] "To achieve our objectives," John Carter Vincent, Director, Office of Far Eastern Affairs, Department of State, went on to say, "we should be powerful, we should be patient, and we should be persevering."[18]

In supporting the objective of non-Communist nationalism in Southeast Asia the United States believed it was building on durable foundations. In the early years after V-J Day Washington wanted to leave the region for good, apart from special ties with the Philippines. It preferred Southeast Asian regimes under nationalist leadership to European colonial governments. But if the choice were between Communist regimes and European colonial governments under the conditions of the Cold War—say mid-1947 in Indochina and Indonesia—the latter were preferable.

---

*The Division of Far Eastern Affairs of the State Department on April 21, 1945, had expressed itself in these words: "Encouragement of and assistance to the peoples of Southeast Asia in developing autonomous, democratic self-rule in close, willing association with major Western powers would not only be in harmony with political trends in that area, but would appear to be the one practical solution which will assure peace and stability in the Far East."[16]

The development of Washington's containment policy with its emphasis on Europe created triangular conflicts of interest among the United States, European colonial powers, and their territories in Southeast Asia. Economic dislocation and political turmoil in Asian dependencies could impair the recovery and security of metropolitan states in Western Europe. The resources the United States was diverting to Western Europe weakened American ability to aid East Asia. But these resources on the whole could be much better used in Europe where the industrial capacity could be quickly built up, where cooperation was forthcoming, and where impetus could be given U.S. objectives.

American policy makers disagreed among themselves concerning the future of Southeast Asia after V-J Day and of American interests there.* Asian specialists tended to stress the importance of nationalism and to believe the European colonial powers would quickly depart.

European specialists were inclined to deemphasize the role of nationalism and to give the European rulers a relatively long future in Southeast Asia. No love was lost between the two sides. If the European specialists had not held the upper hand, and if the Cold War had not interfered, postwar Southeast Asia would probably have become much less of a problem area.

Charles W. Yost, then political adviser in Thailand, answered a query from the Department of State about U.S. prestige in India and Southeast Asia, on December 13, 1945. He observed that the nationalist parties in French Indochina and the Netherlands East Indies were disillusioned when the United States did not positively assist them against foreign pressure, did not get treatment for them comparable to that of the Philippines, and did not restore their economies badly hurt by the war. There was an increasing conviction that Washington was hardly interested in Southeast Asia apart from limited commerce and planned to leave the area entirely to the French, Dutch, and British. Yost asserted that the "unfavorable impression is enhanced by use of US vessels to transport British, French, and Dutch troops and use of American equipment by these troops as well as by Mountbatten's retention of title 'Supreme Allied Commander,' US being generally assumed to be one of the Allies in question."[20] In one of the most prophetic comments of his career he

---

*Shortly after the death of Roosevelt, in the battle of the memos in 1945 between the Division of Far Eastern Affairs and the Division of European Affairs over U.S. policy toward Indochina, the former had urged that in the proposed memorandum for President Truman statements be inserted "as to the increasingly profound interest of the United States in the future of Southeast Asia." In the compromise memorandum (one not even sent to the President) a statement to the above effect was made after stress on the importance of Franco-American ties.[19]

noted: "American abstention . . . does not seem likely to contribute to long term stability in Southeast Asia as it makes probable temporary restoration of prewar arrangements which in fact are often unsuited to present-day conditions and cannot for that reason long be maintained except by force."[21]

Structure at State. The organization of the Department of State in September 1945 is revealing in the light of Yost's comments. Although it is easy to exaggerate the importance of structure, a number of policy makers of the period have very expressly called attention to it. The Office of Far Eastern Affairs included the Division of Southeast Asian Affairs. This division had within its own scope Thailand, and *shared* with other concerned geographic offices and divisions the Netherlands East Indies (Division of Northern European Affairs of the Office of European Affairs), French Indochina and Portuguese Timor (Division of Western European Affairs of the same office), Malaya and British Borneo (Division of British Commonwealth Affairs of the same office), and Burma (Division of Middle Eastern Affairs of the Office of Near Eastern and African Affairs). A Division of Philippine Affairs was also under the Office of Far Eastern Affairs. Significantly the directors of the above offices, like John Carter Vincent of Far Eastern Affairs and H. Freeman Matthews of European Affairs, reported to Secretary of State James F. Byrnes and Undersecretary of State Dean Acheson through James C. Dunn, the Assistant Secretary of State for European, Far Eastern, and Near Eastern and African Affairs. He was an influential "Europe firster." Of course, changes in personnel and in the table of organization occurred (Burma, for instance, was shifted more than once) and other federal agencies were involved in policy making but the basic pattern persisted for some time. Both President Truman and the top leadership in the department were Europe-oriented.

THE REPUBLIC OF THE PHILIPPINES

Washington proceeded in a forthright manner toward the independence of the Philippines and toward the creation of special relations between two sovereign states.* America held to the target date—July 4, 1946—for independence. Suggestions that the date be advanced were as unsuccessful as efforts to delay it. President Truman came to believe that time was needed not only to work out the future relationship between Manila

*Ushering the Philippines into the family of nations was a unique experience for Washington, quite unlike what faced the British in liquidating a world-wide empire. The documentation in footnote 22 reveals considerable tactical confusion at times, with frantic telephone calls to and from Manila as July 4, 1946, neared.[22]

and Washington but also to enable the Philippines to recover from the immediate effects of the war. Although he had shown considerable interest in the islands in April and May 1945 the pressure of world events presumably diminished his attention.[23] After V-J Day he appointed Paul V. McNutt high commissioner to the Philippines, a selection that greatly influenced the course of events.

In October, Commonwealth President Osmeña saw Truman in Washington. The American chief executive approved a directive, prepared in McNutt's office in Manila, which inaugurated a program of reconstruction through the cooperation of eleven departments and federal agencies. Osmeña, however, could not return to Manila with any substantial aid, for legislation was being delayed in Congress. This failure may have cost him the presidency in the national elections of April 1946. Backed among others by the Communist-led Huks, Nacionalista Osmeña lost to Liberal Manuel Roxas who numbered influential collaborators among his supporters. (President Roxas ordered in January 1948 a political amnesty for collaborators.) Osmeña accepted gracefully his defeat by 54 per cent of the 2.5 million votes cast and thereby established a valuable precedent in the transfer of power in the postwar Philippines. In May President-elect Roxas accompanied by High Commissioner McNutt visited Washington where various proposed treaty and other agreements were discussed. It was agreed that after the independence of the Philippines Washington, as requested by Roxas, would represent Manila's interests abroad until it was able to assume the task.

On the day President Truman issued his proclamation withdrawing U.S. sovereignty over the islands and recognizing the independence of the Republic of the Philippines, President Roxas, General MacArthur, and High Commissioner McNutt spoke at a ceremony on the Luneta before the Rizal Monument. In the distance were the ruins of the Legislative Building constructed under the Americans and of Intramuros built under the Spanish. As McNutt spoke, heavy rain began to fall. At 9:15 in the morning the American flag was lowered following by only a brief time in history the Japanese and Spanish banners. Manuel Quezon and José Laurel were not there to witness the ceremony but within a few days the former's body would be returned home in honor on the U.S.S. "Princeton" and the latter would be flown back from Japan under guard. With the raising of the Philippine flag one subsequent president of the republic sensed a feeling of nostalgia. On the occasion of the ceremony MacArthur said to a Philippine friend: "Carlos, America buried imperialism here today."[24]

Independence Settlement. This complex arrangement reflected changes of attitude in both Washington and Manila as a consequence of World War II. The U.S. Congress wanted to keep some of the colonial ties while the administration in Washington shifted to support genuine independence. The Department of State in particular was concerned over Asian and world reaction to the island republic. General MacArthur for his part clearly helped at the beginning to send Manuel Roxas to Malacañang, and Paul McNutt after a period of impartiality between the candidates contributed to Roxas' victory. The High Commissioner's more important handiwork is found in certain aspects of the Bell Trade Act and the Tydings Rehabilitation Act. Although a reservoir of goodwill existed toward the Philippines in Congress, Manila with its postwar conditions and desperate needs did not have much bargaining position with Washington. In fact, the Philippine economy was more dependent on the United States than any state in the Union was dependent upon the rest of the nation. Filipinos in the aftermath of liberation from the Japanese were willing to make concessions to the United States that would have been unlikely in the 1930s.

Political, economic, and military relations were formalized in the independence settlement.[25] A treaty of general relations associated with the transfer of sovereignty was signed in Manila. After frantic efforts involving Truman, Roxas, Acheson, and McNutt an executive agreement implementing the Bell Trade Act was also signed the same day. (Washington had opposed consummation of such an agreement until *after* July 4.) Contrary to the desire of the United States a military base accord was not concluded that day, though an air transport agreement and a treaty of conciliation were signed on November 16. A consular convention was concluded on March 14, 1947, but a treaty of friendship, commerce, and navigation was delayed. The American Congress passed a law enabling Filipinos to become naturalized U.S. citizens and giving them an immigration quota. Formal relations were conducted through the establishment of embassies in Washington and Manila.

The economic settlement expedited by McNutt in Congress during a visit to Washington placed severe restrictions on Philippine economic autonomy. The Bell Trade Act provided for free trade between the two countries for eight years after which tariff increases over twenty years would reach 100 per cent in 1974. The peso was tied by the act to the dollar and the rate of exchange could not be altered without the approval of the American chief executive. Under a parity provision, contributed by McNutt, U.S. citizens and corporations acquired the same economic rights in the development of natural resources and public utilities in the islands as Filipinos. The Tydings Rehabilitation Act provided $620 million in compensation with $400 million of it for people and firms proving they had been the victims of war damage, $120 million for the restoration of public property and services, and $100 million in the form of surplus U.S. military property. Under a linchpin proviso, also contributed by McNutt, private claims of more than $500 would not be paid until Manila accepted the Bell Trade Act. As the parity provision contradicted the constitution of the Philippines, an amendment to the latter was necessary.

The Trade Act reflected a compromise between Manila, which wanted free trade for twenty years, and Senator Tydings, who was eager to terminate trade preferences in five years. Roosevelt shortly before his death favored declining preferences, and Truman participated in a key meeting, November 13, 1945, on the proposed bill. The State, Agriculture, and Commerce Departments in Washington criticized the act on various grounds.[26] The parity provision and the tying of the peso to the dollar, it was argued, violated the principles of reciprocity and independence. Nevertheless, President Truman signed the trade and rehabilitation bills into law on April 30, 1946, and the Philippine Congress and electorate approved the necessary amendment to the constitution.

Military arrangements between the United States and the Philippines were made in the agreement on bases signed March 14, 1947, and that on military assistance concluded a week later. These arrangements were not predicated on a U.S. military role in the rest of Southeast Asia. The American Congress in a joint resolution approved June 29, 1944, had authorized the President to keep or to acquire and hold such bases and related rights as he deemed necessary for the mutual protection of the United States and the Philippines. On May 14, 1945, Truman and Osmeña had signed a preliminary statement on general principles relative to an American naval and military base system in the islands, and the Manila Congress, in a joint resolution approved July 28, had authorized the Philippine President to negotiate the establishment of American bases in the archipelago.

It proved difficult, however, to translate intention into reality. The road to an agreement on military bases was long and winding with many hazards along it. A lively exchange, for instance, occurred between Ambassador McNutt and the Department of State when the former suggested on November 7, 1946, that in an Armistice Day speech at an American Legion banquet he note that the United States and the Philippines "have entered into a solemn compact for the mutual defense of the Philippines believing such defense to be in the interest of both nations."[27] He went on in his proposed remarks to assert that if Manila wanted the withdrawal of U.S. forces and the termination of American protection he was sure Washington would do so. McNutt who had discussed the speech privately with President Roxas believed it would strengthen the Philippine President against members of his administration who were contributing to the attack on the U.S. base program.

After consideration at the "highest levels of the State, War, and Navy Departments" McNutt was quickly informed that the "consensus is that your proposed declaration is inadvisable at this time and that public reference to 'a solemn compact for the mutual defense of the Philippines' would be impolitic in any foreseeable circumstances."[28] The Ambassador on November 10 replied that he found it "extremely difficult to reconcile" the contents of the telegram with the previous U.S. stance relating to a mutual defense compact. "If this is not the settled policy of the US," he asked, "what can I tell Philippine Government?"[29] Three days later the Department of State informed McNutt that Washington did not want to make a public reference to a "solemn compact" pending the conclusion of the base agreement. In fact, that very day, November 13, the Secretaries of State, War, and Navy considered the base problem in the Philippines, and the Secretary of War Robert P. Patterson expressed impatience over Manila's attitude, observing that the U.S. need for forces and bases in the islands was being reexamined.

On November 23 General Dwight D. Eisenhower, Army Chief of Staff, recommended that all American army forces be withdrawn from the Republic of the Philippines. Secretary Patterson six days later in his agreement wrote in a letter to the Secretary of State:

> You will note that General Eisenhower has recognized that the military importance of the Philippines is of lesser weight in our national interest than the future good relations of the two nations and that long term continuance of Army forces in the Philippines would be of little value unless their retention was the result of an expressed desire of the Philippine Government.[30]

Secretary Byrnes agreed with Patterson and Eisenhower. President Truman on December 4 approved the recommendation that all American army forces be withdrawn from the Philippines. President Roxas, however, clearly indicated later in the month he wanted U.S. bases in the islands. He was particularly concerned over American installations near the capital and over the question of jurisdiction over U.S. military personnel.

When the accord of March 1947 was finally reached twenty-three naval, army, or air force bases were involved. In the agreement, the United States acquired for a period of 99 years "the right to retain the use" of a designated list of them and to use designated others if Washington saw "military necessity." Both parties would have to agree before any third state could acquire bases in the Philippines. Washington was free to seek the enlargement or reduction of the areas. The air base at Clark Field and the naval base at Subic Bay were key installations.*

In 1946 the U.S. Congress had passed a military assistance bill for the Philippines indicative of coming American-Philippine military relationships. Under the military assistance agreement of 1947 (replaced in 1953) U.S. aid in the form of training, weapons, and related support was provided and a Joint United States Military Advisory Group was created to assist in the program. Philippine military equipment was thereby related to U.S. sources. The increasingly serious Huk menace was a factor in the deliberations on military aid.

Just as the parity provision and currency arrangements were viewed by many Filipinos as an infringement on their sovereignty, U.S. bases with related problems of administration and jurisdiction caused concern among some Filipinos. In the early postwar period frictions between Americans and Filipinos could be more easily held in check than in subsequent years. In fact, Manila was critical of Washington for not developing its bases faster. Nationalism, however, was on the increase, stressing more and more economic and cultural considerations though not at all ignoring political ones.

The basic foreign policy of the Republic of the Philippines in the early years was established by the independence settlement. Although no formal alliance existed between Washington and Manila until 1951, despite talks on security with mutual understanding, the presence of American bases on Philippine soil ruled out nonalignment as the heart of foreign policy. The bases could draw an attack on U.S. armed forces in the Philippines and they could provide facilities for American military operations outside the islands. It is impossible to isolate foreign bases from the country in which they are located. The host nation can attempt to determine the circumstances under which base facilities are used in warfare but their very existence is a calculation in the plans of friend and foe alike.

Important though the bases are in Philippine foreign policy, they were only symbols of the special relationship between the United States and the Philippines after July 4, 1946—a special relationship resting on historic, political, and economic foundations as well as on security consider-

---

*American interest in Philippine base facilities was related to a diplomatic effort under way in 1946 to acquire base rights not elsewhere in Southeast Asia, but in Pacific islands like Manus, an Australian dependency; Western Samoa, a New Zealand dependency; Viti Levu (Nadi) in the Fiji Islands, a British colony; and others. The old Japanese mandated islands of the Carolines, Marshalls, and Marianas were under American occupation prior to becoming a United Nations strategic trust territory under the United States.

ations. It meant more to the Filipinos than to the Americans, for the United States was a superpower with global interests. Nevertheless, in the world of 1946, Washington had a special relationship with only three countries, Great Britain, Canada, and the Philippines. The Filipinos for their part often claimed that the Americans took them for granted in East Asia, but the time would come when the reverse accusation would be made.

In the early years of the island republic two roles for Manila were frequently mentioned. Some Americans and Filipinos thought of the new state in terms of a "show window of American democracy in Asia" and of a "bridge between Asia and the West." The first concept was not valid in fact and the second was not feasible in practice, and both were condemned by many Philippine nationalists who did not want either.*

The special relationship between Washington and Manila complicated the search of the Filipinos for an Asian identity or more important a national identity. The search would be intensified as the events of July 4, 1946, became less vivid and more a page in a history book. In the early years of the republic, genuine sympathy for non-Communist nationalist movements, loyalty to the principles of the United Nations, cultivation of ties with a number of non-Communist Asian neighbors, and sponsorship or participation in regional gatherings like the Baguio Conference of May 1950 were characteristics of foreign policy. Malacañang upon the independence of the Philippines established diplomatic relations with no Communist state, and considered communism at home or abroad a threat to the security of the republic. The development of the Cold War confirmed the pro-American and anti-Communist stance in Manila.

The hopes for the bright future of the Philippines at the time of independence were drastically curtailed by 1950. Probably too much was expected by Americans who regardless of political party were eager for the Philippine experiment to succeed and by Filipinos who believed the mere acquisition of sovereignty would provide the key to prosperity and peace. The level of expectation for states emerging from colonialism was much higher in the late 1940s than in the 1950s or 1960s.

Three Grave Developments. The Philippines faced three serious situations within four years of independence—an economic crisis, a weakening of political democracy, and the real possibility that a Communist

---

*Salvador P. Lopez, former Secretary of Foreign Affairs of the Philippines, notes that the "show window" role "creates an unflattering image of the Philippines as an American political supermarket in Asia" and that the "bridge" role "places a heavy strain on the capabilities and resources of the Filipino nation which may have little desire to take on this role, being content to be itself, at peace with its neighbors and in fruitful cooperation with them."[31]

regime would take over the islands. All were interrelated and affected Philippine-American ties. The independence settlement was subjected to pressures for revision that produced changes much earlier than anticipated.

Although the United States officially estimated it had given the islands between V-J Day and early 1950 $2 billion worth of overall aid, much of it did not contribute to solid economic development. Controversies arose over unpaid war damage claims, back pay to wartime guerrilla units, "anomalies and irregularities" or graft and corruption, and numerous other subjects. On the positive side of the ledger were the more than doubling of the physical volume of production to prewar levels from 1946 to 1949, the reduction in the cost of living from a 1946 index of 100 to a 1949 index of 44, and the growing entrepreneurial class. But on the negative side were the system of levying and collecting taxes, the low wages of agricultural and industrial workers, the standards of public administration, the reduction of foreign exchange reserves by early 1950 to less than half those in 1945, the mishandling of import and exchange licensing following its imposition in 1949, and the extremely limited resources of the treasury in 1950. Since the big cumulative import surplus from the conclusion of the war to the end of 1949 was matched by net American government expenditures and since the latter were declining with the spending of rehabilitation funds, the Philippines in early 1950 was badly in need of more U.S. aid.

Political democracy in the islands was at stake in the late 1940s. In effect the presidential democracy of Quezon had been replaced by a two-party system with hotly contested elections. After President Roxas' sudden death in April 1948 Vice-President Elpidio Quirino succeeded him. In a hotly contested election in November 1949 Quirino of the Liberal Party defeated José Laurel of the Nacionalista Party for the presidency. The election was characterized by extensive frauds and many instances of terrorism—birds and bees were allegedly called upon to vote and even ancestors reportedly rose from their graves to flock to the polls. The effect was to discredit the electoral process and give support to the Hukbalahaps. The Liberal administration before and after the elections suffered from anomalies and irregularities.

The Hukbalahaps constituted the greatest threat to law and order the postwar republic had faced.[32] Although Communist-led they had considerable support, especially from the peasants in Central Luzon who suffered from longstanding economic and social grievances. Commonwealth officials had failed to keep their promises, and the leaders of the republic, though more sensitive to voting power in a two-party system, had achieved little in the cause of social justice. From a People's Anti-Japanese Army (Hukbalahap is an abbreviation from Tagalog) the Huks gathered political and military strength until they emerged as a People's Liberation Army in February 1950. Their objective was an anti-American people's republic. In many respects from 1946 to 1953 a civil war of guerrilla dimensions was fought between the government and the Huks in Luzon and on occasion in the Visayas. Probably only the American liberation of the Philippines had prevented the Huks from taking over the government (given, of course, Japan's collapse), and after the independence of the country, they made another bid for power. If the islands had been a mainland state adjacent to a people's republic, the cause of communism would have been greatly strengthened. As it was, the outside Communists, especially the Chinese, could give little more than propaganda support and limited advice on tactics and strategy.

Southeast Asian leaders viewed developments in the Philippines from 1946 to 1950 with some interest and much cynicism. Many of them considered the Philippines too closely tied to the United States and few were favorably impressed by developments in the islands. As the first country in South and Southeast Asia to achieve independence after World War II, the Philippines attempted to exert some leadership in Asian affairs. The effort met with little success. The Baguio Conference, for instance, aroused limited interest and produced no significant results. The Indians, Russians, and British were critical of the Philippine experience in sovereignty. In New Delhi the Filipinos were viewed as only enjoying the facade of independence, in Moscow they were considered mere puppets of the United States (another way of expressing the Indian viewpoint), and in London they were looked upon as a bad example for other newly independent peoples. Since the Republic of the Philippines was among the first to emerge of the new states after the defeat of the axis, it suffered from lack of comparison with others.

INDONESIA

American policy toward Indonesia from the surrender of Japan to the Dutch transfer of sovereignty in December 1949 reflected a dilemma. As in the case of the Philippines, the United States was opposed to colonialism, and this attitude eventually dominated American policy. But unlike the Philippines, Indonesia was always a foreign problem and Washington became involved in complex international negotiations inside and outside the United Nations. American policy toward the Dutch in Europe clashed with that toward the Indonesians in Southeast Asia. The development of the Cold War contributed to the shifts in U.S. posture as Washington weighed the importance of Western Europe and East Asia and the relationship of nationalism and communism. By 1949 the United States sought a settlement of the Indonesian question that would acknowledge Indonesian national aspirations and respect Dutch rights, that would prevent the archipelago from going Communist and support the authority of the United Nations, and that would otherwise protect American interests.[33]

Despite Japan's surrender on August 14, 1945,* and Indonesia's proclamation of independence on August 17 allied forces under the Southeast Asia Command though lacking adequate intelligence did not begin to arrive until September 29.[34] The British commander recognized the de facto authority of the Republicans the following day, for the Republic of Indonesia was well established in several areas. It also was armed by weapons turned over by the Japanese. The lack of adequate men and shipping not only had delayed the arrival of the British but also limited their success. They were responsible for disarming and removing the Japanese armed forces, for freeing prisoners of war and internees, and for maintaining order in key areas. Just the internees alone, including some 100,000 people, many being Dutch in Java, created very serious problems of security.

The British military authorities tried to keep out of Indonesian political matters but it was impossible. Although London was sympathetic to The Hague, the latter wanted more support under their agreements. The Dutch and some Indonesians, moreover, were angered when the British used armed Japanese in certain areas to maintain order. Mountbatten himself was critical of Dutch policy at The Hague. As a substantial number of the British-commanded forces were Indians, Congress leaders in New Delhi were aroused over Indians clashing with local nationalists in the archipelago. The appearance in early October of several poorly trained Netherlands East Indies army internal security companies—certainly no military threat but symbols of the future—stirred the Indonesians. It was not until early March, 1946, however, that nine Dutch battalions with Mountbatten's approval landed in Batavia.

During the previous November a Republican cabinet under Soetan Sjahrir had been set up. When discussions between the Dutch and Indonesians broke down, the United States on December 19 after consultation with Great Britain publicly urged their speedy resumption. The Ukraine, probably because of Western opposition in the United Nations to Soviet policy in Iran, condemned British policy in Indonesia as a threat to the peace and called for a UN commission of inquiry. Sjahrir himself had appealed to President Truman on December 25 for U.S. aid

*Japan signed the Instrument of Surrender at Tokyo Bay on September 2, 1945.

at the United Nations. During debate in the Security Council, February 7, 9–13, 1946, the position of the Ukraine was supported only by Poland and the Soviet Union. The United States expressed hope that the talks in progress between the Dutch and Indonesians would succeed and that the results would reflect the purposes of the United Nations Charter and the "legitimate aspirations" of Indonesians for "self-government."*

The Netherlands on February 10 called for the creation of a "Commonwealth of Indonesia" as a "partner in the Kingdom" in control of domestic matters. The Queen as far back as December 6, 1942, had urged the reconstruction of the kingdom after the war based on "complete partnership." As no mention was made in the statement of February 10, 1946, of the Republic per se, the implementation of the goal was difficult to forecast. Sukarno was detested in The Hague. The Dutch under Lieutenant Governor General H. J. Van Mook and the Indonesians under Sjahrir with British support urged in March a federal state in Indonesia associated with the Netherlands, but the role of Sukarno's Republic in terms of territorial extent and degree of influence was controversial. The French agreement with Ho Chi Minh early in the month was considered a helpful precedent.

First U.S. Period. From the end of World War II to the first Dutch "police action" of July 1947 American policy toward Indonesia was relatively passive. The Department of State indicated on October 18, 1945, it did not question the sovereignty of the Dutch but did not intend to help or participate in forceful steps on their part to impose control. John Carter Vincent outlined essential points in October 1946 with reference to both Indonesia and Indochina: "We recognize the sovereignty of the French and Dutch in those areas but we have also endeavored in appropriate ways to encourage the sovereigns and the dependent peoples to get together in agreements which will permit recovery from the war and at the same time give due consideration to the self-governing aspirations of the Indonesians and Vietnamese."[36] The "appropriate ways" were like a driver's use of his low gear in a model-T Ford. Washington desired a

---

*The basic position of the United States in the Dutch-Indonesian dispute was defined in a memorandum of December 26, 1945, for the use of the American delegation to the General Assembly in London. See *Foreign Relations of the United States, 1946*, Vol. VIII, pp. 787–89. It was noted, *inter alia*, that "in connection with the responsibilities relating to the surrender of the Japanese in the Netherlands East Indies there was no thought so far as the United States was concerned of extending the Allied mandate beyond these specific responsibilities." *Ibid.*, p. 788. For London's viewpoint as of January 25, 1946, see directive of the British government to Sir Archibald Clark Kerr who was being sent on a special mission to Batavia to reach a settlement between the Dutch and Indonesians. *Ibid.*, pp. 802–03.[35]

compromise settlement, was willing to help, but did not want to shift to high gear. Meanwhile the British at the end of November withdrew their forces from Indonesia and terminated SEAC.

The United States approved of the Linggadjati Agreement finally reached by the Dutch and Indonesians in March 1947. Lord Killearn of Great Britain had played an important role in the negotiations. In April Washington gave de facto recognition to the Republic of Indonesia, and late in June it indicated willingness to provide financial help in return for the political cooperation of the Indonesian nationalists. Earlier in the year an American movie executive, Matthew Fox, had made them a private loan.

Controversy over the implementation of the Linggadjati Agreement reached a boiling point in the summer of 1947. The Hague had greatly increased its armed forces in the archipelago and believed it could lead from strength. On June 16 President Truman asserted that he did not favor joint good offices as proposed by Great Britain though he supported telling the Dutch and Indonesians of the American hope that they would continue efforts to settle their differences peacefully. The next day Secretary Marshall strongly urged in instructions that the Dutch not use military force in Indonesia to try to break the deadlock and that the Indonesians make further efforts toward a settlement. American opposition to the use of force was later reiterated. It was in vain. Beginning on July 21 the Dutch in their first police action enlarged the territory in Java and Sumatra under their control, especially populated territory. The United States now took a more active role in the controversy both inside and outside the United Nations. In fact, President Truman personally approved a policy that led Washington to tender good offices to the Dutch on July 31 and shortly thereafter to the Indonesians. The former promptly accepted but the latter attached conditions which caused the United States to terminate the offer. On July 30 Australia and India individually brought the conflict to the Security Council.

Second U.S. Period. From the first Dutch police action and up to the start of the second in December 1948 American policy—in terms of the juridical arguments the United States made at the Security Council and in terms of the political techniques the latter adopted largely at U.S. urging—"did in fact," according to Alastair M. Taylor, "work consistently to the advantage of the Netherlands."[37] Washington opposed the withdrawal of troops; it favored the use of good offices in contrast to arbitration. The Dutch took a similar position, believing it worked to their advantage in the archipelago. American officials in Washington and at the United Nations were more favorable in interpreting Dutch intentions than those involved in the discussions under United Nations auspices in Indonesia.

From the beginning Washington had wanted the Netherlands to be moderate in handling the Indonesian crisis. The United States for some time did not urge policies that would run counter to a large and influential body of opinion in the Netherlands. As the containment policy of the Soviet Union was under way in Europe, the strengthening of the Dutch economy and of the influence of the Netherlands in the West was an American objective. At the same time it should be noted that Washington between the two police actions in Indonesia was not simply pro-Dutch per se in the dispute. After the first police action the United States in line with previous steps refused to sell arms to the Netherlands for use in Indonesia;* and both the Dutch and Indonesians experienced at times considerable American pressure.

On July 31 and August 1, 1947, the Security Council debated the Indonesian question, and on August 1 called for a cease-fire by both sides. Although the Dutch and Republicans issued cease-fire orders, the fighting continued. On August 25 the Security Council authorized the creation of a Consular Commission on the spot in Batavia to report on the failure to implement the cease-fire and of a Committee of Good Offices (GOC) to serve in the controversy. By September 18 the membership of the Committee was established—Australia selected by the Republic of Indonesia, Belgium by the Netherlands, and the United States by Australia and Belgium. From now on Washington would have a major role in the field. Dr. Frank P. Graham served on the GOC followed by H. Merle Cochran who also served on its successor, the United Nations Commission for Indonesia (UNCI). In October the GOC arrived in Batavia, and helped in facilitating a twofold agreement approved on January 17, 1948, by the Netherlands and the Republic on the U.S.S. "Renville." With additions two days later, drafted by Graham after consultation with the Indonesians, the Renville Agreements provided for a truce and set forth a statement of principles for a permanent political settlement. For a while it had been touch and go with the Dutch threatening to resume military action. Secretary of State Marshall in Washington let the Dutch know he supported Graham.

The Madiun revolt of Moscow-oriented Indonesian Communists which broke out on September 18 had significant repercussions in later American policy toward Indonesia. President Sukarno and Premier

---

*An exception had been a commitment relating to the equipping of a Netherlands Marine contingent training in the United States before V-J Day. A surplus property credit worth $100 million involving no arms or munitions was extended by the United States to the Dutch in the East Indies on July 11, 1946, to be used before January 1, 1948. Later the United States made available to Indonesia through the Netherlands $101 million of commodity assistance through the Economic Cooperation Administration (ECA).

Hatta quickly put down the revolt without the assistance of Dutch forces. Washington became convinced that the leaders of the Republic were anti-Communists who would be weakened and who would become prey to extremists if their nationalist aspirations were not satisfied. Ho Chi Minh in Indochina was already indicating what a wedding of nationalism and communism in a colonial dependency could produce.

Third U.S. Period. It was the second Dutch police action in December that precipitated a basic shift in American policy in the Indonesian controversy—a shift very much pro-Republic. Discussions on a political settlement between the two contestants had broken down; the good offices approach had not succeeded. Starting on December 19, the Dutch quickly seized the Republican capital of Jogjakarta and captured Sukarno, Hatta, and Sjahrir. The United States, which had tried to prevent the police action, on December 22 suspended economic aid to Indonesia and took vigorous leadership in the United Nations. The Security Council on December 24 called for a cease-fire and for the release of political prisoners, and on January 28, 1949, it also called for the return of the Republican government to Jogjakarta, outlined a timetable for the Dutch to transfer sovereignty to a United States of Indonesia, and strengthened the field machinery of the United Nations by replacing the GOC with the UNCI.

Meanwhile support for the Republic had been marshaled in January at a New Delhi conference of countries in Asia, Africa, and the Southwest Pacific called by Prime Minister Jawaharlal Nehru. In Southeast Asia the Philippines, Burma, and the Republic of Indonesia were represented, and Thailand sent an observer. Recommendations, indicative of rising nationalism in Asia and Africa, were made to the Security Council.

Although the second police action stimulated a course of events that finally led to the independence of Indonesia at the end of 1949, diplomatic and political roadblocks hampered the achievement of *Merdeka* or freedom. The Security Council acting when necessary and UNCI operating on a day-to-day basis made possible the role of the United Nations as a midwife in the birth of Indonesia. In July the Republican government whose leaders had been released from detention returned to Jogjakarta; and on August 1 another cease-fire agreement was adopted.

A round-table conference having significant and widespread representation officially opened on August 23 at The Hague. Along with the United States, Australia, and Belgium as members of UNCI were the Dutch and the Indonesian Republicans and Federalists. The discussions were complicated, for they reflected a heritage of ill will and a snake pit of conflicting interests. On October 31 the Republicans and the Federalists presented to the steering committee a provisional constitution under which the Republic and other Indonesian states would form a Republic of the United States of Indonesia. On November 2 the conference ended with the signing of documents including an instrument for the Dutch transfer of sovereignty, a statute for the creation of a Netherlands-Indonesian Union, and a transitional accord. The Dutch States-General barely approved the settlement, reflecting in part the bitterness in the Netherlands over substantial U.S. pressure. On December 27 Queen Juliana in a historic ceremony formally transferred sovereignty to the United States of Indonesia. A new state was born from a vast colonial empire; President Sukarno now had an opportunity to change from being a successful revolutionary to an effective peacetime leader.

The significant shift in American attitude in the Indonesian dispute reflected foreign as well as domestic considerations. Although still emphasizing the importance of Europe and the containment of the Soviet Union, Washington was worried over the impending fall of mainland China to communism and its effects on the rest of Asia. Indonesia, it was stressed, was potentially the strongest country in Southeast Asia, and nationalism was now considered the best vehicle for keeping it from Communist control. After independence economic and other aid could be effectively used, it was hoped, to help remove the economic and social causes of communism and to help promote political stability. The "speediest acceleration" of trade between Indonesia and the rest of the world had long been urged. Washington was particularly angered over the Dutch use of force in the second police action. For the most part public opinion in the United States and congressional opinion supported Indonesia. The Senate even threatened to cut off economic aid to the Netherlands, and a situation might have arisen wherein The Hague would not accept the North Atlantic Treaty. Pro-Dutch sympathies in some circles of the State Department were greatly weakened. American attitudes toward Indonesia were bipartisan and not the subject of controversy between Republicans and Democrats.

Indonesia was admitted to the United Nations in September 1950. After the President of the General Assembly welcomed the new member, representatives of twenty-eight states joined in the greeting. In reply the Indonesian delegate emphasized the contributions of the United Nations in the winning of his country's independence. As the sixtieth member, Indonesia's in, out, and in role in the world organization would be most unusual.

After *Merdeka,* Djakarta's basic foreign policy was officially termed "independent and active." The republic opposed alignment with any "power bloc," each of the two major world groupings being described in these terms. It became a bitter foe of Western colonialism and a staunch champion of Asian and African nationalism, looking upon the struggle of colonial peoples for independence as the basic issue of the times. Sukarno would later make significant changes in the foreign policy of the country.

The role of the United States in the birth of Indonesia pleased neither the Indonesians nor the Dutch.[38] The Hague believed Washington did too much to advance the cause of Indonesian independence and Djakarta claimed Washington did not do enough at the right times. Dr. Frank P. Graham was influential though rather cautious and thought of himself as basically pro-United Nations; H. Merle Cochran was more forceful and in the end more decisive in the controversy. As the United States changed its role and the emphasis of its policy during the long conflict from a relatively inactive stance to an active one, first largely pro-Dutch in effect and then firmly pro-Indonesian in effect, criticism of Washington by the two contestants varied. In a controversy as complex and bitter as the one between the Dutch and Indonesians, the United States could not fully please either party without completely supporting one against the other.

THE KINGDOM OF THAILAND

In the early postwar years American policy toward the Philippines and in the end Indonesia was comparable in many respects to that toward Thailand. The United States made a sustained effort in negotiations with Great Britain to prevent Thailand from being saddled with the equivalent of an unequal treaty. It was not a case of assisting in the birth of a new state but of seeking to preserve the complete independence of an old.

America versus Britain. During World War II serious divergencies between Washington and London developed concerning the postwar treatment of Thailand. Great Britain was angered at Bangkok's declaration of war despite a treaty of nonaggression, at the use of Thai soil for Japanese attacks on Malaya and Burma, at the role of Bangkok in Japan's New Order, and at the Thai acquisition of territories in Malaya and Burma. London considered Bangkok an enemy and "liable to punishment" in the words of Sir Josiah Crosby, British Minister before the war.[39] Thailand would have to work its passage back, London believed, and the peace settlement should not be just a kiss-and-make-up affair.

In marked contrast the United States, stressing Thailand as the only independent country in Southeast Asia before World War II, wanted it to exemplify independence with political and economic stability for the rest of the area. The traditional American opposition to colonialism was reflected in helping Bangkok preserve its independence. If the Thai lost any of their territory (apart from their gains with Japanese help) or had their freedom impaired, an important American objective in Southeast Asia would be lost despite the major U.S. role in the war against Japan. Washington's refusal to recognize the Thai declaration of war along with its attitude toward the recognition of the Free Thai movement was viewed in London as producing a "curious anomaly"[40] in allied relationships.

It was easier for the United States to concert its policy on Thailand with China than with Britain.[41] As far back as March 12, 1943, President Roosevelt purposely supported Chiang's February 26 disclaiming of territorial ambitions in Thailand, his viewing it as an enemy-occupied country, and calling for its independence.[42] In 1945 Thai efforts toward allied approval for a Free Thai government-in-exile came to a head. The United States eventually favored a liberation committee of Free Thai being established in an allied country without prejudice to a possible government in exile at a later date, but Great Britain wanted to wait for the establishment of a Thai government on Thai soil liberated from Japan. Although Chiang was concerned about developments relating to Bangkok, he took no precipitate action. In the summer of 1945 his desire that the sixteenth parallel established at the Potsdam Conference be extended from Indochina across Thailand went unheeded. (He made it a condition for accepting the division in Indochina.) When Regent Pridi, leader of the Thai underground, indicated in May he wanted his forces to come out openly against Japan the United States urged him not to take premature action. Washington like London believed he should coordinate his plans with SEAC whose support was needed and avoid a Japanese seizure of the Thai government.

In view of developments in Thailand and in the Pacific War and despite the fixed differences by May 1944 on Thai policy Washington made a strong effort in June 1945 to find agreement with London.[43] A key document on June 25 from the Department of State to the British embassy indicated that both countries wanted a free and independent Thailand, that neither had territorial objectives in the kingdom, and that the areas Thailand had recently acquired from Burma, Malaya, and Indochina should be restored to their former owners. At the same time, it asserted, there was no complete agreement (as sought by the United States) on these items: (1) Thailand should enter the United Nations at an appropriate time upon its pledge to cooperate in relevant international arrangements, (2) security agreements pertinent to Thailand should be the subject of joint Anglo-American discussion and accord, (3) all nationals of the United Nations should have fair and equal commercial and economic opportunity with respect to British economic and commercial policies in Thailand after the war, (4) London and Washington should grant prompt recognition to and resume diplomatic relations with a legal Thai government on Thai soil when it repudiated the agreements with Japan along with the war declaration and began open resistance against the Japanese, and (5) Great Britain should discuss with the United States contemplated control measures over Thailand although Washington had decided not to take part in any civil administration or control agency in the kingdom after the war.

On August 14, 1945, the British embassy in Washington informed the Department of State that the terms of the United Kingdom for ending the war with Thailand would be given the Department before the start of Anglo-Thai negotiations. Moreover, if Bangkok disavowed the declaration of war, repudiated the accords with Japan, and dispatched a mission at once to Kandy, Ceylon, for discussion at SEAC headquarters, London would not press for unconditional surrender.

There ensued a remarkable sequence of events in Anglo-American diplomacy involving the Department of State and the British embassy in Washington, the Southeast Asia Command in Kandy, British and American officials in Bangkok, and the U.S. embassy and foreign office in London. On several occasions American pressure on Great Britain was intense; Prime Minister Attlee was once reportedly aroused from his bed. Tempers were frayed more than once in the complicated and long negotiations. Although the Thai were not cognizant of the details of the Anglo-American dispute over their future they were sufficiently aware to use Washington as a lever against London. As so often in their history, the Thai reaped advantages from the differences between major powers. Upon the U.S. resumption of diplomatic relations with Thailand on January 5, 1946, the Department of State calmly and sweetly asserted that Washington had taken a "deep interest" in the Anglo-Thai negotiations, had informed London "in friendly conversation" of its position, and was "pleased with the ready and cordial response" of Great Britain.[44]

After the collapse of Japan, Regent Pridi moved quickly to capitalize on his position as the key figure in the Thai underground during the war and to rehabilitate Thailand among the victors of the conflict. On August 16 he proclaimed that the Thai declaration of war on Great Britain and the United States was null and void and that Thailand was ready to restore at once to Great Britain the territories in Burma and Malaya which Japan had "entrusted" to Bangkok. The proclamation approved by the National Assembly significantly made no reference to recent Thai acquisition of territory from Indochina. In September Bangkok officially informed Tokyo that their alliance of 1941 with related accords was terminated, and subsequently Thailand denounced all other political agreements with Japan made while Pibul was premier.

On August 20 the British informed the State Department of their plans at Kandy to negotiate with the Thai a political settlement solely of British concern and also a military and quasi-military settlement of allied interest. Essentials of the proposed political and military agreements were supplied. The draft political accord included Thai measures of repudiation and restitution and steps of postwar cooperation in the economic and strategic fields. The proposed military agreement called for the Thai to help in disarming Japanese forces in the kingdom and in turning them over to allied authorities and for the release of all allied prisoners of war and internees; the Thai were to accept allied military controls over their country and a military mission; they were to provide a free contribution of 1,500,000 tons of rice; they were to accept an allied rice unit to stimulate the production and control the export of the commodity, and agree to allied controls over exports of rubber, tin, and teak.

The Department of State replied to the British embassy on September 1. As regards the suggested political agreement, Washington questioned the intent and method in obligating Thailand to participate in international arrangements on rubber and tin; it wanted assurance that London required only nondiscriminatory treatment for British interests and nationals; it believed claims arising from Japanese acts in Thailand should await decision on Japanese reparations. Referring to the proposed military agreement, Washington stressed that Mountbatten's command should take no action compromising the position of the United States that it was not at war with Thailand. Also, the agreement should be restricted to matters of allied concern against the common Japanese foe. The rice levy, as the Americans called it, was especially attacked as being unjust since Thailand had been willing to go to war with Japan. Beyond this consideration, its size might be greater than the amount of Thai rice available for export in the coming year.

September was a critical period in the Anglo-American negotiations on Thailand. Early in the month a Thai delegation arrived at SEAC headquarters in Kandy and received twenty-one military and related proposals from the British. The Thai were ordered by their government to accept them and plans were made for signing the necessary documentation as an allied military agreement. At the same time the proposals were leaked, their nature arousing considerable press comment. The unfortunate number twenty-one was linked to the infamous twenty-one demands Japan made on China in 1915. Acting Secretary of State Dean Acheson telephoned Ambassador John G. Winant in London who quickly went to see Prime Minister Attlee late in the evening of September 6. Admiral Lord Louis Mountbatten in Kandy was actually instructed to hold up the signing of the planned agreement. Instead on September 8 he signed a temporary, strictly military accord with the Thai, one agreeable to Washington. Within Thailand itself British and Indian troops arrived by plane from Burma between September 3 and 13, their chief duties being to assume responsibility for the Japanese and to help allied prisoners of war and civilian internees.

The British sharply responded early the same month to the American reaction of September 1 to their proposals. They maintained that SEAC should not be limited to matters relating to the war with Japan; they opposed postponement of claims for damages to the allies until a decision on Japanese reparations was reached; and they were adamant on the rice levy. In their judgment the amount of the levy already existed in Thai stockpiles. There can be no doubt that London placed great stress on the requested Thai contribution of 1,500,000 tons of rice. Serious shortages in 1945 existed in India, China, and various parts of Southeast Asia, and the levy of rice from Thailand could be put to good use. On September 10 the State Department received a revised draft of the proposals of August 20 but the modifications were not major.

On September 19 Washington again informed the British of its opposition to the rice levy, questioning their estimate of available rice and seeking in every way to disassociate itself from the matter. The U.S. resumption of diplomatic relations with Thailand was used as a lever, for it was indicated Washington would delay the step for a reasonable period while the Anglo-Thai negotiations were under way.

Seven days later the State Department presented its views to the British embassy on the proposed political agreement between London and Bangkok as it related to the role of Thailand in postwar strategy. Under British proposal C1 of September 10 Thailand would recognize that the recent war had shown the country's importance to the defense of Burma, Malaya, Indochina, and India and to the security of the Southwest Pacific and Indian Ocean. Washington officials believed the language was historically that of a protectorate and might be interpreted as an advance commitment by Thailand to accept steps the United States opposed. In its place Washington would substitute a proviso that Bangkok should agree to cooperate in relevant international security arrangements under a United Nations. As far as the Kra Isthmus was concerned, the United States was not disturbed over London's request under C3 that no canal should be constructed across Thailand without British consent. It was held at the time that the subject was largely academic.

Washington was irked late in September about the possibility of the British in Kandy under M. E. Dening, Political Adviser to Mountbatten, giving the Thai an ultimatum to sign an agreement without reference to Anglo-American conversations. The United States applied pressure to prevent such a step in London, and threatened to tell the Thai of its position. Further exchanges between the British and Americans over the next two months removed some of the differences but large ones remained into December.

Nerves were hit when Washington on October 25 after again criticizing the matters of the rice levy and claims suggested that the former constitute reparations in kind in compensation for the latter and that the proposed claims be handled by an allied claims commission. On November 12 the British replied that under the plans the rice levy would only come from accumulated stocks, and that it did not constitute reparations but rather "a special measure of reconcilement." Furthermore, the British stated an allied claims commission was not desirable; it was inappropriate for any state not at war with a country to be associated in determining its capacity to pay reparations or in deciding the equitable distribution of claims. In a heated reply on November 29 personally delivered by Undersecretary Dean Acheson to Lord Halifax the United States asserted it was equally concerned with the United Kingdom in settling allied claims against Thailand and in deciding its capacity to pay them. Washington threatened to resume diplomatic relations with Bangkok. Great Britain replied to the United States on December 11 that the two should participate on an equal footing in an allied claims commission.

Meanwhile on December 7 London assured Washington that it had no intention of establishing a protectorate over Thailand or getting a special military position through C1. This provision simply gave London the basis to approach Bangkok for discussions on steps to meet a threat if it arose to British areas in Southeast Asia prior to the establishment of regional security arrangements under the United Nations.

Relations between Great Britain and the United States over Thailand reached a flash point when Washington heard on the afternoon of December 12 that the British in Singapore—Dening once more the architect—had exerted heavy pressure on Thailand to sign an agreement even though Anglo-American conversations were being held. The American Ambassador in London was instructed on December 13 to inform the foreign office at the top level that the U.S. political adviser in Bangkok, Charles W. Yost, would recommend to Thailand that it not sign while the Anglo-American talks were continuing, and that if local British pressure continued, the United States would at once resume diplomatic relations with Thailand and comment to the Thai on the controversial agreement. Great Britain was asked to drop the rice levy or agree to an impartial determination of the amount of surplus stocks in Thailand. Furthermore, the United States would not acquiesce in C1, maintaining it still had the appearance of a protectorate.

The chips were now down; a real impasse was reached. The Thai had already decided to sign but they delayed after receiving the American recommendation. On December 18 the American Ambassador informed the Department of State that London had indicated the rice levy would be set at an amount equal to the Thai accumulated surplus subject to a maximum of 1,500,000 tons and compatible with keeping an adequate amount of rice for the internal needs of the kingdom. The exact figure would be decided by the planned Anglo-American-Thai rice commission. Three days later the Ambassador reported that London had agreed to a formula whereby C1 would be altered to meet U.S. objections. On December 22 Yost was informed by the Department of State that discussions with the United Kingdom were now concluded and that Washington therefore withdrew its recommendation to Bangkok that it delay signing. At the same time the Thai should be told that this step did not constitute U.S. approval of the agreement and Bangkok should be fully informed of Washington's position during the long Anglo-American talks.

At Government House, Singapore, on New Year's Day 1946 the "Agreement between the United Kingdom and India with Siam for the Termination of the State of War" was signed.[45]* It was the first postwar pact ending a war with a member of the axis. Among the many provisions a number called for a restoration of the status quo ante bellum. Thailand renounced the territory it had seized in Burma and Malaya; British property including concessions and tin and teak stocks would be restored; the commercial and banking firms of Great Britain could resume activities. Compensation for damages and losses to the British would be paid by Bangkok. London could veto the construction of a canal across the Kra Isthmus. The United Kingdom and India would support Thailand's application for membership in the United Nations. Thailand recognized in view of the recent war its importance to the defense of Malaya, Burma, Indochina, and India and to the security of the Indian Ocean and the Southwest Pacific and agreed to cooperate fully in all security agreements which were approved by the Security Council or the United Nations relevant to itself and particularly in such agreements that would relate to the countries or areas cited. As regarded rice, Thailand would prohibit its export until a period not later than September 1, 1947, except in accordance with the suggestions of a special body to be consti-

*Australia which had declared war on Thailand in 1942 signed a peace agreement with Bangkok on April 3, 1946. There was a lively debate between Washington and Canberra over a clause giving Australia a special privilege relative to concluding commodity arrangements not granted other nations. London and Paris supported Washington.

tuted; the Thai would make available free of cost to a British-designated organization an amount of rice in Bangkok equal to the surplus in the kingdom at the date of the pact with a maximum figure of 1,500,000 tons or, if agreed, would make available an equivalent in paddy or *loonzain;* Thailand, furthermore, would turn over at an agreed price to the same organization until a date not later than September 1, 1947, all rice produced in the country beyond the amount required for its domestic needs. The reparations in free rice, it was planned, would not become the property of the British government but would be made available for allocation to rice-deficient countries by an international organization.

It is clear that the British settlement with the Thai was much more lenient as a result of the American role. "American diplomacy," it has been reliably asserted, "exhibited resourcefulness and tenacity in softening British demands and ironing out ambiguities of language which might have been construed to affect the political and economic independence of Thailand or to restore Great Britain's prewar position of economic and financial primacy there.[46] A very small number of people interested in Thailand in the Department of State generated the pressure for the U.S. posture in the Anglo-American negotiations. A memorandum had even been prepared for possible use by Roosevelt at Yalta. For the British the future of Thailand was not a high priority among world problems of much greater importance. Prime Minister Churchill had inspired the original British attitude toward the Thai, and his successor Prime Minister Attlee was slow in revising policy toward both Thailand and Burma. In the end his government did—under real American pressure in the case of the former and without it in the case of the latter.

The agreement of the United Kingdom and India with the Thai on January 1, 1946, had a short duration. In an exchange of notes on January 14, 1954, it was terminated as regards London and Bangkok, some provisions having lapsed, others having been carried out, and a few being updated in the current exchange. Events had indicated that all the rice clauses of the pact of January 1946 could not be implemented. In many respects the Chinese, not the Americans, British, or Thai, had the final say! The Chinese in Thailand controlled the trade in rice and they had no interest in a free grant by the Thai of 1,500,000 tons of it. Smuggling the commodity to Hong Kong or Malaya could bring substantial profits. The rice provisions were revised in May and December in an effort to cope with illegal channels.

For a short time after World War II Great Britain had the strongest impact of any outside power in Thailand. As the best customer and a neighbor in both Malaya and Burma, its influence was substantial. From 1948, after Burma's independence in January and especially after the return to the premiership of Pibul Songgram in April, the United States gradually replaced Great Britain in influence.

Washington, Bangkok, Paris. In contrast to a role sympathetic to the Thai against the British, Washington opposed the Thai in their efforts to keep the territory taken from the French in Indochina in 1941. America had an influential role in the final settlement of the controversy. As John Carter Vincent said in October 1946, the United States was in the middle of the dispute and was helpful "when and as our help is solicited."[47] The basic American position was that Thailand should restore the territory and France should then negotiate with the Thai on border and related issues.

After the war the French, it is clear, were eager to regain their prestige in the world. One of the ways of reaching this goal in Asia, they believed, was to return to Indochina with its prewar boundaries. Thailand had made the settlement of May 9, 1941, acquiring territories in Laos and Cambodia, with the government of Vichy France but the Free French had never accepted it. Bangkok maintained that it had been concluded with a legal French government and that no declaration of war had been made. Negotiations between France and Thailand were stormy, punctuated by the end of April 1946 by increasingly serious border incidents. The French accused the Thai of permitting Indochinese rebels to use bases in the kingdom to plunder in Laos. Incidents in Cambodia added to the mounting tension.

Thailand called the attention of the United Nations to the situation in a memorandum of May 31 to the Secretary General. France in late July suggested that the territorial controversy be submitted to the International Court of Justice, and Thailand accepted the proposal in principle. It became evident in August that Bangkok could not be approved by the Security Council for admission to the United Nations as France indicated it continued to view itself in a state of war with the kingdom. The Soviet Union also came to oppose the membership of Thailand, with whom it had no diplomatic relations.

Bangkok wisely changed its policy on the boundary controversy in view of American and even stronger British sympathy for France, of the firm French posture, and of its admission problems to the United Nations. After informal discussions in Washington between the French and the Thai a settlement was reached in October on a number of proposals. On November 17 the agreement was formally signed in Washington providing for the Thai transfer of the disputed areas in Indochina to France (who would restore them to Laos and Cambodia), for the resumption of diplomatic relations between Paris and Bangkok (marking the termination of the war), and for the end of French opposition to the admission of Thailand to the United Nations as well as for the withdrawal by Bangkok of its complaint to the Security Council. In order to soften the Thai transfer of territory, a matter which shook the Bangkok cabinet, a Conciliation Commission, as provided in a Franco-Thai treaty of December 7, 1937, would be appointed. It would examine the issues of the controversy and allow Bangkok to present its case for a revision of the frontier on geographic, ethnographic, and economic grounds. If Thailand and France could not agree on compensation for previous damages, the Conciliation Commission would also pass on the matter.

The full extent of the role of the United States in the settlement of the controversy only became known outside official circles in 1971.[48] Involved were efforts to coordinate Anglo-American policy (usually but not always successful), attempts to prevent the controversy from becoming a major issue in the United Nations (generally effective), and steps to remove the sting of border incidents through observers in the field and to resolve the controversy through the extension of good offices (the efforts of the former hard to evaluate but the results of the latter clearly successful). Considerations of saving Thai face and of meeting French pride could not be submerged in the long confrontation. In the later phases of the controversy Dean Acheson was directly involved.

Washington was prepared to take a more active role than it actually did in the end. On May 27 the Thai Prime Minister had appealed to President Truman as well as other prominent leaders and the Secretary General of the United Nations for sympathy and cooperation in the face of French "attacks" on Thai territory. The American chief executive replied on June 7 urging both Paris and Bangkok to prevent further border incidents. After France indicated that the dispute over the territory should be referred to the International Court of Justice, Paris made a suggestion that Acheson thought was of "significant importance" to necessitate consultation with President Truman. On July 31 the former wrote the latter that "to preserve the rights and prestige of both countries and to prevent any political or economic action prejudicial to either party pending the Court decision, the French wish Siamese agreement on an interim administration of the disputed territories under third power, preferably United States, auspices."[49] Acheson recommended that if Thailand agreed to this approach the President should designate an American to be a "Conservator" with a small staff. Truman approved the next day the Acheson suggestion and a draft telegram to Bangkok on the subject. In the end the Thai preferred secret, direct negotiations with the French in Washington under U.S. good offices without, for the present, submitting the case to the International Court of Justice and accordingly, without an interim administration of the disputed territories under a Conservator. The French, in fact, withdrew in late August their offer to take the case to the Court because of a recent boundary incident.

The terms of the settlement, it is clear, reflected American influence on Thailand. Edwin F. Stanton, the U.S. Minister in Bangkok, reported on October 17 that Thai acceptance was "largely because we urged that they [the French proposals] be accepted as a basis for effecting an amicable and lasting settlement of the matters in dispute . . . and, furthermore, because they [the Thai] believe that we will see to it that justice is done to Siam."[50] American and British official observers were present when the territories were restored to the French. But Washington's role was not yet over.

An American was chairman of the International Commission of Conciliation which met in Washington on May 5, 1947. The other four members were Peruvian, British, French, and Thai. In a report on June 27 the Commission backed none of the Thai claims to territory but called for a number of changes in border relationships. (The boundary dispute over Preah Vihear was left to fester.) The report as a whole was badly received in Thailand where it was uncertain for some time of the government's approval. In May 1948 Premier Pibul Songgram whose regime France was the first to recognize asserted that Thailand accepted the territorial claims of Paris and that the matter was closed. A heritage of ill will against France, however, remained to plague relations between Paris and Bangkok, its intensity varying with developments in Indochina.

The Security Council unanimously approved Thai admission to the United Nations in December 1946. Theoretically Thailand could have been vetoed by any one of the five permanent members. The Soviet Union approved admission, for agreement had been reached on the establishment of diplomatic relations and Bangkok had lifted its ban on communism. Nationalist China approved since a treaty of amity had been signed on January 23, 1946, establishing diplomatic relations for the first time between Thailand and China. (Washington had urged a reluctant Bangkok to take the step.) Great Britain and France approved admission to the United Nations since postwar settlements had been reached in each case. The United States approved—after all, it had played a major role publicly and privately in the rehabilitation of Thailand in the postwar world community.[51]

Course of Thai-American Relations. Soon after diplomatic relations between Washington and Bangkok were resumed on January 5, 1946, the former announced that treaties and other international agreements in force between them before the outbreak of the war continued "in full force and effect." President Truman told Edwin F. Stanton, the first U.S. postwar minister to Thailand, that the United States should give the kingdom political and material help. On September 9 the Department of State reported that Thailand would welcome American capital in developing its minerals, and in August 1949 plans were announced for a U.S. mineral resources survey mission to go to the country. An American loan of $10 million was made involving the Thai purchase of railroad equipment and the rehabilitation of the transportation system. The United States supported efforts to increase the foreign exchange reserves of Thailand. American trade greatly expanded, and Washington bought rubber and tin for stockpiling, and purchased rice for South Korea, China, and U.S. forces in Japan. In the fall of 1949 General MacArthur was instructed to release certain earmarked gold in Japan for the Bank of Thailand. As far back as August 1947 Bangkok had agreed to terms of reference for settling the claims of American nationals against the government arising from the recent conflict. At the initiative of the United States the previous March Thailand had concurred in raising their respective diplomatic missions to embassy level. Within a few years after the war Bangkok came to rely to quite an extent on American economic and financial support.

In its attitude toward domestic politics in the kingdom the United States was basically cautious. Washington was not willing to support London in putting pressure on the Thai to try and punish Pibul and other collaborators. He had been brought to trial under a War Criminals Act but the Thai High Court in March 1946 dismissed the case on the grounds that the act could not be applied retroactively. In May 1947 Thailand in an exchange of notes with Great Britain was agreeable to "the apprehension and trial of persons accused of war crimes or notable for affording active assistance to Japan."[52] For all practical purposes, however, the collaboration issue was dead.

The tragic and mysterious death of King Ananda Mahidol on June 9, 1946, led to the Thai appointment of a Special Commission of Inquiry which included American and British physicians. The majority indicated that the King, who was found shot to death, had not killed himself. The search for the guilty party or parties had long and deep ramifications in Thai politics, the circumstances of the King's death leading to bitter charges and countercharges. American doctors have quite an impressive record in preserving the health or restoring the well-being of a number of prominent Southeast Asian leaders but rarely are the physicians involved in investigating the death of any of them.

In the drafting of the Thai constitution of 1946 Pridi asked Charles W. Yost and Kenneth P. Landon, currently of the American mission in Bangkok, for literature on democratic government and copies of foreign constitutions. A coup in November 1947 overthrew the Pridi forces and restored the military to power. The military leaders, however, initially exercised restraint in the new government and remained in the background, for they were apprehensive over the attitudes of Great Britain and the United States. Both London and Washington, being concerned over the future of democratic institutions in the kingdom, were angered over the coup. Washington finally gave recognition to the new regime in March 1948, acting on the realities of the situation. When Pibul Songgram returned to power as premier in a coup the next month American and British recognition of his military regime was quick in forthcoming. Pibul soon proved himself strong, conservative, and anti-Communist. The American containment policy of the Soviet Union was well under way and China was moving fast toward communism. The United States appeared less interested in helping the development of constitutional democracy in Thailand than in building positions of strength to stop Communist expansion.

Some Questions and Some Answers. Thai foreign policy from 1945 to 1950 was in flux.* Bangkok had to give first priority to the liquidation of its role in Japan's New Order in Greater East Asia, to its acceptance by the victorious powers, and to its admission to the United Nations. For all practical purposes these objectives had been accomplished by the end of 1946. Soon Thailand would have to adjust to relations with independent states on all its borders instead of relations with the colonial powers.

*Nevertheless, Kenneth T. Young, former U.S. Ambassador to Thailand, believed the Thai have established over the centuries a number of principles in foreign policy. (Kenneth T. Young, "The Foreign Policies of Thailand" [a manuscript].) *Self-reliance* stands out, for the Thai believe they must depend upon themselves for survival as a nation. Another principle is *independence* from foreign domination. "The objective of Thai foreign policy," Young asserted, "has always been to secure and maintain the independence and freedom of the Thai nation—of 'Muang Thai' —from outside control." (*Ibid.*, p. 3.) *Multiplicity* is a third principle reflected in various Thai contacts with governments over many years and in Bangkok as a current international diplomatic center. A fourth is *counterweight*, which calls for external support by a power to bolster Thai efforts against another. At the same time, Young observed, the Thai believe "a counterweight must not counter too far nor weigh too much." (*Ibid.*, p. 5.) *Plasticity*, he asserted, is a fifth principle. And here another American ambassador to Thailand, Edwin F. Stanton, has aptly noted from many years of experience that the Thai "have perfected the art of polite verbal acquiescence, but this is not necessarily followed by action if the matter is deemed not to be in their national interest." (Edwin F. Stanton, *Brief Authority: Excursions of a Common Man in an Uncommon World*, Harper, New York, 1956, p. 184.) He quotes an official as saying: "We Thai bend like the bamboo but we do not break." (Quoted in *ibid.*, p. 171.) Thailand, it seems clear, has managed to maintain its independence partly because of its diplomats. At the same time the rivalries of outside powers like the British and French in colonial Southeast Asia should not be discounted.

Burma was first, followed by Cambodia, Laos, and Malaya over a period of almost ten years. But for a while Bangkok could not be certain of what the future held in Southeast Asia. Basic questions needed answers. Would the forces of Mao Tse-tung overrun all the mainland of China? Would Ho Chi Minh be able to withstand the French? Would the United States really be willing to stop Communist expansion in Southeast Asia?

By the middle of 1950 Premier Pibul Songgram believed he had the answers to a number of basic questions affecting the future of the region and of the kingdom of Thailand. Mao Tse-tung had clearly won in mainland China; Ho Chi Minh as a consequence had been strengthened in his struggle against the French; and the United States was showing a genuine interest in the future of Southeast Asia. Thailand decided it wanted the United States as a counterweight to the threat of Communist China and Communist Vietnam. Washington would respond cautiously, and some four years would elapse before a formal alliance was made.

THE UNION OF BURMA

In contrast to the American role in Thailand in the early postwar period Washington took a much less active role in Burma. During World War II the United States evidenced neither a long-range nor a short-range policy toward the country.[53] Churchill wanted Burma restored to its prewar political status, and a government-in-exile in Simla, India, made careful plans for its return after the defeat of the Japanese. In October 1945 the Simla government arrived in Burma with Sir Reginald Dorman-Smith as governor but it faced a much different political situation from that before the Japanese invasion. Bogyoke Aung San who had in effect organized the Anti-Fascist People's Freedom League (AFPFL) in 1944 and had led his own defense troops against the Japanese in early 1945 represented the most influential nationalist force at the end of the war. The immediate postwar policy of Great Britain, even under Prime Minister Attlee, was not sufficiently progressive either in the political or economic fields to meet the demands of the Burmese nationalists. London placed considerable priority on speeding the economic recovery of Burma before taking major steps toward self-government. Admiral Lord Louis Mountbatten, however, had personally thrown his support behind Aung San in the wake of Japanese military reverses, support which won for him the sympathy of many Burmese.[54]

Aung San and the AFPFL exerted pressure for recognition on both the British military government and its successor in October, the civil government. In September 1946 after considerable friction the AFPFL agreed to enter a new Executive Council of the governor with a majority of the seats and with Aung San as deputy chairman. By now Major General Sir Hubert E. Rance who had served under Mountbatten had been appointed governor of Burma and Prime Minister Attlee was launching India on the road to independence. In December Great Britain announced its intention of granting full self-government to Burma.

The next month a mission led by Aung San reached agreement in London with Great Britain on steps that would lead to Burma's independence either within or outside the British Commonwealth. The Executive Council became an interim government although the assassination of Aung San and a number of his colleagues in July 1947 deprived the country of able leadership. A constituent assembly drew up a constitution for a Union of Burma which was adopted in September. On October 17 the Nu-Attlee Treaty provided for basic relations between Burma and Great Britain outside the British Commonwealth and included a defense agreement made on August 29. A Burma Independence bill which was severely criticized by Churchill was approved by the British parliament and became law on December 10. Astrologers were consulted on the most auspicious time for independence and chose January 4, 1948. Their wisdom is questionable in view of subsequent events, for Burma's freedom was sorely tested in the domestic upheaval that quickly racked the country.

Only after London and Rangoon had reached agreement during the previous January on the future of Burma did Washington evidence much more public interest in developments. And until 1950 this public concern was basically kept at low key. In 1946 during the months when British policy was shifting toward Rangoon the United States quietly but officially expressed more than once to London its "concern and interest" in Burma's "peaceful transition" to "self-government." Washington's policy, as indicated in a cable from Acheson to the U.S. embassy in Great Britain on November 8, was based on a number of considerations. It was frankly stated that "Burmese strategic position on projected American air routes, as buffer between India and China and as potential major rice exporter justify American interest in peaceful and orderly constitutional progress" and that "failure Burma to secure rapid constitutional progress and assurances further progress might cause large numbers non-communists to become discouraged and to join Communists. . . ."[55] Washington suggested to London the example of British treatment of India as being applicable to Burma but the United Kingdom stressed that the Indian case was not a good parallel for the Burmese.

After Attlee's invitation on December 20 to Burmese leaders to come to Britain to discuss the political future of their country the United States publicly asserted the next day, though "informally and orally," that it was "our confident hope London talks will result in future progress toward agreed goal of full self-govt for that important Asiatic country [Burma]."[56]

Under the Aung San-Attlee agreement of January 1947 Burma's interim government could determine matters of defense and foreign policy. The next month American and Burmese officials in London reached a lend-lease agreement whereby the United States made available to Burma military and other supplies in the country at the end of the war. Also in February Washington took steps to caution Aung San against including Communists in his government. In June Secretary of State Marshall sent "sincere good wishes" to Thakin Mya, chairman of the constituent assembly, and received a cordial reply. Aung San, it might be noted, had at least twice praised the Navy Day speech of President Truman in 1945 focusing on the principles of U.S. foreign policy.

Even before Burma's independence the United States raised its consulate general in Rangoon to an embassy and plans were made for Washington and Rangoon to exchange ambassadors. The American chargé d'affaires told the Burmese press on September 19, 1947, that his country wanted cultural and economic relations with Burma for the benefit of both. In December a procedure for filing war claims in Burma was announced and an agreement for a Fulbright program was signed. The American envoy to Thailand, Edwin F. Stanton, represented the United States at the Independence Day ceremonies in Rangoon. President Truman on the occasion sent greetings to the new republic, and in April 1948 the United States joined with other countries in welcoming Burma into the United Nations.

The outbreak of civil war in the Union raised questions of American policy. Basically Washington left the matter of aid to the beleaguered government up to the British. True, a few patrol boats and some lend-lease arms were provided Prime Minister U Nu, but in September, Washington rejected a Burmese request for military aid indicating that Rangoon should look to London and to American commercial interests. As regards the latter, arms were subject to U.S. export controls which would probably not be easily relaxed in Burma's case. Although the British reportedly wanted priority and exclusiveness in providing arms to Rangoon, the United States, having no major political, economic, or security interests in Burma, was not aroused over the matter.

The White Flag Communists of the Burma Communist Party started their insurrection in late March after Moscow-inspired meetings in Bombay, November to December 1947, and in Calcutta, February to March 1948. Communist revolts erupting in Burma, Indonesia, and Malaya in 1948 as well as the continuance of the older insurrections of the Viet Minh in Indochina and the Huks in the Philippines indicated that communism was on the offensive in Southeast Asia.[57] Other dissidents in Burma who fought against the government in the early years of independence included the Red Flag Communists of the Communist Party (Burma), the White Band People's Volunteer Organization, the Karen National Defense Organization, and separatists in Arakan.

Fortunately for the early existence of the Rangoon government the revolts of the dissidents were not simultaneously planned and no alliance among all of them could be established. Even so the regime of Prime Minister U Nu came very close to collapse and Burma very near to anarchy. Great Britain at the most serious time did not supply Rangoon with the needed weapons although India provided arms to its small neighbor at a critical period. The personal friendship of Prime Ministers Nehru and Nu was a major consideration in Indian-Burmese relationships in the years when both were in power. As a result of the London Conference of Commonwealth Prime Ministers in April 1949, a Burma Aid Committee of the ambassadors from India, Great Britain, Pakistan, and Ceylon in Rangoon came into being which led on June 28, 1950, to a loan agreement of five Commonwealth countries to help Burma. Although the loan was not drawn upon, it was a gesture of sympathy for Rangoon.

In the United States there was a tendency for a while to write Burma off to anarchy. The country was considered a poor risk for assistance. The American Ambassador, J. Klahr Huddle, was away from his post in Rangoon for many months on detail to the Kashmir commission of the United Nations during the worst period of the insurgency. A number of minor agreements were signed by Burma and the United States in the early period after the former's independence but the visit of the Burmese foreign minister, Dr. E. Maung, and deputy prime minister, General Ne Win, to the United States in the summer of 1949 in search of arms was not successful.

The government of Prime Minister U Nu, obviously much to the surprise of many observers, survived the insurrection. In addition to profiting from the division among the "multicolored" rebels and the limited military aid from abroad, U Nu used military force on the one hand and tried to remove many of the grievances of the rebels, on the other. Equally significant, outside powers despite their interests did not intervene in an attempt to overthrow the legally constituted government.

As the policy of the United States toward Southeast Asia began to change by early 1950, the Union of Burma was soon given more attention and better relations ensued. It no longer appeared on the verge of collapse but its future was very uncertain. The fall of mainland China to the forces of Mao Tse-tung entered into the decision making of both Rangoon and Washington. The Union was the first non-Communist country to recognize the People's Republic of China while the United States came to lead world opposition against recognition.

After postwar Burma emerged in the family of nations its foreign policy jelled. In the words of U Nu the country was a "tender gourd among the cactus."[58] At first the Union favored alignment; both Aung San and U Nu at one time or another had spoken for it. Burma's security, it was believed, could come through alliance and through the United Nations. The defense agreement of 1947 with Great Britain was an important cornerstone. Although limited to three years it would continue unless terminated on a year's notice by either party. Any military alliance that might be made, it was asserted, was not prejudiced by the defense agreement. Foreign Minister E. Maung when he visited Washington in the summer of 1949 indicated Burma was willing to consider a Pacific security pact. The United States was opposed to such an alliance and was supporting Prime Minister Nehru in his opposition to it. In September U Nu began to alter his viewpoints on alignment and by December he clearly favored neutralism.

The decision of Burma to follow a neutral policy was probably more influenced by the Communist takeover in China than by the attitude of the United States toward a Pacific defense pact. John Scott Everton, a former U.S. ambassador to Burma, has written: "It would be safe to assume that no major policy decision is made, no action taken, without consideration of the effect of such decisions and actions on Burma's relation to mainland China."[59] Prime Minister U Nu's policy of neutralism was expressed in the context of the so-called power blocs waging the Cold War. At the same time he believed Rangoon's interpretation of positive neutrality enabled Burma to make decisions on foreign policy on the merits of issues. In other respects the Prime Minister's foreign policy put considerable stress on the promotion of Theravada Buddhism and Asian socialism. Like all postwar Burmese leaders, U Nu was strongly opposed to colonialism. A "tender gourd among the cactus" would long characterize the plight of his country and explain the limitations of its international role.

INDOCHINA

From the collapse of Japan to the diplomatic recognition by the United States of the State of Vietnam, the Kingdom of Laos, and the Kingdom of Cambodia in February 1950, American policy toward Indochina was relatively passive. At the beginning of the period and especially toward the end Washington evidenced more interest but during most of the time it was basically an observer. No one could have predicted that the United States would be involved in a major war in Indochina within twenty years of V-J Day. With the benefit of hindsight two questions emerge like Banquo's ghost to haunt the corridors of time. Did the United States in the year 1945 and into 1946 miss a golden opportunity by not upholding the regime of Ho Chi Minh in the hope that his Vietnam (Communist but nationalist) would play a role later exemplified by Tito's Yugoslavia? Some Americans think so. Did the United States at a later period miss another opportunity by not maximizing the "Bao Dai formula"—a non-Communist Vietnamese nationalist alternative to Ho Chi Minh—when American influence could have been best employed? Here again, some Americans think so.

These questions never really can be answered, and the variables in the Indochinese situation are so numerous and complex that they challenge the most courageous analyst. The substantial capture of the Vietnamese nationalist movement by the Communists under Ho Chi Minh and the determination of Paris to keep Indochina in the French orbit created an impasse that was only broken by over seven and a half years of war.[60] Moreover, the concepts of an Indochinese Federation with Vietnam, Cambodia, and Laos and of the French Union with the mother country and its overseas domain were subject to interpretation. France was politically unstable at home and badly divided on Indochina, the Communists calling for an end of *la sale guerre* and the conservatives desiring to keep the French Empire. As a consequence of conflicting interests, French negotiations first with Ho Chi Minh and then with alternative leaders were long, complex, and frequently acrimonious. Nor could events in Indochina be isolated from world developments. The victory of Mao Tse-tung in mainland China led to a Stalin-Mao-Ho alignment across Eurasia affecting the future of Vietnam, Cambodia, and Laos. The containment policy of the United States in the development of the Cold War produced a Franco-American alliance in a multilateral framework of the North Atlantic Alliance with definite implications for Indochina. Nationalism, colonialism, and communism were important ingredients in a witch's brew which poisoned the international atmosphere, in Shakespeare's words: "Fair is foul, and foul is fair; hover through the fog and filthy air."

OSS and Ho Chi Minh. In the latter part of 1944 contacts definitely developed between Ho Chi Minh and a number of Americans in southern China. The exact circumstances and extent of the American role are still a mystery. Chester L. Cooper has aptly pointed out from his OSS experience in the China-Burma-India Theater that the Office of Strategic

Services was a "freewheeling organization" particularly in "out-of-the-mainstream places" like the southwestern part of China.[61] It may be that one or more OSS agents had established contact with Ho Chi Minh several months before Roosevelt's orders of October 1944 about doing nothing regarding resistance groups in Indochina.

The four secret visits of Ho Chi Minh to OSS Kunming headquarters in late 1944 and early 1945 were quite likely under the auspices of one or more OSS men. Ho wanted weapons and ammunition. In return he would provide intelligence through his network of informers in Tonkin, would continue to help rescue allied fliers downed in the jungle, and would conduct sabotage operations against the Japanese. Charles Fenn, an OSS agent, later revealed through the press that Ho was enlisted by OSS as Agent 19. Fenn also indicated through the news media that he took Ho Chi Minh at his request to see General Chennault, and that the Viet Minh leader agreed to create a rescue team in Vietnam for downed allied fliers. Paul E. Helliwell, an OSS chief in China during the four mentioned visits of Ho to the Kunming headquarters, has revealed, however, that Ho Chi Minh's requests for arms and ammunition were each time rejected as OSS followed "its policy of giving no help to individuals such as Ho, who were known Communists and therefore obvious postwar sources of trouble."[62] A major factor in the decision was the fact that Ho Chi Minh, thinking of the French, would not pledge to restrict the use of American arms to combat with the Japanese. Nevertheless, Ho did get a few revolvers and some ammunition from Helliwell, and the supply grew in time from various American sources including OSS.

In the spring of 1945 the cooperation of OSS with Ho Chi Minh was much more extensive. By the end of May a few of its personnel had walked or parachuted into the headquarters of the Vietnamese leader in northern Tonkin. Americans increased in numbers, working closely with Ho in his jungle camp. One of them, an army lieutenant who came to know the Viet Minh leader well over a period of several months, subsequently revealed that Ho tried to get help from him in preparing a declaration of independence from France. The American was unable to quote the language of the U.S. declaration of 1776 but Ho was really more interested in the spirit of it. When the Declaration of Independence of the Democratic Republic of Vietnam was issued on September 2, 1945, it reflected both the 1776 declaration of the United States and 1791 Declaration of the Rights of Man and of the Citizen of France, the two countries against which ironically Ho Chi Minh would wage bitter wars threatening the peace of Asia and the world. The Viet Minh leader, however, once indicated that the U.S. declaration was employed as a model since his people viewed America as the country most likely to sympathize with them.

Ho used the OSS portable radio of the lieutenant to contact the Free French in China about the postwar future of Vietnam. This subject was not conducive to cordiality between the Americans and the Free French. OSS, following a change in Roosevelt's orders to do nothing about resistance units in Indochina, had started in April to retrain and arm a sizable number of French soldiers who had escaped into Kunming after the Japanese coup of March. The objective was to drop teams of Americans and French into Indochina to organize guerrilla bands against the Japanese. The French, it became clear, wanted American aid but without a direct U.S. role in Indochina. Helliwell observed: "It was perfectly obvious by June of 1945 that the French were infinitely more concerned with keeping the Americans out of Indochina than they were in defeating the Japanese or in doing anything to bring the war to a successful conclusion in that area."[63] On the other hand, Jean Sainteny indicated that the Americans in the summer were blinded by *"anticolonialisme enfantin."*[64]

OSS personnel in Vienna through their personal ties and contacts were very much impressed by Ho Chi Minh and his guerrillas. The Americans dropped arms to them, and during the final months of the Pacific War OSS officers were "actually leading and training Viet Minh guerrillas."[65] An American medic in July 1945 may well have saved Ho's life. In retrospect, however, U.S. material aid to Ho Chi Minh during the closing phase of the conflict was probably not excessive. United States help to resistance groups in Indochina, as the American Joint Chiefs realized, could obviously not be decisive in the U.S. objective of defeating Japan.[66] But the aid, even though small scale, could help to maintain active resistance to the Japanese in Indochina, and this consideration could not be overlooked.

For Ho Chi Minh the American support of his resistance forces against the Nipponese had important psychological consequences. He claimed his people were a part of the United Nations war effort against Tokyo. He at least hoped, he may even have expected, that the United States would back him in winning independence from France. Ho Chi Minh was impressed by Washington's setting a date for Philippine independence and he highly praised the attitude of Roosevelt toward colonialism. The United States did have Ho's goodwill in the closing months of the Pacific War.

Shortly after Japan's defeat Ho wrote the American lieutenant urging the United States to inform the United Nations that the Viet Minh begged them "to realize their solemn promise that all nationalities will be given democracy and independence. If United Nations forget their solemn promise & don't grant Indochina full independence, we will keep fighting until we get it."[67] Ho also wrote Captain Charles Fenn expressing regret that American friends would be leaving soon and noting that future Vietnamese-American relations would be "more difficult."

An interesting memorandum, it should be noted, was prepared by OSS Director Donovan for the Secretary of State on August 22 reporting that representatives of the Central Liberation Committee from Hanoi had recently indicated in Kunming that they wanted the United States to intercede with the United Nations to prevent the French and Chinese from occupying Indochina. The contents of the memorandum could also be interpreted to mean that the Central Liberation Committee representatives had shown a desire to have Vietnam become an "American protectorate." (If this interpretation is accepted, the Viet Minh were probably thinking in terms of U.S. tutelage over the Philippines prior to independence.)

When the tidings of Tokyo's surrender reached Kunming on August 15 the Americans and Free French were caught by surprise. Major Jean Sainteny, head of French Mission 5, was instructed by Paris to take what action he thought appropriate. He decided to travel to Hanoi but wanted local members of OSS to provide him with transport. (The communications and transportation equipment of OSS was at a premium.) An agreement was reached that the French group under Sainteny would be accompanied by a party from OSS under Major Archimedes L. Patti who was locally responsible for collating U.S. intelligence on Indochina. After some delay—General Wedemeyer was hesitant to approve the departure of Sainteny—the combined group possessing no credentials flew on August 22 to Hanoi where the Japanese who met them were quite perplexed about what to do. Sainteny convinced the Japanese that he had come to view the conditions and needs of the French prisoners and Patti had arrived to make arrangements for a coming visit of an Allied Commission to take the surrender of local Japanese troops.

A crowd hostile to the French gathered before the hotel in Hanoi where the new arrivals were housed. The Japanese believed the French should go elsewhere. At the suggestion of Sainteny they were allowed to move into the former residence of the French governor general. Here the French lived in semicaptivity for several days, the Viet Minh and the Japanese restricting their activities. On September 9 the French were forced to move again in order to allow General Lu Han, the commanding officer of the occupying Chinese forces, to live in the residence. Meanwhile the Americans from OSS, free to travel about Hanoi, were flattered by the Viet Minh who had taken over the city and much of Vietnam in an "August Revolution" whose character is still debatable.

Other Americans arrived on the scene and they were well received by the Viet Minh. In addition to OSS personnel whose task was to make preparations for the Japanese surrender were the Military Advisory and Assistance Group (MAAG) under Brigadier General Philip E. Gallagher, which was involved in assisting and advising the occupation forces of the Chinese Nationalists and through them trying to preclude violence; the Military Government Group (G5) under Colonel Stephen Nordlinger, which was largely concerned with the release and rehabilitation of the allied prisoners of war; and a number of American journalists.

The sympathies of Americans on the scene, OSS officers like Patti and journalists for instance, were for Ho Chi Minh. (He often met with some of them.) General Gallagher was courted through the local news media partly to impress the French and Chinese. A Vietnamese-American Friendship Association was formed in Hanoi on October 17 with expressions of friendship from both parties. The sympathies of the Americans, however, were essentially based on their perception of Ho's leadership of a nationalist movement and on their concern for a colonial people seeking independence.

The MAAG apparently assumed that a United Nations trusteeship would in time be created for Indochina. In the meantime General Gallagher dealt with the Viet Minh government; his orders on August 24 like those to Colonel Nordlinger were to be politically neutral. This approach, of course, disappointed both Ho Chi Minh and the French. A shift in policy occurred in late September, it is contended, when the Americans under Gallagher and Chinese under Lu Han in northern Vietnam were ordered to facilitate the French recovery of power.[68]

In Saigon various Americans were critical of the French and expressed sympathy for the nationalistic aspirations of the Viet Minh.[69] It was very influential in the city in a Provisional Executive Committee. American attention was directed to Saigon on September 26 when Lieutenant Colonel A. P. Dewey, head of a small OSS mission in southern Indochina, was ambushed and killed. Neither General Gallagher nor Colonel Nordlinger in Hanoi was certain of Dewey's activities. Ho Chi Minh apologized to Gallagher though the Viet Minh leader was not sure whether the incident was staged by the French or by his supporters. Ho also sent a letter on September 29 to President Truman asserting that "we are as profoundly affected by death of any American resident in this country as by that of dearest relatives."[70] He expressed his admiration and friendship for the American people and their representatives in Vietnam. The French disliked the activities and attitudes of OSS officers in South Vietnam as in the North and also in Laos (a number arrived in

Vientiane shortly after the war and Souphanouvong, with American help, was flown to Hanoi to meet Ho). In addition the French were generally critical of American correspondents. General de Gaulle later wrote that "we regarded the presence in the area of United States personnel for the combined task of economic prospecting and political indoctrination as ungracious but, generally speaking, without great effect."[71]

In time the Department of State came to assert more influence over the activities of OSS in Indochina. It was believed that OSS people were too independent in their operations and became too involved in policy matters outside their field of competence. Certainly they were not spokesmen for the United States. OSS reduced operations, but Major Frank White for several months occasionally talked with Ho. The Department of State had no desire to assist Ho Chi Minh despite Viet Minh hopes that the United States would be willing to provide political backing for the independence of the Democratic Republic of Vietnam in exchange for economic concessions.

Ho's Appeals to Washington. From the fall of 1945 to the Franco-Viet Minh agreement of March 1946, it has been revealed, a series of appeals and/or suggestions were sent by Ho Chi Minh to the President of the United States or the Secretary of State.[72]* Ho also made various appeals to Chiang Kai-shek and Attlee; Stalin too was approached. Ho Chi Minh even tried to have the "Indochina issue" brought before the United Nations. The outbreak of fighting between the French and Viet Minh in South Vietnam in late September 1945 provided a stimulus for Ho's appeals against the French although his major war effort in North Vietnam did not begin until December 1946 after the Franco-Viet Minh accord on March 6 had collapsed.

On October 17, 1945, Ho Chi Minh in an effort to facilitate the recognition of his government as the spokesman of Vietnam in world councils and to prevent France from that role sent a telegram to President Truman urging that the Democratic Republic of Vietnam and not France sit on the Far Eastern Advisory Commission. He claimed that the absence of Vietnam would lead to instability in the Far East. The White House on October 17 referred the telegram to the Department of State which indicated on November 15 that "no action" on it should be taken. Apart from seeking information on the attitudes and policies of Ho Chi Minh, the Department pursued this basic approach.

Five days after the telegram of October 17, Ho appealed to Secretary of State Byrnes for "immediate interference" in South Vietnam and asked for the recognition of the "full independence" of his country by the

---

*There were often time delays in the receipt in Washington of Ho's appeals as he had to use difficult channels at different times.

United Nations. He submitted several documents for the information of the United States—one of them being the Declaration of Independence of the Democratic Republic of Vietnam. About the same time Ho appealed by radio in Hanoi to Truman, Attlee, and de Gaulle, asserting his government planned to hold a plebiscite within two months to provide a constitution for Indochina.

President Truman's Navy Day speech on October 27 was particularly noted in Hanoi. The second, fourth, and sixth "fundamentals" of U.S. foreign policy (relating to self-government) were praised. Although Truman spoke in generalities and did not in any way refer to Indochina, Ho Chi Minh hoped these "fundamentals" would be applied to Vietnam. He also frequently referred to the Atlantic Charter—once as the "foundation of future Vietnam"—and to the San Francisco Charter of the United Nations. They implied, he indicated, the eradication of "all forms of colonial oppression."

On November 1 Ho wrote Byrnes seeking to send to the United States about 50 young Vietnamese to study agriculture, engineering, and other specialties. The students would also serve the interest of "friendly cultural relations." He noted that the Vietnamese intelligentsia for many years had been "keenly interested in things American." In another communication to Byrnes Ho Chi Minh strongly protested the absence of Vietnam on the Far Eastern Advisory Commission.

On or about November 8 the Viet Minh leader sent a letter to Truman accusing the French of aggression in South Vietnam and asserting his people would fight any French forces coming into the country. Strongly indicting French policy before, during, and after the Pacific War, he asserted any future bloodshed was the responsibility of France. About two weeks later Ho Chi Minh appealed to Truman and the Director General of the United Nations Relief and Rehabilitation Administration for help to fight starvation caused in his viewpoint by drought, flood, and the Chinese and French.

Reacting to the appointment of General Marshall on a special mission to end the Chinese civil war, Ho sent letters on January 18, 1946, to both President Truman and the General. The Viet Minh leader asked Truman for intervention to find a quick solution of the Vietnamese crisis. American aid was sought both in the cause of independence and reconstruction. Pointedly Ho asserted that "peace is indivisible," relating French aggression and world security.

The next month he again wrote President Truman. On February 16 the former asked the United States "to take a decisive step" on behalf of Vietnamese independence. He wanted what had been given the Philippines, and asserted that the goal of Vietnam like that of the Philippines was "full independence and full cooperation" with Washington. At the same time Ho raised the question of "complicity" or "connivance" on the part of the "Great Democracies" in the interests of the French. Two days later in an appeal to the American, British, Chinese, and Russian governments, Hanoi asked them for "urgent interference"—for "mediation"—to halt the bloodshed in South Vietnam and also asked them to present the issue of Indochina to the United Nations.

On February 27 the State Department received from Kenneth P. Landon, an official who had been on temporary assignment in Hanoi, a message to the effect that he was transmitting to Washington two letters Ho Chi Minh had handed him for President Truman and a petition. Landon had planned to spend only a few days in Hanoi but remained there longer on Ho's urging. In their conversations the Viet Minh leader sought U.S. aid for his cause. The Franco-Viet Minh accord of March 6 led to the end of Ho's correspondence with Washington but some links did remain especially until he left Hanoi in December.

It is impossible to state what was the maximum and what was the minimum role Ho Chi Minh would have accepted for the United States. Early in 1946 he suggested to an American journalist, Stanley M. Swinton, an interest in some kind of a U.S. guarantee of independence within ten years if Hanoi let the French return. General Gallagher reported in late January his belief that Ho would perhaps settle for the tutelage of France if subject to the control of other nations. On another occasion Gallagher recalled that Ho Chi Minh had told him Vietnam was not yet ready for independence, that the U.S. handling of the Philippines was exemplary, and, as Gallagher interpreted Ho's train of thought, the United States might do the same for Vietnam. Colonel Nordlinger for his part has indicated that Ho was willing for some kind of U.S. authority over his country. It is also possible that he would have accepted a United Nations trusteeship for a very limited duration. Looking into the future, Ho after World War II once even remarked he could be neutral like Switzerland in the emerging contest between the West and communism.

The failure of Washington to capitalize on the goodwill in Hanoi existing for a while after the defeat of Japan—goodwill so well expressed by Vo Nguyen Giap at independence ceremonies on September 2—cannot easily be laid to rest. If the United States had followed the opposite policy, what would Ho Chi Minh have done? Americans familiar with the scene at the time differ in their answers. In the light of subsequent developments there is a tendency to consider the American failure a lost opportunity.[73]

Application of Potsdam Decision. Meanwhile the application of the Potsdam decision to divide Indochina at the sixteenth parallel and President Truman's general order No. 1 to MacArthur, August 15, 1945, on behalf of the allied powers relating in detail to Japanese surrender in East Asia and the Pacific had caused severe reverberations in the French dependency. The Southeast Asia Command under Admiral Mountbatten —he assumed the widened command August 15—had the responsibility for providing forces for southern Indochina (Cambodia, Cochin China, southern Annam, and southern Laos) with Major General Douglas Gracey appointed to command the British and Indian troops involved in the operation. They were to be replaced by French forces as soon as possible. Gracey's orders were to round up and disarm the Japanese in the area and to get the release of allied prisoners of war and internees. He was expected to avoid unnecessary intervention in local political affairs but to maintain law and order in necessary areas in carrying out his assignment. On September 21 Gracey issued a proclamation expressing his determination to maintain order in all Indochina south of the sixteenth parallel. Mountbatten then told him to "confine operations of British/Indian troops to those limited tasks which he had been set."[74] Subsequently the British supported Gracey in his proclamation. True, he was faced with an extremely difficult task—how to carry out his instructions in a very fluid and often chaotic situation—but it was widely believed that he went beyond the Potsdam mandate.

In the first week of September advance parties of Gracey's command arrived in Saigon where they found a Communist-dominated Provisional Executive Committee under the leadership of Tran Van Giau which had been established on August 25. Discussions for a basis of negotiations on the future of Indochina between the French Commissioner for Cochin China, H. J. Cédile, and Giau quickly collapsed as did later efforts. When Gracey arrived in Saigon near the middle of September he faced the growing danger of an armed revolt. The Japanese were reluctant to be responsible for security (though they helped) while Gracey had only 1,600 officers and men at his command. He reluctantly took a major step by arming 1,400 French prisoners of war of the 11th Colonial Infantry Regiment who had been confined to barracks. In the words of Donald Lancaster, a former British diplomat in Saigon, the step "was to have momentous consequences."[75] Disliked by the Vietnamese and by a small unit of Free French troops who had just arrived, the newly freed prisoners were exasperated, eager for action, and provocative toward the local populace. Incidents occurred, and the French community in Saigon was delighted when soldiers of the Regiment on the night of September 23–24, with Gracey's sanction, occupied the public buildings in the city expelling the Executive Committee from the town hall. The British general, now embarrassed by developments as critically reported by American and British journalists, disarmed the French troops and had them confined to barracks.

Tran Van Giau took over the leadership of armed resistance to the French which spread through Cochin China. General Philippe de Haute-cloque Leclerc who had been selected to command the military forces of France in Indochina arrived in Saigon on October 8. He had been assured by Mountbatten in a meeting at Kandy that arms and stores would be available to the French Expeditionary Corps from stocks in Ceylon. Leclerc and Gracey divided their responsibilities. The British agreed to keep law and order in Saigon and clear an area to the north for the concentration of Japanese troops. Leclerc's forces quickly began the pacification of the countryside of Cochin China which soon led to the reestablishment of French control over the towns and chief roads.

In Cambodia the role of France was rather easily reestablished in a modus vivendi of January 7, 1946, under which the kingdom received the status of an autonomous state in the French Union subject to severe restrictions required by Paris. A small number of troops, British and French officers being the leaders, had gone to Phnom Penh the previous year after the Japanese surrender. When Gracey left Saigon on January 28, 1946, the French were practically in the driver's seat in Indochina south of the sixteenth parallel. Indeed, their position had been carefully guarded in Anglo-French accords the previous August and October.

To the north the Chinese Nationalist forces had crossed the border near the end of August 1945. General Lu Han's troops, moving toward Hanoi from the Red River valley and from Lang Son, looted and plundered along the way. Moreover, the Chinese occupation of northern Indochina (Tonkin, most of Laos, and northern Annam) was characterized by economic exploitation. Sainteny in the winter of 1945 contacted Paris seeking an appeal to the United Nations to investigate Chinese conduct. He was supported by the local American and British representatives.

The Chinese in contrast to the British worked with the Viet Minh on a de facto basis.* They were not sympathetic to communism but they disliked the French. Furthermore, Ho was much stronger in Tonkin than in Cochin China. General Lu Han advised non-Communist Vietnamese nationalists who came in the wake of the Chinese troops to negotiate with the Viet Minh for a role in the government. Ho Chi Minh sought to capitalize on the situation. He wanted to use the Chinese against the French, but he also desired to use the French to get the Chinese out of

---

*In fact, Mountbatten later indicated that putting northern Indochina under Chiang's control "sowed the seed" of greater conflicts. It was widely believed in London that Ho acquired such a strong position he could not be removed.

northern Indochina, seeking to conserve his strength for an eventual showdown with Paris if it became necessary. Ho, possibly trying to assure Washington he was not under the control of Moscow, officially dissolved the Indochinese Communist Party on November 11, 1945, and replaced it with an Association for Marxist Studies. Elections for an Assembly held on January 6, 1946, in Tonkin, Annam, and secretly in parts of Cochin China, though the voting was often irregular and sometimes fraudulent, produced a clear majority for the Viet Minh and were somewhat indicative of public opinion.

France and China finally reached a complicated settlement on February 28 which in effect provided for the evacuation of Chinese troops at the expense of French interests in China and Indochina. Among other considerations the Chinese were worried over Communist strength in Manchuria. Chiang Kai-shek had again indicated on August 24, 1945, that his country had no territorial ambitions in Indochina. He preferred it independent but he revealed he would neither assist an independence movement nor help the French crush it. Although China agreed on February 28, 1946, to withdraw its troops from Indochina by the end of the next month, all of them did not leave until the summer. This delay was a major factor in retarding an agreement between France and Laos, where the Chinese were sympathetic with the local nationalists. A modus vivendi was reached on August 27 whereby the paramount influence of France in Laos was reestablished, but many *Lao Issara* (Free Laotian) leaders fled to Bangkok where they sought Anglo-American support. When the Chinese Nationalist forces finally left northern Indochina, the French were thus restored to all of Laos but their future in northern Vietnam vis-à-vis the Viet Minh was very uncertain.

Hanoi and Paris: The Road to War. The course of relations between Ho Chi Minh and the French in 1946 from the Franco-Chinese settlement of February to the outbreak of open hostilities in December was characterized by lost opportunities on both sides. On March 6 a preliminary agreement with a military convention was signed by Viet Minh and French officials whereby France recognized Ho's republic as a "free state, having its own government, parliament, army and treasury, belonging to the Indo-Chinese Federation and to the French Union."[76] French military forces would return to Vietnam north of the sixteenth parallel replacing the Chinese, but the strength and composition of the former were fixed and they would be withdrawn and replaced by Ho's troops progressively over a five-year period. On the question of the national unification of Vietnam, France agreed to hold a referendum in Cochin China and to accept its results. Ho later remarked to Paul Mus that smelling French feces for a short time was preferable to eating Chinese manure for a lifetime.

The good faith of both parties has been questioned with history providing no absolute verdict. The French and the Viet Minh were both stalling for time, for they believed they could use it to their respective advantage. On the world stage the Cold War had not achieved a significant momentum between Washington and Moscow, and mainland China, where the Marshall Mission was in progress, was some years from a complete Communist takeover. Moscow, moreover, was far away from Hanoi. Ho Chi Minh complained in early 1946 that the Russians were preoccupied with Eastern Europe and not providing him the financial help he wanted and that the French Communists were soft-pedaling the question of freedom for Indochina in an attempt to get votes at home. Basically Ho wanted full independence but he was apparently willing at the time for a French economic and cultural presence and for a political link with France in a very loosely structured French Union. Paris, emphasizing overseas empire as a key component of power in the world community, was not willing to accept a Canada or Australia in a French commonwealth of nations. The Brazzaville Conference in early 1944 of the Free French and many of their colonial dependencies had significantly ruled out the attainment of "self-government" in the colonial areas. Moreover, the French community of administrators, businessmen, and settlers in Indochina should not be underestimated. It did not realize the depth of Vietnamese nationalism and believed the prewar edifice could be restored with the proper use of French force. As Cochin China was the main center of French economic interests and was a colony in contrast to the rest of the area, France did not want the unification of the three Kys—Tonkin, Annam, and Cochin China—an objective ardently desired by Vietnamese nationalists whether Communist or not.

The major issues between the Viet Minh and the French during most of 1946 boiled down to independence and unification. Just what was a "free state" in the Indochinese Federation (whatever that might be) and in the French Union (which did not technically come into existence until the adoption of the constitution of the Fourth Republic in October 1946)? Conferences between the Viet Minh and French at Dalat in April–May and at Fontainebleau in July–September failed to break the stalemate although Ho Chi Minh, perhaps convinced the Communists were coming to power through elections in France, agreed to a modus vivendi the night of September 14. Meanwhile Vice Admiral Thierry d'Argenlieu, who had been appointed French High Commissioner and Governor General, the highest ranking office in Indochina, in August 1945 went ahead to organize an autonomous Republic of Cochin China and a second Dalat Conference, this time for Indochina without the Viet Minh.

With the failure of the Fontainebleau Conference relations between the French and Viet Minh authorities in Hanoi further deteriorated. Incidents multiplied in a tense environment as both sides violated their agreements. On November 23 the French bombarded the port of Haiphong after Ho's forces had refused to leave the Chinese quarter. Finally the Viet Minh on December 19 attacked the French in Hanoi followed by assaults on French garrisons in northern Annam and Tonkin.[77]

United States Policy in the Growing Crisis. During these events the United States exerted no meaningful influence. As is clear, American priority in Asia was given to Japan, China, and the Philippines with the European colonial possessions of Southeast Asia coming after them. Furthermore, since Japan surrendered earlier than expected, American planners had far less time to shift from the problems of postwar Europe to postwar Asia, let alone Southeast Asia. In addition, the Potsdam decision relative to the responsibility of the British and Chinese in their zones of Indochina was not precise, and the United States proved passive in letting the British, Chinese, and French make their own interpretations. Since General Wedemeyer was Chiang's chief of staff, Washington could have exerted considerable influence, at least in northern Indochina.

Later, in 1946, it is doubtful if American pressure on Paris to implement the March settlement with the Viet Minh would have basically modified French policy. The Marshall Plan with its aid program for France did not become operative until early 1948. Thus its leverage was not present in 1946 when basic policy decisions were made in Paris toward Indochina. Furthermore, French Communists were in the cabinet; Washington did not want to do anything that might strengthen them. And when the chips were down, the United States was far, far more concerned about the role of France in the Atlantic community than in French colonialism in Southeast Asia and the fate of the Communist-dominated Democratic Republic of Vietnam.

Nevertheless, Acting Secretary Acheson on October 5, 1945, had informed the American chargé in China of a position on August 30 that "it is not the policy of this Govt to assist the French to reestablish their control over Indochina by force and the willingness of the US to see French control reestablished assumes that French claim to have the support of the population of Indochina is borne out by future events."[78] As already indicated, it is contended the United States in late September decided to facilitate the French recovery of power. John Carter Vincent in a speech at the Foreign Policy Association, October 20, did not question French sovereignty in Indochina but reiterated "it is not our intention to assist or participate in forceful measures for the imposition of control by the territorial sovereigns."[79] Washington was willing, he said, to help reach a peaceful settlement of the controversy if it were asked.

In the same month, October 24, Secretary Byrnes warned the allies, the French, Dutch, and British, not to employ against "natives" American-labeled lend-lease equipment. He indicated rather weakly, however, that Washington would not urge the return of such lend-lease military supplies. In fact, by early fall French troops in American-made uniforms and with U.S. lend-lease weapons were pouring into southern Vietnam. American ships significantly were also used to transport French forces. France was allowed to purchase $160 million worth of U.S. surplus supplies for use in Indochina.

On January 15, 1946, the State Department pointedly informed the Acting Secretary of War, according to a circular telegram eight days later, that "it is not in accord with policy this Govt" to use American aircraft or flag-vessels to carry troops of any nationality to or from French Indochina or the Netherlands East Indies nor to allow the use of such craft to transport weapons, ammunition or military equipment to these areas.[80] On February 14 the State Department informed the War Department that the purpose of the stated policy was to prevent the employment of American aircraft or vessels in carrying supplies and units "for military use" in French Indochina or the Netherlands East Indies.

Dean Acheson, however, discussed with President Truman a question raised by H. Freeman Matthews from the Office of European Affairs on January 18 about allowing the British in Indochina to turn over to the French some 800 trucks and jeeps which the United States had given the British under lend-lease and which were then in Indochina. Matthews had noted it was now contrary to U.S. policy to allow the French to purchase arms and military maintenance supplies to be used in the area but American military authorities favored, as did the British and French, the transfer of the jeeps and trucks. The President told Acheson he agreed to the step, for no new equipment was being brought into Indochina and the removal of the vehicles was impracticable. Ho Chi Minh, of course, drew his own conclusions from the developments in the field of arms and supplies.

After the Franco-Viet Minh agreement of March 6 Washington, along with London and others, did not grant Ho's request for recognition comparable to that recently given by Paris. American representation in Indochina remained modest. Consul Charles S. Reed, II, reported to the State Department from Saigon where the consulate was raised to a consulate general in May. After Reed talked with Ho Chi Minh in Hanoi in late April, he reported that the Viet Minh leader had stressed to him the "utmost necessity" for having American technicians and capital in Vietnam. The American Vice Consul in Hanoi, James L. O'Sullivan, had more frequent contacts with Ho Chi Minh in 1946.

O'Sullivan reported on June 5 that Ho would probably call at the

American embassy (in Paris) and that he had "constantly" given the Vice Consul the impression that he (Ho) would give "great attention to any suggestions" of the Department. It was not until September 11 near the end of the negotiations associated with Fontainebleau that the Viet Minh leader at his request made a visit to the American Ambassador. Jefferson Caffery informed the Department on the same day that Ho had said some " 'help' " from the United States in his struggle for a united independent Vietnam in a French Union would be appreciated although he was not at all specific in his comments. Ho claimed he was not a Communist. The Ambassador reported:

> From the general fuzziness of his remarks, I gathered that he would like us to get into the game and he would be very pleased if he could use us in some way or other in his future negotiations with the French authorities.
> I expressed our interest in Indochina and the people of Indochina but made no commitments.[81]

The evening of September 11, George M. Abbott, First Secretary of the American embassy, at the request of Ambassador Caffery called on Ho Chi Minh. In a memorandum the next day Abbott noted that Ho had recalled his contacts with Americans from OSS officers during the last war up to the recent meeting with the Ambassador. Ho expressed admiration for President Roosevelt, for the United States, and for its policy in the Philippines. Again Ho denied he was a Communist. Abbott stated in his report:

> Ho Chi-minh spoke at various times of the aid which he hoped to get from the United States, but was vague except as regards economic aid. With regard to the latter, he explained that the riches of his country were largely undeveloped, that he felt that Indochina offered a fertile field for American capital and enterprise.[82]

The Viet Minh leader made a vague reference, Abbott noted, to the role of France, his country's needs, and to "military and naval matters" specifically mentioning the naval base at Cam Ranh Bay.

In October John Carter Vincent observed that the situation looked more promising for a settlement in the French-Viet Minh impasse. He favored an agreement permitting recovery from the recent world war and giving consideration to the "self-governing aspirations" of the Vietnamese. In the same month the State Department pointedly asked Consul Reed about the origins and meaning of the Vietnamese flag. Despite the Communist dimension considerable sympathy for Ho Chi Minh as a nationalist leader still existed among Americans in Indochina.

Late in the year—on the verge of sustained hostilities between Ho and the French—Abbot Low Moffat, then Chief of the Division of Southeast

Asian Affairs in the State Department, visited Hanoi and met Ho and other Viet Minh leaders. In a communication of December 5, one Moffat did not get until after his departure from Hanoi on December 9, the Department, on the assumption he would talk with Ho, offered a summary of its current thinking as a guide. Moffat was told to "keep in mind" the "clear record" of Ho Chi Minh as an "agent international communism." In the viewpoint of the Department the "least desirable eventuality would be establishment Communist-dominated, Moscow-oriented state Indochina."[83] At the same time the March 6 accord and the September 14 modus vivendi were considered the basis for a settlement, and both parties to them should not prejudice the future by a resort to force. The economic rehabilitation of Indochina was important; France and Vietnam should cooperate to mutual advantage. Although the United States was not undertaking any "formal intervention" at this time and did not want any publicity it was planned that Caffery would speak frankly with the French as Moffat would to Ho Chi Minh.

Consul Reed transmitted Moffat's report to Washington on December 12. After analyzing basic difficulties between the French and Viet Minh, Moffat concluded that "not only new faces are needed but neutral good offices or even mediation may be essential."[84] A week later he went further: "Believe possibility US assistance should be earnestly considered despite risk of rebuff or unpopularity."[85] On the same day Reed drew attention to the viewpoint of a "long time resident" in Indochina who warned that failure in the negotiations between the French and Vietnamese and apparent indifference in Washington could only push the latter into the Russian sphere of influence.

Meanwhile three days before the Viet Minh attack on the French, in Hanoi, December 19, Ho made it a point to see two American correspondents from *The New York Times* and praise Franklin D. Roosevelt and the "Four Freedoms."[86] In a genial mood though recovering from a fever attack he gave no indication of the coming bloodshed. Ho emphasized his hope for cordial relations with the United States.

Shortly after the outbreak of the fighting John Carter Vincent in a memorandum to Undersecretary of State Acheson on December 23 stressed the seriousness of the situation, criticized French policy, and observed that guerrilla warfare might continue indefinitely. When Acheson talked with the French Ambassador that afternoon the former indicated Washington would not offer to mediate under the current conditions but was willing to take steps the French might think helpful in finding a settlement. Paris, of course, would resent and reject good offices or mediation.

The Bao Dai Formula. As the fighting continued between the Viet

Minh and the French, Paris gave increasing attention to the creation of a Vietnamese government that would provide a realistic alternative to Ho's regime and win Vietnamese backing. The government might also make a military effort in the defeat of the Viet Minh and attract international support. But around whom should the government center and what powers should be transferred to it? No Vietnamese government under French auspices could attract the non-Communist nationalists or the *attentistes* (fence sitters) unless France offered it at least the equivalent of the agreement made with the Viet Minh in March 1946. In the end the type of independence for the State of Vietnam proved the greatest obstacle, for the French National Assembly in May 1949 removed a major one when it reluctantly agreed to the relinquishment of the colony of Cochin China in the interests of the unification of the three Kys. French-sponsored efforts for a provisional government in Cochin China under Nguyen Van Thinh (he hanged himself), Le Van Hoach, and finally Nguyen Van Xuan were not successful.

Paris needed a person of considerable stature to lead the Vietnamese. The French turned increasingly to Bao Dai, emperor of Annam under previous French and Japanese rule and former supreme councillor to the Democratic Republic of Vietnam. Bao Dai whose sympathy was sought by the Viet Minh as well as the French wanted an independent and unified Vietnam in the French Union. In the end he rejected the Viet Minh advances. William C. Bullitt, former American ambassador to France, while on a private tour, visited him in Hong Kong late in 1947 and told him U.S. help for Vietnam would come more easily if a Communist-run government did not ask for it. Later Bullitt conferred with French officials in Paris, reportedly favoring the former emperor. Whatever the motivation or channel, Bao Dai decided to negotiate independently with the French. In the course of long discussions punctuated by discord and by agreement and reflecting the vicissitudes of French politics, Bao Dai compromised his original objective of an independent Vietnam in the French Union. His long trips to France, however, were partly motivated toward applying pressure on Paris, and possibly he achieved as much as any Vietnamese could under the circumstances.

On December 7, 1947, the former emperor initialed his first agreement with the French high commissioner, Émile Bollaert—a joint declaration with a secret protocol—which in essence was restrictive (he later disavowed it); another agreement, still restrictive, was signed on June 5, 1948, by the two men and by Nguyen Van Xuan, now head of a provisional central government, on a French cruiser in the Bay of Along; and a third, an exchange of letters between French President Vincent Auriol and Bao Dai, the Elysée Agreement of March 8, 1949, confirmed the statement of principles of the joint declaration of June 5, 1948. Later Bao Dai and Léon Pignon, the French high commissioner, exchanged letters, dated June 13, 1949, to effect the Elysée Agreement pending approval of the French National Assembly. Similar basic agreements were made by France with Laos on July 19 (leading to the return of many exiles of the *Lao Issara* movement) and with Cambodia on November 8. The French were motivated by the military victories of Mao Tse-tung and their own failure to defeat Ho Chi Minh in 1948.

On June 14, 1949, the State of Vietnam was inaugurated in Saigon with Bao Dai as chief of state. Ngo Dinh Diem, a prominent nationalist, refused office largely because he thought Vietnam should have the status of an India or a Pakistan. The *attentistes* were not impressed, the non-Communist nationalists were divided among themselves by personal and regional rivalries, and the Viet Minh loudly charged the Saigon government was simply a collection of French puppets. Late in December Bao Dai and Pignon approved a number of conventions on the implementation of the Elysée Agreement worked out by joint committees. The French National Assembly, reflecting government instability, was slow in approving the basic agreements made with Vietnam, Laos, and Cambodia in 1949, but it finally acted and the bill became law with the signature of the President on February 2, 1950.

The United States and the Bao Dai Formula. As the Bao Dai formula was being implemented in the early years, 1947–50, the United States took no decisive steps to pressure Paris into granting full and quick independence to Vietnam. On January 8, 1947, France indicated to the Department of State appreciation for Acheson's remarks to the French Ambassador December 23 but stressed that Paris must handle the Indochina situation singlehandedly. Secretary of State Marshall in public comment in January after the outbreak of the fighting simply hoped that "a pacific basis for adjustment" could be found.

The United States in a cable to the American embassy in Paris reiterated on January 8 its policy which called for sales to France of reasonable amounts of military supplies except for instances appearing to relate to Indochina. As in the past, this policy was more easily stated than fully implemented. On September 27, 1948, for instance, a policy paper of the State Department noted that "we have allowed the free export of arms to France, such exports thereby being available for re-shipment to Indochina or for releasing stocks from reserves to be forwarded to Indochina."[87]

On February 3, 1947, Secretary Marshall told the American embassy in Paris for use in frank conversation with French leadership that "there are two sides" to the Indochina problem and that "frankly we have no solution" to propose. On the one hand, Marshall observed that the French had a "dangerously outmoded colonial outlook and methods" and on the other hand that "Ho Chi Minh has direct Communist connections and it should be obvious that we are not interested in seeing colonial empire administrations supplanted by philosophy and political organizations emanating from and controlled by Kremlin."[88] The Secretary noted that the United States has a "vital interest" in the well-being, political and economic, of the area.

Marshall indicated a few weeks later on May 13 in a cable to the American embassy in Paris that Washington was "increasingly concerned" over the "slow progress" toward settling the dispute in Indochina. He stressed for relay to the French that setbacks in Southern Asia to the long-range interests of France would adversely affect those of the United States, Great Britain, and the Netherlands as all were "essentially in the same boat." Once more the French were to be told that Washington was ready to do anything it could that might be viewed as helpful.

In the late summer, September 11, the United States took steps to caution Paris against a dry season military offensive, for it would affect the congressional attitude on financial aid to France in view of its needs at home. The caution was given in vain. In another direction, not pleasing to Washington, the French high commissioner for Indochina, Émile Bollaert, made a significant speech on September 10 about policy toward the area. Vice Consul O'Sullivan in a report to his government two days later indicated the speech was a "definite retreat" from the accord between the French and Viet Minh of March 6, 1946.

By the summer of 1948 the State Department had firmly concluded that France could not achieve a military solution under the current circumstances, that the continuation of the parade of puppets in Vietnam would strengthen Ho Chi Minh and might well produce a Communist-dominated state most likely oriented to Moscow, and that it was of "the highest importance" that a non-Communist regime be given concessions that would attract the largest possible number of non-Communists. This conclusion, however, did not mean that the United States would throw its support at once or without reservation behind the person of Bao Dai. But despite deep apprehension and real worry in Washington the trend of U.S. policy was in this direction.

On July 14 the American Ambassador in Paris was given the authority to "apply such persuasion and/or pressure" best calculated to produce the "desired result," namely the prompt and unequivocal approval of the principle of Vietnamese independence in the French Union and the unification of the three Kys. Once the Bay of Along agreement of June 5 between France and Bao Dai and the status change of Cochin

China were approved in Paris, it was indicated, Washington was willing to give public support to the French action. Again on August 30 the Department stressed this approach in a cable to the American embassy in Paris. The next month the U.S. Ambassador told a French foreign office representative that Washington was also willing under comparable circumstances to consider helping France through ECA with financial aid for Indochina providing "real progress" was made toward a non-Communist solution founded on the "cooperation of true nationalists."

The policy statement of the Department of State on Indochina, September 27, was an excellent exposition of the subject produced at a critical time in the gestation of the Bao Dai alternative.[89] The analysis in realistic terms concluded:

> The objectives of US policy can only be attained by such French action as will satisfy the nationalist aspirations of the peoples of Indochina. . . . We are naturally hesitant to press the French too strongly or to become deeply involved so long as we are not in a position to suggest a solution or until we are prepared to accept the onus of intervention. The above considerations are further complicated by the fact that we have an immediate interest in maintaining in power a friendly French government, to assist in the furtherance of our aims in Europe. This immediate and vital interest has in consequence taken precedence over active steps looking toward the realization of our objectives in Indochina.[90]

It almost has been forgotten that from at least 1947 into 1950 the Viet Minh ran a news service in New York. Prior to March 1948 they issued *Releases* and after that a *Bulletin*. The latter was under the auspices of the Viet-Nam–America Friendship Association which held a banquet in New York in 1948.* While the French were trying to sell the Americans on the Communist threat of Ho Chi Minh—d'Argenlieu's comments back in 1946 had some of the ring of the later domino theorists—the Viet Minh were portraying themselves as pure anticolonial nationalists.

The American Consul General in Saigon, George M. Abbott, it is interesting to note, observed as late as February 1949 that "one peculiar thing about Vietnam Communism" was the fact that propaganda against the United States has been "very little." Ho Chi Minh, he pointed out, was careful to stop any public propaganda against America in the press, on the radio, or in speeches. (This attitude as from November 1948 did not apply inside party circles and to word of mouth.) Abbott in his report of February 1949 indicated the prestige of the United States was

*Some informal contact between U.S. officials and the Viet Minh existed via the American embassy in Bangkok in 1947.

"still high," and Ho apparently hoped he could get U.S. backing or at least acceptance of a Vietnam run under his leadership. Nevertheless, the Consul General, it should be noted, reported on November 5, 1948, that "from the point of view of Moscow, prospects are excellent that Ho Chi Minh will eventually force the withdrawal of the French and set up the first 'New Democratic Republic' in Southeast Asia."[91]*

American policy toward the Bao Dai formula finally jelled in the course of 1949. On January 17 Washington had informed the U.S. Ambassador in Paris that it wanted France to make a settlement with Bao Dai or any really nationalist grouping but it did not at the time want to irretrievably commit itself to a regime that might virtually become a puppet existing only with the support of the French military forces.

The Elysée accords of March 8 introduced a significant dimension. Secretary Acheson subsequently observed that in 1949 they "moved in the direction of United States aims in Asia, though the Department doubted whether they moved far enough or would be carried out fast enough."[92] Southeast Asia specialists questioned if they would work as presently written while Western European specialists believed that U.S. pressure on the French would only irk them. As a consequence Washington tried to work with London in getting Philippine and Indian assistance in the effort to persuade the Saigon Vietnamese and French to be realistic. Meetings between Acheson and Robert Schuman of France and among Acheson, Schuman, and Ernest Bevin of Great Britain in 1949 were not productive despite the Anglo-American solidarity against the French. Paris was stubborn, very stubborn.

On May 2 the American Consul General in Saigon was specifically instructed in the light of the situation to take no action that might be viewed as "premature endorsement or de facto recognition" of Bao Dai. At the same time Washington did not want to convey the impression it opposed or wanted to hinder him.

The United States had the advantage of some very perceptive reporting from its Consul General in Saigon. As a consequence of the holding of an American Foreign Service conference in New Delhi in the early spring, Abbott and his staff prepared extensive background memoranda on the situation in Indochina and on the development of American policy there.[93] These memoranda together with the policy statement of the Department of State on the previous September 27 constitute a gold

---

*Efforts by the United States to discover a firm or direct link between Moscow and Ho Chi Minh for some years after the Pacific War were not successful. In 1948, for instance, this conclusion emerged in an appraisal of the Department of State in the summer and again in the fall. It was not doubted in Washington that Ho was a Communist, but his role as a puppet of the Kremlin did not seem likely.

mine of information on U.S. policy in Indochina in the late 1940's. At the time of the preparation of the memoranda there was no American news service in the French area.

On May 10 the U.S. Consul General in Saigon was informed that "at proper time and under proper circumstances" Washington was ready to recognize Bao Dai and consider his possible request for American arms and economic aid. Such an assistance program, it was noted, would need congressional approval. Ten days later the Department sent cables to Saigon and Hanoi reflecting further thought on the Bao Dai formula. The Consul General in Saigon was told Washington hoped France would carry out the Elysée Agreement with "generosity and expedition" but that the United States should at this stage avoid a "conspicuous position" of any kind. The Consul in Hanoi was instructed to caution Vietnamese nationalists about accepting a coalition government with Communist Ho Chi Minh. The point was made that the question of whether Ho was as much a nationalist as a Communist was "irrelevant."

The State Department sent to the American Ambassador in Paris on June 6 a remarkable memorandum giving its frank views on the Elysée Agreement for presentation to the French government. The Secretary of State had participated in a conversation leading to the paper. The fact that the memorandum was delivered only orally and in part due to the embassy's assessment of French reaction does not detract from the significance of Washington's viewpoints.[94] The memorandum presented an excellent perspective on nationalism and colonialism in Southern Asia, almost in university seminar terms. Viewed against this background the Elysée Agreement was seen as a step in the right direction but still not sufficiently appealing to Vietnamese nationalists. In short, it was believed, Vietnam must be allowed to control its own destiny or the Communists will succeed.

The United States blandly welcomed on June 21 the "formation of the new unified state of Vietnam" under Bao Dai.[95] Washington, of course, now had the leverage of American aid to France under the Marshall Plan but it was not utilized. Ho Chi Minh was becoming increasingly hostile to the United States and its "Marshallization of the world" as he expressed it; Mao Tse-tung was taking over the Chinese mainland; the Chinese and Russian Communists were cooperating; and the Cold War was being actively waged. If American pressure had been applied on France in respect to Bao Dai before 1950, perhaps the best period would have been the months following the Elysée Agreement. After the United States became involved in the Korean War, other priorities were quickly established. American diplomats in Saigon disagreed among themselves about how much support should be given Bao Dai and how much pressure should be put on the French. Bao Dai himself got along well with the Americans, a fact that was not appreciated by the French in Saigon.

The United States had been impatient about the French slowness to approve the Elysée Agreement. On January 27, 1950, Ambassador-at-Large Philip C. Jessup gave a note to Bao Dai calling for a "closer relationship." Five days later Secretary Acheson issued a public statement asserting that Moscow's recognition of Ho Chi Minh should destroy any illusions about the "nationalist" aspect of his aims. It revealed, Acheson said, the "true colors" of Ho as the "mortal enemy of native independence."

On February 2 the Secretary in a memorandum to President Truman sought his approval for U.S. recognition of the legal governments of Vietnam, Laos, and Cambodia after France completed the necessary legal formalities. The Secretary's reasons were precise:

> Among them are: encouragement to national aspirations under non-Communist leadership for peoples of colonial areas in Southeast Asia; the establishment of stable non-Communist governments in areas adjacent to Communist China; support to a friendly country which is also a signatory to the North Atlantic Treaty; and as a demonstration of displeasure with Communist tactics which are obviously aimed at eventual domination of Asia, working under the guise of indigenous nationalism.[96]

The President the next day gave his formal consent. On February 4 the American Consul General in Saigon was telegraphed formal letters of recognition to Bao Dai, "Head of State of the Republic of Vietnam," and to the Kings of Cambodia and Laos.

Only five days after the final French approval of the Elysée Agreement Washington recognized on February 7 the State of Vietnam, the Kingdom of Laos, and the Kingdom of Cambodia "as independent states within the French Union." The recognition, it was stated, "is consistent with our fundamental policy of giving support to the peaceful and democratic evolution of dependent peoples toward self-government and independence."[97] The American consulate general in Saigon would be raised to a legation and the U.S. minister would be accredited to Vietnam, Laos, and Cambodia; the United States looked forward to an exchange of diplomatic representatives with them. Noting the establishment of "the independence of Viet Nam, Laos, and Cambodia as associated states within the French Union," the United States anticipated that the "full implementation" of the various agreements ratified and awaiting ratification between France and the three states "will promote political stability and the growth of effective democratic institutions in Indochina."[98] It was significantly stated that the United States was considering "what steps it may take at this time to further these objectives and to assure, in collaboration with other like-minded nations, that this development shall not be hindered by internal dissension fostered from abroad."[99] Despite the American recognition Washington, it is clear, was still concerned over the "self-government and independence" of the State of Vietnam, Cambodia, and Laos. Great Britain granted recognition on February 7 to the three countries as "Associate States within the French Union." Other countries closely tied in most cases to the Western alignment followed in granting recognition. Washington and London had, however, failed in efforts to get some Asian states to assume the lead.

Meanwhile Ho Chi Minh on January 14 had publicly appealed for diplomatic relations with any state willing to treat the Democratic Republic of Vietnam "on a basis of equality and mutual respect of national sovereignty and territory."[100] He took the position that the sole legal government of the Vietnamese people was the government of the Democratic Republic of Vietnam. Communist China recognized Ho as the head of the legal government of Vietnam on January 18, the Soviet Union on January 30, and other Communist states followed. Ho Chi Minh moved quickly into the Moscow-Peking camp.

By early 1950 a polarization had clearly occurred between Ho Chi Minh's Democratic Republic and its friends and Bao Dai's State of Vietnam and its supporters. Both the United States and Communist China were on the verge of playing important roles in the future of Indochina. But neither Washington nor Peking could foresee where their policies would lead them in the vortex of Vietnam, Cambodia, and Laos.

4 WASHINGTON, PEKING, AND SOUTHEAST ASIA (EARLY 1950-MAY 1954)

The establishment of the People's Republic of China in 1949 altered the course of American policy toward Southeast Asia.

Three U.S. missions the next year reflected concern over the future of the region. Although they varied in their focus they tried to cope with common problems. Two of the missions significantly preceded the outbreak of the Korean War and one followed it. They did not have the importance of President Kennedy's in 1961 but in perspective they gain stature.

From early 1950 to May 8, 1954, when the Geneva Conference on Indochina opened, the course of the Korean War (June 1950 to July 1953) and the growing intensity of the First Indochinese War in the early 1950s dominated the East Asian scene. The outbreak of the Korean War and the entrance of Communist China into it speeded the Japanese peace settlement of 1951 and the building of the American alliance structure in East Asia and the Pacific. Both the Korean War and the Japanese peace settlement directly and indirectly affected the several countries of Southeast Asia, many newly independent. The First Indochinese War, fought within the area itself, aroused over the years varied concern and different reactions in Southeast Asian capitals. The fall of Dien Bien Phu on May 7, 1954, symbolized the end of an era but the contours of the future were blurred.

The United States was deeply involved in these momentous events in East Asia and the Pacific. How Communist China looked to American policy makers and what it actually did before and after the events of the Korean War in 1950 helped set the stage for the conclusion of the Japanese peace settlement. The American sense of threat from Peking was a significant aspect in U.S. policy as the First Indochinese War intensified. But in contrast to Washington's direct engagement in the Korean War, its engagement in the First Indochinese War was indirect. In any transition period of history conflicting priorities against the background of changing events always weigh heavily, but the trend in American policy was toward the watershed of U.S. commitments to mainland Southeast Asia in 1954.

During these years the Republicans replaced the Democrats in the White House with the Eisenhower-Dulles team in foreign policy replacing Truman and Acheson. Although the Korean War was brought to a conclusion as a result of various developments, some beyond American control, the First Indochinese War was allowed to escalate in terms of U.S. involvement, with the opening of the Geneva Conference on Indochina in early May 1954 marking a final phase of a tragic and bloody conflict.

IMPLICATIONS OF THE ESTABLISHMENT OF THE PEOPLE'S REPUBLIC OF CHINA

In many respects the postwar period for the United States in East Asia lasted only five years, for the defeat of Japan in August 1945 was followed by the outbreak of the Korean War in June 1950. The international firmament was drastically altered on October 1, 1949, by the establishment of the People's Republic of China, one of the major developments of the twentieth century. The changing of the Decree of Heaven in China had fateful consequences for Southeast Asia and for the American role there.

The policy of the United States in the "China tangle," as it had been aptly named even before the Marshall Mission,[1] was expressed in the summer of 1949 in the famous letter from Secretary of State Acheson to President Truman transmitting the so-called White Paper on American relations with China especially from 1944 to 1949. Washington's effort to help the Nationalists assert control over as much of China as possible and to prevent a civil war through compromise having failed, Acheson pointedly asserted that "the unfortunate but inescapable fact is that the ominous result of the civil war in China was beyond the control of the government of the United States."[2] Turning to the future, however, the Secretary of State frankly said: "One point . . . is clear. Should the Communist regime [of China] lend itself to the aims of Soviet Russian imperialism and attempt to engage in aggression against China's neighbors, we and the other members of the United Nations would be confronted by a situation violative of the principles of the United Nations Charter and threatening international peace and security."[3] This warning to Mao Tse-tung bore fruit in Korea the following year and was to be reiterated with reference to Southeast Asia.

As for the Nationalist government which fled to Taiwan, Washington asserted in early January 1950 it would continue economic assistance but not provide military aid or advice. It indicated that the resources on Formosa were sufficient for the Chinese Nationalists to get the items they considered necessary for the island's defense. For its part Washington wanted no special rights or military bases on Formosa. American policy was now clearly directed toward noninvolvement in the Chinese civil war. In many respects the dust was settling and the particles could fall where they might. In fact, it was generally believed Chiang Kai-shek would not last long on Taiwan. If this proved true, Southeast Asia could not escape the impact of only one Chinese state.

Washington's posture toward China provoked severe controversy in the United States. The American public was disturbed and confused over the situation. Some blamed Moscow for the defeat of Nationalist China and others accused the State Department of treason. Bipartisan foreign policy, particularly toward China, was under severe criticism in Republican circles. As a general rule, the Democrats supported President Truman and the Republicans were critical of him. The influence of the China Lobby was not insignificant. The attack by Senator Joseph R. McCarthy against Secretary Dean Acheson and the Department of State was at a zenith the first half of 1950.[4] Politically the Secretary was not permitted to forget his allow-the-dust-to-settle reference to China. John Foster Dulles, a prominent Republican and a key consultant to the State Department, did not desist from serving despite the controversy.[5] The domestic attacks on American policy toward China were an *important* factor in causing Washington decision-makers to give more attention to the future of Southeast Asia. This region, it was argued, must not become another China.

A diplomatic revolution occurred when mainland China moved from Nationalist to Communist control. The consequences of the change could not accurately be foreseen in either short- or long-range terms. Peking's policies toward various powers would markedly vary in some cases and remain relatively constant in others.[6] Its tactics would alter from the revolutionary posture in 1949 and thereafter, to the ambivalent stance of the transition years, 1952–54, and thence to the phase of peaceful coexistence.*

The People's Republic of China long considered the United States a major foe. Washington personified Peking's concept of a capitalist, imperialist, aggressive power bent on encircling and destroying China. After the United States took a strong position for the Nationalists on Formosa, Chinese unification, a very important objective in the foreign policy of Communist China, stood for many years in the way of meaningful negotiations between Washington and Peking.[7] But even in the period from the founding of the People's Republic to the outbreak of the Korean War, Mao Tse-tung showed little interest in normal relations with the United States. Indeed, various deliberate incidents discouraged American initiative toward recognition, even had President Truman chosen to face the domestic strife such recognition would have incurred. The presumption, however, was that Washington would recognize Peking, and Truman would probably have taken the step. The American termination of official representation in Communist China was personally approved by the President with full knowledge of its international and domestic implications. In a short while the U.S. official presence in mainland China ended and practically every unofficial contact terminated. All trade between the two countries was halted in late 1950. Washington sought a diplomatic quarantine of Peking through opposing recognition by various states and through leading the opposition to Communist China's seating in the United Nations.

Toward the Soviet Union, Communist China's attitude in 1949 and for some time after was one of support for close alignment. Even before October 1, 1949, Mao Tse-tung had stressed his determination to "lean to one side" in the world conflict. On February 14, 1950, the Soviet Union and the People's Republic of China, as one of the consequences of a memorable visit by Mao to Stalin, signed a treaty of friendship, alliance, and mutual assistance and at the same time concluded a number of related agreements. An attack by Japan or "states allied with it" on either Communist China or the Soviet Union would bring the victim military and other aid from its ally. In Washington's eyes communism appeared close to a monolith. The Chinese Communists were believed to be under the influence of the Soviet Union, therefore serving the interests of a foreign power. Basically, it should be stressed, communism until

*The Chinese tactics of peaceful coexistence reached their zenith in 1955 and 1956 with the last half of 1957 ushering in a period of Peking's strong championship of national interests at the expense of good ties with the leading neutralist governments in Southern Asia, India and Indonesia.

Stalin's death in 1953 did have many of the characteristics of a monolith. The Sino-Soviet alliance was a living reality in world politics. Moscow's influence on Peking, however, was probably smaller than claimed in many Western circles. In fact, Mao Tse-tung later revealed Stalin's opposition in 1945 to a Chinese civil war and lack of confidence during the negotiations leading to the Sino-Russian alliance of 1950.[8] As the years passed, the monolithic aspect of communism increasingly lost even external validity with Peking becoming more assertive and taking more initiative. China's Inner Asian frontier with the Soviet Union and the Mongolian People's Republic felt the impact of the new relationship.

As regards colonial and semicolonial peoples, Liu Shao-chi, a prominent Chinese Communist, stressed in remarks in November 1949 at the Peking meeting of a Trade Unions Conference of Asian and Australasian delegates that the path of the Chinese Communists in crushing imperialism and establishing the People's Republic was the one various colonial and semicolonial peoples should use in fighting for national independence and for "people's democracy." Before an audience that included Communist and left-wing leaders from Southeast Asia Liu urged his listeners to create whenever and wherever possible liberation armies and to back "wars of national liberation" in Asia. Praising first the Viet Minh, he then mentioned liberation warfare efforts in Burma, Indonesia, Malaya, and the Philippines. U Nu, Sukarno, and Nehru were viewed as puppets of Western imperialism and not genuine nationalist leaders. A Trade Union Liaison Bureau was set up at the Peking conference as a nerve center for contacts and support. Moscow soon praised the revolutionary approach of Comrade Liu Shao-chi.

In contrast, as Peking's tactics shifted away from revolutionary zeal toward peaceful coexistence, it held an Asian and Pacific Peace Conference in October 1952 with many participants from Southeast Asia. Instead of stressing the advantages of violence and revolution the Conference emphasized the benefits of peace and coexistence. It called for an end of hostilities in Vietnam, Malaya, and elsewhere and for fair settlements through negotiations. It also set up a Liaison Bureau—Madame Sun Yat-sen became its head—to enhance contacts.

Peking's Objectives. With the rise to power of the Chinese Communists the global and regional objectives of Peking became a matter of real concern in many foreign offices. No definitive statement has been made about Communist China's objectives. The differences between long-range and short-range goals further complicate any analysis. Moreover, some of the objectives have changed or been given higher or lower priority. Different tactical approaches over a period of time have occasionally drawn more public attention than the goals themselves. Regardless of the question of agreement among observers on the objectives of Communist

China, the crucial fact was that official policy in Washington was made on the assumption that certain Chinese goals existed. Adolf Hitler's race concepts were false but his belief in them killed millions of innocent people.

Two schools of thought on Communist China should be identified although numerous variations can be found. One school in the United States, Great Britain, France, and elsewhere essentially believed that China was not expansionist, that the Communist impact on the Chinese and their civilization was exaggerated by foreigners, and that Washington's policies precipitated some or much of Peking's militant reaction to the world. The contrasting school of thought officially held in the United States and in some other countries, at least in the 1950s and 1960s, was that China constituted a threat to peace and security in Asia and the world, that the Communist ideology of Mao Tse-tung was an essential aspect of the threat, and that Washington reacted to, rather than partly caused Peking's militant policies.*

*Significant articles published in *Foreign Affairs* and the *Department of State Bulletin* reflected contrasting interpretations of the alleged Chinese threat. Richard M. Nixon writing as a private citizen in 1967 asserted:

"The common danger from Communist China is now in the process of shifting the Asian governments' center of concern. During the colonial and immediately post-colonial eras, Asians stood opposed primarily to the West, which represented the intruding alien power. But now the West has abandoned its colonial role, and it no longer threatens the independence of the Asian nations. Red China, however, does, and its threat is clear, present and repeatedly and insistently expressed." (Richard M. Nixon, "Asia after Viet Nam," *Foreign Affairs*, October 1967, p. 113.)

William P. Bundy, Assistant Secretary of State for East Asian and Pacific Affairs, spoke of Peking's threat as of August 1967 in these words:

"None of us can say categorically that the Communist Chinese would in due course move—if opportunity offered—to dominate wide areas of Southeast Asia through pressure and subversion. But that is what the Chinese and their maps say, and their Communist doctrine appears to add vital additional emphasis. . . . Surely Adlai Stevenson was right that the threat of Communist China is not so fanciful that it should not serve as a valid assumption of policy." (William P. Bundy, "The Path to Viet-Nam: A Lesson in Involvement," *Department of State Bulletin*, September 4, 1967, p. 287, or Department of State Publication 8295, Released in September 1967, p. 12.)

John K. Fairbank, Director of Harvard's East Asian Research Center, wrote in 1969:

"One may conclude that the best way to stimulate Chinese expansion is for us to mount an over-fearful and over-active preparation against it. History suggests that China has her own continental realm, a big one; that Chinese power is still inveterately land-based and bureaucratic, not maritime and commercial; and that we are likely to see emerging from China roughly the amount of expansion that we provoke." (John K. Fairbank, "China's Foreign Policy in Historical Perspective," *Foreign Affairs*, April 1969, p. 463.)

The global objectives of Communist China in late 1950 as perceived in Washington and reflected in U.S. policy were the expansion of communism throughout Asia and the world; a special and critical role in the underdeveloped countries and the revolutionary movement in Africa, Asia, and Latin America; the isolation of the United States in Asia and throughout the world; and the establishment of the People's Republic of China as a great power in regional and global affairs. With its large area, strategic location, many natural resources, and huge population Communist China, it was argued, could speedily advance its objectives.

Peking's goals toward Southeast Asia were considered in Washington basically threefold. One objective was to secure the frontiers of China through buffer areas. Preferably they should be Communist as in the case of the Democratic Republic of Vietnam after the defeat of the French, but mainland China would settle temporarily for a neutralist regime like Burma and, as envisioned in 1962, like Laos. Another objective was the complete disengagement of the United States from the area. The American presence was viewed as the single most important threat to the goals of Communist China in the region. Washington saw a third objective as establishment of Chinese paramountcy in Southeast Asia. This paramountcy was not one of conquest and direct rule but rather one where the political, military, and economic policies of Peking would be implemented by cooperative Communist regimes in the region. In some respects the model might historically resemble the suzerain-vassal relationship between powerful Chinese emperors of the Middle Kingdom and local rulers in Southeast Asia. Peking's control, however, would probably be greater, resembling more in this respect Japan's New Order in Greater East Asia. The first objective was short-range and the second, associated closely with the third, was long-range.*

After Chinese Communist troops reached the borders of Southeast Asia in December 1949, the reactions among the countries there varied. The Philippines and Thailand continued to recognize the government of Nationalist China but Burma and Indonesia came to exchange ambassadors with Communist China. North Vietnam's diplomatic relations with Peking and South Vietnam's ties with Taipei were not surprising. Cambodia and Laos eventually exchanged envoys with Peking while

---

*The Chinese Communists will fight, according to Professor Fred Greene, a former American government official, in the following situations: "(1) to attain and secure what they consider to be the country's proper boundaries, (2) to protect the survival of a fellow Asian Communist state, (3) to avert a humiliating public defeat, if there is no other way out, and (4) to counter a substantial assault on the homeland." (Fred Greene, *U. S. Policy and the Security of Asia,* McGraw-Hill for the Council on Foreign Relations, New York, 1968, p. 213.) Although Peking ardently wanted Taiwan, the Pescadores, and the offshore islands of Quemoy and Matsu it did not desire war with the United States.

Malaya and Singapore upon independence established ties with neither China. There were fluctuations in various cases, and the future would produce more.

All Southeast Asia was well aware of the changing of the Decree of Heaven but no agreement was possible on what it meant and how to cope with it. The contrasts among neighbors in diplomatic relations with the two Chinas were indicative of the disagreement. To some Southeast Asian leaders who opposed alignment Prime Minister Nehru was the person who could best support them in Peking; to others who favored alignment Washington was their main source of hope in standing up to Communist China.

Peking's relationships in Southeast Asia, it soon became apparent, were official or unofficial, overt or covert, and conventional or popular. The impact of the People's Republic of China was evident in the various Communist parties of the region and among the more than 12 million overseas Chinese in 1950. Peking sought to use both for intelligence, propaganda, communications, and subversion. "People's diplomacy" or "popular diplomacy" whereby the Chinese Communists tried to influence important private individuals through trips to "New China," by various goodwill missions, and other means was used when possible. Conventional diplomacy was reflected in Chinese programs of trade and aid negotiated under government auspices. Propaganda was disseminated through Radio Peking, subsidized publications, and other mass media.

One consequence of Mao's victory directly affecting China's neighbors was the flight of substantial numbers of Nationalist or Kuomintang (KMT) troops into Indochina and Burma. In December 1949 around 30,000 with dependents crossed from Kwangsi into Tonkin and in the following month about 5,000 arrived from Yunnan. They surrendered their arms and were interned. The French were worried about the impact of these forces on relations between Communist China and France. The agreement between Ho Chi Minh and Mao Tse-tung in January to establish diplomatic relations ended for some years the possibility of French diplomatic recognition of Communist China. The majority of the refugee Nationalist troops were sent to the island of Phu Quoc in the Gulf of Siam from which in May and June 1953 almost all were transported to Taiwan. In contrast events in Burma took a more serious turn.

The Burmese Aberration. No better words can be chosen for this episode in American foreign policy. It was essentially a consequence of the Chinese Communist victory and belonged to the issue of whether Washington should back Chiang Kai-shek in his ambitions to return to the mainland. Yet it also directly related to American ties with a country in Southeast Asia. Although the episode stands as an aberration in Truman's basic China policy its relevance to Burmese-American relations cannot be minimized. In fact, the presence of Kuomintang troops and their activities in Burma became over the years a serious international issue which impaired the relations of Rangoon with Washington and Bangkok, involved very much the interests of Nationalist and Communist China, and drew the United Nations into a delicate and complex dispute.

In early 1950 some 1,700 Nationalist troops crossed from China into Kengtung in the Shan State. They moved on and established headquarters at Mong Hsat near the Thai-Burmese frontier as a result of pressure by Burmese forces. By early 1953 their number had risen to possibly 12,000. Refusing to leave Burma or submit to disarmament and internment, the Chinese troops were under the leadership of General Li Mi, who was known to fly from Mong Hsat to Taiwan and to be supplied partially by airlift from the outside. The Nationalist troops administered certain areas, smuggled opium to Thailand, and cooperated with some rebel Karen units. They even invaded Yunnan in July 1951 in an effort directed toward the overthrow of Mao Tse-tung, but were forced back into Burma. Other incidents occurred. The Rangoon government of U Nu, already badly harassed by various rebels, was forced to divert some of its limited military resources to cope with the Kuomintang forces. It was attacked by the opposition in parliament but refused to join the Communists and other rebels in a common campaign against the Chinese Nationalists.

Burma was apprehensive lest Peking use the situation to move into the country to liquidate the Kuomintang troops. In 1946 Chiang Kai-shek had dispatched a force into Burma on the excuse of looking for deserters. In retrospect Communist China exercised considerable restraint although Rangoon and Peking cooperated on one occasion in the long history of the crisis in a military effort against the KMT forces. Burma firmly believed the Central Intelligence Agency (CIA) of the United States actively supported the Nationalist troops. Rumor had it in Rangoon that Americans were working with the KMT forces and that they were being given U.S. arms and supplies. General Ne Win once reportedly criticized a U.S. ambassador at a diplomatic reception. Although high-ranking American officials in Washington and Rangoon denied U.S. involvement Burma wondered if the CIA might be operating independently of the State Department. Rangoon considered Chiang Kai-shek's China under the control of the United States and Pibul's Thailand subject to its influence. If the United States applied pressure, Burma believed, Chiang would have to stop aid and direction to the Kuomintang forces in the Union and Thailand would have to take a strong stand against providing them (and the Americans) a rear base for any activity. The Thai Interior Minister, General Phao Sriyanond, was not popular in Rangoon, for he was suspected of involvement with the KMT in the opium trade and of working with CIA agents.

On March 2, 1953, U Nu in a speech to parliament asserted that Burma had asked the United States to use its good offices with Chiang Kai-shek to secure the withdrawal of the Chinese troops and that it had requested India to help in every way possible in the solution of the controversy. He indicated that neither these diplomatic efforts nor the use of Burmese military force had achieved the desired result. Although Burma was concerned about Peking's reaction to taking the matter to the United Nations, U Nu asserted this course of action was now necessary.

In January 1952 the Soviet Union had attacked the United States in the United Nations on the Kuomintang issue in Burma, and in February Foreign Secretary Anthony Eden had suggested in the House of Commons a United Nations mission to get the facts of the situation. It was not until March 25, 1953, however, that Burma officially brought its complaint regarding "aggression" against the Union by the "Kuomintang Government of Formosa"[9] before the United Nations and asked that it be placed on the agenda of the seventh session of the General Assembly. In a companion step Burma on March 17 terminated the American program of economic and technical aid as of the end of June.

Discussion and action in the United Nations over the "foreign forces" in Burma extended for a period of time and contributed to a substantial though not total solution of the controversy. The General Assembly passed basic resolutions on April 23 and December 8, 1953, and on October 27, 1954. Burma received widespread sympathy but several countries did not blame Nationalist China for the activities of the Chinese troops in the Union. As a general rule Western delegates were more cautious than were the Asian and Communist ones. Indonesia fully supported Burma; Thailand believed the troops should be disarmed and evacuated or interned but did not favor a condemnation of Nationalist China; the Philippines was much closer to the position of Thailand than to that of Indonesia. In contrast to the Soviet Union which staunchly backed Burma, the United States believed the best settlement would be to get Nationalist China to agree to help in a solution that would lead to the disarming and evacuation of the soldiers.

A resolution of the General Assembly on April 23, 1953, passed fifty-nine to zero with China abstaining and Burma approving. It condemned the presence of the "foreign forces" in the Union and "their hostile acts" against it; these forces were to be disarmed and interned or leave Burma forthwith; all states were urged to give no help to them, and upon Rangoon's request, to assist in their peaceful evacuation; and the continuation of negotiations through the good offices of certain United Nations members was recommended.

A Joint Military Committee of Burma, Nationalist China, Thailand, and the United States discussed ways of carrying out the resolution. In late June it was agreed, subject to the approval of the respective governments, that the "foreign forces" would be evacuated from Burma to Taiwan through Thailand under the supervision of the Joint Military Committee. Although the implementation of the plan encountered numerous obstacles—the Kuomintang forces were reluctant to leave, the Burmese became impatient, the Thai were aroused over criticism from Rangoon and the burden they had in the evacuation—by the time it ended on September 1, 1954, almost 7,000 people, foreign forces with their dependents, had been evacuated from Burma to Formosa. A considerable number of Chinese troops remained (possibly 3,000 or more) with a significant amount of arms, much to the distress of Rangoon. In March Burmese forces had captured Mong Hsat; in May General Li Mi announced the end of his command; and the Nationalist Government of China disclaimed all responsibility for Chinese troops in Burma who had refused repatriation. Some of them continued to stay in the Union and others fled to Thailand and Laos.

The KMT controversy in Burma created serious problems for U.S. policy makers, especially in 1953. They had been concerned about the matter from almost the beginning. From 1951 to the spring of 1953 Washington achieved no success in finding a solution. There was apparent indifference in high government circles for some time. Some senior officials hoped the potential of a second front in Yunnan against the government of Mao Tse-tung could be preserved, limited though it was. This hope was often associated with the conviction, still remaining in some circles, that Burma would fall into the hands of the Communists or disintegrate as a state and that Washington should therefore write it off in policy planning.

At the same time, Chiang Kai-shek could not be considered amenable to every American suggestion, and he had only limited control over the Chinese forces in Burma. As far as U.S. influence is concerned, subsequent issues over Quemoy and Matsu should not be forgotten. Nationalist Chinese sources have indicated that the CIA was at first involved in providing arms and supplies to General Li Mi but later stopped all such activities. Taipei has asserted that in response to American requests it agreed to ban the clearance of all planes to the Burmese border area and it attempted to prevent the collection of money by agents of the Chinese forces in Burma.

Determined efforts were made by two American ambassadors and two chargés d'affaires in Rangoon to persuade the Department of State, during the presidencies of Truman and Eisenhower, to remove the KMT irritant in relations between Rangoon and Washington. Ambassador David McK. Key and his belated successor, William J. Sebald, believed the best approach was the effective use of American influence in Taipei. In 1952 denials of U.S. aid to the KMT forces were made by Secretary of State Dean Acheson, by John Sherman Cooper, then an American delegate to the United Nations General Assembly, by Henry B. Day, U.S. Chargé d'Affaires in Rangoon, and by Lincoln White, press officer of the Department of State. White indicated his statement was based on a thorough investigation by the Department. These denials, however, did not stop a number of prominent American journalists from continuing to write dispatches on the KMT buildup, some of the writers saying or implying that Americans were involved.

In October 1953 Prime Minister U Nu reportedly sent a personal letter to President Eisenhower on the KMT controversy. Washington officially indicated at the United Nations the President was taking a personal interest in the situation. In November Vice-President Nixon on a Far Eastern tour visited Rangoon where he was briefed by the U.S. embassy on the crisis. The United States provided the airlift of the Chinese forces to Taiwan, and was influential in its diplomacy through negotiations in Rangoon, Bangkok, and Taipei.

In retrospect, Washington was aware of the assistance to General Li Mi from Taiwan with all its ramifications and implications, and it seems certain that the United States facilitated the aid during an early period; but eventually Washington made sincere though somewhat belated attempts to resolve the controversy. The issue of the KMT forces, however, rose again in 1961 early in the Kennedy administration.

United States Concern for Southeast Asia before the Korean War. The implications of the victory of the Chinese Communists on mainland China for the United States in Southeast Asia began to be studied by American officials in 1949 and they stimulated the field missions of 1950. Moscow's first nuclear explosion in September 1949 added another dimension of concern. The outbreak of the Korean War the following June gave emphasis to the evaluations and precipitated further policy actions. Indeed, the year 1950 can be established as the beginning of several very concrete steps in Southeast Asia that would develop into major commitments. In that year both the United States and the People's Republic of China began to view the area as an arena of potential confrontation. Instead of relative disengagement from Southeast Asia Washington slowly started down the road of engagement unable, of course, to see the end of it.

Almost a year before the outbreak of the Korean War Secretary Acheson on July 18, 1949, sent a top secret memorandum to Ambassador-at-Large Philip C. Jessup. It read: "You will please take as your assumption that it is a fundamental decision of American policy that the United States does not intend to permit further extension of Communist domination on the continent of Asia or in the southeast Asia area."[10] A few weeks earlier, June 10 to be exact, Secretary of Defense Louis Johnson had requested that the staff of the National Security Council (NSC) undertake a study of American security policy toward Asia in view of Communist advances. He wanted a comprehensive plan in terms of long-range interests instead of a country-by-country day-to-day approach. The Mutual Defense Assistance Act, as finally approved on October 6, added impetus to the consideration of a broad approach to East Asia.

The National Security Council staff study was finally submitted on December 23. Providing the basis for discussion at a meeting of the Council seven days later, the report on the "Position of the United States with Respect to Asia" was comprehensive (Asia was defined for the purposes of the study as the part of the continent east of Iran and south of the Soviet Union with the major offshore islands) and general (political, strategic, and economic considerations were presented with some basic conclusions). It pointed out that in the past "we have consistently favored a system of independent states [in Asia] and opposed aggrandizement of any powers which threatened eventual domination of the region."[11] As for the present, it noted:

> The extension of communist authority in China represents a grievous political defeat for us; if southeast Asia also is swept by communism [the target for a Kremlin-coordinated offensive] we shall have suffered a major political rout the repercussions of which will be felt throughout the rest of the world, especially in the Middle East and in a then critically exposed Australia.[12]

The Soviet Union, not the People's Republic of China, was viewed as the chief Communist threat to U.S. security interests in Asia.

On December 30 President Truman presided at the meeting of the National Security Council where the conclusions of the staff study were approved as duly amended. A basic security objective in Asia was identified in terms of:

> Prevention of power relationships in Asia which would enable any other nation or alliance to threaten the security of the United States from that area, or the peace, national independence and stability of the Asiatic nations.[13]

As far as Southeast Asia was concerned, Washington should give "particular attention" to French Indochina and "immediate consideration" to Indonesia in the light of the recent Round Table Conference at The Hague and of Communist pressures.

American policy toward Indochina was the subject of a report in early 1950 which the Department of State wanted the National Security Council to consider on an urgent basis. Although the report was formally submitted to the Council on February 27 by its executive secretary, President Truman did not approve its basic conclusions until late April.

Meanwhile on March 7 Deputy Undersecretary of State Dean Rusk in a note to the Defense Department, outlined his Department's policy toward Indochina and Southeast Asia. It was flatly asserted that "within the limitations imposed by existing commitments and strategic priorities, the resources of the United States should be deployed to reserve Indochina and Southeast Asia from further Communist encroachment."[14] Rusk indicated that the State Department had already engaged its "political resources" for this objective, was currently examining the use of "additional economic resources," and believed the Defense Department should now "assess the strategic aspects" and consider from the military viewpoint how the United States could best help to prevent further encroachment by the Communists.

On April 5 the Joint Chiefs of Staff through General Omar N. Bradley accepted the conclusions of the State Department on Indochina and Southeast Asia and recommended the speedy implementation of military assistance programs for a number of areas, namely, Indochina, Thailand, Burma, Indonesia, and the Philippines. These programs should be carefully controlled and definitely related to the American political and economic effort.

The conclusions President Truman approved in late April were significant for the future of U.S. policy—Indochina was "a key area of Southeast Asia" and subject to an "immediate threat"; if it fell to the Communists, Thailand and Burma could be expected to have the same fate, and the rest of Southeast Asia would be in "grave hazard"; the Departments of State and Defense, therefore, should on a priority basis formulate a "program of all practicable measures" to protect American security interests in Indochina.

The State Department on April 25 finalized a draft position paper on Indochina and another on Southeast Asia. Seven days later, still several weeks before the Korean War, the Joint Chiefs of Staff commented separately on the two papers, stressing the quick establishment of a military aid group in Indochina and a more positive and forceful American position in Southeast Asia—in fact, leadership among the Western powers.

Meanwhile, on July 30, 1949, Acheson announced that two consultants on Far Eastern problems, Raymond B. Fosdick and Everett Case, had been appointed. They would work with Philip C. Jessup and other State Department officials.[15] Ambassador-at-Large Jessup left Washington on December 15 on a tour of Asia to review the international situation and make recommendations to his government.

The highlight of Jessup's trip was a conference in mid-February 1950 of American ambassadors from Korea to Pakistan and officials from Washington held in Bangkok.[16] This gathering assumes more importance in the perspective of time. The Secretary of State had suggested holding such a regional conference in view of developments in East Asia. The situation was considered serious with mainland China in Communist hands, with Communist guerrillas very active in many countries of Southeast Asia, and with Peking calling for the liberation of the overseas Chinese in the region. After surveying the impact of Communist China on the countries of Asia, the Americans considered what the United States could do and should do to assist its friends to help themselves meet the Communist threat. With respect to Southeast Asia it was agreed that the cornerstone of American policy must be the independence of the countries of the area; the importance of nationalism in the struggle against colonialism and the need of preventing communism from capturing nationalism were fully recognized. The conference favored American economic and technical aid and in particular cases military assistance to countries in Southeast Asia seeking to maintain their independence in the face of Communist threats. Information and cultural programs could help if properly adapted to local conditions.* There was marked disagreement at the gathering on what the United States should do in French Indochina. W. Walton Butterworth, Assistant Secretary of State for Far Eastern Affairs, who had flown to Bangkok for the conference, cabled Washington on February 17 that no aid should be committed to Indochina unless Paris gave the "requisite public undertakings" on "further steps leading to status" comparable to that of Indonesia. He stressed that Bao Dai was considered a French puppet in the eyes of Asian neighbors and that the "missing component" was not U.S. aid, nor recognition, but further French action to put Vietnam in the "category of independent states."[18]

Although the mission of Jessup focused attention on Southeast Asia —his statement in Singapore, for instance, in early February that the United States would regard armed aggression against Indochina as "a very grave matter" not passing unnoticed—it was the Griffin economic survey mission to Indochina, Thailand, Burma, Indonesia, Malaya, and

---

*On April 13, 1950, Jessup publicly reported on the highlights of his tour of December 15, 1949 to March 15, 1950.[17] The report was influenced by the Bangkok conference.

Singapore in March and April, a companion to the Bell economic survey mission later that year to the Philippines, which produced concrete results. And the Melby-Erskine military survey mission to Southeast Asia shortly after the outbreak of the Korean War was a significant development in the evolution of U.S. military aid to various countries of the region.

The Griffin mission, hastily put together, was not only in the wake of the victory of the Chinese Communists (unexpectedly quick toward the end) on the mainland of China but also in the wake of the criticism of many Republicans like Senator William F. Knowland and Congressman Walter H. Judd of American policy in East Asia. "Neglect" was a favorite word. The mission sought to demonstrate American interest in the people of the countries of Southeast Asia, to strengthen the governments, and to counteract at least to some extent the political and psychological impact of the victory of Mao Tse-tung. It also reflected the widespread conviction among the Asian specialists in the Department of State about the importance of the new governments of Southeast Asia, a recognition, of course, not emphasized by the "Old Europe" school. Much of the public relations of the Griffin mission focused on Point Four of Truman's inaugural speech rather than on anticommunism.

The concept of the Griffin mission was cleared with key members of Congress, and R. Allen Griffin himself was a Republican and a personal friend of Senator Knowland. Samuel P. Hayes was the able deputy chief. The effort was bipartisan though not organized at the ambassadorial level; it represented an attempt to bridge the gap between the Democratic administration and many Republicans in Congress. The mission's cabled recommendations on Indochina, Thailand, Burma, and Indonesia but not on Malaya and Singapore, a total of some $66 million, were welcomed in Washington. Funds were made available to mount the program, and recommended services and commodities were soon put into procurement. The recommendations for technical and economic aid, made for a period of roughly fifteen months from the date of the visit, emphasized "quick impact" projects. The mission was well aware of the military value, direct or indirect, of the program. But its recommendations were no Marshall Plan for Southeast Asia, something Harry Truman told Clement Attlee in December 1950 he had been considering in some form.

When the Griffin economic survey mission was in Tokyo in early March on the way to Southeast Asia its head was received by General MacArthur, and Major General Charles A. Willoughby, Chief of Intelligence, briefed the group. Willoughby told the members that the strategic key to Southeast Asia was Vietnam and that the reestablishment of law and order was the chief problem there.[19]

In each country the Griffin mission visited, it analyzed the current political, economic, and financial conditions. Its reports represented a valuable analysis of the situation as of March and April 1950 shortly before the outbreak of the Korean War. Long-range problems of Southeast Asia were also identified; they related to national unification, social integration (particularly the overseas Chinese), perpetuation of colonialism, and political and economic development. The reports revealed an appreciation of the military, economic, and political significance of Southeast Asia as a whole to the United States, a consideration brought out in the discussions between members of the group and American diplomats in the area. In fact, the very sending of the mission as well as the Melby-Erskine one that followed in 1950 indicated this appreciation.

The modest recommendations of the Griffin mission for Malaya and Singapore were overruled in Washington (it was believed these areas should be left to the initiative of the British who might be undercut by an aid program). However, the group's visit resulted in the establishment (after differences in Washington on organization) of special technical and economic missions (STEMs) in Thailand, Burma, Indonesia, and Indochina. Economic and technical cooperation agreements were made with Burma, Thailand, and Indonesia in 1950 and with Vietnam, Cambodia, and Laos in 1951. The United States Information Service gave extensive publicity to the aid program.

Meanwhile a number of significant statements having a bearing on Southeast Asia were issued by high-ranking American officials. One of the most important was an address by Secretary of State Acheson at the National Press Club in Washington on January 12, 1950. Here he defined the "defensive perimeter" of the United States in the Pacific as running from the Aleutians to Japan, the Ryukyus, and the Philippines. (MacArthur listed the same March 1, 1949.) Acheson did not mention in the perimeter Taiwan, Korea, or Southeast Asia, apart from the Philippines, but he asserted that a guarantee against military attack in "other areas in the Pacific," i.e., those not in the perimeter, is "hardly sensible or necessary within the realm of practical relationship."[20]* At the same time Acheson noted that if such an attack occurred the "initial reliance" must be in the resistance of the people attacked but subsequent reliance existed in the commitments of the members of the United Nations

---

*Acheson's "defensive perimeter" was in line with current U.S. military thinking. This point was clearly indicated in the staff study of the National Security Council on the American position with respect to Asia, December 23, 1949. The Joint Chiefs on January 26, 1950, flatly asserted that the American long-range strategic concept in the event of war with the Soviet Union was—"the United States, in collaboration with its allies, will seek to impose the allied war objectives upon the USSR by conducting a strategic offensive in western Eurasia and a strategic defensive in the Far East." *United States-Vietnam Relations, 1945–1967*, Book 8, p. 273.

"which so far has not proved a weak reed to lean on by any people who are determined to protect their independence against outside aggression."[21]

The Secretary observed that conditions in the Southeast Asian countries were difficult; he believed American opportunities and responsibilities were limited. The United States as one of many nations could only help when invited; the direct responsibility rested with the new countries. "American assistance," he noted, "can be effective when it is the missing component in a situation which might otherwise be solved."[22] Although he believed the "susceptibility" of many states in the Pacific area to "subversion and penetration" could not be prevented by "military means"[23] Washington could help strengthen the new governments and aid them in economic recovery and development.

Acheson analyzed briefly the situation in specific countries of Southeast Asia as he viewed it at the beginning of 1950. In the Philippines, he stressed the independence of the nation and noted that an attack on the islands "could not and would not be tolerated by the United States."[24] In Burma the "immediate government" of the state was "utterly disrupted" but in Malaya progress was being made, with the British working well with the people. In Indonesia the recent conclusion of the Round Table Conference at The Hague was praised, the future of relations between the Dutch and Indonesians was considered bright, and the situation encouraging though still difficult. In Indochina progress was also being made with the French moving, though slowly, in transferring authority to local administration and in getting the support of the people. Acheson hoped the French would make further progress quickly although he was aware of their problems.

A few days later, on January 31, Assistant Secretary of State George C. McGhee in a speech stressed the importance of more trade between the United States and South Asia and the mutual advantages of American investment. His brief political analysis of Burma closely resembled that of Acheson on January 12.[25]

On March 27 Loy W. Henderson, ambassador to India, spoke at the Indian Council of World Affairs, on American objectives in Asia. He indicated the United States was sympathetic to the non-Communist states of Asia in their efforts to preserve their political independence, maintain their territorial integrity, and achieve economic stability. Ho Chi Minh, he asserted, was "a Moscow-recognized Communist" and subservient to a foreign state. Henderson showed considerable sympathy toward the problems of Southeast Asia. Washington, he said, "approaches special situations and problems in Asia from the point of view of its general foreign policies."[26] (On the same day, it might be noted, Dean Rusk was publicly named Assistant Secretary of State for Far Eastern Affairs.)

Secretary Acheson for his part pointedly called attention the same month (March 15) to President Truman's belief that Washington must help the free peoples who are resisting subversion by armed minorities or by external pressures.[27]

Thus, even before the outbreak of the Korean War, the victory of the Chinese Communists and the first Russian nuclear explosion in the early fall of 1949 had helped to precipitate public statements of policy, the Jessup and Griffin missions, and the decision to provide aid to various Southeast Asian countries including the Associated States of Vietnam, Cambodia, and Laos. Moreover, after considerable spadework in Washington, the President had decided on January 31 to go ahead with research for the hydrogen bomb, and the National Security Council, following a long review of military and foreign policies, had adopted on April 25 NSC-68, directed toward meeting the threat of the Soviet Union (whose top priority was viewed as world domination) by specific steps to strengthen the United States and the Free World.

The reaction in Southeast Asia to American policy in 1950 before the outbreak of the Korean War was generally sympathetic though there was suspicion of U.S. motives (encouraged by some remaining European advisers). It was certain that economic and technical aid would be widely welcomed and military assistance would be accepted in many countries. The United States was generally viewed as anticolonial although it was thought American policy toward colonialism did not always match American sentiment. Southeast Asian leaders publicly and privately varied in their reaction to Washington's China policy. Still in the future were the Korean War and a peace settlement with Japan requiring key policy decisions in the new states of the region.

THE KOREAN WAR

In the complex relationships of Washington, Peking, and Southeast Asia the Korean War was a factor of the first magnitude. It altered the course of American policy in East Asia and the Pacific. It established the power and enhanced the influence of Communist China in Asia and the world. It helped make Southeast Asia an area of confrontation between Peking and Washington.

The Korean War was limited in area, objectives, and choice of weapons.[28] It was fought in Korea with Manchuria a "privileged sanctuary" for the Communist forces and Japan for the United Nations forces. Both sides sought to unify Korea but not to the extent of carrying the war outside the peninsula. Conventional weapons were employed throughout the conflict. The United States had clear-cut nuclear superiority, though the Soviet Union by instigating the North Korean attack on the Republic of Korea indicated willingness to risk a local war that might escalate into a general conflict. Late in the struggle, President Eisenhower has revealed, Washington warned Communist China that if the truce negotiations failed it would employ nuclear weapons.*

The Three Phases. The Korean War or "police action" had three phases, each with its diplomatic and military components. The first phase began with the North Korean invasion of South Korea across the thirty-eighth parallel on June 25, 1950, and ended with the Chinese Communist intervention in November (some authors prefer October). Surprises or miscalculations were in store for practically all parties concerned. The United States and South Korea did not expect the invasion (nor for that matter did MacArthur expect Chinese intervention) and the Soviet Union and North Korea did not believe the United States and the United Nations would fight despite their important roles in the establishment of the republic.

After launching the offensive North Korea ignored the resolutions of the United Nations Security Council on June 25 and 27 actively pushed by the United States with the Soviet Union not present to veto them.† President Truman ordered American sea and air support for the Republic of Korea's armed forces south of the thirty-eighth parallel. The American chief executive made the final decision on U.S. intervention, informing congressional leaders, and the United Nations Security Council favored it.

President Truman issued on June 27 one of the most important policy statements of his career. "The attack upon Korea," he said, "makes it plain beyond all doubt that communism has passed beyond the use of subversion to conquer independent nations and will now use armed invasion and war."[29] He announced measures he had taken that would affect

---

*"The lack of progress in the long-stalemated talks—they were then recessed—and the nearly stalemated war both demanded, in my opinion, definite measures on our part to put an end to these intolerable conditions. One possibili·y was to let the Communist authorities understand that in the absence of satisfactory progress, we intended to move decisively without inhibition in our use of weapons, and would no longer be responsible for confining hostilities to the Korean Peninsula. We would not be limited by any world-wide gentleman's agreement. In India and in the Formosa Straits area, and at the truce negotiations at Panmunjom, we dropped the word, discreetly, of our intention. We felt quite sure it would reach Soviet and Chinese Communist ears. Soon the prospects for armistice negotiations seemed to improve."—Dwight D. Eisenhower, *The White House Years: Mandate for Change, 1953–1956*, Doubleday, Garden City, 1963, p. 181.

†On June 27 the Security Council recommended that the members of the United Nations furnish the Republic of Korea such aid as needed to "repel the armed attack and to restore international peace and security in the area." S/1511, June 27, 1950. See also *Yearbook of the United Nations, 1950*, Columbia, New York, 1951, pp. 223–24, for text of resolution.

the future of Korea, Taiwan, the Philippines, and Indochina. American sea and air support, as just mentioned, was given South Korea's armed forces; the U.S. Seventh Fleet was ordered to "prevent any attack on Formosa" while the government of Chiang Kai-shek was requested to stop sea and air operations against mainland China; American forces in the Philippines would be strengthened and military aid to the islands would be speeded; military assistance to France and the Associated States of Vietnam, Cambodia, and Laos would be accelerated and a military mission sent there. In retrospect three of the four areas mentioned by the President involved or would involve American crisis diplomacy: wars in Korea and Indochina and the crises of 1955 and 1958 over Formosa and the offshore islands.

The North Korean blitzkrieg resulted by mid-August in driving the defenders into a small beachhead in southeast Korea around the port of Pusan. By the end of June the United States considered it necessary to commit ground forces and extend the area of operations of American air and naval units to North Korea. Early in July the Security Council of the United Nations asked Washington to designate a commander who would head a unified command, under the United States, of United Nations forces. In August the Soviet Union pointedly terminated its boycott of the Security Council. The next month the United Nations commander, General Douglas MacArthur, launched a counterattack. Soon all South Korea was liberated, and toward late October his forces were approaching the Yalu River boundary between China and Korea (some South Koreans reached it). On October 7 the General Assembly passed a resolution that was widely interpreted as allowing the United Nations forces to unify the country.

The second phase of the Korean War began with the intervention of the Chinese Communists in November and ended with the beginning of negotiations for an armistice agreement in June 1951. Peking's decision to enter the conflict changed radically the character of the war.[30] As MacArthur's forces approached the Manchurian-Korean border, Peking apparently believed its vital interests were threatened even though it was ill prepared for a war with the United States and needed full time for its own economic reconstruction.

The "volunteers" of Communist China soon drove the United Nations forces out of North Korea and advanced deep into the south. By mid-1951, however, the United Nations forces had made a recovery and the war was stalemated very close to the thirty-eighth parallel. On April 11 President Truman relieved General MacArthur of his command over the fundamental question of whether (as the latter put it "in war . . . there can be no substitute for victory."[31] President Truman and his administration, in the face of vigorous criticism from many Republicans, opposed widening the war by taking military measures against the territory of Communist China. After MacArthur's dismissal, the hearings in 1951 before the Senate Armed Services and Foreign Relations Committees on the "military situation in the Far East" provided an opportunity for one of the most significant debates in American history on U.S. policy in Northeast Asia. (There was no General MacArthur in the Second Indochinese War!) In the end the President's position stood although he lost considerable influence. Meanwhile the General Assembly on February 1 condemned the People's Republic of China as an aggressor in Korea and on May 18 approved an embargo on the export of strategic items to North Korea and Communist China.

The final phase of the Korean War began with negotiations for an armistice in June 1951 and ended with the conclusion of an armistice agreement on July 27, 1953. The negotiations were suspended from August to October 1951; they were recessed on October 8, 1952, but resumed on April 26, 1953. Changes in leadership occurred in both the Soviet Union and the United States. Joseph Stalin died in March 1953 and his departure probably facilitated the armistice in July. Dwight D. Eisenhower, stressing the Korean War in his campaign, had become President of the United States the previous January. After heavy loss of life (33,629 American dead and 103,284 American wounded alone) and great destruction of property the Korean War ended in a military, political, and diplomatic stalemate. Both sides could claim achievements but neither accomplished its maximum objectives.

Implications and Results. What implications did the Korean War have for the future? In terms of warfare its meaning was highly significant. General Matthew B. Ridgway has pointedly written: ". . . Korea taught us that all warfare from this time forth must be limited. It could no longer be a question of *whether* to fight a limited war, but of *how* to avoid fighting any other kind."[32] He went on to add that "one mistake we avoided in Korea was an insistence on 'total victory' or 'unconditional surrender' or even a 'halt to aggression' before talking peace."[33] As a limited war the conflict in Korea influenced the dimensions of the Second Indochinese War.

William P. Bundy observed on January 23, 1965, that American action in Korea "reflected three elements [all having a bearing on the future in Indochina]":

—a recognition that aggression of any sort must be met early and head-on or it will have to be met later and in tougher circumstances. We had relearned the lessons of the 1930's—Manchuria, Ethiopia, the Rhineland, Czechoslovakia.

—a recognition that a defense line in Asia, stated in terms of an island perimeter, did not adequately define our vital interests, that those vital interests could be affected by action on the mainland of Asia.

—an understanding that, for the future, a power vacuum was an invitation to aggression, that there must be local political, economic, and military strength in being to make aggression unprofitable, but also that there must be a demonstrated willingness of major external power both to assist and to intervene if required.[34]

The armistice negotiations in Korea also had direct bearing on later events relating to Indochina. Fighting continued during the negotiations, and American loss of life was heavy. The discussions were long, difficult, and acrimonious. A special report of the United Nations Command to the Secretary General of the United Nations on August 7, 1953, stated: "the hopes of the Unified Command for quickly concluding an agreement that would stop the fighting soon proved illusory. Time after time the Communists stalled, injected extraneous issues, endeavoured to use the negotiations for propaganda purposes, and otherwise indicated a lack of good faith."[35] But an armistice was eventually concluded, and in many respects the Korean question was put on ice. As in the military case of limited war in Korea, the negotiations for an armistice terminating that conflict have a bearing on negotiations ending future limited wars. Panmunjom was a symbol of things to come.

The Korean conflict stands as an example of the circumstances under which Communist China and the United States went to war. Chairman Mao Tse-tung apparently could tolerate a South Korea but not a North Korea in unfriendly hands. President Harry Truman despite an evaluation by his advisers of Korea's not being an area vital to American security believed the Communist invasion of June 25, 1950, had such serious implications for the United States, the United Nations, and the world that it must be repelled. Another President, Lyndon B. Johnson, in another decade, in another peninsular war of Asia, would consider the consequences of U.S. acquiescence to be equally serious. Both chief executives had their conceptualization of the Communist threat to U.S. interests challenged at home, especially as the Korean and Indochinese conflicts dragged on.

One of the early moves in Washington after the outbreak of the Korean War was the formal sending of the Melby-Erskine military survey mission to Southeast Asia. It was based on a White House decision to provide military aid to all Southeast Asian countries who desired it and would accept it. The reception of the mission varied decidedly from country to country. In the Philippines and Thailand the welcome mat was out, and in Vietnam the French and the Vietnamese they sponsored were very cooperative. The trips to Cambodia and Laos were pleasant but not fruitful. (Sihanouk received a helicopter.) The British in Malaya were primarily interested in support for building a road across the Kra Isthmus to help stop infiltration from Thailand. (Washington opposed the mission's favorable recommendation.) Burma would only allow a Coast Guard captain to visit the country, for it only wanted river boats. Indonesia was sympathetic though it reluctantly accepted less military aid than it really desired.

It was Indochina where conflicts of policy were pronounced, reflected in communications to Washington. On August 5 Major General Graves B. Erskine, Chief of the Military Group of the mission, reported that the French forces in Indochina were stalemated, that those of the Viet Minh had steadily become stronger, aided by the Chinese Communists, that the assistance so far requested by the French from the United States was not adequate, that military aid must be provided the French "on a considerable scale," and that "a political solution, which includes concessions on the part of the French, and definite plans for eventual independence of Viet Nam is a necessary complement to military action."[36] A telegram from the American Minister in Saigon on August 7 focused on the conclusion of the work of the survey mission for Indochina. But another aspect should be noted.

After being in Saigon for a while John F. Melby, the civilian head of the mission, strongly recommended to Washington that any U.S. aid to Indochina be provided only after the French left or, as a minimum, upon ironclad assurances of a French withdrawal by a date all Vietnamese factions approved. Melby firmly believed that U.S. assistance under other conditions was folly. Donald R. Heath, the American envoy in Saigon, did not agree, but the U.S. mission was divided. In Washington the Bureau of Far Eastern Affairs in the Department of State generally backed Melby while that of European Affairs, reflecting the influence of Paris, opposed him. Assistant Secretary of State for Far Eastern Affairs Dean Rusk reportedly did not commit himself. European Affairs, as was so often the case, won the day. It was an important decision for the United States, for it did not alter the momentum under way. Significant military assistance to Indochina, and to some other areas of Southeast Asia, came in the wake of the Melby mission.

The Korean War was an underlying factor in producing the overall American alliance pattern in East Asia and the Pacific. (In view of the Japanese peace settlement the words *underlying* and *overall* are carefully chosen.) The First Indochinese War gave a further impetus to the undertaking. Communist China was the foreign power whose militant attitude, Washington believed, provided the direct threat to both Northeast and

Southeast Asia. The direct threat from the Soviet Union, it was also thought, was restricted to Japan and Korea although in many circles the Sino-Soviet alliance of 1950 was believed to buttress Moscow at least for a few years in Southeast Asia. If the United States withdrew from East Asia it was reliably estimated in the late 1950s that Communist China had the military capability of overrunning first mainland and then insular Southeast Asia and of overrunning Taiwan, South Korea, and, with the help of the Soviet Union, Japan. Whether Peking would do it, of course, was another question.

The basic limits of American security policy in East Asia before the Korean War had been publicly defined by Secretary Acheson in his celebrated speech on the defensive perimeter. The Aleutians, Japan, the Ryukyus, and the Philippines were islands off the coast of East Asia where superior American sea power and air power could be brought to bear. The defensive perimeter did not include any territory on the mainland of Asia where U.S. ground forces would be needed. Even so it was an extension of the basic triangle of defense that long existed before Pearl Harbor, a triangle focused on Alaska, Hawaii, and Panama in the Pacific.

On May 17, 1951, some time after the outbreak of the Korean War, President Truman approved a National Security Council policy statement which asserted that the United States should "maintain the security of the off-shore defense line: Japan-Ryukyus-Philippines-Australia and New Zealand. Deny Formosa to any Chinese regime aligned with or dominated by the USSR and expedite the strengthening of the defensive capabilities of Formosa. Attempt by all practicable means to forestall communist aggression in South and Southeast Asia."[37] It was flatly stated that "Soviet control of the off-shore islands in the Western Pacific, including Japan, would present an unacceptable threat to the security of the United States."[38] Washington, moreover, should "detach China as an effective ally of the USSR and support the development of an independent China which has renounced aggression."[39]

Later, on August 20, 1954, a policy statement of the National Security Council under President Eisenhower called for maintaining the security and increasing the strength of the "Pacific off-shore island chain"—Formosa was included—as "an element essential to U.S. security." The Council favored an eventual collective defense arrangement extending from Japan and the Republic of Korea to Australia and New Zealand with U.S. participation.[40]

As a consequence of the Korean War, the Japanese peace settlement, and the First Indochinese War, the defensive perimeter thus came to include the island ladder of the Aleutians, Japan, the Ryukyus, Taiwan, the Philippines, Australia, and New Zealand; and even more significantly, parts of two peninsulas on the land mass of East Asia, Korea in the north and mainland Southeast Asia in the south. The forward strategy of the United States in the Pacific, aimed at keeping a potential enemy as far away as possible from American shores, had extended to the land mass of East Asia.

The end of the Korean War in July 1953 came as a mixed blessing in Southeast Asia. The United States believed at the beginning of the truce negotiations that an armistice would free Peking for probes and perhaps military action in the area. In many respects the Korean War bought time for the United States and France in Southeast Asia, time which was not effectively used by the French and probably not by the Americans in Indochina. President Truman in an address given on April 11, 1951, the day of General MacArthur's dismissal, had significantly stated: "Our resolute stand in Korea is helping the forces of freedom now fighting in Indochina and other countries in that part of the world. It has already slowed down the timetable of conquest."[41] Apprehensive about the future, the sixteen members of the United Nations that had sent armed forces to Korea warned the Communists on July 27, 1953, about the grave consequences of renewing the war as the resulting hostilities with the allies "in all probability" would not be limited to the area of Korea. They ominously stated their belief "that the armistice must not result in jeopardizing the restoration or the safeguarding of peace in any other part of Asia."[42]

Role of Southeast Asia. The reaction of the countries of the region to the Korean War varied. As the war moved from the North Korean to the Chinese Communist phase, attitudes shifted. In view of the key role of the United States in the conflict the attitudes of Southeast Asian countries to it reflected in large measure their policy toward Washington.

The outbreak of the Korean War came as a great surprise to the Philippines and precipitated a war scare in the country. The first reaction of the Filipinos was to rally behind the United States even more than behind their own government. Manila supported the important resolutions of the Security Council and then of the General Assembly in defense of South Korea against North Korea and later Communist China. It was pleased with President Truman's announcement of June 27, 1950, involving the strengthening of U.S. armed forces in the Philippines and the speeding of U.S. military assistance to the young republic. As a result of mounting domestic pressure, Manila, despite the serious Hukbalahap menace and grave financial difficulties, decided to send troops to Korea. The role of the Philippines in the Korean War reflected the loyalty of the new republic to the principles of the United Nations and its close ties with Washington.

Thailand's reaction to the Korean War was comparable to that of the Philippines. Bangkok was shocked by the North Korean invasion which served to convince many doubters outside cabinet circles that Thailand should align itself with the United States. The role of the United Nations in the crisis was praised, and Bangkok supported its important resolutions whether directed at North Korea or Communist China. Prime Minister Pibul asked U.S. Ambassador Stanton for advice about answering the appeal of the United Nations for aid. Stanton indicated he favored an offer of rice but had doubts about sending armed forces, for they might be needed at home. Pibul quickly decided to contribute both to the United Nations cause in Korea. He correctly believed it would be a major factor in strengthening American support for Thailand.

Burma and Indonesia pursued different policies in the Korean War from the Philippines and Thailand. Rangoon and Djakarta unlike Manila did not have close ties with the United States; nor did Washington for that matter in 1950 desire an alliance with them. Both Burma and Indonesia, moreover, differentiated between the roles of North Korea and Communist China in the conflict.

The Burmese government took a more sympathetic attitude toward the United Nations position in the Korean War than Indonesia. Rangoon supported the Security Council resolutions of June 1950 because it believed North Korea was guilty of aggression and because it feared it might sometime be in a comparable position and need United Nations assistance. At the same time Rangoon sought friendly relations with all countries. It made a contribution of rice toward the relief of South Korea but sent no armed forces there. Burma favored the important resolutions of the General Assembly up to 1951. It voted in February against the General Assembly resolution naming Communist China an aggressor and in May it abstained on the one calling for an embargo on strategic items to North Korea and Communist China. In effect, however, Rangoon for the most part upheld the embargo.

Indonesia was not a member of the United Nations at the beginning of the Korean War. Djakarta wanted to stay out of the conflict and was apprehensive lest membership in the United Nations would compromise its attitude. It was inclined to view Korea as a pawn in the struggle between Washington and Moscow. After admission to the United Nations in September 1950 Indonesia abstained on General Assembly resolutions which approved the decisions of the Security Council in June, which branded Communist China an aggressor, or which imposed an embargo on strategic items. Indonesia, of course, sent no armed forces to Korea but it did eventually make a small contribution to the United Nations Korean Reconstruction Agency. Some Indonesians contrasted the U.S. stance in the Korean War with that in the Dutch-Indonesian conflict. Djakarta did not differentiate between the North Korean and the Chinese Communist roles in the war as clearly as did Burma. Nevertheless, it was worried lest Peking's entrance in the conflict lead to a global conflagration.

The Associated States of Vietnam, Cambodia, and Laos, being under strong French influence and not members of the United Nations, had no role to play in the Korean War. The State of Vietnam was sympathetic to the stance of the United Nations. It contributed to Korean relief and supported the United Nations embargo on strategic items to North Korea and Communist China. Both Cambodia and Laos viewed the Korean War as far away but were sympathetic to the United Nations cause. Cambodia gave rice and salted fish to South Korea. In contrast, the Democratic Republic of Vietnam was sympathetic to the Communist cause in the conflict. But like the State of Vietnam it had serious problems at home. In one peninsula of East Asia Koreans were fighting Koreans and in another Vietnamese were fighting Vietnamese.

THE JAPANESE PEACE SETTLEMENT

Integral components of the Japanese peace settlement of 1951, hastened by the outbreak of the Korean War, were the Treaty of Peace and the Security Treaty between the United States and Japan, both signed on September 8; the Mutual Defense Treaty between the United States and the Philippines signed on August 30; and the Security Treaty among Australia, New Zealand, and the United States (ANZUS) signed on September 1. Associated with the Korean War but not unrelated to the Japanese peace settlement were the Treaty of Mutual Defense between the United States and the Republic of Korea signed on October 1, 1953; and in some measure the Treaty of Mutual Defense between the United States and the Republic of China signed on December 2, 1954.

Indicative in many respects of events to come in the Western Pacific was the policy statement of the National Security Council approved by President Truman on May 17, 1951. As regards Nippon, Washington should "assist Japan to become a self-reliant nation friendly to the United States, capable of maintaining internal security and defense against external aggression and contributing to the security and stability of the Far East."[43] Accordingly, Washington should "proceed urgently" to finalize a peace settlement based on the "position already determined by the President," making "urgent efforts" to get as many countries as possible who participated in the Pacific War to agree to this position. Likewise the United States should "proceed urgently" to negotiate bilateral security arrangements with Tokyo on the "position determined by the President," the arrangements to be finalized at the same time as the peace treaty. After the peace settlement Washington should help Japan in the "development of appropriate military forces" and should take "all practical steps to achieve Japanese membership in the United Nations and participation in a regional security arrangement."[44]

The policy statement of the National Security Council also called for the conclusion of a "security arrangement" with New Zealand and Australia and the maintenance of "security relationships" with the Philippines. The United States should "consider the desirability"—the words "conclude" or "maintain" were not used—of "security arrangements with other countries of Asia, either on a bilateral or multilateral basis."[45]

The Treaty of Peace. John Foster Dulles as the special representative of President Truman was in many respects the architect of the Japanese peace settlement.[46] This accomplishment may well emerge as his greatest contribution to American policy in the Pacific. Although somewhat concerned about the domestic political implications Truman placed in Dulles' hands in September 1950 primary responsibility for the complex diplomatic negotiations (with their significant ramifications in the Senate and Pentagon), and one year later on September 8, 1951, forty-eight allied powers in San Francisco signed a treaty of peace with Japan. General MacArthur had indicated in June 1950 in conversations with Dulles and others his conviction that the Japanese had earned a peace treaty and that American occupation could not continue much longer without assuming the character of "colonialism." The Communist aggression in Korea in the summer was widely viewed in Washington as having the ultimate objective of encircling Japan with Soviet power and of making it a Communist state. President Truman and General MacArthur at a historic meeting on Wake Island in mid-October discussed a Japanese peace treaty and the promotion of peace and security in the Pacific. The United States was opposed to a defenseless Japan serving as a "vacuum of power" which would fall prey to Communist neighbors. The best solution appeared to be a multilateral treaty of reconciliation and a bilateral pact where Japan requested and received American protection.

The peace treaty at San Francisco, restoring Japan as an independent, sovereign nation, included provisions on territorial arrangements, security, trade and commerce, property rights, and reparations. Nippon lost its overseas empire but no restrictions were placed on its economy or on its right to trade. Japan agreed to the principle of reparations though figures were not set. No treaty restrictions were placed on Japanese rearmament. Tokyo committed itself to the principles of the Charter of the United Nations and it promised to resolve its international disputes through peaceful means.

The Japanese peace treaty attracted great interest in Southeast Asia, an interest not surprising in view of Nippon's conquest of the area. All the countries realized the key role of Washington in the pact, and its provisions influenced bilateral relations between the United States and various Southeast Asian countries.*

In terms of the San Francisco treaty the estimates and objectives of the Philippines and the United States varied. Despite the mutual defense pact made by the two countries in 1951, the Philippines delayed ratification of the Japanese treaty of peace. Manila had attended the San Francisco conference and signed the treaty but it became a hot issue in domestic politics. Only after protracted intermittent negotiations with Japan leading to the signing of a reparations agreement on May 9, 1956, did Manila formally approve the San Francisco peace treaty, opening the door to normal diplomatic relations. The Philippines had wanted the support of the United States, but Washington did not desire to become too deeply involved in the negotiations. Although the United States believed Japan should pay reparations to the Philippines, the exact terms should be negotiated by Manila and Tokyo.

Burma and Indonesia made peace settlements with Japan separate from the San Francisco treaty. Burma, aroused over the reparations issue, even refused to attend the peace conference, but Indonesia, also concerned over the matter, went to San Francisco and signed the treaty of peace. On November 5, 1954, Tokyo and Rangoon formally concluded an accord embodying a peace treaty and a reparations and economic cooperation agreement. The United States regretted the absence of Burma from the San Francisco peace conference but was pleased to see Burma and Japan break the log jam in Nipponese reparations settlements.

When the Indonesian delegation went to San Francisco it had no mandate to sign the Japanese peace treaty. Prime Minister Shigeru Yoshida of Japan gave Indonesia public assurances on reparations and fisheries at the gathering and an exchange of notes between the Japanese and Indonesian delegations occurred via Dean Acheson, president of the conference. The Indonesia cabinet by a vote of ten to six authorized its delegation to sign the Japanese peace treaty. Subsequent negotiations were protracted and complex between Djakarta and Tokyo. In August 1953 Indonesia announced it would try to establish normal relations with Japan as soon as possible through a bilateral accord. In late 1957 a

---

*It is interesting to note that the Griffin mission in Southeast Asia upon instructions examined the prospects for the use of Japanese technicians in the area and the development of trade with Japan. The mission found a general willingness to sell, a reluctance to buy, and a "uniformly negative response" to the employment of Japanese technicians.

reparations formula was reached between the two countries, and on January 20, 1958, a peace treaty and a reparations accord were formally concluded.

Attending the Japanese peace conference at San Francisco, the State of Vietnam signed the treaty of peace and subsequently ratified it. In his speech at a plenary session on September 7, 1951, the principal Vietnamese delegate was critical of the reparations provisions, affirmed the right of his country to the Spratly Islands and the Paracel Islands in the South China Sea, and called for a "collective security system" in his part of the world. Subsequent negotiations between Tokyo and Saigon led on May 13, 1959, to a settlement on reparations. The Democratic Republic of Vietnam was not represented at San Francisco. It strongly opposed Japan's position that negotiations on reparations be held only with the Saigon government; it claimed reparations for itself as a consequence of World War II and refused to recognize the accord of May 13 as binding on Vietnam. Formal diplomatic relations between Tokyo and Saigon contrasted with informal ones between Japan and the Democratic Republic.

Laos and Cambodia signed and ratified the Japanese peace treaty. They subsequently waived reparations claims but Japan made an agreement for economic and technical cooperation with Laos on October 15, 1958, and with Cambodia on March 2, 1959. The presence of the State of Vietnam, Laos, and Cambodia at San Francisco marked their debut in a major international gathering. They were delighted; the Americans were pleased; the French were satisfied.

The Thai, of course, were not participants at the conference. After the treaty of peace signed there went into effect Bangkok and Tokyo resumed diplomatic relations. In 1955 an agreement was reached on Thailand's claims against Japan arising from the issue of yen military scrip to Japanese occupation forces during the recent conflict.

It would not be realistic to consider Japan's reparations agreements with various Southeast Asian countries without emphasizing their origins and long-range significance. The United States had strongly opposed specific reparations agreements in the treaty of peace, much to the discomfort of the claimants. On the other hand, Washington was later active in urging the Japanese under the broad terms of the peace treaty to make individual settlements with various countries and to fulfill them. These agreements provided significant aid to Southeast Asian states and also served as a wedge for a Japanese comeback to the area. By May 13, 1959, Japan had specifically pledged to pay a total sum equivalent to $1,012,080,000 under reparations agreements (excluding accords on economic cooperation). The annual average for a while came to $75

million corresponding to 2.6 per cent of Tokyo's exports in 1958 or 0.3
per cent of the national income. In addition Japan agreed in the negotiations to provide in long-term loans and investments to various countries
the equivalent of at least $716,600,000. Japanese payments in goods and
services as well as government and private loans have assisted economic
development in Southeast Asia.

The Security Treaty. The Security Treaty between Washington and
Tokyo permitted U.S. forces to stay in Japan to protect the nation
against "armed attack from without," and if Tokyo requested, to help the
government suppress large-scale riots and disturbances instigated by an
outside power or powers. Japan could not grant bases to third powers
without American approval. The United States could use its forces in
Nippon in any way Washington thought necessary for the "maintenance
of international peace and security in the Far East."[47] Although the
duration of the pact was indefinite, it was replaced by the Treaty of
Mutual Cooperation and Security of January 19, 1960, which could be
terminated upon one year's notice by either party ten years from its
coming into force (June 23, 1960). Essentially each partner recognized
that "an armed attack against either Party in the territories under the
administration of Japan" would endanger "its own peace and safety" and
each "would act to meet the common danger in accordance with its constitutional provisions and processes."[48] American armed forces
remained in Japan but consultation provisions in the treaty arrangement
were significant. In due course Nippon became the most important ally
of the United States in the Pacific. Not without reason did the Senate
Committee on Foreign Relations assert as far back as February 14,
1952:

> A free, prosperous, and democratic Japan could exert an important
> stabilizing influence in the Far East. Japan occupies a strategic
> position in the Far East; it has a large, energetic, and skilled popu-
> lation; it is the only industrial nation in the Far East; and it lies
> athwart the American defense line in the Pacific.[49]

Directly Related Defense Treaties. The Mutual Defense Treaty
between the United States and the Philippines formalized the ties that
had existed for some time. On April 18, 1951, President Truman publicly stated that "an armed attack on the Philippines" would be considered by the United States as "dangerous to its own peace and safety and
that it would act accordingly."[50] Dulles had visited the Philippines in
mid-February before going to Australia and New Zealand, and in August
Washington formally proposed to Manila a mutual security treaty comparable to that planned for Australia and New Zealand. The treaty was
signed in the same month before the presidents of the two republics.

The Philippines was deeply concerned over the proposed Japanese peace treaty, for Manila believed it was "too soft" on Tokyo. It feared the resurgence of Japanese militarism, disliked American support for Nippon's economic recovery, and condemned the absence of a specific reparations agreement from the peace settlement. With the Huks constituting a serious challenge to the government and with the Korean War under way, Manila was worried about the Communist threat at home as well as abroad. Furthermore, Senator Claro M. Recto was raising questions about the nature and value of the American commitment.

The heart of the Mutual Defense Treaty was found in Article IV: "Each Party recognizes that an armed attack in the Pacific Area on either of the Parties would be dangerous to its own peace and safety and declares that it would act to meet the common dangers in accordance with its constitutional processes."[51] The armed attack under Article V was deemed to include one on the metropolitan territory of the Philippines or the United States, or the island territories under the jurisdiction of either in the Pacific, or on American or Philippine public ships, aircraft, or armed forces in the Pacific Ocean. The parties alone and together would develop their capacities to resist armed attack, and would consult each other from time to time on the pact and whenever either believed the "territorial integrity, political independence or security" of either was threatened by "external armed attack" in the area of the Pacific. The duration of the treaty was indefinite but either party could end it on notice of one year.

Certain provisions of the Mutual Defense Treaty should be stressed. The terms of Article IV are so broad that an "armed attack in the Pacific Area" from a militant Japan, aggressive Communist China, or expansionist Indonesia on one of the parties could lead to the implementation of the alliance. Moreover, Article V is very broad, and numerous situations could arise directly affecting its implementation. On the other hand, Washington has no commitment under the treaty to intervene in internal disturbances in the Philippines, even those instigated by the Huks. The nature of the American commitment under Article IV is less specific than the one found in the North Atlantic Treaty. It reflects the language and formula of the Monroe Doctrine. Nevertheless, this point is legalistic, for the presence of American bases in the Philippines and subsequent statements from the highest sources in Washington indicate the depth of the U.S. obligation.

Like the Philippines, Australia and New Zealand were apprehensive about future Nipponese militarism and agreed to the proposed Japanese peace treaty providing the United States would give them a security commitment. ANZUS, as the security treaty came to be called, differs in only a few respects from the Mutual Defense Treaty between the United States and the Philippines.[52] Article IV of ANZUS, the heart of the treaty, is practically identical with Article IV of the Philippine-American pact. Article V of both alliances dealing with the treaty area has almost identical language. The consultation provision in both ANZUS and the Philippine-American pact calls for consultation under comparable circumstances, except in the former the threat is not specifically limited to "external armed attack" as in the latter. ANZUS formally established a council of foreign ministers or their deputies for the implementation of the treaty. It would be so organized that it could meet at any time, and it could consult with the states, organizations, and authorities in the Pacific. Both treaties had the same time duration.

Australia and New Zealand were concerned about the absence of Great Britain from ANZUS. London would have liked membership and was hurt by its exclusion (even of observers from Council meetings) but Washington was definitely opposed to giving security commitments to the British dependencies of Hong Kong and Malaya. The Philippines was also interested in membership but settled for a bilateral pact with the United States.

Canberra would have preferred an alliance with stronger commitments from Washington and with better built-in diplomatic machinery. It was not until the ANZUS Council meeting in August 1952 that the U.S. Commander in Chief Pacific rather than the Joint Chiefs (as desired by the Australians) was clearly identified as the focus for ANZUS military planning and liaison. However, the terms of Articles IV and V have proved a mixed blessing. For instance, they caused concern in Washington, Canberra, and Wellington in the offshore island crises involving U.S. support of the Nationalist Chinese against Peking and in the confrontation crisis involving the suppport of Australia and New Zealand foɪ Malaysia against Indonesia.

Indirectly Related Defense Treaties. The mutual defense pact between the Republic of Korea and the United States was the first U.S. treaty commitment of its kind in history to the mainland of East Asia. Associated primarily with the Korean War it reflected the sacrifice of the American people to prevent a Communist takeover in South Korea. It also represented a concession to President Syngman Rhee in order to get him to support an armistice and to soft-pedal his efforts to carry the war to the north. The basic American and South Korean commitments under Article III are comparable to those under Article IV of ANZUS and the Philippine-American pact. The treaty specifically relates to an armed attack in the Pacific on either of the signatories "in territories now under their respective administrative control, or hereafter recognized by one of the Parties as lawfully brought under the administrative control of the other."*

In another relationship, the security pact between the United States and the Republic of China obligated each party to come to the other's defense in case of "armed attack in the West Pacific Area" against either signer's territory. The formula of commitment was like the one used in ANZUS and the Philippine treaty. The Chinese area covered by the pact was Taiwan and the Pescadores but other territories could be added by mutual agreement. Significantly President Eisenhower had disagreed with Secretary Dulles and had removed from the draft treaty the inclusion of the offshore islands of Quemoy and Matsu which were under Chinese Nationalist control.[53] The United States received the right to station defense forces in Taiwan and the Pescadores as decided by mutual accord. The parties agreed to maintain and develop alone and together their capacity "to resist armed attack and communist subversive activities directed from without against their territorial integrity and political stability."[54] The treaty was indefinite in duration though either party could end it on a year's notice.†

---

*American Foreign Policy, 1950–1955: Basic Documents, Vol. I, p 897. The treaty also contained consultation provisions, gave the United States the right to station forces in the Republic of Korea as decided by mutual agreement, and had the same time duration as ANZUS.

†An exchange of notes on December 10, 1954 confirmed that the use of forces from territories under the control of Nationalist China would be a matter of joint agreement subject to self-defense in an emergency situation, and that such forces as represented joint contribution would not be removed from the treaty area to the extent that its defensibility was substantially affected without mutual agreement. The Senate Committee on Foreign Relations defined further the U.S. obligations under the treaty in three understandings: the pact did not modify the legal status of Taiwan and the Pescadores (leaving Washington uncommitted on ultimate sovereignty); the United States would act only if Nationalist China fought in self-defense; and any expansion of the treaty area must be approved by the Senate.

Final approval of the pact was somewhat delayed as the Senate attended to an urgent message from the President on the developing critical situation in the Formosa Strait. Eisenhower requested on January 24, 1955, authority from Congress to use American armed forces to protect against armed attack Formosa, the Pescadores, and related territories and positions under Nationalist Chinese control. In effect he wanted to use, if necessary, U.S. forces to protect the offshore islands if he believed an attack on them was really directed at Formosa and the Pescadores. Congress approved a joint resolution on January 28 meeting the President's request, and the mutual security treaty between Taipei and Washington entered into force in March.

The American defense of Taiwan had significant implications for Southeast Asia. Truman's statement on June 27, 1950, and subsequent

U.S. policy toward the Republic of China on Taiwan meant that two Chinas were here to stay, at least for the foreseeable future. Accordingly, the overseas Chinese in the various Southeast Asian countries would be subject to attempted influence from Taipei and Peking. Also, questions of recognition and of attitudes in the United Nations could not but raise serious problems for the leaders and diplomats of the states of the region.

The American alliances with Japan, the Philippines, Australia and New Zealand, Korea, and Nationalist China had a fundamental objective: to deter aggression by a potential enemy. This approach represents a radical peacetime departure in the foreign policy of the United States from the nonalignment characteristic of most of its diplomatic history. It can be argued that a number of major wars of this century arose through miscalculation and might have been avoided. At the same time the American alliances in East Asia and the Pacific concluded between 1951 and 1954 were not ironclad but provided for flexibility. Furthermore, the enemy or enemies would have to attack in several treaty areas to bring all of them into play.

A recurring theme in most of the alliances was the hope for a broad multilateral treaty in the Pacific. It is expressed in the phraseology "pending the development of a more comprehensive system of regional security in the Pacific Area"[55] or a variation of it. Indeed, the Senate Committee on Foreign Relations in reporting on the mutual defense treaty with Korea on January 21, 1954, observed that the "security of the Pacific area would be measurably enhanced if the nations of that region would join and work together for their regional and collective self-defense."[56] Secretary Dulles had informed the Committee that a "Pacific security system" was desirable but did not seem likely "at any early predictable date" due to the political and cultural differences and the physical separation of the countries of the area. Multiplicity of motivation characterized the partners of the pacts already in existence, and the signers, not to mention the nonparticipants, could not agree on a common Pacific security system.

Other U.S. Relationships. With the events of the Korean War and the Japanese peace settlement, American policy toward, and the response of the countries of Southeast Asia reflected the new international environment in East Asia and the Pacific. These bilateral relations merit particular attention. In the Philippines the outbreak of the Korean War affected domestic politics, at least to some extent, for it has been pointed out the country was undergoing a financial crisis, the Hukbalahaps were threatening to overthrow the government, and the recent national election had been marked by corruption. As far back as the winter of 1950 President Quirino had urged President Truman to send a U.S. economic survey mission to the Philippines. Arriving in Manila in July, the mission under the able leadership of former Undersecretary of the Treasury Daniel W. Bell undertook a careful survey. In its October report, the Bell mission urged basic fiscal, land, social, and economic reforms by the Philippine government, and recommended, subject to this effort, support by the American government up to $250 million in carefully supervised grants and loans over a five-year period. The report created a stir in the island republic, especially its criticism of public administration. A basic Philippine-American agreement on the implementation of the Bell recommendations, however, was reached in Baguio in November, initiating a program of U.S. economic and technical assistance. The Philippines was jealous of its newly won sovereignty and questioned American supervision but the United States was convinced conditions in the republic called for reforms and the effective use of American aid. As the ties between Manila and Washington were still strong and both agreed on the Communist threat in Asia, the latter's use of the carrot and the stick was possible.

The Huks by the summer of 1950 had around 15,000 men in their armed forces, chiefly in Central Luzon, and a much larger number of sympathizers and supporters in Luzon and the Visayas. They had begun as a People's Anti-Japanese Army during the Pacific War, fighting the invaders and their "Filipino puppets" and urging social and economic reform. Through the early postwar years they might possibly have worked under the leadership of Luis Taruc in the constitutional framework of the country. Then their leadership was completely captured by the Communists, their goal was openly the overthrow of the Philippine government by the People's Liberation Army, and the Huk movement became a real part of the Communist effort in Asia.

Although the Communist Party of the Philippines (PKP) with its People's Liberation Army won support from many peasants it was not able to win widespread backing from organized labor, college students, or the Chinese. Only limited aid came from these groups. In Huk propaganda the Pyongyang radio of North Korea was constantly quoted for news on the Korean War, sympathy was expressed for the Communists fighting in Indochina and Malaya, the victory of Mao Tse-tung in China and the achievements of Stalin were praised, and the U.S. role in the Philippines and the world was damned. In July 1950 the Huks expected a People's Republic of the Philippines within two years.

The general election of November 1949 in which President Elpidio Quirino defeated José Laurel under conditions of considerable fraud and terrorism convinced the Huks they could not achieve power through constitutional means. President Quirino's eventual appointment of Ramon

Magsaysay to the defense post in his cabinet was the most important selection of his career. Magsaysay became the key man in defeating the Huks; he also stood for honest elections. The American military mission in the Philippines provided advice and equipment to its army and constabulary in the fight against the guerrillas. Americans also were active in a program of economic and social reform.

In the national elections of November 1953 Magsaysay defeated Quirino for the presidency. The elections were generally free, honest, and peaceful, and led to the "outs" taking over power from the "ins."[57] Washington followed the campaign and the voting carefully, was officially neutral but unofficially highly sympathetic to Magsaysay, and indirectly worked hard to affect the outcome. Magsaysay, it should be stressed, was not a creation of the United States; Washington's chief role was to publicize him (which was perhaps not needed) and press for free elections (which probably was needed).[58] As President of the Philippines, Magsaysay was able to use his great power to intensify efforts against the Huks and to push a program of economic and social reform in the islands.

In contrast to its role in the Philippines, Washington during the Korean War was much less active in Indonesia. Djakarta was pursuing its "independent and active" foreign policy between the "power blocs" and championing the cause of anticolonialism. It was giving considerable attention to the Netherlands-Indonesian Union with its agreements on foreign relations, defense, financial and economic relations, and cultural ties. The West New Guinea controversy was emerging as a major factor in the collapse of the Union. On August 10, 1954, Djakarta and The Hague signed a protocol and exchanged notes to end the Statute and many related provisions, but the Union was destined to suffer a long and agonizing death.

As for the United States and Great Britain, Vice-President Mohammad Hatta significantly asserted in April 1953 that Indonesia was "bounded by the British Navy and the American Navy, which control the Indian and Pacific Oceans. But no one can say that Britain and the United States have evil designs on Indonesia. On the contrary, they are desirous of seeing Indonesia remain independent and become prosperous."[59] At the same time Hatta noted that his country had no common boundaries with the Soviet Union or China and a "direct threat from that direction to Indonesian independence neither exists nor is possible."[60] Djakarta believed it had considerable freedom in foreign policy.

Washington was not hostile to Indonesia's "independent and active" foreign policy. In the last full year of Truman's presidency he told Assistant Secretary of State for Far Eastern Affairs John M. Allison, about to leave on a tour of Southeast Asia, that he could inform Indonesia and Burma that Washington fully understood their interest in being neutral and in settling their domestic problems before being involved in international problems. "We did exactly the same thing," Truman said, "when we were young!"[61] Allison believed he presented these viewpoints to good effect in various countries in Southeast Asia.

Although the United States and Indonesia differed on the recognition of the China of Mao Tse-tung and the Vietnam of Bao Dai as well as general policy in the Korean War, it was American aid to Indonesia which caused a crisis in relations between Washington and Djakarta. As a consequence of strong Western influence on its economy, Indonesia was particularly sensitive to any political implications of American assistance.

In February 1950 the Export-Import Bank extended Djakarta a development loan of $100 million. The visit of the Griffin mission, April 11–22, provided the occasion for a survey of Indonesia only a few months after the achievement of independence.[62] It recommended that

American aid should be dissociated from the influence of Dutch personnel. Special attention should be given to avoiding any appearance of ulterior United States interest, and projects of particular interest to the leaders in Jogjakarta should be stressed.[63]

An agreement on October 16 provided for U.S. economic and technical aid to the island republic.

The previous August 15 Washington had made Indonesia a grant for small arms to help in equipping its constabulary. In fact, President Truman on May 1 had approved $3 million in military aid items. Under the Mutual Security Act of 1951 Indonesia in receiving certain aid was expected to pledge to contribute to "the defensive strength of the free world." Jealous of its "independent" position, Djakarta, unlike Manila, did not want to make the pledge, but Foreign Minister Subardjo and Ambassador Cochran worked out a formula whereby Indonesia would receive assistance with the phrase "contribute to the strength of independent and sovereign nations" replacing the one originally desired by the Americans.

After the aid agreement was signed on January 5, 1952, and the terms became known, a storm of protest arose in Djakarta. Subardjo's resignation was accepted on February 21 and the Sukiman government fell two days later. It was not until December 30 that the Indonesian cabinet approved an accord with the United States terminating the Subardjo-Cochran arrangement and replacing it with an agreement whereby American aid was administered by the Technical Cooperation (Point Four) Administration and special provision was made for delivery of the constabulary equipment not yet received. Indonesia reaffirmed it would act in conformity with its United Nations obligations in "promoting international understanding and good will, in maintaining world peace, and in eliminating causes of international tensions."[64] As a type of U.S. aid, the J. G. White Engineering and Management Consultant Services for some time from 1952 acted as engineering consultant to Djakarta.

Behind the scenes Washington gave considerable thought to American security policy toward Indonesia. On May 17, 1951, President Truman approved a policy statement of the National Security Council which included the following:

> In Indonesia, the United States should seek to strengthen the non-communist political orientation of the government, promote the economic development of Indonesia, and influence Indonesia toward greater participation in measures which support the security of the area [Southeast Asia] and Indonesian solidarity with the free world.[65]

Along with the policy statement was a staff study of the National Security Council which stressed, *inter alia*, the importance of Indonesia. On March 3, 1952, the Joint Chiefs of Staff observed:

> In the event of the imminent or actual fall of Malaya to communism, [the United States should] consider in the light of circumstances existing at the time, what if any measures, including military, the United States in its own self-interest should undertake to prevent the fall in Indonesia to communism.[66]

Although Washington could not foresee the course of future events it was aware of the need to watch developments.

The policy of the United States toward the purchase of natural rubber and tin, important exports of Indonesia, directly influenced relations between the two countries. Prices boomed in 1950 as a consequence of the Korean War, began to decline in 1951, and created serious financial and economic troubles for Indonesia in 1952. Djakarta resented U.S. efforts to lower the prices of tin, rubber, and other raw materials. In March 1952 the two countries reached an agreement for three years on the American purchase of tin, and an increase in the price of rubber, 1954–55, brought some relief to the island republic.

American relations with Malaya and Singapore, both British dependencies, were also affected by the prices of tin and rubber since the United States was a key purchaser.* The Korean War, of course, had

*For a perceptive statement on U.S. relations with Malaya and Singapore in 1950, see the report of the Griffin mission in Hayes, *The Beginning of American Aid to Southeast Asia*, pp. 127–49. "The United States," it was asserted, "in common with the rest of the non-Communist world, ... has an important stake in the peace and in the economic health and development of Singapore and the Federation of Malaya and in their political development within the democratic traditions of the United Kingdom and toward their eventual goal of responsible self-government." *Ibid.*, pp. 131–32.

various effects on the prices, some good and some bad. Natural rubber and tin generate an international diplomacy of their own.

During the Emergency which the British declared in Malaya after the Communist uprising in June 1948 Washington allowed shipments of arms to help defeat the rebels. It appreciated many of the problems the British faced in counterinsurgency. The United States encouraged the Thai to cooperate with Great Britain against Communist guerrillas trying to evade British forces and moving into the Thai jungle for refuge and recoupment. American loans and grants to assist in the economic recovery of the United Kingdom indirectly helped it to make various contributions to Malaya after World War II.

Washington's security policy toward Malaya and Singapore shifted from 1950 to 1954. A staff study enclosed in a policy statement of the National Security Council approved by President Truman on May 17, 1951, called for the United States to coordinate its operational planning with Great Britain as regards "Malaya and adjacent areas." Another staff study on February 13, 1952, pointed out that given the assumption that the Western powers control the sea Malaya offered a "defensible position" even in the face of a "full-scale land attack." This defense, it was indicated, would protect Indonesia against "external communist pressure." The Joint Chiefs of Staff for their part on March 3 asserted that:

> Although the world situation generally and the situation in the Far East specifically will be controlling, it may be possible for the United States to provide those reinforcements which are essential for a successful defense of Malaya at the Isthmus of Kra, thus insuring the retention by the British of Singapore while concurrently decreasing the danger of a successful communist invasion of Indonesia.[67]

The Joint Chiefs believed the American effort, if undertaken, should be part of a collective action by the United Nations or in conjunction with Great Britain and any other friendly government. President Eisenhower on January 16, 1954, approved a policy declaration of the National Security Council calling for fitting American military action against Communist China if Peking made an overt armed attack against Malaya.

As dependencies of Great Britain, Malaya and Singapore had no independent voices in the Korean War or the Japanese peace settlement. The Communist insurrection in Malaya, however, spurred the Malays in their opposition to the spread of communism. The British embargo on rubber to the People's Republic of China as part of the United Nations effort in Korea clearly affected Malaya and Singapore. When Great Britain made peace with Japan it included as a matter of course the two dependencies.

Questions of war damages and reparations were presumably all but resolved from confiscated Japanese property, and before the peace settlement at San Francisco, advance reparations payments had been made. The matter, however, was not dead.

The Korean War speeded the *entente cordial* developing between the United States and Thailand. The Thai government, eager for American economic and military aid, received warmly both the Griffin and Melby-Erskine missions. When the former was in Bangkok joint Thai-American committees discussed possible U.S. economic and technical help and agreed on the kinds of assistance. The Griffin mission emphasized in its reporting the need for speed in assistance stressing the impact on Thai leadership. Proposals for an aid agreement were forwarded to Washington and negotiations followed. The original aid provisions of the United States were patterned after its agreements with European countries and were not suitable for Thailand. Washington modified some of its terms, and an economic and technical cooperation agreement was signed on September 19, 1950. The Thai were worried over speed in congressional appropriations, but by January 1951 the program was under way and thirty American experts had arrived.

Military aid from the United States raised a different set of problems. By training and equipping Thai armed forces, Washington would tend to strengthen the military regime of Pibul Songgram. At the same time Ambassador Stanton believed the Communist threat in Southeast Asia justified U.S. military aid. He thought Thailand should have small but well trained and well equipped armed forces to cope with border guerrilla activities and to help the police fight subversion from within. While the Melby-Erskine mission was in Bangkok it conducted careful discussions with the Thai on military needs. After intense negotiations the United States and Thailand signed on October 17, 1950, a military assistance agreement. In a significant statement on the occasion Ambassador Stanton asserted that the agreement was neither a military alliance nor a defense pact; furthermore, it made no provision for American bases in Thailand. A number of U.S. servicemen functioned as a military assistance advisory group, adding to the growing official community of the United States in Bangkok. In January 1951 Ambassador Stanton formally presented U.S. military equipment to the prime minister of the kingdom.

Increasing American interest in Thailand was indicated by the opening of a consulate in Chiang Mai, an important northern city, in November 1950. An educational exchange agreement, praised by Stanton, had been concluded the previous July. Bangkok later gave the assurances required to receive U.S. military aid under the Mutual Security Act of 1951.

The role of Thailand in American security policy came to receive increasing attention in Washington. A National Security Council staff study on February 13, 1952, analyzed the "strategic interdependence" of countries in Southeast Asia giving considerable attention to Thailand. A few days later on March 3 the Joint Chiefs stressed measures *"other than military"* that "may be determined as feasible to forestall an invasion of Thailand or a seizure of power by local Thai communists."[68] Consideration of American security policy toward Bangkok continued unabated in 1953. On January 16, 1954, President Eisenhower approved a policy statement of the National Security Council that called for the United States to "take appropriate military action against Communist China" if it committed an overt attack on Thailand.[69] The President's Special Committee on Indochina under General Walter Bedell Smith reported on April 5 that "the U.S. should undertake the immediate organization within the several states of Southeast Asia of an increased number of military units, including guerrilla and para-military organizations, as well as anti-subversion police forces. In particular, this should be accomplished in Thailand and if possible in Indonesia and Burma."[70] These high-level considerations pointed toward increased U.S. involvement in the security of Thailand.

American policy toward Burma in 1950 reflected changes in the international climate. Burma was a neighbor of Communist China and the Korean War cast a long shadow. Ambassador Philip C. Jessup had visited Rangoon in connection with the Bangkok conference and explained American interests in Southeast Asia in the light of the success of Mao Tse-tung. The Griffin mission was well received in Rangoon, and on September 13 "the Bilateral" or agreement on economic cooperation was signed whereby Burma would receive American economic and technical aid. In November the United States agreed to provide Rangoon with a number of river patrol craft under the Mutual Defense Assistance Program. Washington originally wanted a crash effort to promote economic development in the Union aimed at stopping further Communist inroads there and elsewhere, but did not realize the scope and complexity of the task. For a brief period, as one specialist observes, it "wished to exact a political price for its support. This in the early days of the aid relationship included acquiescence in the role of the KMT on Burmese soil."[71] Rangoon accepted the American crash approach but wanted extensive long-range planning and industrialization to destroy the "colonial" economy.

In implementing a program of economic and technical aid, Americans were aware of the sensitivities of the Burmese. Washington sought to promote political stability in the country and to demonstrate U.S. friendship but there were definite limits to its advice. Furthermore, Americans had little prior peacetime experience in Burma, or knowledge about it, and many of them found it hard to adjust to living conditions in the country.* A Special Technical and Economic Mission from the United States worked with a Burma Economic Aid Committee to handle the assistance.[72] Prime Minister U Nu took a personal interest in the effort. Programs were activated in such fields as transportation, public works, and communications, agriculture, health and sanitation, education, and industry and natural resources. An economic and technical survey of the Union was undertaken by Knappen, Tippets, Abbett, McCarthy, Engineers, in association with Pierce Management, Inc., and Robert R. Nathan Associates, Inc.†

The first American economic aid program weathered two storms but failed to survive the third. Rangoon was opposed to giving the specific assurances required under the Mutual Security Act of 1951 but reaffirmed in an exchange of notes with Washington in February 1952 that "it will act in conformity with its obligations under the United Nations charter and in accord with the principles and purposes of the United Nations charter in promoting international understanding and good will and maintaining world peace and eliminating causes of international tension."[73] Aid without strings was a subject of discussion in Burma that did not die easily.

The sudden transfer of the assistance program in July 1952 from the Mutual Security Administration in Washington to the Technical Cooperation Administration of the State Department created another crisis in Rangoon, for the latter drastically cut the proposed budget of Burma aid for fiscal year 1953. Neither American nor Burmese officials in Rangoon had been consulted, and Burma suspected the reduction was due to its attitude on the assurances. A compromise program for fiscal 1953 was ultimately reached, and went into force on October 24, 1952.

The issue of the Kuomintang troops in the Union came to a head in March 1953 when Rangoon took the controversy to the United Nations and terminated the U.S. economic aid program as of June 30. An informal agreement between the American embassy and the foreign minister of Burma had led to the latter's removal in the notification of a refer-

*As for Burmese leaders, they were not well acquainted with America, and the Griffin mission urged a program of increased contacts especially through visits to the United States.

†It is interesting to note that the American embassy in Rangoon in April 1949 and the Griffin mission the next year recommended U.S. support for an agricultural and industrial school for the Kachin State. In view of the help the Kachins gave American forces in Burma in the Pacific War the project was viewed in some respects as "a joint United States-Burma war-dead memorial."

ence to the provocation of the KMT troops in the Union.[74] The close-
out procedures, however, were phased; and Rangoon took over responsibility for some unfinished projects and retained some contractual services
formerly financed by American government funds.

Although the U.S. aid program to Burma was central in direct day-to-
day relations between Rangoon and Washington, 1950–53, a number of
additional matters arose to cause difficulties. Gordon Seagrave, an American medical missionary of many years experience in the country, was
charged by the government with helping the rebels, and in January 1951
sentenced to imprisonment for six years. Later the sentence was reduced,
and in November the Supreme Court quashed the conviction. In a quite
different matter Burmese leaders were becoming concerned in 1953 over
American disposal of surplus rice in various countries seeking the commodity. In 1954 a prominent Burmese official indicated the U.S. dump-
ing of rice in Asia would force Rangoon to tie its economy to Communist China.

Despite the fact that Burmese-American relations were difficult and
that the United States had long considered Burma an area of British military responsibility, President Eisenhower on January 16 approved a
policy statement by the National Security Council under which an "overt
Chinese Communist attack" on Burma would cause the United States to
"take appropriate military action against Communist China."[75] It was
Indochina, however, not Burma, that became a storm center.

THE FIRST INDOCHINESE WAR

Although this bloody struggle began in December 1946 and ended in
July 1954, technically it became polarized in January and February
1950 when leading powers in each rival bloc formally decided to enter
into diplomatic relations with the government of Ho Chi Minh or Bao
Dai. Its climax came with the fall of Dien Bien Phu on May 7, 1954,
and the opening of the Geneva Conference on Indochina the next day.[76]
This span of time from January 1950 to early May 1954 constitutes one
of the most significant periods for Southeast Asia in world diplomacy.
The United States over the years increasingly supported France and the
Associated States of Vietnam, Cambodia, and Laos while the People's
Republic of China increasingly aided the Democratic Republic of
Vietnam.[77] The Korean War affected in various ways the roles of
Peking and Washington in Indochina but its end in July 1953 did not
bring the two powers to open war in Southeast Asia. Both approached
the banks of the Rubicon in their policies though unlike Caesar neither
chose to cross it.

The First Indochinese War, however, acquired a new and highly significant orientation in its last years. Washington no longer considered it a local colonial struggle in a remote part of the globe, but a holding action of the Free World in a strategic area to prevent the expansion of monolithic communism represented by the Russians, Chinese, and Viet Minh. In this context the Americans were holding up the dam in Korea, the British, in Malaya, and the French, in Indochina.

As for the United States in Vietnam, two observers have noted, "anticommunism preempted anticolonialism or pronationalism in importance."[78] Although some critics would qualify this statement, it cannot be denied that the Vietnamese Communists were able to capitalize on nationalism at home far more than their opponents were able to capitalize on anticommunism. To many influential leaders in newly independent countries in South and Southeast Asia, the Viet Minh, moreover, stood for nationalism and the opposition for colonialism. On the global stage the final dimensions of the First Indochinese War were indicated by the great power participants at the Geneva Conference which ended it—the United States, the Soviet Union, Great Britain, France, and the People's Republic of China.

American policy toward Indochina between 1950 and 1954 officially called for steadily urging Paris to move quickly toward giving genuine independence to Indochina and for providing "economic and growing military assistance to the French."[79] The roots of this involvement are found in the Truman administration but they were well nourished during the Eisenhower presidency and sustained a robust plant during the Kennedy and Johnson administrations.

Truman's New Directions. After U.S. recognition of Vietnam, Cambodia, and Laos in February 1950 as independent states in the French Union, the American consulate general in Saigon was raised to a legation and a minister resident in Saigon was accredited to each of them. Questions of the representation of the Associated States abroad and of their negotiations with Washington soon arose, causing considerable diplomatic difficulty.

Both French and Vietnamese officials in February, moreover, began to speculate in earnest about the direct American aid that they wanted and expected. A formal French request was made on February 16 after Paris had decided to tell Washington that the alternative to long-term American aid in Indochina was a very possible French withdrawal from the area. The request, of course, raised a number of questions for American policy makers. How much would there be in the new aid program? What would be the nature of the economic and military assistance? How—and this was a very important how—would it be administered in Indochina? Would there be American strings to it? The new prime minister in

Saigon, Nguyen Phan Long, was pro-American, and boasted in early 1950 he could defeat the Viet Minh in six months with enough direct U.S. assistance. He lost his post in early May and was succeeded by Tran Van Huu who immortalized the "fructify" expression. The French, eager that aid really go through them and not directly to the Associated States, made a convincing case in 1950 as regards military assistance but were less persuasive with respect to economic aid. Apprehensive that the Americans might seek to use assistance as a condition for complete independence of the Associated States, the French fell back upon their version of the Elysée Agreement of March 8, 1949. As for the friends of Ho Chi Minh, a large crowd of Communist sympathizers with pictures of their leader and Viet Minh flags demonstrated in March in Saigon against the visit of two U.S. destroyers. Thus by May 8, when Secretary Acheson formally announced the extension of military and economic aid to the Associated States of Vietnam, Cambodia, and Laos and to France, many of the elements of the Indochinese puzzle for the United States were already present.

   Dean Acheson has indicated that the decision of May 8 proclaimed in the interests of the "restoration of security" and "the development of genuine nationalism" in the Associated States was made after some hesitation:

> The hesitation came from the belief of some of my colleagues that, even with our material and financial help, the French-Bao Dai regime would be defeated in the field by the Soviet- and Chinese-supported Viet Minh. All of us recognized the high probability of this result unless France swiftly transferred authority to the Associated States and organized, trained, and equipped, with our aid, substantial indigenous forces to take over the main burden of the fight.[80]

At any rate the policy had been agreed on after discussions with various members of Congress domestically and with Bevin and Schuman internationally. President Truman had approved it.

   It should be stressed that American options at the time Washington was informally reaching a decision in February and March to provide aid to France and the Associated States were sharply defined. The Secretary of Defense in a memorandum for Truman on March 6 flatly noted that "the choice confronting the United States is to support the legal governments in Indochina or to face the extension of Communism over the remainder of the continental area of Southeast Asia and possibly westward."[81] Involved in the Secretary's thinking were his perception of the Communist threat, his concern for a line of containment, and his belief in the domino premise.

Formal agreements followed the U.S. announcement of May 8, and the American official presence in Saigon was substantially expanded. On May 24 the President of the French Union and the chiefs of state of Vietnam, Cambodia, and Laos were officially informed of the U.S. decision to establish a special economic mission in Saigon to work with the three Indochinese governments and the French High Commissioner. The economic and technical aid would reinforce not supplant the joint effort of Vietnam, Cambodia, Laos, and France "on whom rests the primary responsibility for the restoration of security and stability."[82] Only a modest sum for economic and technical aid was initially available— $23.5 million for the fiscal year ending on June 30, 1951.* In terms of military assistance Truman approved $10 million in aid on May 1, 1950, and seven Dakota planes were formally presented to French officials in Saigon at the end of June, the first such items in a long and bloody sequence. President Truman's June 27 announcement in connection with the outbreak of the Korean War that he was accelerating military assistance to France and to the Associated States in Indochina and was sending a military mission there brought Indochina into the broad scope of American military policy in East Asia and the Pacific.

In August the President, speaking to Vietnam in the first Voice of America broadcast to that country, expressed the hope that the Associated States in the French Union "may take their place" with the other nations in the Free World. In the same month a Special Technical and Economic Mission was established in Saigon, and a Military Assistance Advisory Group (MAAG) was set up to administer military supplies.

By the middle of September Washington and Paris had concluded that the only way to salvage the situation in Indochina and keep the French army in Europe was to establish indigenous armed forces in the former. The French maintained they needed U.S. assistance in funds and military equipment to raise them while the American mission in Saigon stressed the need for the forces and urged giving the Associated States a genuine role in the preparations. In October France suggested in its planning increasing Vietnamese battalions from twelve to thirty and adding ten divisions to the French army serving in Europe. Although Washington agreed to greatly increase its military aid in Indochina Paris thought the amount was not sufficient. But in November the French National Assembly approved the establishment of national forces in the Associated States. A key agreement was signed in Saigon on December 23 by repre-

---

*This figure was recommended by the Griffin mission which also observed that "the aid which the United States has extended to France through the ECA is of major assistance to the French in carrying the present load in Indochina, but little U.S. aid has been given to Indochina directly."[83]

sentatives of the United States, France, Vietnam, Cambodia, and Laos on "mutual defense assistance in Indochina." It was provided that U.S. military aid would be turned over to the French High Command and direct relations between the Military Assistance Advisory Group and Vietnam, Cambodia, and Laos would not be allowed.

By the time of the agreement of December 23 the intervention of Peking in the Korean War had further shifted the emphasis from Soviet communism to Chinese communism in Southeast Asia. In fact, a National Intelligence Estimate (NIE 5) of December 29 indicated that direct intervention in Indochina by Chinese Communist troops might take place at any time. (In later estimates the probability declined and then stayed low.) NIE 5 also asserted that the French position in Indochina was "precarious."

The Joint Chiefs of Staff in a significant report on November 28 to the Secretary of Defense reexamined American policy in Indochina. They had reviewed a report of October 11 by the Southeast Asia Aid Policy Committee (the formation of which they had recommended in April) and one by Brigadier General Francis G. Brink, Chief of the Military Assistance Advisory Group in Saigon. The short- and long-term objectives of American policy in Indochina, as expressed by the Joint Chiefs, continued to be relatively basic in U.S. policy during the rest of the First Indochinese War. Although subject to some modifications in later recommendations the subsequent record actually shows that the short-term objective listed first on November 28 still stood when the war was over, namely, "the United States should take action, as a matter of urgency, by all means practicable short of the actual employment of United States military forces, to deny Indochina to communism."[84]

After considerable debate with the French on legal terminology, the United States signed on September 7, 8, and 9, 1951, bilateral agreements on economic and technical aid with Vietnam, Cambodia, and Laos. "Letters of intent" had been provided by the Associated States the previous fall. Washington, having failed in 1950 to get the French to give more autonomy to Bao Dai, was especially determined that it should get credit for its economic assistance. Despite French opposition to bilateralism, economic aid would be channeled directly to the people of Indochina. The Associated States later gave the assurances required under the Mutual Security Act of 1951. Relations between Cambodia and the United States were enlivened when Norodom Sihanouk offered an elephant as a gift to Harry Truman. It brought back memories of King Mongkut's offer of 1861.

Meanwhile events in Indochina were affecting the balance of forces. By late 1950 the Viet Minh, helped by the use of training facilities in

China and by Russian and Chinese arms, wrested from the French the frontier zone in Tonkin along the China border and forced the French to retreat to the Red River delta. In February 1951 the Lao Dong or Workers' Party was created by Ho Chi Minh with an honorary presidium of Joseph Stalin, Mao Tse-tung, Kim Il Sung, and Maurice Thorez. Three months later American, British, and French military representatives with Australian and New Zealand military observers held staff talks in Singapore on defense problems in Southeast Asia, it being understood that governments were not committed. The same month, May 17 to be exact, the President with the National Security Council formally determined that in Indochina the United States should "continue to increase the military effectiveness of French units and the size and equipment of indigenous units by providing timely and suitable military assistance without relieving the French authorities of their basic military responsibilities or committing United States armed forces."[85]

Apart from the Communist inroads, Indochina in terms of being an embryonic federation was facing disintegration. Cambodia, Laos, and Vietnam at a conference with France at Pau from June to November 1950 revealed clear-cut nationalistic and individualistic tendencies. In the course of the negotiations the Vietnamese appealed without success to the Americans and British to moderate the French.

In December General Jean de Lattre de Tassigny was appointed French High Commissioner and Commander in Chief of French Union Forces in Indochina. "Le Roi Jean" was energetic and dynamic and had the flair of General MacArthur. He called for a crusade against communism, and aroused sympathy in America for the French role in Indochina, claiming the Associated States were independent and French colonialism was dead. Although he restored morale among the French forces, stemmed the Viet Minh drive, and took the offensive, he made no big changes in the conduct of the war and *la sale guerre* gained credence in France. During a visit to Washington in September 1951 de Lattre (who favored a buildup of national forces in Indochina) received assurances of a more speedy delivery of American aid and of a larger amount of it. At the same time he did not like inquiries about French military plans. A statement by the U.S. Departments of State and Defense on September 23 in connection with the visit revealed that the "participants were in complete agreement that the successful defense of Indochina is of great importance to the defense of all Southeast Asia."[86] Yet late the previous month the Joint Chiefs of Staff had warned against promising American armed forces to Indochina.

The visit of de Lattre to Washington was somewhat complicated by the arrival of Prime Minister Tran Van Huu of Vietnam fresh from the Japanese peace conference. "Le Roi Jean" was conducting negotiations partly on behalf of the Vietnamese government but without coordination with its prime minister now in the American capital. After meeting President Truman, Tran Van Huu departed without further ado.

A few weeks later a little-known congressman by the name of John F. Kennedy who had recently visited Vietnam candidly observed: "In Indochina we have allied ourselves to the desperate effort of a French regime to hang on to the remnants of empire. There is no broad, general support of the native Vietnam Government among the people of that area."[87] His most important source of information in Saigon was a U.S. official, Edmund Gullion, whom he had previously met, whose viewpoints he respected, and whom he would eventually appoint as an ambassador. General de Lattre did not like Congressman Kennedy and complained about him to the American Minister. Neither the Congressman, later Senator, later President of the United States, nor the General, later Marshal of France, would live to see the outcome in Vietnam. For de Lattre the end was very near; he returned to France in late 1951 where he died of cancer in January 1952. For some time, however, Bao Dai continued to be portrayed in many official circles in Washington as a leader with considerable nationalist support exercising real political power.*

While the General was in Indochina the United States was deferential to him. After the establishment of diplomatic relations the key Americans in Saigon were the Minister (later Ambassador) Donald R. Heath, his deputy, Edmund Gullion, and Robert A. Blum, head of the economic aid mission. Gullion and Blum with CIA officials differed from Heath in their evaluations and recommendations. The relations of de Lattre with Heath were cordial but not particularly so with Gullion and Blum. In fact, the General told Blum to his face that he was "the most dangerous man in Indochina."[88] Heath was basically sympathetic to the French and believed the United States should go slowly in pressuring them. Gullion, more forceful in his outlook, favored a target date for the complete independence of the Indochinese states. The outbreak of the Korean War, he realized, made it harder to urge the French to take such a position, and he was well aware of their argument that they were participating in a widespread conflict with communism in Asia.

When Blum left Saigon toward the end of 1951, fateful indeed were

---

*The Department of State long considered it necessary to urge Bao Dai to exercise much stronger and more aggressive leadership. On October 18, 1950, for instance, the American Minister in Saigon was instructed to see Bao Dai immediately after his return from a sojourn in France and firmly impress upon him the need to personally assume the reins of state and lead Vietnam into immediate and energetic opposition to the Communists. For this revealing telegram from Acheson to the American legation in Saigon, see *United States-Vietnam Relations, 1945–1967*, Book 8, pp. 388–90.

his conclusions—namely that "the situation in Indochina is not satisfactory and shows no substantial prospect of improving, that no decisive military victory can be achieved, that the Bao Dai government gives little promise of developing competence and winning the loyalty of the population, that French policy is uncertain and often ill-advised, and that the attainment of American objectives is remote."[89] As Blum's economic and technical aid had gone directly to the Indochinese at the village level, he had good sources of information. The French, especially the old colonial hands, were critical of the aid program, its personnel, and its publicity, believing that it undermined their preferred position. The growing American military assistance to the French, Blum believed, vastly weakened the psychological benefits of U.S. economic and technical aid. Yet the United States did not exert nor try to exert leverage upon the French authorities commensurate with its assistance.

Deepening U.S. Involvement. In 1952, the last full year of the Truman administration, the First Indochinese War assumed greater international dimensions. At the same time the Viet Minh substantially infiltrated the Red River delta. In Paris it was announced in early April that Jean Letourneau was to be French high commissioner in Indochina but keep his post as minister for the Associated States and General Raoul Salan was to serve as commander in chief. Progress was slow in the formation of a Vietnamese national army as agreed by Bao Dai and the French authorities in December 1950. The great majority of the officers were French; and Paris, insisting that the army be trained by the French, opposed American participation even by successful U.S. instructors from the military mission in Korea. Bao Dai at the civilian level made little inroads among the *attentistes*.

The United States during 1952 stepped up its diplomatic and financial efforts in the war. On January 28 John Sherman Cooper, indicating concern over Peking's possible direct intervention in Indochina, Thailand, or Burma, told the First Committee of the United Nations General Assembly that "his government had instructed him to state that any such communist aggression in south-east Asia, would, in its view, be a matter of direct and grave concern requiring the most urgent and earnest consideration by the United Nations."* In May Indochina was discussed by American leaders at the White House. Letourneau in a visit to Washington the next month was promised more U.S. military and economic aid,

---

*United Nations, General Assembly, Sixth Session, *Official Records*, First Committee, 503rd Meeting, January 28, 1952, p. 267. This was as far as the American Joint Chiefs of Staff would go. The British and French took a comparable position at the United Nations. Acheson, in *Present at the Creation*, pointedly observed that "this still left undetermined what, if anything, any or all of us would do about such an intervention," p. 675.

raising to more than 40 per cent the American support of French expenditures in the war. The French would use the additional assistance to build up the national armies of Vietnam, Cambodia, and Laos. A communiqué issued on June 18 significantly asserted that "the struggle in which the forces of the French Union and the Associated States are engaged against the forces of Communist aggression in Indochina is an integral part of the world-wide resistance by the Free Nations to Communist attempts at conquest and subversion."[90] The United States, it was noted, had a large part of the burden in Korea and France had the primary task in Indochina. At the same time Washington did not get the information and action it wanted in the latter. At the end of June Acheson, Eden, and Schuman could not agree on what to do should Peking ignore a warning about direct military intervention in Indochina. Acheson indicated only U.S. naval and air participation could be considered.

On June 25 President Truman in approving a statement of the National Security Council reached his last major conclusions on American objectives and courses of action in Southeast Asia. The conclusions of the Council and the President were reached only after considerable discussion in the highest government circles for several weeks. The basic issue was whether the United States was willing to go to war with Communist China to prevent Southeast Asia from falling into the Communist camp. Clearly the Joint Chiefs did not want to commit ground forces in Indochina, Thailand, or Burma nor join a combined military command to defend them. Involved in the discussions was not the question of the importance of Southeast Asia to the United States but rather the problems in holding the area.[91]

The conclusions of the Truman administration on June 25 merit particular attention; they would be carefully noted by President Eisenhower and his advisers. It was frankly asserted that "Communist domination, by whatever means, of all Southeast Asia would seriously endanger in the short term, and critically endanger in the longer term, United States security interests."[92] The consequences, expressed in domino terms of multiple repercussions, extended essentially to Japan and to "the stability and security of Europe." Therefore, an overt attack by Peking on Southeast Asia must be "vigorously opposed." The "successful defense of Tonkin," it was claimed, was "critical" to keeping mainland Southeast Asia in non-Communist hands.

If a Chinese overt attack did occur in Indochina, the United States, working with France, Great Britain, and any other friendly government, or under the auspices of the United Nations, would as a minimum provide "air and naval assistance as might be practicable" for the "resolute defense of Indochina itself" and would furnish the major forces (with at least British and French token ones) to interdict "Chinese Communist communication lines including those in China." Significantly France along with the Associated States would provide the ground forces to defend Indochina.

In a conclusion worthy of special note the statement of the National Security Council stressed that Washington should "make clear to the American people the importance of Southeast Asia to the security of the United States so that they may be prepared for any of the courses proposed herein."[93] The need of American public support was thus clearly identified. The implementation of the decision would leave much to be desired.

As relations between the United States and the State of Vietnam became more important, the American legation in Saigon was duly raised to an embassy and a Vietnamese embassy was established in Washington. On October 12 the 200th American ship bearing military aid arrived in Saigon. The North Atlantic Council meeting in Paris adopted a resolution on December 17 acknowledging that the "resistance of the free nations in South-East Asia as in Korea is in fullest harmony with the aims and ideals of the Atlantic Community" and agreeing that "the campaign waged by the French Union forces in Indo-China deserves continuing support from the NATO governments."[94]

Secretary Acheson's postmortem on American policy in Indochina, 1950–52, is caustic. He frankly says: "our conduct was [accurately] criticized as being a muddled hodgepodge, directed neither toward edging the French out of an effort to re-establish their colonial rule, which was beyond their power, nor helping them hard enough to accomplish it or, even better, to defeat Ho and gracefully withdraw."[95] After commenting on the limitations of coercing France he concludes: "So while we may have tried to muddle through and were certainly not successful, I could not think then or later of a better course."[96]

President Truman and Acheson were spared the perils of partisanship in American policy toward Indochina and Southeast Asia. Years later Truman emphatically responded on the bipartisan aspect behind policy.

President-elect Eisenhower was well aware of the seriousness of the situation in Indochina. As John Foster Dulles observed, they discussed the situation in December when Eisenhower was returning from Korea on the cruiser "Helena."

We realized [Dulles later asserted on May 7, 1954] that if Viet-Nam fell into hostile hands, and if the neighboring countries remained weak and divided, then the Communists could move on into all of Southeast Asia. For these reasons, the Eisenhower administration from the outset gave particular attention to the problem of Southeast Asia.[97]

Significantly the briefing of the President-elect in the White House by Secretary Acheson in the presence of President Truman spotlighted the situation in Indochina. Acheson noted that Washington, London, Paris, Canberra, and Wellington in military discussions had not been able to devise "agreed military solutions against the contingency of overt Chinese intervention in Indo-China." The French now wanted political discussions on the subject and "this is an urgent matter upon which the new administration must be prepared to act."[98]

Eisenhower Takes Up and Carries On. When President Dwight D. Eisenhower went to the White House on January 20, 1953, his administration reviewed the situation in Southeast Asia. Although the United States was deeply involved in Indochina it had not reached a point where American credibility or reliability was overwhelmingly committed. Public attention in the United States was focused on the Korean War. The new administration could have altered course, especially as one party had replaced its rival in the White House. President Eisenhower and his Secretary of State John Foster Dulles, however, accepted the basic guidelines of U.S. policy in Indochina developed by President Truman and Secretary Acheson. A Republican administration did not alter the course formulated by a Democratic one. Eight years later, when the Democrats returned to power in the White House, and eight years after that, when the Republicans took over again, questions of continuity of policy in Southeast Asia would again arise.

The key figure in American foreign policy during most of the Eisenhower administration was Foster Dulles. Although the President occasionally intervened, he had such confidence in his Secretary of State that the latter was given considerable leeway. Assistant Secretary of State for Far Eastern Affairs Walter S. Robertson also had significant influence. Allen W. Dulles, a brother of the Secretary, was head of the CIA. As a result of the outlook and temperament of the President, Secretary Dulles (with his personal relationships) was in many respects for a number of years the architect of U.S. policy in East Asia.

A few days after assuming office, Foster Dulles in a broadcast to the nation noted the importance of the rice bowl of peninsular Southeast Asia to the Soviet bloc. "And you can see," he said, "that if the Soviet Union had control of the rice bowl of Asia that would be another weapon which would tend to expand their control into Japan and into India."[99] In May Congressman Walter H. Judd, influential in administration circles on East Asia, along with three colleagues issued a report of their special study mission in Asia, noting that "if Indochina should fall, Thailand and Burma would be in extreme danger; Malaya, Singapore, and even Indonesia would become more vulnerable to the Communist-power drive" and asserting that "the Communists must be prevented from achieving their objectives in Indochina."[100] The domino theory, later popularized by President Eisenhower, had its roots, as already indicated, in the Truman administration. As far back as early 1950, for instance, Dulles had written about it with respect to Indochina in *War or Peace*,[101] and the outbreak of the Korean War had served to highlight the relationship of events in one Asian country to others. In all likelihood the loss of mainland China to the Nationalists was germinal in the theory. At any rate it is well reflected in relevant National Security Council papers after then in the First Indochinese War.

In his first message on the State of the Union President Eisenhower on February 2, 1953, associated the war in Korea with the "same calculated assault" being pressed by the aggressor in Indochina and Malaya. His instructions to the Seventh Fleet to cease shielding Communist China from the Nationalists—the so-called unleashing of Chiang Kai-shek— were related to the "two flanks" concept being considered in 1953. Korea was one flank and Indochina the other, with Communist China in the middle. If Nationalist China created "some sort of a threat in the center," U.S. policy might be more successful in the flanks.[102] The United States, however, did not pursue this approach to its logical conclusion, namely, support for the return of Chiang Kai-shek to the mainland.

Eisenhower and Dulles were eager to end the First Indochinese War on favorable terms, for among other reasons this might speed French ratification of a treaty creating the European Defense Community (EDC). Establishing an army from six states in Western Europe—Germany, Italy, France, Belgium, the Netherlands, and Luxembourg—the EDC plan had been proposed by France in September 1950, and the negotiated treaty had been submitted by the French government to the National Assembly for approval in January 1953, the month Eisenhower assumed power. The Soviet Union strongly opposed EDC and sought to link an end to the First Indochinese War with the French rejection of the treaty. Moscow, a Eurasian power, like Washington, an Atlantic-Pacific power, found itself occasionally torn between giving priority to objectives in Europe and in Asia.

The process of linking the Korean and Indochinese wars, well under way during the Truman administration, was persistently continued by Eisenhower. On March 28 Washington and Paris agreed that if Peking took advantage of a Korean armistice "to pursue aggressive war elsewhere in the Far East" such a step would conflict with the foundations upon which any Korean armistice would rest.[103] High Commissioner Jean Letourneau and Prime Minister René Mayer had made a trip to

Washington that month in search of more U.S. aid for Indochina under a plan quickly drawn up by General Salan and later revised and adopted by General Henri Navarre. The Americans approved the principles of the plan and began to study the financial aspects of its implementation.

Around the middle of April U.S. policy toward Southeast Asia further crystallized in speeches by Eisenhower and Dulles, with a spring Viet Minh invasion of Laos providing static in the background. On April 16 the President, urging Moscow to cease its "direct and indirect attacks" in Malaya and Indochina, raised the possibility of "united action" by the Free World against Communist aggressions in both Korea and Southeast Asia. The united action appeal—more dynamic in effect than a call for collective security—would take on more significance the next year. Two days later Secretary Dulles stressed the new dimensions of "priority and urgency" for East Asia in current U.S. policy, mentioning that Japan, Korea, Formosa, Indochina, and Malaya faced a "single hostile front" requiring cooperative effort by the countries of the Free World.

The invasion of Laos by the Viet Minh led to Washington's statement of sympathy for its people on April 17 and its making available for Laotian defense some cargo planes with American civilian pilots. The French, of course, did all they could to aid the landlocked kingdom but strongly urged that an appeal to the United Nations be channeled through Paris. The Thai, aroused over the Viet Minh invasion of a neighbor along the Mekong, especially since Peking only in January had announced the establishment of a "Thai Autonomous People's Government" in southern Yunnan, sought help from the United States. Dulles announced on May 9 that small arms and ammunition had been delivered and other emergency military aid would follow. Testifying for the Mutual Security program, the Secretary had stressed the seriousness of the situation in Indochina and of the "chain reaction" if it were lost. In May General Navarre arrived in Vietnam to replace General Salan.

Criticism of French policy in Indochina was evident in both London and Washington, powers with colonial experience in Southeast Asia. On May 11 Prime Minister Winston Churchill in an address to the House of Commons criticized in effect the refusal of France to take the war to the United Nations. Eisenhower thought Paris should place the conflict before the world organization. Some French military leaders believed an effort should be made to get an international guarantee of the territorial integrity of Laos so that the French High Command in Indochina would be relieved of major responsibilities there. Despite all the pressures Paris under the circumstances was opposed to taking the war in Indochina to the United Nations—to "internationalizing" it—viewing the conflict as a matter of domestic concern.

In 1953 criticism of the French failure to provide complete independence for the Associated States was more pronounced than ever. On July 3 Joseph Laniel, who had recently become Prime Minister, announced that France intended to "perfect" the independence of the Associated States through negotiations with them. Privately Bao Dai reportedly remarked—"What do they mean 'perfect'? What's the matter with the French—they're always giving us our independence. Can't they give it to us once and for all?"[104] The declaration of July 3 did not remove the widespread doubts about the intentions of France. In October the Laotian and French governments concluded a "Treaty of Amity and Association" but the Laotians were not certain of their exact degree of independence as a member of the French Union. Cambodia, however, as a consequence of a vigorous and dramatic campaign waged by King Norodom Sihanouk in France, Canada, the United States, Japan, and Thailand, as well as at home, obtained concessions between August and October which enabled him to return triumphantly in November to his capital. By the following February Cambodia had achieved almost complete autonomy. Formal negotiations between France and the State of Vietnam after bitter discussions and considerable maneuvering in Saigon were delayed until 1954.

American congressional criticism of the French on the independence issue was especially noteworthy. The report of Congressman Judd and others in May made the point in no uncertain terms and the House Committee on Foreign Affairs in June emphasized the need for assurances on "ultimate independence." In June Senators Everett M. Dirksen and Warren G. Magnuson after a study mission called for a "target of independence" for Vietnam. In May Senator John F. Kennedy had been informed by the Department of State that France had gone beyond the point of no return in transferring control to Vietnam, Cambodia, and Laos and that they had become sovereign states. On June 30, however, Kennedy in a Senate speech asserted that "genuine independence as we understand it is lacking in this area [Indochina]" and "regardless of our united effort, it is a truism that the war can never be successful unless large numbers of the people of Viet-Nam are won over from their sullen neutrality and open hostility to it and fully support its successful conclusion."[105] After Senator Barry Goldwater in July wanted to amend the Mutual Security Act so as to withhold funds from France until it agreed to set a target date for complete independence of the Indochinese states, Kennedy sought to soften the wording so as to use U.S. aid to encourage the granting of independence. Neither man succeeded. Later Kennedy sarcastically asserted that "every year we are given . . . assurances . . . that the independence of the associated states is now complete;

... [and] that the independence of the associated states will soon be completed under steps 'now' being undertaken."[106] In October Senator Mike Mansfield, after a study mission to Indochina, warned that the "entire issue" there might be thrown "into doubt" if "the indigenous power latent in nationalism" were not utilized.[107] Later in the year a survey team under Senator H. Alexander Smith of the Senate Committee on Foreign Relations and another under the auspices of the House Committee on Foreign Affairs visited Southeast Asia and their observations were comparable.

President Eisenhower subsequently wrote in his memoirs that the French government while he was NATO Commander "apparently saw no need to publicize any ... sincere, simple, and selfless pronouncement [on independence and self-determination upon military victory],"[108] fearing its effect on other parts of the French Empire like Algeria, on the French prosecution of the war, and on French prestige in the world. He noted that "it was generally conceded [in 1953] that had an election been held, Ho Chi Minh would have been elected Premier."[109] The President was well aware that the insistence of France that the conflict was domestic in nature, despite the threat, created a situation where the United States could not support the maintenance of a colonial empire but at the same time felt the need to defeat Communist aggression. Ambassador Heath in Saigon, the American on the receiving end of the instructions, tried to persuade key Vietnamese that they would surely receive their full independence, but that they would have to await the conclusion of the fighting lest a French grant of immediate sovereignty lead to a withdrawal of the Expeditionary Corps. The French, however, never really answered the key question: When will the Vietnamese receive their full independence after the war?

On July 14 representatives of Great Britain, France, and the United States after a conference in Washington in which they discussed the security of East Asia and the international implications of an armistice in Korea stated that the effort in defense of the independence of Vietnam, Cambodia, and Laos "against aggressive Communism is essential to the Free World."[110] Franco-American discussions also occurred on U.S. aid to Indochina. Eisenhower, it should be noted, did not want France to follow his example of settling for a divided Korea. The occasion of the Korean armistice and of the sixteen-nation declaration on July 27 enabled Foreign Minister Georges Bidault to assert that collective security had triumphed in the Korean War. General Navarre soon noted that Peking's direct involvement in Indochina would produce a United Nations and United States response, risking a third world conflict. Yet the French government hoped the Korean armistice would lead to a cease-fire in Indochina. On September 10 at a meeting of the ANZUS Council Australia, New Zealand, and the United States discussed both Indochina and Korea where it was indicated "Communist aggression has led to outright hostilities."[111]

President Eisenhower, Secretary Dulles, and others in the administration steadily stressed the dangers of Communist aggression, the role of Peking, and the importance of Indochina to Southeast Asia, the United States, and the Free World. During the early summer a special U.S. military mission was in Saigon and elsewhere in Indochina to survey the situation. In August the President in a speech at the annual conference of governors emphasized the chain reaction in Southeast Asia if Indochina fell to the Communists. On September 2 Dulles asserted in an address that "a single Chinese-Communist aggressive front extends from Korea on the north to Indochina in the south."[112] He went on to issue a grave warning to Peking against sending its army into Indochina as it had in Korea: "The Chinese Communist regime should realize," he said, "that such a second aggression could not occur without grave consequences which might not be confined to Indochina."[113] Dulles had moved from the President's comments the previous month on Peking-backed subversion of Indochina and its "most terrible significance" for America to comments on outright aggression by Peking and its consequences for Communist China. It is significant that the Secretary of State was now warning that American reaction might be at the very source of the Communist aggression. Undersecretary of State Bedell Smith three days later stressed the direct relationship of Indochina to the security of the United States. Official Washington, however, did not actually believe that Peking would mount an invasion of Indochina on the Korean model.

On September 29 the United States in an agreement with France undertook in effect to underwrite the Navarre Plan by providing additional aid up to $385 million before the end of 1954. The Plan called for the quick buildup of indigenous forces in Indochina to assume static defense duties so that the French Expeditionary Corps, also increased, could deal with regular Viet Minh units and intensify the war. By 1955 the latter would be decisively defeated. Although the U.S. role in the conflict was increased through the support for the buildup of the indigenous forces and theoretically also through a number of French undertakings[114] at American request in the conduct of the war, Paris was still in the driver's seat. Moreover, Washington's desire for France to ratify the EDC treaty was a factor in the additional U.S. aid.[115] Interested congressional leaders had been informed of the new program prior to the announcement of the Franco-American agreement.

On October 27 Premier Laniel, citing American policy in Korea and reflecting strong sentiment in France and Britain, told the National Assembly that he favored the Navarre Plan but stressed the importance of an honorable peace through local or international negotiations. The reaction to Laniel's speech in Washington was quick. In early November Vice-President Nixon who was visiting the battle area flatly said that "it is impossible to lay down arms until victory is completely won."[116] Ho Chi Minh complicated the situation by proposing peace negotiations.

Meanwhile, near the end of October, President Eisenhower and the National Security Council adopted a "basic national security policy" vis-à-vis the Soviet Union. It called for the development and maintenance of "a strong military posture, with emphasis on the capability of inflicting massive retaliatory damage by offensive striking power."[117] Nuclear weapons in the event of hostilities would be considered "to be as available for use as other munitions." Indochina and Formosa, it was asserted, were "of such strategic importance to the United States that an attack on them probably would compel the United States to react with military force either locally at the point of attack or generally against the military power of the aggressor."[118]

Early in December a summit conference was held in Bermuda by Eisenhower, Churchill, and Foreign Minister Bidault in place of Laniel who was ill. Here in pleasant surroundings the "vital importance" to Free World defense of the French war effort was stressed, and preconditions for agreeing to a Moscow proposal for a conference of five powers including Communist China were approved. On December 29, Dulles at a press conference praised the Navarre Plan and indicated his belief that the war would be over in a year.

Dien Bien Phu, however, entered the bloody equation. Both Laos and Vietnam were involved in the military calculations. In late December, for instance, the Viet Minh again invaded Laos, this time heading toward Savannakhet, but they soon returned to Vietnamese territory. General Navarre's valley fortress at Dien Bien Phu in western Tonkin was designed over a period of time to hold up the access of the Viet Minh to Laos and the Red River delta, to impair the flow of Chinese supplies, and to draw the enemy into a costly and self-defeating frontal attack against his 12,000 elite troops. In mid-December the General believed his chances of success against Viet Minh assaults were 100 per cent, but on January 1, 1954, he realistically indicated apprehension in a secret report to Paris. Nevertheless, two American chiefs of MAAG and many higher ranking U.S. officers in Washington believed the Dien Bien Phu operation was sound. Eisenhower did not agree. Meanwhile the fighting along the northern delta of the Red River favored Ho's forces; they achieved real victories in 1953. Moreover, Peking gave Ho increased aid after the Korean War in terms of training, supply, and equipment. According to a map of General Navarre in May, the Viet Minh controlled the greater part of Vietnam, large zones in Laos, and a few areas in Cambodia.[119] Maps in the near future would be less optimistic.

At the close of 1953 the United States was inclined to resist directly at places of its choice an armed attack by Communist China on Indochina, but for the present it was trying to counterbalance Peking's aid to Ho Chi Minh. Washington was not willing to send American combat forces to aid the French though a Chinese attack might alter the situation; nor was it willing to use or threaten to use nuclear weapons only on behalf of the French in Indochina. The United States wanted real independence for Vietnam, Cambodia, and Laos, but if the French Expeditionary Corps withdrew—a development Washington did not favor during the war—the Bao Dai regime, weak and unpopular, would collapse, and Indochina would be Communist. Dilemmas, inconsistencies, and ambiguities confronted Washington and Paris as they approached the new year.

Toward Possible Intervention. On January 12, 1954, the Secretary of State after consultation with his influential brother about the forum delivered a major address on the "New Look" in defense policy before the august and influential Council on Foreign Relations in New York. In the background was the war in Indochina. Dulles favored a "massive retaliatory power," "a maximum deterrent at a bearable cost," "a great capacity to retaliate, instantly, by means and at places of our choosing."[120] In his speech he was warning the aggressor about counting upon a future sanctuary and he was publicly indicating that nuclear weapons used in retaliation would be viewed as conventional. It was evident that great stress was placed on U.S. air power and less emphasis on U.S. ground power. The speech was sufficiently broad to receive several interpretations and constructions and to produce various clarifications and qualifications. It created little stir in London or Paris but aroused concern in Moscow and Peking. Although Dulles said in March the address was not connected with the current situation in Indochina it was bound under the circumstances to be applied to U.S. policy in the area. Reflecting on the one hand an effort to be more tough with international communism by going beyond mere containment but without committing U.S. ground troops in brush fires along the vast periphery of the Soviet-Chinese bloc, and reflecting on the other hand an effort to economize through a stretchout in the cost of national defense, the New Look was a product of controversy among the armed services and civilian government officials. The possible use of tactical and strategic nuclear weapons in limited and general war was particularly an issue. In many respects the New Look, partly based on the experience of the Korean War, did not stand the test of international events.

In the same month, January 1954, President Eisenhower approved a policy statement of the National Security Council on American objectives and courses of action in Southeast Asia.[121] It was comparable in major respects to the one Truman supported in June 1952. The "falling domino" metaphor was clear. The keystone in defending the mainland of Southeast Asia, except for the possibility of Malaya, was identified as the "successful defense of Tonkin." An immediate aim was to assist the French to "eliminate organized Viet Minh forces by mid-1955." The possibility of U.S. involvement in all-out war with Communist China and even the Soviet Union was recognized. It was stressed that the importance of Southeast Asia to U.S. security should be made clear to the American people so that they might "be prepared for any of the courses of action" proposed in the policy statement.

Despite American optimism about the outcome of Dien Bien Phu the President announced on February 6 that 40 B-26 bombers and 200 U.S. technicians would go to Indochina. The Air Force technicians would help service planes turned over to France since French personnel were not acquainted with them. The Americans joined 125 other technicians in Indochina under MAAG but they were scheduled to leave by mid-June.* A number of American civilians flew "flying boxcars" provided France by the United States in supply missions in Indochina under contract between General Claire Chennault's famed Civil Air Transport in Taiwan and France. In April American Air Force planes were ordered to fly "certain French Union personnel" to Indochina from France and North Africa. Although the United States in the First Indochinese War never sent armed forces into combat, its use of personnel in Air Force assignments came very close to it. Answering a question bearing on American involvement in the war in Indochina, President Eisenhower asserted on February 10 in a news conference: "I cannot conceive of a greater tragedy for America than to get heavily involved now in an all-out war in any of those regions, particularly with large units."[122] On the same day he significantly informed Dulles, who was in Berlin, that "General O'Daniel's most recent report is more encouraging than given to you through French sources."[123] "Iron Mike" John W. O'Daniel, just on another special military mission to Indochina where he visited Dien Bien Phu, was highly regarded at the White House. Later he was assigned as Chief of MAAG in Saigon, as a consequence of National Security Council action, in an effort to increase American influence in the prosecution of the war.

Providing U.S. material assistance to the French in Indochina was less

*As far back as December 1952 Washington approved a temporary loan of twenty-five to thirty American Air Force personnel to participate in the maintenance of C-47s turned over to the French.

dangerous in terms of American intervention than offering U.S. personnel, especially men in uniform. The MAAG Chief there was informed in December 1953 that Indochina had the highest priority for military assistance. By the middle of 1954 it was estimated that the United States was paying 78 per cent of the total war cost, a rise from 60 per cent after the $385 million grant of September 1953. Between June 1950 and May 1954 the United States, it is claimed, provided military and economic aid worth $2.6 billion in the war effort against the Communists in Indochina. By far the greater proportion was military ranging from small arms to trucks, tanks, planes, and warships. Mars in Indochina was heavily armed by weapons arriving from both the United States and Communist China.

Meanwhile official American expressions about the favorable military outcome of the war were steady regardless of Democratic or Republican administrations. Senator John F. Kennedy publicized in a Senate speech on April 6, 1954, a list of bright predictions made between February 1951 and March 1954.[124] Prophets listed were General Francis G. Brink of MAAG, February 1951, Secretary of State Dean Acheson, June 1952, President Dwight D. Eisenhower and Secretary of State John Foster Dulles, May 1953, General John W. O'Daniel, Assistant Secretary of State Walter S. Robertson, and Secretary Dulles later in the year, Secretary of Defense Charles E. Wilson and Undersecretary of State Walter Bedell Smith, February 1954, and Chairman of the Joint Chiefs of Staff Admiral Arthur W. Radford and Secretary Dulles in March. Curiously omitted from Kennedy's list was Harold Stassen who had recently visited Indochina as head of the Foreign Operations Administration and had reported in early March: "I returned from the Far East with the strong conviction that the forces of freedom are growing stronger and that the Communist position is weakening."[125]

In January and February American military maneuvers in the Western Pacific, alone or with friends, accentuated U.S. interest in the area. In February President Syngman Rhee of Korea indicated his willingness to offer one division to help the government of Laos resist the Viet Minh. He first sought the approval of Washington. After giving the subject some thought the Joint Chiefs on March 1 expressed opposition to the proposal as not being in the best interests of the United States.[126]

The foreign ministers of the United States, the Soviet Union, Great Britain, and France at a meeting in Berlin from January 25 to February 18 (essentially on European problems) decided to call a conference in Geneva on April 26 on Korea and Indochina. As regards the latter it would consist of their own countries plus Communist China and other interested states. The decision was interpreted in many circles as a propaganda victory for Moscow and Peking. Premier Laniel, however, was under mounting pressure to stop the fighting in Indochina through nego-tiations. In other words, the French wanted to end the war if honorable terms were possible. (France indicated at Berlin it would not make any arrangement that directly or indirectly turned Indochina over to the Communists.) Dulles, worried over the coming conference and the gen-eral situation, was convinced some regional defense was needed in Southeast Asia to back the French. He wanted to create a position of strength before going to the conference table. As a number of prominent Americans foresaw, the Chinese Communists between the end of the Berlin Conference and the beginning of the Geneva Conference (Febru-ary 18 and April 26) stepped up their aid to Ho Chi Minh who strove to achieve a knockout blow at Dien Bien Phu.

On March 13 General Vo Nguyen Giap began the siege of the for-tress. Three days before, President Eisenhower had stressed the United States would not be involved in the war unless Congress declared it. Sen-ator John F. Kennedy on March 9 informed the Senate that a partition of Vietnam "would be the first step toward the seizure of complete con-trol in that area by Communist forces" and believed the United States at the Geneva Conference should take a stand that "the war should be con-tinued and brought to a successful conclusion."[127]

In preparation for the American position at Geneva the Joint Chiefs of Staff in a memorandum for Secretary Wilson on March 12 called for a continuation of the fighting with military victory the objective. They op-posed a cease-fire prior to a satisfactory settlement, a coalition govern-ment in any of the Associated States, the partition of any one, and self-determination through free elections. It was frankly asserted that a "set-tlement based upon free elections would be attended by almost certain loss of the Associated States to Communist control."[128] A comparable position was taken five days later by the Subcommittee of the President's Special Committee on Indochina, the first being headed by General Graves B. Erskine and the second by Bedell Smith. Representatives of the State Department on the Erskine committee reserved their position. Secretary Wilson expressed himself on March 23 as fully in accord with the viewpoints of the Joint Chiefs and General Erskine's committee.

To Intervene or Not to Intervene. On March 20 General Paul Ély, Chairman of the French Chiefs of Staff, came to Washington to discuss the situation in Indochina, to get speedier help for the war effort, and to determine the U.S. reaction if airplanes based in Communist China inter-vened in Indochina. Only recently the French had rejected the idea of an American army training mission. By the time Ely arrived, General Navarre was already requesting air and parachute help in driving off the Viet Minh attacks at Dien Bien Phu.

The stage was set for a climactic period in U.S. policy toward Southeast Asia. The discussions between the French General and President Eisenhower, Admiral Radford, Secretary Dulles, and other high-ranking American officials revealed Washington's deep concern over Dien Bien Phu. The President as a former military officer took a professional interest in the matter. He told Radford, according to Ély, to give France the means to prevent the fall of the fortress.[129] As requested by Ély, the United States agreed on March 25 (so Ély thought) to provide U.S. air support should the Chinese air force intervene.[130] Radford himself in a letter to Eisenhower on March 24 said "no commitment was made" but that the matter was referred to Dulles. (The Joint Chiefs on April 8 recommended that U.S. action should depend upon the circumstances.) Radford asked Ely to stay another twenty-four hours and suggested the possibility of a future American air raid by night along the perimeter of Dien Bien Phu. *Vulture*, a limited action in target and time, would involve around 60 B-29 heavy bombers from Clark Field in the Philippines escorted by 150 fighters from the Seventh Fleet. Radford stressed the raid was only an offer; France would have to approve the action; and then Washington would want to review *Vulture* further as it meant U.S. entrance into the conflict.[131] According to Ély, Radford believed he had Eisenhower's support.[132] He returned home on March 27 not only with his belief in assurances of U.S. reaction should the Chinese send their planes into the conflict, but also with a promise of an immediate loan of 25 more B-26s for the war effort. He had opposed the idea that France accept an American military role in training indigenous forces in Indochina and, of course, he had to refer *Vulture* to his government for decision.[133] There was no basic change in MAAG as a supply organization, nor in French control of military aid and of intelligence and planning.

Vulture, however, a product of staff planning, never reached the operational stage although it would be a source of great contention and would not die easily. As if in preparation for U.S. intervention, President Eisenhower on March 24 stressed "the most transcendent importance" to America of Southeast Asia. A week later at a news conference he implied, at least to some observers, that U.S. intervention, if it came, would primarily be with air power and sea power, ground forces being used only as a last resort. "What we are trying to do," he said, "is to make our friends strong enough to take care of local situations by themselves."[134]

Concerned over developments in the Navarre Plan and the consequences of its failure in Indochina, and following consultation with several senators, representatives, and ambassadors, Secretary Dulles on March 29 in a major pronouncement before the Overseas Press Club sought a "united action" approach to the crisis and for all practical purposes opposed negotiations and partition. Prophetically he asserted: "If the Communist forces won uncontested control over Indochina or any substantial part thereof, they would surely resume the same pattern of aggression against other free peoples in the area."[135] The Secretary proclaimed: "Under the conditions of today, the imposition on Southeast Asia of the political system of Communist Russia and its Chinese Communist ally, by whatever means, would be a grave threat to the whole free community."[136] The significance of "by whatever means" should not be underestimated, for Dulles was clearly enlarging the scope of the warning.

The remarks of President Eisenhower and Secretary Dulles in late March aroused concern, apprehension, and controversy in Congress. Was it being prepared for U.S. intervention? Would it really be consulted? What did it actually know about the critical military developments in Indochina? Senator Hubert H. Humphrey on March 31 complained of the administration's reluctance to keep responsible congressional committees fully informed.

Conflicts of interest and policy among Paris, London, and Washington could not be submerged and came to a head in April. Basically Dulles wanted to warn Peking through a coalition to stop its aid to the Viet Minh or face possible naval and air action against its coast, and to create a collective security arrangement to assure the future of Indochina and Southeast Asia. Basically the French favored American military action to rescue a limited target in Vietnam but wanted no broader steps in Indochina or against China that would jeopardize the outcome of the Geneva Conference and "internationalize" the war. Bascially the British opposed any allied warning to China or any allied military effort in Indochina before the Geneva Conference but were willing like the French to join in some kind of a collective security arrangement for Southeast Asia after it.

Meanwhile Dien Bien Phu was "hell in a very small place."[137] At first General Navarre was skeptical about *Vulture* much to the surprise of Ély, but on April 4 he favored the plan if implemented before April 11. The success of the Chinese in the delivery of antiaircraft guns and heavy artillery to General Giap at Dien Bien Phu was altering the course of battle. By the first week of April the fortress was imperiled, and the possible implementation of *Vulture* became a matter of triple priority by its advocates.

On April 3, allegedly "the day we didn't go to war," Radford and Dulles secretly discussed *Vulture* with a small number of influential members of Congress including Senators Lyndon B. Johnson and

Richard B. Russell and Congressmen John McCormack and Joseph P. Martin.[138] Dulles reportedly wanted a joint resolution of Congress authorizing the President to use naval and air power and ground forces in Indochina. Admiral Radford gave a briefing on the military plan as currently conceived: the air attack would involve 200 planes from aircraft carriers in the South China Sea and further air support from U.S. bases in the Philippines. Nuclear weapons were available for the planes on the carriers, it would appear, but would be used only in the event of direct massive Chinese intervention. Questions about American ground support if the air attack failed, about the backing of U.S. allies, and about the possible intervention of Communist China were raised. It developed that only Admiral Radford of the Joint Chiefs favored *Vulture*, that ground forces were not considered an immediate need but would be used if necessary, that the allies had not yet been consulted, and that Secretary Dulles did not think Peking would intervene as in Korea.

The congressional delegation of five Democrats and three Republicans gave Radford neither a green nor a red light for *Vulture* but rather a yellow one. Senator Johnson reportedly raised very searching questions, and he urged the need for allies.[139] The congressional group made three conditions for its backing, conditions which were vital in subsequent developments: a coalition must be formed including Great Britain (the United States must not intervene alone); France must agree to speed independence for the Associated States (Washington must not be placed in the position of fighting a war for colonialism); and France must agree to keep the Expeditionary Corps in Indochina if U.S. forces entered the conflict (congressional recognition of the realities of power in the area was clear though somewhat contradictory to the goal of real independence).[140] American forces, it should be noted, would not have served under French command. As Eisenhower was critical of Truman's way of involving the United States in the Korean War and as he believed congressional backing and allied aid were imperative for intervention, the three conditions were backed by Eisenhower and stood at a White House meeting of the President, Radford, and Dulles the evening of April 4.* Intervention, however, was not yet ruled out.

At the suggestion of Dulles, Eisenhower wrote to Prime Minister Churchill on the same day and called for "a new, ad hoc grouping or coalition" of nations having a "vital concern" in stopping Communist expansion in East Asia—the United States, Great Britain, France, Australia, New Zealand, Thailand, the Philippines, Vietnam, Cambodia, and

---

*Dulles himself by now did not think an air strike was the best way to enter the war and he realized more than ever the United States should not act alone.

Laos.[141] The coalition of countries must be strong and willing to fight. Such a coalition would serve to warn Peking to stop helping the Viet Minh or face allied intervention in Indochina. The proposal confirmed British impressions about the thrust of American policy. As for the question of actual military intervention, Churchill believed, according to Eden, that what London was "being asked to do was to assist in misleading Congress into approving a military operation, which would in itself be ineffective, and might well bring the world to the verge of a major war."[142]

Meanwhile the French who thought that *Vulture* was really what the Americans meant by intervention officially decided on April 4 to approve the military operation, indicating their belief it would not extend the war. The decision was conveyed to Ambassador C. Douglas Dillon who mentioned the role of Congress in any effort but forwarded the request on April 5. On April 3 Dulles had told French Ambassador Henri Bonnet in Washington of the need for an immediate coalition before the opening of the Geneva Conference capable of speedy action and willing to warn Peking, as the sixteen nations had done with respect to Korea on July 27, 1953. The Secretary made it a point to condemn the ideas of partition or coalition government in Indochina. Paris soon realized that *Vulture* was no longer the focus of "united action"; the focus, involving a wide range of policy decisions, was a coalition of Western and Asian powers directed against a Communist takeover in Indochina and against Peking's aid to Ho Chi Minh. Dillon, acting with the authority of Eisenhower, informed Bidault on April 5 that U.S. intervention would require the approval of Congress and the help of allied states in addition to France. Paris was apprehensive about the time lost in activating *Vulture* while "united action" in terms of a military alignment was being discussed.

Dulles and Eisenhower, convinced more than ever of the need to rally support, made statements on April 5 and April 7, the former before the House Committee on Foreign Affairs and the latter at a press conference. The Secretary stressed the expansion of the military aid in technicians and matériel of the Chinese Communists to the Viet Minh at Dien Bien Phu and reiterated his warning to Peking of March 29. The President for the first time made explicit the " 'falling domino' principle," Indochina being the first domino in a row. The possible results of the fall of Southeast Asia to communism, he said, "are just incalculable to the free world."[143]

On April 6 the National Security Council formally decided (with the subsequent approval of President Eisenhower) that military and mobilization planning should be promptly started in case American intervention became necessary and that the United States before the

Geneva Conference should try to organize a regional grouping to defend Southeast Asia against the Communists along with seeking British support for American objectives in East Asia and pressing Paris to quicken its program for the independence of the Associated States. The President's viewpoint was noted that if the regional grouping could be created congressional authorization for American participation should be requested.

Still not firmly decided by the time Dien Bien Phu fell was the question of whether Washington was actually prepared to commit combat forces in the near future, if possible in some kind of a regional effort, to prevent the partition or loss of Indochina. Before the National Security Council on April 6 was NSC Action No. 1074-A which in its annex analyzed alternative forms of American military intervention. The previous day the President's Special Committee on Indochina had produced a report on long-range policy and courses of action relative to possible contingencies in Southeast Asia not yet covered by established National Security Council action. The lack of decision, a source of great anguish to the planners, left the future still in the lap of events.

Senator Kennedy for his part in a Senate speech on April 6 though warning that a coalition government or a partition in Vietnam would lead to "eventual domination" by the Communists focused on French failure to give genuine independence to the country. Without independence, the Vietnamese would not fight; nor would Asian nations join the United States in a coalition. If American troops were sent into the war, he believed, they would face the same difficulties as the French unless the Vietnamese and other Asians really gave support. He was convinced U.S. intervention was "virtually impossible in the type of military situation which prevails in Indochina."[144] Republican Senator Everett M. Dirksen reacted to Kennedy's speech. Dirksen did not want to see a repetition of Korea in Indochina. In Korea, he noted, the United States had provided 90 per cent of the troops and funds, and he "would be the last to go along with a program of that sort."[145]

On the same day France decided to reject the proposal for a coalition and for a warning to Peking prior to the Geneva Conference, Dulles being informed of the decision two days later. Churchill in a letter to the President received on April 7 said his government was willing to talk with the Secretary. The British, now thinking largely of negotiations and a possible partition of Vietnam, were skeptical on both political and military grounds of the American approach to the crisis. They were worried about the implications for Indochina and the world and about the stress on air power vis-à-vis ground power. Dulles, who by April 7 had dropped his idea of a joint warning to Peking and wanted simply a statement of common purpose, left for London on April 10, but in earnest talks on united action with Churchill and Eden could not alter their policy. In the communiqué of April 13 only "the possibility" of collective defense for Southeast Asia and the Western Pacific could be examined. Eden later drafted a position paper which was approved by the cabinet and the contents were given Dulles.

The Secretary of State had no greater success in Paris. The war in Indochina was greatly agitating the French public and was threatening to overthrow the Laniel government. On April 9 Premier Laniel told the National Assembly resistance at Dien Bien Phu would not stop the effort for an honorable peace at Geneva. A statement of Dulles and Bidault on April 14 pointedly noted that on the eve of the Geneva Conference the Communist aggression in Vietnam was at a new climax at Dien Bien Phu; the invasion of Laos had been renewed; and Cambodia had been attacked. Agreement was reached, however, only to "examine the possibility" of a collective defense of Southeast Asia and the Western Pacific.

The situation at Dien Bien Phu continued to worsen. Although some Americans like Bedell Smith had likened the battle to a "modern Thermopylae" it was believed with good military reason that France could lose the garrison and the fortress but still keep up the war in Indochina. But Dien Bien Phu, even without benefit of modern television, had been magnified far beyond its value. It had become such a symbol that its collapse would have major psychological repercussions on the will of France to continue the war.* The home front in the later years of the conflict was far more serious than the military front.

Meanwhile Vice-President Nixon asserted in off-the-record remarks on April 16, probably as a trial balloon, that Washington could not afford to sustain another retreat in Asia and might have to face realities and send forces to Indochina. The Department of State in effect supported Nixon's remarks, but soon both the Vice-President and Secretary of State backtracked on any implications of unilateral military action. Nevertheless, the National Security Council late in April strongly opposed any unsatisfactory settlement negotiated by France, and in that event, suggested to the President ending U.S. aid to Paris and possibly continuing the war essentially as a U.S. effort.

Dulles in a tactical step called for a meeting of the United States and of representatives from various missions in Washington on April 20 to discuss the organization and work of an ad hoc preliminary body on

*A National Intelligence Estimate approved April 28 concluded that the fall of Dien Bien Phu as far as Indochina was concerned would be primarily important for its psychological and political effects on the French Union position. For text see *United States-Vietnam Relations, 1945–1967*, Book 9, pp. 400-05.

defense in Southeast Asia. He thought he had the support of the United Kingdom but on April 18 the British Ambassador, Sir Roger Makins, was ordered to avoid the meeting. Dulles was furious and believed Prime Minister Nehru was responsible for the decision. Eden, however, wanted not only to escape "united action" before Geneva but also to keep open the question of membership on the international ad hoc body. It is also true that Nehru in late March began to take an active public interest in the Indochinese crisis and to exert pressure abroad, for he feared the struggle might escalate into a global war. The proposed gathering on April 20 was altered to focus on Korea.

As the First Indochinese War crested at Dien Bien Phu, the neighboring countries of South and Southeast Asia quite naturally took a much greater interest in the pros and cons of united action. Thailand, of course, had been deeply concerned about the war and its international implications especially since 1950. Bangkok was aroused over the Viet Minh invasions of Laos in 1953 and 1954 and of Cambodia in April 1954. It promptly approved of the united action plan of Secretary Dulles, who announced the decision on April 10 as he was leaving for London. Eden a few days later indicated to Dulles London was prepared to discuss a guarantee of Bangkok. The Philippines was increasingly concerned over developments across the South China Sea, but Manila though anti-Communist did not want to appear to support French colonialism. On April 18 President Magsaysay reacted to Dulles' united action appeal by saying his country was willing in principle to back a joint declaration with Washington "against Communist aggression in Indo-China" but also wanted in the statement "an affirmation of the rights of all peoples to freedom and independence."[146] Two other Southeast Asian states, Burma and Indonesia, joined India, Pakistan, and Ceylon as Colombo Powers in their first meeting in Ceylon, April 28 to May 2, where their prime ministers gave considerable attention to the Indochinese War. They urged France to commit itself to complete independence for Indochina and called for an immediate cease-fire agreement and a negotiated settlement by the principal parties. Foreign Secretary Eden who was very sensitive to the influence of Asian Commonwealth members in the crisis was in frequent touch with them. On April 29 he sent the Prime Ministers of India, Pakistan, and Ceylon a telegram asking them what they were willing to do to back an Indochinese settlement if they approved of it.

On April 20 Dulles again headed for Paris, this time to attend a NATO Council session of foreign ministers. Here in the City of Light rose again the question of an allied military effort to help the French. As the situation at Dien Bien Phu was desperate, Bidault on April 23 asked

Dulles for an American air strike to save the fortress. The latter indicated it was too late to prevent its fall but Bidault disagreed. Dulles cabled Eisenhower who told Bedell Smith that a united front was needed and British support should again be sought. Dulles reportedly informed Eden that night that if London would agree to united action he would recommend to the President that he ask Congress for support. Eden was unmoved. On April 24 Radford who had arrived from Washington ardently pressed Eden in the presence of Dulles for approval of an air intervention. Once more and again that day Eden refused to change his mind, though he decided to return to London to consult Churchill. The British cabinet in an emergency session on Sunday, April 25, supported Eden's viewpoint on no intervention before the Geneva Conference. It agreed to join in guaranteeing a settlement made at Geneva, or if no settlement were reached, in considering other joint action. (London was also willing to join Washington, according to Dulles, in a *secret* study of possible steps to defend Thailand and the rest of Southeast Asia if Paris capitulated in Indochina.) The French Ambassador in London pressured Eden to change his mind on intervention but the British cabinet in a second meeting on April 25 refused.

Aftermath and Postmortem (Early May). With the position of the British solid as the Rock of Gibraltar and with the veto power given them at the time by Washington, the Eisenhower administration began to alter its course and move nearer to the position of London. But it was only nearer. The President spoke in Washington on April 26, when the Geneva Conference on Korea and Indochina opened (Korea being the first topic for discussion), and stressed a "modus vivendi" in Indochina. He linked the conference with the atomic age. Was he hinting that if the meeting failed and the Communists continued the war, the United States might use nuclear weapons? Eisenhower compared Indochina to a "cork in the bottle"; and noted that the outcome of the struggle was "going to have the greatest significance for us, and possibly for a long time into the future."[147] On the same day the President told a group of congressmen that the United States was not about to "carry the rest of the world on our back,"[148] and three days later he talked about a "practical way of getting along."[149]

After Dulles turned over to Bedell Smith on May 3 the chairmanship of the American delegation at the Geneva Conference on Korea and Indochina and returned home shortly thereafter he faced criticism in and out of Congress on his handling of the call for united action and of the entire Indochina crisis. President Eisenhower partly in a move to defend his trusted associate stated on May 5 that plans for creating a security arrangement for Southeast Asia were progressing, a fact which could have an "important bearing" on the Geneva Conference. There was, he noted, a "general sense of urgency."[150] Two days later Dulles himself in an address to the nation, one reflecting changes in conversation with the President, asserted that the current situation did not justify U.S. military intervention in Indochina. But he clearly warned that if an armistice or cease-fire at Geneva opened the road to a "Communist takeover and further aggression," the United States "would be gravely concerned."[151] Work would continue on a collective defense system in terms of participation and commitment. On the same day Eisenhower also discussed with Dulles necessary preconditions for U.S. military intervention in Indochina as well as a possible approach on the matter to France.

Between the President's and Secretary's statements Senator Lyndon B. Johnson spoke on May 6 to a Jefferson-Jackson Day Dinner in Washington under the auspices of the Democratic Party. He called the French defeat in Indochina the most "stunning reversal" in the history of U.S. foreign policy; America's enemies had caught it "bluffing" and America's friends were "frightened and wondering"; the United States was "in clear danger of being left naked and alone in a hostile world."[152] Although the speech was made in the partisan atmosphere of a fund-raising dinner, it became more important in the perspective of Johnson's presidency.

By the time Dien Bien Phu fell on May 7 after an epic siege of many long days and nights and by the time the Indochinese phase of the Geneva Conference began on May 8 disunity was a major factor within the United States—on the Hill, in the Pentagon, and in the administration. Disunity was a major concern among the key Western allies—the United Kingdom, the United States, and France. And disunity was a major consideration among the non-Communist forces within Indochina itself.

Congress opposed unilateral intervention but even more strongly, any intervention at all.[153] Many members were confused about the situation in Indochina and about the administration's postures. It was not until February 1954 when the President announced the sending of Air Force noncombatant technicians to Indochina that debate rose beyond negligible proportions in Congress. Eisenhower's action aroused apprehension and concern in the Senate, and he had difficulty persuading some of the members the step was necessary. Nevertheless a few voices in Congress were raised in favor of U.S. intervention, and the President, if he had gone before a joint session asking for it at the height of the Dien Bien Phu crisis, might have secured a favorable resolution.

In the Pentagon differences of opinion were marked between Admiral Radford and General Matthew B. Ridgway, Army Chief of Staff, who was supported by his Chief of Plans and Development, General James M. Gavin. Ridgway later wrote:

> when the day comes for me to face my Maker and account for my actions, the thing I would be most humbly proud of was the fact that I fought against, and perhaps contributed to preventing, the carrying out of some harebrained tactical schemes which would have cost the lives of thousands of men. To that list of tragic accidents that fortunately never happened I would add the Indo-China intervention.[154]

Ridgway had sent an army team of experts to Indochina to make a survey, and its report on the needed resources there of a major intervention in the light of U.S. available resources at the beginning was read carefully.* (Eisenhower later observed that the concept of an air strike was "silly.")

Administration differences focused in April on immediate U.S. military intervention in Indochina, if necessary alone, and allied approval of united action as a precondition to American military intervention. Nixon favored the former approach while Eisenhower supported the latter. Moreover, there were still differences of opinion on how far the United States should push the French toward giving full independence to Indochina. Dulles privately believed the French had gone as far as they could, given the war and given the capacities of the people of Indochina for self-government. But publicly he usually had to reflect the pressure from Congress and others to urge further steps. The independence issue remained like the sword of Damocles. France and the State of Vietnam on April 28 agreed on two treaties, one of independence and the other of association in the French Union, but the basic issue was not removed.† The fears of a number of prominent Americans materialized: After the military effort of the French collapsed, they would leave behind them non-Communist nationalism in Vietnam in the doldrums, and this would prove one of the greatest assets of Ho Chi Minh. To this dismal analysis some Americans would add the European dimension. As a major U.S. policy objective was to secure French approval of the European Defense

*For the basic viewpoint of the army see *United States-Vietnam Relations, 1945– 1967*, Book 9, p. 332. For instance it was flatly asserted that "a military victory in Indochina cannot be assured by U.S. intervention with air and naval forces alone" and that "the use of atomic weapons in Indochina would not reduce the number of ground forces required to achieve a military victory in Indochina."

†When the settlement of April 28 went into effect on June 4 upon French ratification, the State of Vietnam was technically responsible for international agreements that France had previously made on its behalf. Paris after the cease-fire in July quickly moved to divest itself of "civil administration" responsibility in its zone. In fact, it has been argued that legally no such responsibility existed as of June 4.

Community, its final rejection confirmed the viewpoints of the critics that Indochina and EDC should never have been linked in the first place.

Disunity in April among Washington, London, and Paris on military intervention in Indochina and on a united front in Southeast Asia, involving attitudes toward Communist China and Indochina and questions of timing before or after the Geneva Conference, gave the Communists an advantage. In the end the French joined the Americans in blaming the British for the failure of intervention. The French price of defeat even without conscripts was heavy: 65,000 men killed and 82,000 wounded in the course of the war. In contrast to allied disunity the Communist ranks of the Soviet Union, the People's Republic of China, and the Democratic Republic of Vietnam before Geneva were relatively solid.

President Eisenhower wrote the postmortem on the First Indochinese War when he stated: "I am convinced that the French could not win the war because the internal political situation in Vietnam, weak and confused, badly weakened their military position."[155] During the conflict he successfully maintained a policy of indirect U.S. involvement, notwithstanding great pressure, in contrast to a policy of direct U.S. involvement adopted in the Second Indochinese War.

And so by May 8 the United States had traveled a tortuous road to the Geneva Conference on Indochina, a road that began with the success of the Chinese Communists in 1949 and with the Russian nuclear explosion of September; then encompassed the Korean War and the Japanese peace settlement; and finally the intensified course of the First Indochinese War overlapping the previous two. Each of these developments in its own way drew Washington deeper into the waters of Southeast Asia. But how deep should the United States plunge? Or should it retreat to the shoreline, properly attire itself, and return to its more traditional environs?

||| THE WATERSHED OF 1954

The Geneva Conference on Vietnam, Cambodia, and Laos producing the settlement of July 20 and July 21, 1954, followed by the Manila Conference in September leading to the signing of the Southeast Asia Collective Defense Treaty and the creation of the Southeast Asia Treaty Organization marked the watershed in U.S. policy in the region.

The two conferences were related to Washington's fundamental question of how to organize international security in the area. The Senate did not want to be involved in a war in Southeast Asia but was willing to undertake significant treaty commitments in an effort to prevent one. At a later time when deterrence failed, Congress would come to resent the ensuing war and to question previous U.S. commitments; it would not want to support new ones. Ironically the administration of President Dwight D. Eisenhower made the basic commitments of 1954 and the administration of his Republican successor, President Richard M. Nixon, had to cope with the senatorial disillusionment evident in the resolution on "national commitments" in 1969.

Through the events of 1954 emphasis in U.S. policy in Southeast Asia fully shifted from decolonization to security. The sun had almost set on the Western empires, but many in Washington feared it was now rising on a future Communist realm. The implications of this concern would condition American policy for many years. The origins of the Second Indochinese War stem to a substantial extent from the events of 1954.

At this critical period the United States was not really prepared in foreign policy formulation or decision making to cope most effectively with the mounting problems of Southeast Asia. (Perhaps no country ever was or is!) All the elements of the mix, as the Pentagon Papers so well show, were present in Washington—the White House, Congress, State, Defense, CIA, and the aid and information establishments. But how foreign policy actually emerged and jelled, apart from the obvious roles of key personalities, was a mystery even to many people who had access to the highest classified sources. A very large number of little decisions on Southeast Asia—and sometimes bigger ones—were made on a daily basis by lower-echelon officials like desk officers with the consequent "bubble up" process taking place. Also a number of the same people in or from various departments and agencies kept turning up in one capacity or another to influence U.S. policy in the region. These observations, of course, are not limited to that part of the world but they are certainly relevant to it.

Military assistance to Southeast Asia and particularly Indochina, it should be stressed, gave the Pentagon considerable influence in the development of foreign policy before, during, and after 1954 while CIA activities in the area were definitely pronounced though obviously not televised. Some departments and agencies were clearly more influential than others and acted more independently. CIA was a case in point. At the summit in policy formulation was the National Security Council under the President, which was especially active during the Eisenhower years.

The relations between the White House and Congress continued to reflect the separation of powers and the jealousies between the executive and legislative branches. In 1954, however, President Eisenhower did not finally ask for a Gulf of Tonkin resolution in connection with the First Indochinese War (as President Johnson did in 1964 in connection with the evolution of the second) and congressional leaders in April 1954 were not sympathetic under the circumstances to saving Dien Bien Phu or intervening later in the spring (as they were in August 1964 to backing the White House in the wake of the Gulf of Tonkin episode).

5 THE GENEVA AND MANILA CONFERENCES

GENEVA SETTLEMENT ON INDOCHINA

Conference Diplomacy. Lasting from May 8 to July 21 the Geneva Conference on Indochina was the first time the five major powers to emerge from World War II met to discuss a crisis of common interest in Southeast Asia.* The gathering was no Paris Peace Conference of 1919 or

*A few inside accounts of the Geneva Conference have been published. One of these is Anthony Eden's chapter "The Geneva Conference, April–July 1954" in *The Memoirs of Anthony Eden: Full Circle*, Houghton Mifflin, Boston, 1960, pp. 120–63. For a book reflecting considerable contact with French official sources see Jean Lacouture and Philippe Devillers, *La Fin d'une guerre: Indochine, 1954*, Éditions du Seuil, Paris, 1960. A revised version of the book is Philippe Devillers and Jean Lacouture, *End of a War: Indochina, 1954*, Praeger, New York, 1969. Significant for an American view is Chester L. Cooper's chapter "Blueprint for a House of Cards: Geneva, 1954" in his *The Lost Crusade: America in Vietnam*, Dodd, Mead, New York, 1970, pp. 75–101. Accounts in the Pentagon Papers afford considerable insights. See *United States-Vietnam Relations, 1945–1967*, Study Prepared by the Department of Defense, Book 1, Government Printing Office, Washington, 1971, The Geneva Accords, 1954, and Book 2, Origins of the Insurgency, 1954–1960. An excellent analysis of the Geneva Conference is found in The Senator Gravel Edition, *The Pentagon Papers: The Defense Department History of United States Decisionmaking on Vietnam*, Vol. 1, Beacon, Boston, 1971, pp. 108–78.

Congress of Vienna of 1814–15 in terms of rank and protocol, but Messrs. V. M. Molotov, Chou En-lai, Anthony Eden, Georges Bidault, and later Pierre Mendès-France were prominent figures on the international scene. And John Foster Dulles in Washington guided the activities of Walter Bedell Smith at Geneva as Jawaharlal Nehru in New Delhi supervised those of V. K. Krishna Menon. In fact, the diplomacy of the conference was conducted not only in Geneva but also (often adversely) in binational or multinational meetings from Washington to New Delhi. Plenary sessions of the Geneva Conference especially at its beginning and conclusion (eight in all) were significant; at least eighteen restricted sessions were also held much to the general dislike of the Americans and of the press; but a large part of the work was done in the course of informal private discussions among various individuals and in military subcommittees. During a period of the conference after June 20 the participants were almost entirely men of much lower rank in the absence of their superiors.

Like the fighting during the negotiations of the Korean War, bloody conflict continued in Indochina. The Viet Minh registered significant military gains and the French, badly weakened in morale, retreated in the face of the enemy or simply evacuated zones. The negotiations, of course, could not but be influenced by the fighting in Indochina. Prime Minister Pierre Mendès-France on July 7 believed it necessary to inform the National Assembly that if his efforts for an honorable peace failed, he would seek before resignation to secure approval for the next French government to send draftees to Indochina, and he pointedly gave orders for inoculation of French troops in Germany against yellow fever. Undoubtedly these French troops were not enthusiastic about either getting shots for yellow fever or going to Indochina. However, it can be observed candidly that escalation of a war through inoculation is not a major step on the ladder of deterrence.

It was the backstage rattling of the sword (irrespective of the bluffing involved) by Foster Dulles and others in Washington that had greater impact on Molotov and Chou En-lai. The possibility of American military intervention could not be completely discounted in Moscow and Peking, and it probably was a major consideration in their urging a reluctant Ho Chi Minh to agree to the temporary partition of Vietnam set at the seventeenth parallel and to accept an independent Laos and Cambodia. Several reports of American interest in intervention received publicity in Geneva, greatly annoying Eden when he believed the chances for a settlement might be jeopardized. Nevertheless, he thought the deterrent power of the U.S. hydrogen bomb aided the success of the Geneva Conference and prevented a major war. Also, as offstage plans for some kind of a collective security arrangement for Southeast Asia developed, spearheaded by Dulles, Peking became aware that the region would not become a quick power vacuum despite French difficulties.

The United States for all practical purposes was not a full participant in the Geneva Conference on Indochina. It followed an ambiguous course in the negotiation of the settlement. Dulles himself did not attend,[1] and for a while it appeared that even Undersecretary of State Bedell Smith would not lead the American delegation toward the end of the conference. (U. Alexis Johnson and Walter S. Robertson were members.) Dulles was very much opposed to giving sanction to any agreement that served to recognize Communist territorial expansion by force of arms. Eden's suggestion about "regrouping areas" in Vietnam on May 25 aroused Smith as well as many Indochinese. The Eisenhower administration was partly motivated by political considerations at home since a congressional election was due in November. As many Republicans had accused the Democrats in the 1952 presidential campaign of selling China down the river to the Communists, the administration did not want to appear to be selling any part of Indochina to them. At the same time Eisenhower knew he had won votes in 1952 on his pledged efforts to end the war in Korea and he realized American military intervention in the First Indochinese War would not be popular.

Nevertheless, the President on the evening of May 10 met with Dulles, Radford, and Wilson to discuss a statement received that day made by Laniel to Dillon that the former "would . . . require definite information from me as to what the US Government might be prepared to do in the way of military effort."[2] At the meeting Eisenhower asked Dulles to draft a message the President could present before a joint session of Congress wherein he would ask authority in a resolution to commit U.S. forces to Indochina. A draft joint resolution was prepared and circulated in government circles.

In a key telegram on May 11, one approved by the President himself and only for the eyes of Ambassador Dillon, Dulles instructed the latter, under the given circumstances, to present orally but not in writing to Laniel the "general terms" required for military intervention. It was believed they would have some influence on "current French decisions in [the] military field in Indo-China and in [the] political field in Geneva."[3] A significant shift was the fact that the United Kingdom was no longer given a veto. Furthermore, the conditions of American military intervention would have to be accepted by the French cabinet and backed by the French National Assembly.

As a result of requests authorized by President Eisenhower, numerous studies at the highest levels of government were prepared by departments and agencies on the assumption that American armed forces did intervene in Indochina and on the alternate assumptions that Peking did or did not militarily intervene. The Joint Chiefs of Staff in their report on May 26 reiterated what they had indicated on May 20—that from the American viewpoint bearing in mind all East Asia *"Indochina is devoid of decisive military objectives and the allocation of more than token* U.S. armed forces *in Indochina would be a serious diversion* of limited U.S. capabilities."[4] In the event of intervention the United States should utilize limited naval and air forces; the deployment of ground forces was not supported but American training of those of the Associated States was urged. It was pointed out that "the employment of atomic weapons is contemplated in the event that such course appears militarily advantageous."*

The Department of State in its planning focused on the questions of economic warfare against Peking, United Nations action, and the juridical relations in the French Union aimed at giving effect to the independence of the Associated States. Other branches of the government such as the Central Intelligence Agency, the Operations Coordinating Board, and the Bureau of the Budget submitted relevant reports. Indeed, the effort involved in contingency planning must have consumed a considerable amount of time, and the possibility of American military intervention must have seemed more than a passing fancy.

Yet it is interesting to note that Foster Dulles on June 14 stressed that as far back as May 17:

> I ... pointed out that probably the French did not really want intervention but wanted to have the possibility as a card to play at Geneva. I pointed out that the Geneva game would doubtless be a long game and that it could not be assumed that at the end the present U.S. position regarding intervention would necessarily exist after the Communists had succeeded in dragging out Geneva by winning military successes in Indochina.[6]

Meanwhile the Secretary of State on May 11 in a news conference significantly asserted that "what we are trying to do is create a situation in Southeast Asia where the domino situation will not apply."[7] He implied that the security of Southeast Asia could be maintained even if Vietnam, Cambodia, and Laos were lost. He unfortunately added that Laos and Cambodia were not "essential parts" of Southeast Asia, a comment later deleted from the official record. The President on the same day observed that collective defense would offset the falling domino principle, and on May 12 he indicated a row of dominoes could be built sufficiently strong through united action to survive the fall of one of them. Also on May 12

---

*On May 21 the Joint Chiefs had stressed that if Indochina fell to the Communists the *concept* for the defense of Southeast Asia should not be a static one (Korea model) but an offensive one to attack the source of "military power of the aggressor [China]."[5]

Smith in Geneva was given written instructions whereby he could under certain circumstances withdraw the American delegation from the conference. The telegram personally approved by the President after considerable consultation and a meeting of the National Security Council on May 8 opposed a "cease-fire, armistice, or other settlement" that in effect would cause the peoples of Indochina to be "amalgamated into the Communist bloc of imperialistic dictatorship."[8] The United States supported the position of Nguyen Quoc Dinh, the foreign minister of Bao Dai, given in a speech on the same day: opposition to partition, sole recognition of the State of Vietnam under Bao Dai, free elections under the auspices of the United Nations when the Security Council believed they could truly be free, and an international guarantee of the State's political and territorial integrity.*

In early June dismal reports circulated in Washington on the military situation in Indochina fathered by Secretary Wilson who had returned from a visit to East Asia and by General James A. Van Fleet who had also made a tour. Van Fleet testified before two Senate committees on June 3, and four days later reportedly told Eisenhower that forces from the United States, South Korea, and Formosa should be prepared to go to Indochina. At the suggestion of Australia on May 15 a high level staff conference of Great Britain, France, the United States, Australia, and New Zealand met in Washington June 3–11 to assess the military situation. Earlier, it is interesting to note, Washington had authorized a team of Americans under Colonel Edward G. Lansdale to go to Vietnam and start covert operations against the Viet Minh.

On June 4 Dulles told the Senate Foreign Relations Committee that the situation in Indochina was grave but not hopeless. Focusing in a series of statements on U.S. military intervention, he held out the possibility but subjected it to various qualifications. He noted at a news conference on June 8 that the "whole nature" of Peking's aggression would have to change and on June 10 in a speech at Seattle he observed that Communist China had not openly invaded Indochina. Conditions for possible U.S. intervention were detailed on May 15 by the Department of State and by Dulles on May 25 and June 11. In a major speech at Los Angeles on the latter date the Secretary of State listed five conditions:

(1) an invitation from the present lawful authorities; (2) clear assurance of complete independence to Laos, Cambodia, and Viet-Nam; (3) evidence of concern by the United Nations; (4) a joining in the collective effort of some of the other nations of the area; and (5) assurance that France will not itself withdraw from the battle until it is won.[9]

*In the course of the conference Washington refused French requests to pressure Saigon in its demands to be more cooperative. But when the chips were down late in the conference the United States gave little support to the Saigon delegation.

At home congressional support was necessary. The Secretary went on to stress that "any future overt military Chinese Communist aggression" in the Southeast Asian or Pacific area "would threaten island and peninsular positions which secure the United States and its allies" and "would be a deliberate threat to the United States itself."[10] Dulles indicated that Washington would take the matter to the United Nations and consult its allies but warned in words inserted by President Eisenhower himself that "the right of self-preservation would demand that we—regardless of any other country—meet the issue squarely."[11] These were frank words!

Actually by the middle of June French reverses in the Red River delta and their effects in Paris contributed to an American decision for all practical purposes that U.S. intervention in circumstances apart from an overt Chinese Communist attack would be useless. The Secretary of State observed on June 8 that France could not have an "indefinite option" on U.S. intervention regardless of adverse developments.

Dulles' speech on June 11, where he also accused the Communists of being "dilatory" in the Geneva negotiations while "intensifying" the fighting in Indochina, came one day after Eden's at the Geneva Conference, where he carefully summarized the state of the negotiations. Concerning the cessation of hostilities, it was agreed a cease-fire should be simultaneous in Vietnam, Cambodia, and Laos, the Vietnamese problem being examined first; as regards armistice supervision, it was agreed some type of international supervision was essential but opinions differed on the procedures, powers, and composition of the international armistice commission. As for the future of Cambodia and Laos, the conference was deadlocked. Here Eden, who stressed the differences in ethnic background, language, religion, and culture between Cambodia and Laos on the one hand and Vietnam on the other, reflected the stubborn efforts of the Democratic Republic of Vietnam to secure conference representation of its puppet "Pathet Lao" and "Khmer" resistance governments at the expense of the Royal Governments of Laos and Cambodia.

Eden accompanied Churchill to Washington in late June during the absence from the Geneva deliberations of the ranking Russian, Chinese, French, and American representatives. There was evidence, during mid-June at least, that Washington wanted the conference to fail. On June 12 Laniel had resigned as premier of France, and on June 18 Mendès-France had replaced him pledging to resign by July 20 if he failed in reaching an honorable peace in Indochina. In Washington Churchill and Eden discussed the overall situation with Eisenhower and Dulles against a background of U.S. concern over Eden's suggestions for a Locarno settlement in Southeast Asia. The two powers drew up a secret list for Mendès-France of minimum terms later known as the "seven points" they were willing to respect in an Indochina settlement. These conditions focused on the independence and integrity of Cambodia and Laos and safeguards for a "retained Vietnam" at a line drawn not further south than one "running generally west from Dong Hoi."[12] This line was about halfway between the seventeenth and eighteenth parallels. (The French had originally sought the latter.) A joint statement of Eisenhower and Churchill on June 28 indicated both governments would "press forward with plans" toward a collective defense arrangement in Southeast Asia regardless of the outcome in Geneva. The Communists there were warned about unacceptable demands on France. A meeting of the ANZUS powers on June 30 calling for collective defense in the region and shortly thereafter sessions of an Anglo-American study group on Southeast Asia set up by the two leaders emphasized the summit decisions. The study group considered how a Geneva settlement on Indochina might be guaranteed and how collective defense in Southeast Asia might be organized. On June 29 Eisenhower and Churchill agreed in a declaration—called but quickly forgotten the Potomac Charter—that "in the case of nations now divided against their will, we shall continue to seek to achieve unity through free elections supervised by the United Nations to insure they are conducted fairly."[13] The next day President Eisenhower in a press conference talked about "peaceful coexistence" without "appeasement."[14]

Secretary Dulles like Admiral Radford was apprehensive lest elections in Vietnam result in a victory for Ho Chi Minh. On July 7 he cabled Paris that no date should be set for them now. Later he complained to Mendès-France about the "whittling-away process" from the minimum terms Britain and America had agreed upon in Washington. Shortly before the conclusion of the Geneva Conference Dulles regretted in a cable to Smith the absence of a United Nations role in Vietnamese elections.

As Eden, Mendès-France, Molotov, and Chou En-lai were going in mid-July to attend the final sessions of the Geneva Conference, the British and French leaders were especially eager that Dulles or Smith represent the United States lest allied harmony before the Communists be even more impaired. Dulles, mindful of unrest in Congress, was adamant, but agreed on July 12 to accept an invitation from Mendès-France for a meeting in Paris along with Eden. After discussion among the three men the conditions drawn up in Washington by the British and Americans were confirmed by Mendès-France, and Dulles publicly stated on July 15 that a "formula for constructive allied unity" had been devised. Bedell Smith left for Geneva the next day with new instructions.

Eden and Molotov as cochairmen of the Geneva Conference on Indochina worked rather closely during it. Their private meetings helped to iron out difficulties and prevented it from breaking up. Each in some respect had the task of moderating one of his allies—Eden with respect to the absent Dulles and Molotov with respect to the absent Ho Chi Minh. Both cochairmen had their own national interests in a negotiated settlement. Eden wanted particularly to end the fighting lest the First Indochinese War escalate into a wider conflict in East Asia or throughout the world; Molotov, as already indicated, especially desired to use a settlement in Indochina to prevent French ratification of EDC.

Pierre Mendès-France was eager to end quickly a costly and unpopular war on the best possible terms. Facing the Vietnamese, Chinese, and Russian Communists, he wanted to salvage as much as he could of the French presence in Indochina. Here expectations centered on economic interests and cultural values. His setting a date for resigning the premiership if he could not get an honorable peace was dramatic and a play to the public, but it did serve to speed developments. It also aroused concern in Western circles over the future of EDC.

Chou En-lai was particularly interested in implementing the tactics of peaceful coexistence through a settlement at Geneva that both the French and Viet Minh could accept and that could enhance the stature of Communist China in the Afro-Asian world. On April 29 New Delhi and Peking had reached an agreement on Tibet which embodied the Five Principles of Peaceful Coexistence: mutual respect for sovereignty and territorial integrity, nonaggression, no interference in each other's internal affairs, mutual benefit and equality, and peaceful coexistence.* When Chou En-lai visited Nehru in New Delhi, U Nu in Rangoon, and Ho Chi Minh along the Chinese-Vietnamese border during the period of the Geneva Conference when the ranking individuals were away, the Five Principles were on his mind. Chou En-lai also was conciliatory in meetings in June with Eden and Mendès-France. Peking's courtship of the Colombo Powers and tactics of peaceful coexistence would produce dividends at the Bandung Conference the following April.

Despite the image Chou En-lai was trying to project at Geneva he proved a tough negotiator. Like Molotov and the Viet Minh, he wanted an Indochina that was openly in the hands of the Communists or dominated by them. But Chou En-lai, like Molotov, was willing to take half a loaf in the hope of a whole loaf in a reasonable period of time. Peking, having emerged from the costly experience of the Korean War without driving the Americans into the sea, wanted to concentrate on economic

*The Five Principles were the result of long correspondence between New Delhi and Peking, Nehru first calling them the *Panch Shila* as a result of a visit he later made to Indonesia.[15]

development. A war or showdown with the United States over Indochina was not desired in either Peking or Moscow. And after all, they believed time was on the side of communism in Indochina. It is difficult, however, to assess the strength of the pressure Moscow and Peking placed on the Viet Minh at Geneva; suffice it to say, the representatives of Ho Chi Minh apparently were not able to play one comrade against the other.

The maximum desiderata of the Viet Minh were presented by Pham Van Dong, Deputy Prime Minister, in his speech at a plenary session on May 10. France in a blanket settlement was asked to recognize the independence and sovereignty of the Democratic Republic of Vietnam and of Pathet Lao and Khmer (the resistance governments in Laos and Cambodia) and to withdraw its armed forces from Indochina. French economic and cultural interests would be recognized and the three Indochinese countries might enter the French Union. Free elections, supervised by local committees, would take place in each country to establish for each a unified government, the elections being held under conditions providing for "freedom of activity for the patriotic social parties, groups and organizations."[16] A cease-fire would be effected after the above measures were implemented; entry of arms and military forces from the outside would end; and mixed commissions of the belligerents would supervise the settlement. Chou En-lai and Molotov supported the speech although the latter pointedly suggested on May 14 a commission of neutral nations should supervise the armistice.

The retreat of the Democratic Republic of Vietnam from the maximum demands of May 10 must have been painful for Ho Chi Minh especially since the military initiative was on his side and the Viet Minh forces were on the road to victory. Within only a few days Molotov and Chou En-lai influenced the Viet Minh to acquiesce to the idea of a cease-fire before a political accord. This was an important development in a chain of events.

The question of the seating of Khmer and Pathet Lao representatives also was not resolved to the satisfaction of Ho. It is significant that Pham Van Dong in his remarks on May 10 was thinking of an Indochinese settlement favorable to communism, not just a Vietnamese one. Even before he spoke it had been widely understood by his major colleagues that the participants at the conference from Southeast Asia would be the three Associated States and the Democratic Republic of Vietnam. Although the subject of seating certainly was not dead Moscow and Peking in the end solved it by the device of indefinitely postponing the topic. Eden who had been in touch for some time privately with Molotov about the Viet Minh demands on representation was pleased when Chou En-lai around the middle of June indicated it would not be hard to get the Viet Minh to withdraw their "volunteers" from Cambodia and Laos. The Chinese leader favored bilateral military talks between the commands of the Democratic Republic of Vietnam and those for the Royal Governments of Cambodia and Laos. The breakthrough on the issue probably prevented the Geneva Conference from collapsing.

Another retreat for Ho Chi Minh came in connection with the partition of Vietnam. In late May the Viet Minh revealed a temporary partition was possible. At an unofficial secret meeting on the night of June 10 between Ta Quang Buu, Vice-Minister for National Defense, and Brigadier General Henri Delteil of France along with two others further indications pointed to the fact that the Viet Minh would approve an armistice involving the division of Vietnam, providing the demarcation line was acceptable. Chou En-lai reportedly urged Ho Chi Minh when they later met to be flexible on the line. In the end, at the suggestion of Molotov in Geneva, the Viet Minh settled for the seventeenth parallel instead of the thirteenth as originally sought.

As regards national elections, the Democratic Republic agreed to holding them in July 1956 contrary to its recommendation of six months after the cease-fire. Molotov on July 19 was influential in setting the date. Also, the attitude and role of Chou En-lai and Molotov as regards the final composition and powers of the International Control Commission were not very pleasing to the Viet Minh. Finally, late the very night of July 20, Molotov gave concessions to Cambodia on its international status as a sovereign state. Disturbing likewise to the Democratic Republic was the assurance of Chou En-lai two days earlier to Mendès-France that he would no longer support Viet Minh claims for creating an autonomous Pathet Lao government in a part of Laos, the provinces of Sam Neua and Phong Saly.[17]

Pham Van Dong and other Viet Minh leaders were reportedly bitter over the alleged betrayal of their cause by their Communist allies. Tillman Durdin, a distinguished correspondent of The New York Times, and Jean Lacouture and Philippe Devillers, prominent French authors, have commented on the Viet Minh reaction. However, Ho Chi Minh had fought a long, costly war and he could use time to recoup his losses. Moreover, he did not want to take the risk of open American military intervention should the Geneva Conference fail and the fighting continue. Furthermore, South Vietnam might collapse anyway. Besides, if the Geneva settlement was implemented as he desired, the transfer of the struggle from the military field to the political arena would have successful results.

The Associated States of Indochina did not have an influential role in the overall settlement at Geneva. After Ngo Dinh Diem formally became prime minister on July 7 (another "Double Seventh") his viewpoints were officially represented at the conference. However, Dr. Tran Van Do bitterly complained at the failure of the French to consult him while they were in frequent contact with Pham Van Dong. The former official was reduced to the pathetic role of criticizing from the fringes of the Geneva gathering the decisions being made about his country. The delegations from the Royal Governments of Laos and Cambodia strongly opposed any representation by the Pathet Lao and Khmer resistance regimes at the conference and were pleased to see their attitudes confirmed.

Lurking in the background at Geneva was V. K. Krishna Menon who had arrived on May 22 for informal talks. Prime Minister Nehru in a speech on May 15 had indicated India would welcome an invitation to participate in a settlement. Menon's role was not major in the Geneva negotiations but India's participation in the implementation of the settlement would be important. In view of the close ties between Nehru and Menon the presence of the influential Indian official was not without significance.

The Geneva Accords. The Geneva settlement on Indochina was the result of genuine negotiations.* No one at the beginning could have predicted the terms of the final accords. It can be argued that the phraseology was often legally defective, inexact, and ambiguous precisely to enable agreement. Consensus for the most part existed only on a cease-fire. Anthony Eden's handling of the final plenary session is a lesson in glossing over differences. Significant also are the methods of achieving assent to various accords—signature, verbal approval, and silence. The settlement reflected the military situation that one side despite its great advantages had not inflicted surrender on the other, which in turn might conceivably alter the military situation by getting the intervention of a major outside power. The making of the accords could have been torpedoed at Geneva by the Soviet Union, Communist China, France, and the United States as well as by the Democratic Republic of Vietnam. It is

*For an analysis of the conference and settlement see George McTurnan Kahin and John W. Lewis, *The United States in Vietnam*, Dell, New York, 1967, pp. 43–63. See also Donald Lancaster, *The Emancipation of French Indochina*, Oxford for the Royal Institute of International Affairs, London, 1961, pp. 313–37. The most detailed analysis, legal in its thrust, is Robert F. Randle, *Geneva 1954: The Settlement of the Indochinese War*, Princeton, Princeton, 1969. He has utilized the Dulles Oral History Collection and private papers of the late Secretary. A comparison of Randle, Eden, Cooper, Lacouture and Devillers, and the Senator Gravel and Government Printing Office Pentagon Papers, all previously cited, reveals the complexity of events and the differences in interpretation. Just what did happen, for instance, on certain important days in the spring of 1954? It is doubtful if any definitive study on the Geneva Conference and Accords can ever be written.

doubtful if Great Britain, given its military stance in East Asia and its degree of influence, or the State of Vietnam, which only had nuisance impact at the time, could have torpedoed them. Eden was the architect insofar as any architect existed, his role being perhaps too fulsomely recognized by Molotov at the final session.

The Geneva settlement, like Sun Yat-sen's San Min Chu I, evoked praise from people of political persuasions as far apart as A is from Z. It looked like King Arthur's Camelot (in its better days) to many in the Second Indochinese War. Indeed, the nearest consensus for many years was founded on a return to Geneva. But, of course, each wanted to interpret for his own benefit what a return to Geneva really meant. Chester L. Cooper has flatly characterized the agreements as a "hasty, slapdash potpourri containing a few lofty principles."[18]

In terms of documentation the Geneva Accords were complex. Three cease-fire agreements, dated July 20, were *signed*, the titles of the signers being significant: one for Vietnam by Brigadier General Henri Delteil for the French Union Forces in Indochina and by Ta Quang Buu for the People's Army of Vietnam; one for Laos by the same French officer and by the same Vietnamese officer, this time donning an additional hat on behalf of the fighting units of Pathet Lao; and one for Cambodia by General Nhiek Tioulong for the Khmer National Armed Forces and by the same Vietnamese officer, only this time wearing a third hat on behalf of the Units of the Khmer Resistance Forces and the Vietnamese Military Units. Six unilateral declarations, two each by France, Cambodia, and Laos, were made. The Final Declaration of the Geneva Conference on July 21 was *not signed*, as often claimed; it took note, *inter alia,* of certain agreements and declarations and was adopted in the words of Mendès-France "by the ensemble of the Conference."[19] A unilateral declaration of the United States, which constitutes an important part of the Geneva settlement, was made at the final plenary session. Indeed, the verbatim record of this session on July 21 was one of the significant documents of the conference.

The cease-fire agreement for Vietnam, the details of which were worked out by Colonel Michel de Brébisson and Colonel Ha Van Lau, called for a specific "provisional military demarcation line" roughly along the seventeenth parallel with a demilitarized zone on either side.[20] French Union forces would evacuate the Hanoi perimeter in 80 days, the Haiduong perimeter in 100 days, and the Haiphong perimeter within 300 days of the armistice becoming effective, and Viet Minh forces would evacuate areas south of the demarcation line in periods varying from 80 to 300 days. Left, in effect, were two Vietnams with regrouped forces— the Democratic Republic to the north and the State of Vietnam to the south. Technically, however, Vietnam was a single sovereign state with two rival governments claiming all of it. Civilian internees and prisoners of war would be released and given help in getting to their homes or chosen homes. Civilians from the time of the armistice going into effect until the completion of the regroupment of forces could move and take up residence north or south of the parallel. Reprisals against persons or organizations for activities during the war were forbidden, and their "democratic liberties" were guaranteed by the two parties.

Foreign troops and other military personnel or war material could enter Vietnam only on a basis of the specific rotation of personnel and replacement of material in the country at internationally supervised points of entry. No new or foreign military bases could be established in Vietnam, and the two signers of the cease-fire should ensure that "the zones assigned to them" do not make a military alliance and "are not used" to resume hostilities or further aggression. A Joint Commission with joint groups of Viet Minh and Franco-Vietnamese representatives was set up to carry out the terms of the cease-fire while an International Commission for Supervision and Control, with India as chairman and Canada and Poland as other members, with fixed and mobile inspection teams, was created to supervise the "proper execution" of the cease-fire and the points of entry. Decisions here would be generally reached by a majority vote but unanimity was needed on some important matters. In case of a failure of unanimity on subjects involving a threat to the peace the Commission would report to the members of the conference. Under the cease-fire agreement general elections to unify Vietnam were foreseen in Article 14 (a). The signers of the cease-fire and their successors under Article 27 were made "responsible for ensuring the observance and enforcement" of the agreement. The Democratic Republic of Vietnam looked to France to carry out the Geneva Accords in Vietnam.

In the case of Laos the cease-fire agreement called for the withdrawal of the French and Vietnamese People's Volunteer forces within 120 days of the armistice coming into effect.[21] The fighting units of Pathet Lao significantly were allowed to concentrate in a regroupment area, the provinces of Phong Saly and Sam Neua, with a connecting corridor "pending a political settlement." Reinforcements from outside Laos of troops or military personnel were forbidden, but France could maintain a military mission with a maximum figure of 1,500 men to train the Laotian national army, and have two military establishments not exceeding in personnel 3,500 men, one at Seno and the other in the Mekong valley in the province of Vientiane or downstream. No "new military bases" could be set up in the kingdom. Prisoners of war and civilian internees would be freed and repatriated under given conditions. Except for a specified quantity of arms in specified categories "necessary for the defense of Laos," no armaments of any kind could be introduced into the kingdom. A Joint Commission with joint groups would implement the cease-fire. An International Control Commission, India as chairman and Canada and Poland as members, with inspection teams would supervise the execution of the armistice.

In the Cambodian cease-fire, all French Union and Viet Minh forces would leave the kingdom within ninety days of the armistice coming into effect.[22] The "Khmer Resistance Forces" would be "demobilized on the spot." Significantly no regroupment area was created. Civilian internees and prisoners of war would be freed and repatriated under given conditions. A Joint Commission was set up to implement the cease-fire, and it might establish joint groups. India as chairman with Canada and Poland as members constituted an International Control Commission to supervise the armistice with the help of inspection teams.

The French, Laotian, and Cambodian declarations merit careful attention.[23] France agreed in one declaration to withdraw its troops from Vietnam, Laos, and Cambodia upon request of the respective party concerned except where it had an agreement with a government for "a certain number" of troops staying "at specified points and for a specified time." In another declaration it agreed to "proceed from the principle of respect for the independence and sovereignty, the unity and territorial integrity of Cambodia, Laos and Viet Nam" as regards settling all problems related to the "reestablishment and consolidation of peace" in them.[24] One declaration of Laos related to domestic policy and the other to foreign affairs with the same division obtaining for Cambodia's declarations. In the one on domestic matters the Royal Government of Laos agreed to "integrate all citizens, without discrimination, into the national community," affirmed all citizens might freely participate as candidates or electors in general elections through secret ballot, and promised "special representation" before elections in the administration of Phong Saly and Sam Neua for the Laotian nationals who had not backed the Royal Government during the fighting.[25] Cambodia's declaration on domestic policy, unlike the Laotian, was inserted in its cease-fire agreement. It promised that the Royal Government would integrate without discrimination all citizens into the national community allowing them "freely [to] participate as electors or candidates in general elections by secret ballot."[26]

The Laotian declaration on foreign policy resembled the Cambodian, apart from a few aspects like the limited French military presence.[27] Since the former owed its escape clauses to Khmer efforts, the Cambodian declaration as the model should be stressed. It pledged the Khmer kingdom neither to make a military alliance "not in conformity with the principles of the Charter of the United Nations" nor to allow foreign bases "as long as its security is not threatened." In the period between the cessation of hostilities in Vietnam and the final settlement of political problems in Cambodia Phnom Penh would not seek foreign military aid in matériel, instructors, or personnel "except for the purpose of the effective defense of the territory."[28] These provisions, unlike the Laotian, were also inserted in the cease-fire agreement. The qualifying statements, as just quoted, were the result of Cambodian insistence which held up for a few hours on the night of July 20 the signing of the cease-fire.* It was one of Cambodia's finest hours when shortly before and for some time after midnight at Eden's villa it successfully maintained its claims before Molotov, Eden, Mendès-France, and Pham Van Dong. (The North Vietnamese leader was really irked!) At Geneva Phnom Penh had fought against recognition of the Khmer resistance government, had opposed a regroupment area for the dissidents in Cambodia, had resisted the neutralization of the kingdom—and *mirabile dictu* had won. It even attempted at the final plenary session to press its claims for Vietnamese territory provoking the "most express reservations" of Pham Van Dong for the Democratic Republic of Vietnam!

The Final Declaration of the Geneva Conference on July 21 began by listing the participants, a device which dropped names. Earlier plans for affixing signatures, as desired by Chou En-lai, were relinquished when it became known the United States would not sign. Eden and Molotov worked out the solution to the problem. In the Declaration the Conference took "note" of the three cease-fire agreements and indicated "satisfaction" at the end of hostilities.[29] It also took "note" of the Laotian and Cambodian declarations on general elections "which, in conformity with the constitution of each of these countries, shall take place in the course of the year 1955, by secret ballot and in conditions of respect for fundamental freedoms."

In regard to Vietnam, Paragraph 6 of the Final Declaration stressed that the "military demarcation line is provisional and should not in any way be interpreted as constituting a political or territorial boundary." The next paragraph proved to be one of the most fateful provisions of the Geneva settlement. Since the devil can quote scripture for his own purpose, Paragraph 7, though long, merits quotation instead of paraphrase.

The Conference declares that, so far as Viet-Nam is concerned, the settlement of political problems, effected on the basis of respect for the principles of independence, unity and territorial integrity, shall permit the Viet-Namese people to enjoy the fundamental freedoms, guaranteed by democratic institutions established as a result of free general elections by secret ballot. In order to ensure that sufficient progress in the restoration of peace has been made, and that all the

*A high-ranking Cambodian diplomat, Nong Kimny, gave the author the information about the qualifying terminology.

necessary conditions obtain for free expression of the national will, general elections shall be held in July 1956, under the supervision of an international commission composed of representatives of the Member States of the International Supervisory Commission, referred to in the agreement on the cessation of hostilities. Consultations will be held on this subject between the competent representative authorities of the two zones from 20 July 1955 onwards.

Although the language is subject to various interpretations a time schedule was established and the membership of the international supervisory commission determined.

In the Final Declaration the cease-fire provisions against reprisals in Cambodia, Laos, and North and South Vietnam were stressed; also emphasized (in its words) was the armistice provision to "allow everyone in Viet-Nam to decide freely in which zone he wishes to live." The Conference noted the two French declarations on Vietnam, Laos, and Cambodia, the clauses in the cease-fire in Vietnam concerning foreign military bases and alliances and the introduction of foreign troops, military personnel, munitions, and arms, and the declarations by Laos and Cambodia on these subjects. All members of the conference in their relations with Vietnam, Cambodia, and Laos undertook "to respect the sovereignty, the independence, the unity and the territorial integrity of the abovementioned states, and to refrain from any interference in their internal affairs."

Under Paragraph 13 of the Final Declaration, the consultation clause, the members agreed "to consult one another on any question which may be referred to them by the International Supervisory Commission, in order to study such measures as may prove necessary to ensure that the agreements on the cessation of hostilities in Cambodia, Laos and Viet-Nam are respected." The consultation clause involved possible discussions among participants who in some cases were not on diplomatic speaking terms.

Highly significant is the formal unilateral declaration of Bedell Smith on behalf of the United States at the final plenary session. After reiterating that his government was "not prepared to join" in the Final Declaration, he asserted that the United States took "note" of the three cease-fire agreements and of all the paragraphs except Paragraph 13 of the Final Declaration. He declared with reference to them that it would "refrain from the threat or the use of force to disturb them" in accordance with the Charter of the United Nations, Article 2 (4), and it would "view any renewal of the aggression in violation of the aforesaid agreements with grave concern and as seriously threatening international peace and security."[30] Referring to the item in the Final Declaration on free elections in Vietnam the United States called attention to the declaration by

President Eisenhower and Prime Minister Churchill in Washington on June 29 about their policy toward "nations now divided against their will." The United States, it was stressed, would not join in any arrangement which would impair the right of peoples to determine their own destiny.[31]

The government of the State of Vietnam protested the Geneva settlement on Vietnam and sought in vain to amend the Final Declaration. It had even suggested to conference participants on July 19 placing all Vietnam under "provisional UN control." However, Saigon agreed not to employ force to oppose the procedures for implementing the cease-fire. It did not approve the Final Declaration nor did any representative of Saigon sign the cease-fire document.

Reactions. The reactions to the Geneva settlement varied among the participants. It was highly praised in some capitals, severely criticized in a few, and philosophically accepted by others. President Eisenhower issued a statement on July 21 indicative of the American role in the negotiations. He stressed the United States had not been a belligerent and that the "nations" which did the fighting had the "primary responsibility for the settlement." He noted that "the United States has not itself been party to or bound by the decisions taken by the Conference" and that the "agreement contains features which we do not like."[32] On the other hand, the President called attention to the formal declaration of Bedell Smith at Geneva, hoped that the settlement would lead to peace "consistent with the rights and the needs of the countries concerned,"[33] and frankly asserted that much depended on how the settlement worked in practice.

In an effort to strengthen Cambodia and Laos as fully independent and sovereign nations Eisenhower announced he was asking them to agree to an American ambassador or minister resident in Phnom Penh and Vientiane. The U.S. embassy in Saigon, of course, would be maintained. The President concluded by directing attention to the fact that the United States was "actively pursuing discussions with other free nations with a view to the rapid organization of a collective defense in Southeast Asia in order to prevent further direct or indirect Communist aggression in that general area."[34] He was setting the stage for a major step in U.S. policy in the region—the Manila Conference and the Southeast Asia Collective Defense Treaty. The President later wrote in his memoirs that France had got at Geneva the best it could have under the circumstances.

Dulles in a statement on July 23 stressed that Washington should not "mourn the past" but "seize the future opportunity to prevent the loss in northern Viet-Nam from leading to the extension of communism throughout Southeast Asia and the Southwest Pacific."[35] Dulles was thinking both of the coming collective defense arrangement and of building up Cambodia, Laos, and South Vietnam. He believed the United States had a new asset in the effort—Dien Bien Phu had marked the end of French colonialism.[36] Both Assistant Secretary of State Walter S. Robertson and Undersecretary of State Bedell Smith summed up the American attitude when the former asserted it would be "an understatement" to indicate the United States did not like the cease-fire terms, and the latter flatly said that "diplomacy has rarely been able to gain at the conference table what cannot be gained or held on the battlefield."[37]

Whether the United States followed the right policy at the Geneva Conference is debatable. It has been contended that Washington should have taken a front seat in the negotiations. It was also rigid in its approach. By forthrightly championing non-Communist nationalism in Indochina and actively participating in making the Geneva Accords the conditions of settlement might have been more favorable at the outset and the subsequent American stand at the Manila Conference might have seemed less essential.

In France the end of the war was greeted with a national sigh of relief and almost universally hailed. Prime Minister Mendès-France told the National Assembly on July 22 that the harsh content of the settlement "consecrates cruel facts." He believed France could keep "her presence" in East Asia, noted the concessions made by the Communists, mentioned that the end of the "nightmare" in Indochina might strengthen French policy in Africa and Europe, and praised the roles of Great Britain and the United States at Geneva. Mendès-France had been concerned about the future of Roman Catholics in Tonkin especially those living in the bishoprics of Phat-Diem and Bui-Chou and was pleased over Ho Chi Minh's and Pham Van Dong's assurances of religious freedom. Pham Van Dong, moreover, wrote Mendès-France giving assurances that French businessmen in North Vietnam would be allowed to continue their work (they should even be encouraged) and that French property rights would be respected. French cultural establishments would also be permitted to function.

Anthony Eden spoke in terms of qualified optimism about the Geneva settlement to the House of Commons on July 22. Prime Minister Churchill praised Eden for his work at the conference, and the Foreign Secretary was supported by the British public in general. London took the position that the settlement was the best under the circumstances—a global conflict had been avoided. The final test of the Accords, as viewed from Britain, would be the way the Communists implemented them. Canada and India, it was noted, were Commonwealth members and two of the three participants of the International Control Commissions in Vietnam, Cambodia, and Laos. Great Britain and the Soviet Union as cochairmen of the Geneva Conference, furthermore, would have roles to play in the implementation of the settlement.

Moscow and Peking greeted the Geneva Accords with enthusiasm. In the pursuit of national goals they attempted to conceal their partial sellout of a Communist partner in Southeast Asia. They were pleased over the discomfiture of the United States. Molotov stressed that the Accords were a triumph for the national liberation forces in Vietnam, and Mao Tse-tung in a message to Ho Chi Minh called them a victory for peace in the world. *Pravda* crowed in an editorial on July 22 that "the world prestige of the U.S.S.R. is today at an unprecedented high"[38] and Chou Enlai thinking of the future stressed that the three Indochinese states would make no military alliances and have no foreign bases. (He believed that Eden had given him assurances on their neutrality with no foreign [American] bases.) Both Moscow and Peking counted on Poland as a member of the three International Control Commissions to do its duty for the Communist cause. And the Soviet Union, of course, rejoiced when the French National Assembly rejected EDC on August 30.

Ho Chi Minh though disappointed in certain respects was probably basically satisfied but Ngo Dinh Diem made no effort to hide his frustration and anger. Ho Chi Minh on July 22 told his people the demarcation line was "temporary and transitional"; he made a great effort to stress that the seventeenth parallel was not a partition. Ngo Dinh Diem in a broadcast on the same day denounced the Geneva Accords and ordered flags flown at half-mast for three days. Tran Van Do, bitter at the outcome of the Geneva Conference, resigned as foreign minister though he withdrew his resignation at Diem's request. The Royal Government of Laos issued a statement praising the Geneva settlement. At the same time it was very much interested in how it would be implemented. Cambodia which had every reason to be pleased over its accomplishments at Geneva issued a communiqué on July 25 expressing satisfaction over the "appreciable results," especially the withdrawal of Viet Minh forces from its soil and the sole recognition of the Royal Government.

In the other countries of Southeast Asia reaction to the Geneva Conference and Accords varied. Although they were nonparticipants Indonesia and Burma like the other Colombo Powers had a role separate from Thailand, which was deeply and directly concerned, or from the Philippines which though apprehensive was less involved.

Despite the facts that the Colombo Powers at their first meeting in Ceylon had made on May 2 their proposals for a settlement of the Indochinese crisis, that Anthony Eden had suggested on June 8 they should make up the membership of the international control commission in Vietnam acting by a majority vote, and that they approved the settlement made, they still took no concrete steps as a group. Yet Nehru in comments on July 21 after calling the Geneva Accords "one of the outstanding achievements of the post-war era"[39] indicated his belief that the Colombo Powers had exerted real influence on the discussion leading to them.

During the Geneva Conference Thailand after consultation with the United States finally had asked the Security Council on May 29 in view of the Viet Minh threat from Indochina to provide for direct observation in the kingdom under the Peace Observation Commission. The Security Council discussed the subject on June 3, and the Soviet Union opposed placing it on the agenda on the grounds the talks at the Geneva Conference might be hindered. Moscow intimated Washington through Bangkok was trying to torpedo the conference. The Council overruled Soviet objections by a vote of ten to one, the United States being in the majority. A Thai representative took his place at the Council table and presented his case. At Bangkok's request the Security Council met again on June 16 and considered a draft resolution for peace observers in Thailand. Reports and recommendations as considered essential would be made to the Peace Observation Commission and the Security Council. At the request of the United States the draft resolution on June 18 was put to a vote—nine states favored it including the United Kingdom, France, and the United States; one abstained, Lebanon; but the Soviet Union vetoed the measure. Dulles quickly condemned Moscow's action. Thailand on July 7 wrote the Secretary General to have the matter placed on the agenda of the General Assembly. However, Bangkok did not press for a meeting in view of Indochinese developments. Later Thailand expressed the hope the armistice agreements on Indochina would "function smoothly" and strongly urged the admission of Laos and Cambodia to the United Nations.

On June 21, shortly after the Soviet veto, Bangkok indicated it would welcome U.S. forces under certain circumstances. And on July 13 Washington announced additional military aid and technical assistance for the Thai. Furthermore, around $3 million would be provided for the building of a road of strategic and economic importance from Saraburi in central Thailand through Korat to Ban Phai, a distance of almost 300 miles. These steps acquired more significance in the perspective of later events.

SOUTHEAST ASIA
COLLECTIVE DEFENSE TREATY

A treaty emerges from the conditions that create it, thrives or languishes in an international environment subject to constant change, and is evaluated in the course of history in terms of the achievement of its objectives. The Southeast Asia Collective Defense Treaty or Manila Pact under which the Southeast Asia Treaty Organization or SEATO* was later created was a product of the bloodshed at Dien Bien Phu and of the Geneva settlement on Indochina. It was signed at a time when international communism was making great inroads in Indochina and anticolonialism was rampant. From July 21 when the Geneva Conference ended to September 8 when the Manila Treaty was concluded, intense and complex negotiations were conducted in various capitals on the terms and membership of SEATO. The negotiations had the benefit of international working groups of prospective members meeting in Washington in June and July on the organization of collective security in Southeast Asia. A Manila working group at a higher level next prepared a treaty draft with several articles having alternatives. As a result, the Manila Conference, only lasting from September 6 to 8, reflected considerable spadework. Unlike the Japanese peace conference at San Francisco in 1951, however, the final text of the SEATO Treaty was the consequence of real negotiations at Manila. John Foster Dulles was the chief architect of SEATO from its inception to its birth. His diplomatic spadework and his removal of obstacles to the pact were considered real achievements. He did not live long enough to observe the many vicissitudes of the Manila Treaty.†

The concept of a security pact in the Pacific was not new.[40] As empires declined and new states emerged, various regional pacts were suggested by leaders in newly independent and in Western countries. President Elpidio Quirino of the Philippines, for example, called for a Pacific security pact and a Southeast Asia Union. Other early postwar leaders like Aung San of Burma, Soetan Sjahrir of Indonesia, and Pibul Songgram of Thailand considered some kind of regional organization. The treaty area, the fields of cooperation, and the scope of membership were often vaguely given but so much smoke at times indicated the fire of interest. Indeed, a Southeast Asia League was unofficially set up in Bangkok in September 1947 but it turned out to be a Communist front to help Ho Chi Minh. As the countries from Southeast Asia joined the family of nations, they participated officially—sometimes unofficially

---

*SEATO commonly refers to the Manila Pact and its organization.

†The genesis of the Manila Pact, as well as the history of SEATO, has not been as interesting to authors as the Geneva Conference and settlement of 1954. The best work is one published under Australian auspices: George Modelski, ed., *SEATO: Six Studies,* Cheshire, Melbourne, 1962. Bearing on the subject from British and American points of view are *Collective Defence in South East Asia,* Oxford for the Royal Institute of International Affairs, London, 1956, and Russell H. Fifield, *Southeast Asia in United States Policy,* Praeger for the Council on Foreign Relations, New York, 1963. An interesting though not impartial account is found in *United States-Vietnam Relations, 1945–1967,* Book 1, NATO and SEATO: A Comparison. *SEATO Record,* published every two months by the organization in Bangkok, presents official viewpoints.

before independence—in various international activities having a regional bearing before the Manila Treaty of 1954: the unofficial Asian Relations Conference in New Delhi of 1947; the conference on Indonesia held there in 1949; the Baguio Conference of 1950; the Colombo Powers; the Asian-African bloc in the United Nations; the Colombo Plan; and the Economic Commission for Asia and the Far East (ECAFE) of the United Nations.

Although the Truman administration for several years opposed U.S. participation in a Pacific security pact and rebuffed first British and later French efforts to involve Washington in the defense of Southeast Asia, the American attitude was subject to change. Congress over the objection of the administration had written into the Mutual Defense Assistance Act of 1949 a provision calling for support for a regional security organization of free Asia. In a draft report by the staff of the National Security Council on December 23, it was recommended that Washington, in effect, should back Asian leaders in the objective that any regional arrangement in South and Southeast Asia that might emerge be an association Washington could cooperate with on equal terms and in harmony with the Charter of the United Nations. The National Security Council a week later approved such an approach based on Asian initiative and favored "some form of collective security arrangements." After Dean Rusk became Assistant Secretary of State for Far Eastern Affairs in March 1950, shortly before the outbreak of the Korean War, he indicated in a major speech on "Fundamentals of Far Eastern Foreign Policy" on September 9 that the United States would sympathetically view an Asian regional effort toward security and welfare. In November he spoke of the problems of security in Southeast Asia both internal and external. Dulles who was active as special representative of the President in 1951 in negotiating the treaties with Japan, the Philippines, and Australia and New Zealand gave thought at the time to a general security pact in the Pacific but found it not attainable. On November 6 Rusk stressed (as had Truman) that "initial steps," the alliances of 1951, had been taken toward security in the Pacific area and expressed hope for future developments.

This hope, however, was not easily fulfilled despite the elevation of Dulles to the office of Secretary of State in January 1953 and the urging by the Senate Committee on Foreign Relations on January 21, 1954, for a "Pacific Pact."* Dulles under President Eisenhower found many of the

---

*President Eisenhower himself only five days before had approved a statement of the National Security Council favoring measures to further the "coordinated defense of Southeast Asia" but noting that the "initiative in regional defense measures" must originate with the governments of the area.

same objections among possible participants he had encountered as special representative of Truman. Although the climate on Capitol Hill was changing there was also real concern in the United States about commitments to mainland Asia. Nevertheless John Foster Dulles had drawn two lessons from "the loss" in North Vietnam: collective defense should be organized before aggression was in progress and popular support was imperative in fighting Communist subversion. Undersecretary Smith pointedly remarked at the close of the Geneva Conference, "We must get that pact!"

In August the issues raised by a regional collective security treaty were thoroughly discussed in the Pentagon—prior to the statement of policy of the National Security Council on August 20. Already the term SEATO had actually been used—a cable from Dillon to Dulles on May 31 and from Smith to Dulles on July 18 (quoting a dispatch of Seymour Topping)—but these references did not reflect any pattern. On August 13 the Joint Chiefs after reviewing the report of the Anglo-American study group on Southeast Asia as well as a draft treaty submitted by the U.S. member of the group sent their report to Secretary of Defense Wilson who four days later presented to Dulles the viewpoints of the Defense Department.

The Joint Chiefs listed several provisions that should be incorporated in a "Southeast Asia defense treaty." At the outset was the following requirement:

> The clear purpose of the treaty should be to form a collective security arrangement to deter and, if possible, prevent any further extension of Communist control, by whatever means, within the general area of Southeast Asia and the Southwest Pacific.[41]

The Joint Chiefs gave attention in their recommendations to "overt Communist aggression" and to "indirect aggression" which was considered the "most likely and insidious form of Communist aggression." They opposed a built-in veto and a large-scale economic aid program. Moreover, "no commitment" should be made to "support the raising, equipping, and maintenance of indigenous forces and/or to deploy United States forces in such strengths as to provide for an effective defense of all of the national territory of each signatory."[42] Wilson in his letter to Dulles used the views of the Joint Chiefs as the basis of his comments. The Secretary of Defense stressed that the word "general" should be inserted in the final draft before the "area of Southeast Asia and the Southwest Pacific" and that "military coordination" should be similar to that in ANZUS arrangements.

The statement of the National Security Council on August 20 was a review of American policy in East Asia in the light of the Geneva settlement. As regards the negotiation of a "Southeast Asia security treaty," the following guidelines were established:

a. Commit each member to treat an armed attack on the agreed area (including Laos, Cambodia and South Vietnam) as dangerous to its own peace, safety and vital interests, and to act promptly to meet the common danger in accordance with its own constitutional processes.

b. Provide so far as possible a legal basis to the President to order attack on Communist China in the event it commits such armed aggression which endangers the peace, safety and vital interests of the United States.

c. Ensure that, in such event, other nations would be obligated in accordance with the treaty to support such U.S. action.

d. Not limit U.S. freedom to use nuclear weapons, or involve a U.S. commitment for local defense or for stationing U.S. forces in Southeast Asia.

The U.S. would continue to provide limited military assistance and training missions, wherever possible, to the states of Southeast Asia in order to bolster their will to fight, to stabilize legal governments, and to assist them in controlling subversion.[43]

The American delegation to Manila was subject to four absolute preconditions in the negotiation of the final treaty. Washington would not commit American forces unilaterally; one or more European signers would have to participate if military action was necessitated; the United States planned to provide only air and sea forces with other signatories expected to furnish ground forces; and finally Washington would act only against aggression from the Communists.[44]

The Manila Conference. On August 14 the Department of State announced that a conference at the foreign minister level would begin in the Philippines on September 6 to consider steps to further the common aims of the participants. Meeting at Manila were the United States, Great Britain, France, Australia, New Zealand, Thailand, the Philippines, and Pakistan. Significant by their absence were India, Ceylon, Indonesia, and Burma. In a special category were Cambodia, Laos, and the "free territory under the jurisdiction of the State of Vietnam," not actually represented but directly involved.

The opening addresses of the ranking representatives of the eight powers at Manila set the tone of the conference which then moved into closed session and produced two days later the Southeast Asia Collective Defense Treaty with an "understanding" by the United States, a protocol to the pact, and the Pacific Charter. Secretary Dulles in his opening address warned that the Communists considered their advances in Indochina as bridgeheads for subsequent victories. He wanted to make clear to the potential aggressor that "an attack upon the Treaty area" would provoke a reaction "so united, so strong and so well placed" that it would know in advance it "would lose more than it could hope to gain."[45] In military terms Dulles advocated "the deterrent of mobile striking power, plus strategically placed reserves";[46] he indicated the United States did not favor tying down committed forces in the treaty area. (This constraint in all probability meant a weaker treaty than he had earlier wanted.) Dulles frankly observed that "no simple and no single formula" existed to cover the risks of subversion and indirect aggression. The Secretary advocated a protective mantle over Cambodia, Laos, and Vietnam and hoped the treaty would receive the adherence of more states. He stressed the role of Western powers in meeting the Asian yearning for freedom from "so-called 'colonialism.' "

The Manila speech by Foster Dulles in the light of subsequent developments acquires particular significance. He predicted much of the course of history in Indochina for the next several years. He apparently had more faith in the ways of deterring open aggression than indirect aggression. In fact, a loud chorus of amens from later American practitioners and theorists of counterinsurgency in Indochina would support the Secretary in his observation on "no simple and no single formula" for dealing with subversion and indirect aggression. His opposition to tying down committed forces would not stand the test of events, but even here, American policy makers were hopeful that U.S. forces, particularly ground units, would not long be committed to mainland Southeast Asia.

Anthony Eden did not go to Manila in view of the crisis over the French rejection of EDC, and the Marquess of Reading, minister of state at the Foreign Office, spoke for Great Britain. He asserted that the purposes of the Manila Conference were to prevent another war like the one in Indochina and to warn potential aggressors that the participating countries intended to stay free. He did not want a "Toothless Treaty" and hoped other countries would join in the collective defense effort. A "prolonged period of quiet," he significantly observed, was needed for economic development. France likewise did not send its foreign minister to Manila; Guy La Chambre, a minister of state, called for an organization of collective security but stressed the promotion of economic welfare. He was vague in generally low posture and innocuous remarks. In terms of leadership among the three ranking Western powers it is obvious that the British and the French took a front seat at the Geneva Conference on Indochina and the Americans occupied the preferred box at the Manila Conference. The personal relations between Dulles and Eden were not conducive to Anglo-American harmony, with Southeast Asia and later the Middle East striking fire.

R. G. Casey, Australian minister for external affairs, spoke for his country at Manila. Well aware of differences over whether a NATO-type or an ANZUS-type treaty should be created, Casey believed the real test was the purpose and the attitude of the participants. Here he was asserting one of the great truisms of international relations—the willingness of a state to implement an alliance in a showdown. Hell, it might be observed, is paved with the good intentions of treaty makers. Casey wanted more economic aid for Southeast Asia but did not desire to see the Colombo Plan superseded. He stressed the sovereign equality of the potential signatories. T. Clifton Webb, minister for external affairs for New Zealand, spoke of his country's interest in the pending treaty.

The opening remarks of the Thai, Filipino, and Pakistani representatives tended to be more specific than most of the speeches by Western officials. Prince Wan Waithayakon, Thai foreign minister, was very forthright. He wanted a security commitment "as near as possible to that of NATO"[47] and insisted that subversion be dealt with in the treaty. Thailand was eager to have Cambodia, Laos, and Free Vietnam in the treaty area and was pleased to have the United States, Great Britain, and France, "great powers with world interests," in the alliance. Prince Wan offered Bangkok as the headquarters of the treaty organization. Senator Francisco A. Delgado, speaking instead of Vice-President Carlos P. Garcia for the Philippines, wanted an alliance where the members in case of aggression would act immediately *"one for all and all for one"*[48] and where was stated in an article, not just in the preamble, the "unequivocal recognition of the principle of self-determination for Asian peoples and their right to self-government or independence."[49] The Senator placed particular emphasis on the need for economic cooperation under the planned treaty. Pakistan's minister for foreign affairs and commonwealth relations, Chaudhri Muhammad Zafrulla Khan, stressed that his country had "vital interests" and "responsibilities" in both the Middle East and Southeast Asia but his main thrust was opposition to making "provision against aggression only of a particular variety."[50]

As the opening speeches indicated, the various participants had different viewpoints on the final version of the treaty. Among the issues were the overall type of commitment, the limitation on treaty action in case of armed attack to "Communist" aggression, and the final drafting of the Pacific Charter.

The Manila Settlement. The terms of the Manila Treaty and its protocol, both being signed, bear careful examination. The heart is Article IV, Paragraph 1, of the treaty:

Each Party recognizes that aggression by means of armed attack in the treaty area against any of the Parties or against any State or territory which the Parties by unanimous agreement may hereafter designate, would endanger its own peace and safety, and agrees that it will in that event act to meet the common danger in accordance with its constitutional processes. Measures taken under this paragraph shall be immediately reported to the Security Council of the United Nations.[51]

In an "understanding" accepted by the other participants and inserted above their signatures to the treaty the United States asserted its obligations under Article IV, Paragraph 1, as regards aggression and armed attack only applied to "communist aggression."*

Representing an effort to deal with subversion directed from the outside and indirect aggression, Article IV, Paragraph 2, provided for immediate consultation "in order to agree" on measures for the common defense if any party believed the territorial integrity or political independence of any member in the treaty area or any designated territory or state was threatened by "other than by armed attack" or by "any fact or situation" that might menace the peace of the area. It should be noted that the obligation was to "consult," not to "act." SEATO action, under a provision insisted upon by Great Britain, could be taken in a designated territory or state only with the approval or invitation of the government concerned. Washington, it should be stressed, also agreed in the "understanding" previously mentioned to the consultation formula of Article IV, Paragraph 2, if aggression or armed attack other than Communist occurred.

The description of the "treaty area" was highly significant. The "general area" of Southeast Asia and the Southwest Pacific specifically included the territories of all the Asian members but excluded the Pacific area north of 21°30′ north latitude (Hong Kong and Formosa). Technically this area included at the time the Philippines, Thailand, Pakistan, British Malaya and Borneo, Australia, and New Zealand. But under a provision of Article IV, Paragraph 1, the signatories in a protocol to the treaty unanimously designated the "States of Cambodia and Laos and the free territory under the jurisdiction of the State of Vietnam"[52] as areas where the provisions of the article applied. The words just quoted were very carefully chosen. Provision was made in the Manila Treaty for admitting new members or changing otherwise the treaty area through unanimous decision. Any party could withdraw after one year's notice.

The signatories of the treaty pledged themselves to "strengthen their

*Voting rules for implementation did not appear in the treaty but procedural arrangements were later worked out. Unanimity was originally required for action though abstentions were later allowed. Military planning was not explicitly required.

free institutions" and to work together in further economic steps including technical assistance aimed at promoting their economic and social
progress and well-being. In the protocol Cambodia, Laos, and the "free
territory under the jurisdiction of the State of Vietnam" were made eligible for the benefits of such contemplated economic measures. The parties
of the treaty promised individually and jointly, by self-help and mutual
aid, to "maintain and develop their individual and collective capacity to
resist armed attack and to prevent and counter subversive activities
directed from without against their territorial integrity and political
stability."[53] This provision accentuated the concern over indirect aggression.

The Pacific Charter, reflecting the inspiration of President Magsaysay
and other Filipinos and directed against colonialism, was proclaimed and
signed. As in the preamble of the Manila Treaty, the powers declared
that they upheld "the principle of equal rights and self-determination of
peoples" and would "earnestly strive by every peaceful means to promote
self-government and to secure the independence of all countries whose
peoples desire it and are able to undertake its responsibilities."[54]
Toward these objectives the powers in the Pacific Charter were "prepared to continue taking effective practical measures."[55] According to
Senator Delgado, the original Philippine draft of the Charter did not contain the qualifying words "and are able to undertake its responsibilities"
but they were inserted at the urging of Great Britain, France, Australia,
and New Zealand. Carlos P. Romulo, in fact, had drafted the outline of
the Charter in 1951 in a New York restaurant on the back of a menu.[56]

The Southeast Asia Collective Defense Treaty provided for a council
of all members to assist in its implementation but the provisions on organization were particularly vague. Secretary Dulles in the early stages of
the alliance tried to avoid the word *SEATO* lest an organization like
NATO with its combined command and headquarters arrangement be
implied. He once favored the expression *MANPAC* for "Manila Pact."
When the council under the treaty first met in Bangkok in February 1955
—the foreign ministers of all members but France present—it established
the Southeast Asia Treaty Organization which sired in time an international structure more elaborate than its founding fathers had envisioned
but far from the structural complexity of the North Atlantic Treaty
Organization.

The Manila Treaty has a number of concepts found in various instru-
ments of U.S. foreign policy. The basic approach to subversion, Article
IV, Paragraph 2, is seen in the Inter-American Treaty of Reciprocal
Assistance of 1947 and would be reflected in the U.S. alliance with the
Republic of China signed in December 1954. The "Monroe Doctrine

formula," not the "NATO formula," of involvement is inherent in Article IV, Paragraph 1, and the basic commitment of the Manila Treaty is like that under the previous U.S. alliances with Korea, the Philippines, and Australia and New Zealand. The principle of the Vandenberg Resolution is found in the provision calling for self-help and mutual aid in regional and collective security arrangements. Like the North Atlantic Alliance new members would have to be approved by the Senate. The treaty falls under Article 51 of the United Nations Charter, "the inherent right of individual or collective self-defense," and not under Article 52 on regional arrangements where a Soviet veto could apply to enforcement measures.

Participation. The decision to join or not to join SEATO (as well as the diplomacy before the Manila Conference) reflected the state of international relations in South and Southeast Asia in the latter half of 1954. The various nations had multiple motivation, like couples who decide to go or not to go to the altar. The common denominator among the eight SEATO partners, at least to some extent, was an evaluation of international communism as a threat to their security and a conviction that collective defense was the best approach to the menace. Many other states believed the best way to their security was a policy of noncommitment expressed in a variety of usually flat terminology.

An alliance like SEATO especially at the beginning unites its members in certain objectives and divides them from nonmembers. Such an alliance is a source of unity and disunity; it reflects the diplomacy of alignment and nonalignment. Such a pact can acquire in time significance per se or it can simply represent the sum total of the interests of its members. The alliance can even be used to carry out national policies not directly related to its objectives. The community of interests, made more precise and explicit by a pact like SEATO, must be sufficiently strong to withstand marked political, economic, and cultural diversity and to meet the challenge of change. A state will make an alliance only if it is convinced its national interests at the time are best served by a formal commitment.

To deter an aggressor is a basic objective of allies, but what if deterrence fails? The partners may not be able to agree on common action. The role of an alliance like SEATO in peacetime is quite different from that in wartime. History records few instances where a large multilateral peacetime alliance has ever gone to war. And SEATO certainly is the biggest peacetime alliance ever created in East Asia. A security pact can become merely legalistic and doctrinaire if its members are unwilling to implement it in a showdown. Here arises the key question of vital interests over a long haul. Does SEATO per se maintain them either as national interests or common interests? It takes a very powerful alliance to preserve them in the face of adversity. Furthermore, military and political interests are not always compatible as the nature of a threat varies over time and calls for different responses. The distribution of benefits and responsibilities in an alliance may not be equitable and related to the actual capacity of the partners. Power and responsibility in SEATO have rested largely with Washington from the beginning.

Can the Manila Treaty survive changes in government sometimes made by force? Like a Cassandra was the bloody coup in Iraq in 1958 and its effect on the Baghdad pact. Yet coups occurred in Thailand and Pakistan and governments changed in the Philippines but they remained SEATO members. (Bangladesh was a different situation.) Related to political viability, the capability of many new states to meet their commitments is limited; like fledglings they face the problems of growing up, and often enter the family of nations with no meaningful preparation for statehood. The long-range contractual capability of one or more of the Asian SEATO members was not academic in 1954.

Significantly no Asian partner in the alliance had a common boundary with another; Thai, Philippine, and Pakistani regional troubles involved neighbors who were non-SEATO members. This situation removed possible sources of friction among allies in the treaty area but also increased problems of cooperation. The three Asian countries despite their ties clearly looked more to Washington than to each other.

For the United States, when all is said and done, the Manila Treaty of 1954 was designed to deter overt armed aggression from Communist China in the treaty area and provide a shield to buy time for American and related programs of aid which might lead to the economic and social advance of the people, to greater stability in their governments, and to the reduction of Communist appeal. The "understanding" that American obligations under Article IV, Paragraph 1, applied only to "communist aggression" was stipulated by the United States when the article itself did not limit aggression to "communist." Washington viewed SEATO as a link in the system of alliances in Asia and the Pacific although an integrated security arrangement along the Sino-Soviet periphery was not possible.

The United States in 1954 and 1955 was fully aware of the grave significance of its commitments in mainland South and Southeast Asia under the Manila Treaty. The Senate Committee on Foreign Relations in its report on the pact, January 25, 1955, significantly concluded that it was "not impervious to the risks which this treaty entails. It fully appreciates that acceptance of these additional obligations commits the United States to a course of action over a vast expanse of the Pacific. Yet these risks are consistent with our own highest interests."[57] American policy was based on the belief that a threat of aggression by Peking and Hanoi in Southeast Asia, particularly South Vietnam, Laos, Cambodia, and Thailand, was real, that the fall of any of them to communism would destroy the capacity of other Southeast Asian states to withstand it, that the subjection of more territory through subversion and aggression to the influence of Hanoi and Peking would enhance Communist power and threaten the United States, and that the largely new countries of Southeast Asia deserved support from Washington in the best interests of themselves and the United States to develop as independent nations in the world community. William P. Bundy, writing as Assistant Secretary of State for East Asian and Pacific Affairs in 1967, summarized the choice in 1954 as between "fairly deep involvement in Southeast Asia or standing aside in the face of an estimate that to do so would cause Communist Chinese and North Vietnamese power and domination to flow throughout the area."[58]

In January 1955 the Secretary of Defense made it a point to ask the Joint Chiefs of Staff to furnish "a concept" for the possible use of American military power in implementing Article IV of the Manila Treaty either under the assumption of the prohibition of nuclear arms or of permission to use them. It was a case of unilateral, not multilateral planning.*

Although Washington was becoming deeply involved in Southeast Asia Dulles was particularly concerned over the non-Communist Indochinese successor countries. He looked upon SEATO despite its loose terms as a means of offsetting the Communist gains in Indochina. He placed great stress on the deterrent and probably did not think deeply about the consequences if it failed. Several times Dulles said he did not want to see American ground troops fighting in the jungles of Southeast Asia. Not only did he specifically hope that Cambodia and Laos could be immunized but also that South Vietnam despite the dire forecasts could

---

*Vice Admiral A. C. Davis, the representative of the Department of Defense in the American delegation at Manila, assessed in a revealing memorandum for the Secretary of Defense, September 14, the Manila Treaty as it concerned his Department. Davis indicated the work of the conference represented in large measure an attempt to recover from the "psychological blow" of the recent Geneva settlement. The treaty had "many audiences"—the people at home, the Communists, and the "neutralist" countries. Admiral Davis believed the United States tried to reconcile two conflicting objectives, namely, warning in no uncertain terms the Communists about "effective collective counter-action" and limiting the extent of "advance military commitments" in the interests of freedom of action and constitutional restraints. The Manila Pact, at the moment, according to the Admiral, "serves more a psychological than a military purpose. The area is no better prepared than before to cope with Communist aggression." *United States-Vietnam Relations, 1945–1967*, Book 10, p. 747.

be kept from the Viet Minh. Dulles sought to build up in South Vietnam a powerful government commanding popular loyalty and able to destroy subversion. It is doubtful if he had a real grasp of the complexity of Southeast Asia.

Great Britain placed a somewhat different emphasis on the Manila Treaty from that of the United States. London was more concerned about wide Asian membership, about the relative role of socioeconomic as compared with military considerations, about the full implementation of the Geneva Accords, and about the deliberate anti-Communist image of SEATO. The United Kingdom wanted to preserve the British presence in Southeast Asia; it was particularly concerned over the protection of Malaya and favored giving it a SEATO assurance. The British believed that the Manila Pact was necessary both as a deterrent and a shield, and was the best attainable solution under the circumstances. Still irked by exclusion from ANZUS by the United States, Great Britain saw in SEATO a partial compensation. It firmly believed in the need for working with Asian nationalism.

The question of wide Asian membership involved the British approach to security in Southeast Asia. Although London showed flexibility in the face of changing conditions it had wanted, as Anthony Eden well indicated on November 8, 1954, "a reciprocal international guarantee that would cover the [Geneva] settlement itself, and then a South-East Asian collective defence treaty to balance the existing Sino-Soviet Treaty and the close relationship which, as we know, exists between Vietminh, China, and the Soviet Union."[59] As is clear, the final Geneva settlement on Indochina required no real action by the powers in case of violation. Eden believed an international guarantee of the Geneva Accords failed because of Communist insistence on a veto. (He thought he convinced Washington Locarno was not "a dirty word," a symbol for Munich.) Eden was also disappointed because India and the other Colombo Powers would not guarantee the Geneva settlement. The more they were involved in it, especially India, the greater the chances at the time that Communist China would be more cooperative. Although the British effort for an international guarantee of the Geneva Accords failed, Eden still sought support for a SEATO from the Colombo Powers. Dulles in the past had strongly opposed India's participation in such an alignment. On one occasion he told Eden that if the British brought India in, he (Dulles) wanted Formosa a participant. But on July 30 Eden with U.S. approval appealed to India and the other Colombo Powers to support steps for collective defense in Southeast Asia. London believed Pakistan would agree while Burma and Ceylon might possibly go along. Despite India's refusal the British thought they had moderated Nehru's opposition to the SEATO concept.

As for the non-Communist successor countries in Indochina, Eden favored the protocol extending the protection of SEATO over them. (On occasion he spoke of a "protective pad" or "girdle of neutral states" in Indochina.) London firmly believed the Geneva Accords at least in spirit prevented Cambodia, Laos, and South Vietnam from becoming full members of SEATO. It did not want to impair the implementation of the Geneva cease-fire provisions then going on. Washington which for some time had been consulting Phnom Penh, Vientiane, and Saigon on security arrangements was interested in their active membership but relinquished its viewpoint.

France joined SEATO in 1954 in the hope it would help preserve the French presence in Indochina. It supported the protocol to the treaty as a way of creating a barrier to further Communist expansion. In fact, the French, opposed to SEATO membership for Cambodia, Laos, and South Vietnam, reportedly suggested the protocol idea.[60] Prime Minister Mendès-France, moreover, told the French National Assembly in December that the Manila Treaty was a logical follow-up to the Geneva Accords, and that through it France acquired for Cambodia, Laos, and South Vietnam the legal safeguard Washington had not granted at Geneva. He also wanted to do some fence-mending in French relations with the United States. Some of the other SEATO members were not enthusiastic about Paris as a partner in view of its colonial record. However, it was noted that France unlike the Netherlands in West New Guinea no longer ruled any large territory in Southeast Asia.

For Australia and New Zealand membership in SEATO was a highly significant step. For the first time in history they were making treaty commitments for the security of Southeast Asia. Both having come to realize that their future was greatly involved in the "Near North," they believed the deep commitment of their American ally in the region would advance their own interests. Canberra would have preferred a NATO-like obligation with a military command, specific forces, and an infrastructure. It welcomed Pakistan as an ally, was sorry India was absent, and indicated it would not intervene in a war between two Commonwealth partners in Asia. New Zealand was less sympathetic to SEATO preferring bilateral security pacts to a multilateral treaty with only three Asian signers. But it welcomed the United States as an ally under the Manila Treaty and was pleased to have both Great Britain and the United States as partners especially in view of the British concern over ANZUS. On one occasion Prime Minister Walter Nash personally urged Nehru to bring India into SEATO.

The three Asian signatories of the Manila Treaty in 1954, Thailand, the Philippines, and Pakistan, believed their position in regional and world affairs would be strengthened by the alliance with the United States.

At the same time they were afraid Washington would be unduly influenced by the non-Asian partners. All three hoped for further American military and economic aid and for preferential treatment, stressing they were assuming risks many of their neighbors were unwilling to take. The Philippines and Thailand were more concerned over international communism than was Pakistan. All were more worried over their own security than over the defense of South and Southeast Asia. SEATO did not drastically restrict their freedom of action in foreign affairs.

For Thailand the Manila Treaty was of particular importance, for it provided the long-sought alliance with the United States and brought American commitment to mainland Southeast Asia.* The kingdom was the first state to ratify the pact. Thailand hoped that the treaty would help preserve its own independence and prevent Indochina from falling under the management of hostile leaders either in Peking or Hanoi. Although the Thai were worried over the legal nature of the U.S. commitment and its organizational and military backing, they realized the benefits. Kenneth T. Young observed in 1965:

> Thailand values SEATO first as a *channel* to obtain allies so as not to be left defenseless again with the involuntary option of capitulating to an overpowering enemy, as a *vehicle* to forge lasting links with the United States and other SEATO members to organize as well as insure in advance their participation in Thailand's defense in the event of aggression, and as a *disguise* of multiple choice to cloak the fact of reliance on American preponderance.[61]

The U.S. commitment to Thailand, highly significant in 1954, would gain in importance for both Americans and Thai.

Despite the fact that the Philippines under President Magsaysay joined SEATO, the island republic still viewed its bilateral alliance with the United States in 1951 as more important. The Manila Treaty did not appear to the Filipinos as any radical departure in foreign policy. It is true that Manila extended its commitments under the pact but its military weakness would restrict any big military role on the mainland of Asia. The adroit use of SEATO, however, could facilitate U.S. deployment from bases in the Philippines to other parts of the treaty area. The Manila Treaty was criticized in the island republic for the nature of its "teeth," and the Philippines would have liked to have been headquarters of the organization, but the pact was ratified with no serious difficulties.

*On August 11 the Joint Chiefs of Staff in Washington stressed that they did not favor stationing "token forces in or around Thailand." The National Security Council in a policy statement nine days later called for concentrating "efforts on developing Thailand as a support of U.S. objectives in the area [Southeast Asia] and as the focal point of U.S. covert and psychological operations in Southeast Asia." *United States-Vietnam Relations, 1945–1967*, Book 10, p. 738.

Pakistan's membership had not originally been planned by the United States. Washington was well aware that the Moslem country viewed its participation largely in terms of its power position relative to India. Yet Pakistan had the largest forces of any potential partner located in the treaty area and was willing to assume the obligations of the pact. East Pakistan, it was noted, was a neighbor of Burma although West Pakistan, the main focus of power and activity, was a neighbor of Iran. The Moslem country would have preferred a stronger SEATO in terms of commitment, organization, and combat capacity.

At the time of the Manila Conference Cambodia, Laos, and South Vietnam were in favor of the protocol to the Southeast Asia Collective Defense Treaty. Although Cambodia for a very brief period assumed a marked pro-American and pro-SEATO stance the attitude soon changed. South Vietnam especially in the early years of the treaty unsuccessfully sought adherence. Laos too on occasion indicated an interest. However, only South Vietnam in the end did not turn against the protocol to the Manila Pact. The relationship between the Geneva Accords and the treaty with its protocol remained a subject of controversy. Professors George McT. Kahin and John W. Lewis, for instance, argued that

> if SEATO did not violate the letter of the Geneva Agreements, it clearly violated their spirit, both by implying that the 17th parallel had a political character and by its inconsistency with the neutral status of the southern regroupment zone. . . . Washington . . . utilized the SEATO negotiations to offset the results of the accords reached at Geneva.[62]

On the other hand, Great Britain and France, as already indicated, were architects of the Geneva Accords and also supporters of the Manila Treaty with its protocol. Like the United States, it is argued, they sought a way to prevent the use of force to upset the Accords.

Although the Colombo Powers except Pakistan rejected membership in SEATO their specific attitudes varied reflecting different motivations in 1954. India and Indonesia wanted nothing to do with the Manila Conference, while Burma and Ceylon were not so adamant. India had resisted overtures from the latter two to sponsor some kind of a regional security arrangement. Nehru did, however, make an effort to get Peking to adopt a friendly attitude toward Southeast Asia. The Indian Prime Minister believed Communist China would accept a neutral Indochina; this conviction was one of the basic reasons why he was willing for India to serve on the International Control Commissions in Vietnam, Cambodia, and Laos and why he urged the latter two in particular, as well as Saigon and Hanoi, to follow a policy of neutrality. Nehru strongly opposed the protocol to SEATO. His criticism of the Manila Treaty arose from his basic support for nonalignment, dislike of Pakistan's adherence and apprehension lest it gain strength through SEATO, and finally concern over provoking China accompanied by a desire to accommodate Peking. It should be recalled that New Delhi kept from its own people during 1956–59 government knowledge of China's border incursions and of its terrorism in Tibet.

Indonesia was opposed to SEATO not only because of its nonalignment policy but also because of its particularly anticolonial stance. Djakarta saw SEATO as a means for the leading Western powers to return to Southeast Asia. It even favored a solid neutralist bloc friendly to Peking but Nehru did not want to go that far.

Burma probably never came very close to joining SEATO in 1954. U Nu was influenced by the viewpoints of Nehru, but even more important, Burma did not want to take any step at the time that might antagonize its most powerful neighbor, Communist China. In September 1955 the Burmese Chamber of Deputies unanimously approved a resolution opposing membership in SEATO. Nevertheless, Rangoon was not so vehemently critical as Sukarno's Indonesia. Ceylon under Prime Minister Sir John Kotelawala gave serious consideration to membership in 1954 but partly due to Nehru's influence decided against it in favor of continuing nonalignment.

The reaction of the Democratic Republic of Vietnam to the Southeast Asia Collective Defense Treaty was highly critical. It also reflected the opposition from Peking and Moscow to SEATO. For some time after the Geneva settlement Washington continued to maintain its consulate in Hanoi asserting that it was still accredited to the State of Vietnam as the legal government of Vietnam. The Viet Minh regime on October 27, 1954, announced it did not "recognize" the U.S. consulate, since northern Vietnam under the Geneva Accords was "temporarily placed under the administration of the Democratic Republic of Vietnam."[63] It was not until December 1955, however, that Washington finally closed its office in Hanoi.

Bipartisanship in the United States was pronounced in the making and in the approval of the Manila Treaty. Indeed, little opposition to the pact arose in this country. The treaty was signed not only by Dulles, but by a distinguished Republican Senator, H. Alexander Smith, and by a prominent Democratic Senator, Mike Mansfield. The Senate Foreign Relations Committee in its report noted that

> in the preliminary discussions as well as at the [Manila] conference itself a spirit of cooperation was exhibited between the legislative and executive branches which contributed greatly to the satisfactory outcome of the proceedings.[64]

The Committee approved the treaty and protocol by a vote of 14 to 1. The Senate itself gave its advice and consent by a vote of 82 to 1 on February 1, 1955.

FROM DECOLONIZATION TO SECURITY

The watershed of 1954 in U.S. policy in Southeast Asia marked by commitments to the mainland through SEATO calls for looking around and taking stock. In the early postwar years the United States was concerned over decolonization in Southeast Asia, the formalities of which by the fall of 1954 were almost over. Malaya remained a British dependency until 1957 when it received its independence. It would blossom into Malaysia in 1963 leaving only Brunei (a British-protected sultanate) and Portuguese Timor (technically an overseas province) as dependent territory in all Southeast Asia. In 1962 the Netherlands relinquished West New Guinea to temporary United Nations administration pending transfer to Indonesia, and in 1965 Singapore became independent from Malaysia.

The near completion of the formalities of decolonization in 1954 practically coincided with the extension of U.S. commitment to mainland Southeast Asia. The new obligations did not involve "material changes" in U.S. military planning, for Washington in the words of Dulles on November 2 in his report to the President on the Manila Treaty planned to keep "at all times powerful naval and air forces in the Western Pacific capable of striking at any aggressor by means and at places of our choosing"[65]—which, in fact, could be "the sources of aggression." In retrospect, however, this "mobile striking power" did not prove adequate to cope with the Communist "wars of national liberation" in mainland Southeast Asia. The United States eventually decided to commit, earmark, and pin down standing forces which Dulles, in testifying on the treaty before the Senate Committee on Foreign Relations, observed was a step not "practical or desirable or necessary."[66]

International Implications of Decolonization. The aftermath of decolonization (defined in this section as the actual termination of a state of dependency) raised serious international problems in Southeast Asia. Decolonization restored the area to the power vacuum with its attraction for outsiders that existed prior to the Western colonial era. None of the states though varying in power position was sufficiently strong to dominate the others and they were not willing as a whole to work together in collective defense. There was no voice of Southeast Asia in matters of security but a cacophony of many voices. In terms of power potential, states ranged from Indonesia to Laos and Singapore. A united Vietnam would have the greatest power potential on peninsular Southeast Asia but Indonesia possessing the greatest of the entire region might become a "middle" power. Of course, a truly united insular and peninsular Southeast Asia would be a major force in the world equation of power.

In terms of international relations it can be argued that a subordinate international system arose in the region. The existence of so many variables prevented the formulation of a definitive model but Southeast Asia became a subject of interest for theory-building.[67] The subsystem, consisting in the first instance of states in geographical proximity in a reasonably well defined region—states relatively weak in power with basically local interests as compared with world interests—operated like other subordinate systems in the general international system dominated by the Great Powers. It exercised influence and power through structural arrangements involving patterns of coercion and voluntary consent, of leadership and gradations of subservience, and of cohesion and solidarity. But should Asian neighbors like Communist China and India be added? Should the United States, a superpower with global interests having considerable influence in the region, be included? In a different category, how precisely is power exercised in the area? Do new states have the same behavior pattern as old ones once the element of relative power is introduced? What comparisons exist in the time dimension with the precolonial system in Southeast Asia? With current subsystems in the Middle East and elsewhere? Data-collecting and theory-building, alas, are not always married, and there is a danger that concepts and hypotheses not sufficiently tested will crystallize into assumed realities affecting future conclusions. At the same time meaningful analysis requires a systematic framework within which events and problems can be selected and related to one another and conclusions reached in a reasoned context.

Decolonization has opened a Pandora's box of national rivalries and conflicting interests in Southeast Asia. Responsibility for the maintenance of national boundaries and the handling of minorities has been transferred from the metropolitan powers to the new states. Most of the boundaries, often involving minority problems, were drawn by the colonial powers who were motivated to a large extent by imperial considerations.[68] Although the newly independent states inherited a territorial base often to their disliking, they have usually found it easier to maintain than to alter. After all every neighbor in Southeast Asia except Thailand, Brunei, and Portuguese Timor was also a newly independent state.

Boundary disputes were eventually settled between Burma and Communist China and between Indonesia and the Netherlands but they long remained between Cambodia and South Vietnam, the Philippines and Malaysia, and in the case of the Paracel and Spratly Islands in the South China Sea as well as elsewhere.

Minority problems in the wake of decolonization defy an easy solution.[69] A large Cambodian minority in South Vietnam, an important Vietnamese minority in Cambodia, many Thai in Burma, Laos, and Yunnan, China, an imposing number of Malays in southern Thailand, a small but growing Indonesian minority in the southern Philippines, a highly sensitive Vietnamese minority in Thailand—these and others cause conflict or have a potential for doing so. In addition a large and influential number of overseas Chinese and a smaller and more localized number of overseas Indians raise many common economic, social, cultural, and political problems for Thailand and the newly independent states, not only in domestic policy but also in foreign policy.

Decolonization brought to the surface historical rivalries in Southeast Asia submerged during the colonial period. For instance, the conflicts between Cambodia and Vietnam and between Cambodia and Thailand are better understood in the light of precolonial history. In contrast those between Thailand and Burma were not accentuated in the postcolonial period. A number of rivalries in Southeast Asia do not have deep historical roots. Indonesia, the Philippines, and Malaysia in their current territorial extent are the product of the Western colonial powers far more than many of the mainland states whose territorial heartland was reasonably well established at the time of the imposition of French and British colonial rule.

The states of Southeast Asia vary in their attitudes toward the territorial status quo in the region. When the time dimension is stressed the variation is more pronounced. The relations between Cambodia and its stronger neighbors and among the insular states of Southeast Asia became especially fluid. The conception held by some new leaders of the historical past of their countries acquired particular significance. An effort was made to justify change in terms of assumed verities of the past. But just what is the historical past in many of the newly independent states? What are the national traditions? Some Southeast Asian leaders have been rewriting history to justify their viewpoints and to attempt an adjustment of the new to the old. Maphilindo, a plan for close cooperation among Indonesia, the Philippines, and Malaysia, was falsely viewed as a return to the conditions of the Malay world before the colonial era. National traditions, however, are often the outcome of decisions taken in the early years of statehood. Such decisions become institutionalized and may create predispositions for the future.

The new framework of international relations existing in Southeast Asia in the wake of decolonization has created new dimensions in the foreign policy of interested outside powers. What should be their role in local disputes and rivalries? Issues are not just black and white and do not lend themselves to quick and pat solutions.

Another international implication of decolonization concerns the adjustment of the newly independent state to the former metropolitan power. The Philippine adjustment to the United States, the Indonesian to the Netherlands, the Vietnamese, Cambodian, and Laotian adjustment to France, and the Burmese and later the Malayan, Malaysian, and Singaporean adjustment to Great Britain, both in short-range and long-range terms and across a wide spectrum of relationships, are important. Much depended upon the way *Merdeka* was achieved, the nature of an independence settlement, and the threats that arose from third parties. In the Cold War issues between the so-called East and West the new states of Southeast Asia were divided in support of the former metropolitan powers; but in the relations between the so-called North and South all condemned colonialism and racism and sought better economic treatment from the industrialized states.

Decolonization in Southeast Asia did not quickly end the barriers or compartments set up by the Western colonial powers in the area. Nehru's prediction at the Asian Relations Conference on March 23, 1947, remained unfulfilled: "As that [European] domination goes, the walls that surrounded us fall down and we look at each other again and meet as old friends long parted."[70] The development of a regional consciousness and of good-neighbor ties, separate but related, would be a challenge. The decision of the newly sovereign states in Southeast Asia to be aligned or nonaligned, a decision affected by the colonial heritage, would influence their future relationships.

Southeast Asia may be called a laboratory of the effects of decolonization.[71] Here the policies of the new states since 1946, as compared with those of the single old state, can be observed and the effect of time on behavior studied. Here the impact on domestic and foreign policy of George Washingtons and Simón Bolívars, friends and enemies to one another, and their early pragmatic successors with comparable relationships can be studied. And here in the years after the watershed of American policy would the United States engage in a major war.

How did Washington in 1954 view the total impact of decolonization on Southeast Asia in terms of U.S. foreign policy? First the requirements of the day had to be met and policy makers had little time for philosophical speculation. Next the political, economic, social, and psychological dimensions could not be evaluated in any definitive sense for some time. But there was a full realization beyond these considerations that decolonization was creating many new problems for U.S. foreign policy and that no magic formula existed for coping with them. The situation called for new relationships along a broad spectrum and for Americans who were willing and able to personify them.

Security and Value. As Washington accepted heavy security commitments in Southeast Asia in 1954, just what was the importance or the "value" of the area to the United States at the time?[72] What were the interests being supported by the American assumption of major obligations? The importance of Southeast Asia to Washington clearly had acquired broad dimensions. Direct and indirect values were significant since the United States had to bear in mind the effect of Southeast Asia on American friends with deep interests in the area.

Lying almost wholly in the humid tropics south and southeast of Communist China and east and southeast of India, and stretching over 3,000 miles east and west and more than 2,000 miles north and south, peninsular and insular Southeast Asia had one of the most strategic locations in the world. Through the region ran narrow water passageways linking the Pacific and Indian Oceans, passageways important in world commerce and in naval power. Notable were the Strait of Malacca between Sumatra and Malaya, the shortest water gateway between the two oceans, and the Sunda Strait between Java and Sumatra. In another direction Southeast Asia provided stepping stones from mainland China to Australia in the Southwest Pacific. Vietnam was halfway around the world from Gettysburg, as President Eisenhower once observed, but it was a key part of the "Near North" as seen from Australia.

In the years of the last British Empire Singapore, an island off the tip of the Malay Peninsula, was developed by Great Britain into a major commercial seaport and a significant naval base. It was important in 1954. Seven hundred miles north of Singapore at the narrow strip of land between the Andaman Sea and the Gulf of Siam was the Kra Isthmus in Thailand, long under consideration for a possible canal and viewed as a possible line of defense for Malaya. The Philippine Islands opposite Vietnam on the South China Sea, afforded sea and air bases in 1954 for the United States which were important both for Southeast Asia and for the Western Pacific.

Burma, located at the northwest corner of Southeast Asia, with its giant neighbors of China and India should not be minimized. A Burma Road, a Stilwell Road, and a railroad from Thailand, all built in connection with World War II, revealed how strategic Burma could be. Indochina, as the record of Japanese military penetration indicated, was an important key to Southeast Asia. Some of the international controversy over Laos in 1953 and 1954 arose from the strategic location of the landlocked kingdom along the Mekong River. Thailand should be mentioned last, for its geostrategic relationships to the rest of peninsular Southeast Asia such as Burma to the west and Laos and Cambodia to the east were of great significance.

Of course, the implications of the strategic role of various countries in the Pacific and First Indochinese Wars can certainly be overemphasized in view of vast political and military changes, but a bedrock of reality remained. And new considerations like the rapid expansion of air transportation increased the value of the area. Only a flight of a few hours, for instance, separated Bangkok from Darwin, Hong Kong, or Calcutta.

In broader dimensions the achievement of paramountcy by Communist China over Southeast Asia, it was believed in 1954, would give Peking a strategic position that would clearly endanger the posture of the United States in East Asia, would threaten India and Pakistan in South Asia, and would menace Australia and New Zealand in the Southwest Pacific. The impact, it was thought, would extend from Japan to the Middle East and Europe.

The military value of Southeast Asia in a major nuclear conflict among the Great Powers or for purposes of general deterrence, however, was not very significant. But in limited nonnuclear wars in adjacent countries it was very important. Charles Wolf, Jr., thoughtfully observed some years ago before the Second Indochinese War:

> The United States is a world power with military commitments, allies, and interests in areas remote from its strategic bases at home and abroad. As such we must be concerned with the effect of major changes in the political and military orientation of areas like Southeast Asia on the defensibility of adjacent areas . . . and we must be concerned with the effect on the defense of India and Australia, as well as on the whole balance of forces in the Far East, of a "loss" of Southeast Asia, or of a change in the status of a major portion of the area such as Indonesia.[73]

In economic terms Southeast Asia in 1954 had limited value to the United States although "limited" should be used judiciously. American private direct investments, only five years after U.S. major commitments, were a little more than $600 million for all Southeast Asia out of a total of $29.7 billion for the world. More than 60 per cent of the $600 million was in the Philippines where trade ties were also marked. In contrast $210 million of private direct investments were in Japan and $10.2 billion in Canada. Certain American investments in Southeast Asia like Indonesian petroleum received particular attention.

The value of American exports to and imports from Southeast Asia was relatively minor in terms of total U.S. trade. In 1957, three years after major American commitments, the United States along with Japan,

Canada, and Western Europe exported only $7.6 billion of their world exports of $70 billion to all South and Southeast Asia and imported only $4.5 billion of their total imports of $72 billion from the same area.

These statistics, however, did not indicate the importance of certain exports from Southeast Asia to the United States or to its friends and foes. The denial aspect is a factor of consideration. For instance, if Peking could control the distribution of exports in Southeast Asia, it could direct them to itself and to its friends and deny them to its foes. The latter would have to pay the price of alternate sources of supply or go without. The alternate sources, of course, could be other geographical areas or synthetic production when technically possible.

Southeast Asia produced about 60 per cent of the world's tin and around 90 per cent of its natural rubber, chiefly in Malaysia and Indonesia. When Japan cut off such imports to the United States in the last world war, Washington experienced real shortages. The United States again became an important importer of tin and natural rubber from Southeast Asia but the loss of this source in the future would not be so critical. A large synthetic American rubber industry was developed although both natural and synthetic rubber would have important world markets for a long time. Tin, which cannot be synthetically produced, was systematically and heavily stockpiled in the United States, and attention was given to other geographical sources. Communist China had supplies of tin but imported natural rubber.

Another important export of Southeast Asia was petroleum. In 1958, four years after the basic U.S. commitments, it produced 2.5 per cent of the world's total, mostly in Indonesia and Brunei. None was exported to Communist China which would find the petroleum an asset in its economy and under its control a strategic lever. In 1958 less than 15 per cent of Southeast Asia's petroleum went to the United States which had better sources of supply.

Burma, Thailand, and Indochina have traditionally been the rice bowl of Asia and their exports to rice-deficient countries have been very significant. Conditions at home and abroad have affected at various times the production and export of the commodity. In Southeast Asia, the traditional rice-deficient countries have been Indonesia, the Philippines, and Malaysia. Communist China with its huge and growing population would derive profits from controlling the rice trade of the region either in diverting the exports to itself and its friends or in keeping the staple from others. New high-yield varieties of certain food grains particularly rice would in time greatly increase the production in various countries—the so-called Green Revolution—solving many old problems of food supply but raising new social and economic questions.

Other important exports from Southeast Asia should be mentioned like copra, coconut oil, bauxite, and Manila hemp. Nor should iron ore, tungsten, spices, tea, coffee, sugar, and tobacco be ignored. The United States, it was clear, had a stake in maintaining ocean shipping as well as air routes in the region.

The economic value of Southeast Asia was greater for some of the allies of the United States, like Japan in Asia and certain others in Western Europe, than for itself. Traditional patterns of investment, banking, and trade, once involving colonial areas and metropolitan countries, had not disappeared by the mid-1950s in several instances. Malaysia has been the greatest dollar earner in the British Commonwealth sterling grouping. Southeast Asia's potential as a bigger market for the industrialized nations of the Free World was widely accepted. The Griffin mission in 1950 stressed at the time the triangular pattern of international trade —Western Europe, Southeast Asia, the United States—and its benefits for all. Japan's economic role in Southeast Asia was important both for itself and for its friends.

The political and psychological value of Southeast Asia to the United States in 1954 was even more difficult to evaluate than the military or economic. The people of the area numbered around 190 million, comparable then to the population of the Soviet Union and larger than that of the United States, but much smaller than the population of India or mainland China. Perhaps almost half lived in Indonesia, and between 12 and 13 million resided under Communist rule in the Democratic Republic of Vietnam. In a land area of 1,735,000 square miles, less than half the current size of the United States, the people were very unevenly distributed. Certain areas like Central Luzon, Java, and the Red River delta were overpopulated while Mindanao and the Outer Islands of Indonesia were underpopulated. The general rate of population growth was over 2.0 per cent each year (perhaps 2.5 per cent) but the rate varied from country to country; South Vietnam's rate, for example, was estimated at 2.8 per cent per annum.

It was widely accepted that Southeast Asia could support a much larger population. Furthermore, the region was located near areas like mainland China and India which were overpopulated and whose minorities in Southeast Asia had already shown they could well adjust to the conditions. If Peking could control population movements in the area, this could be a temporary but not a permanent solution to China's population problem. Involved, of course, in the basic equation was the food and population ratio.

Should all the people of Southeast Asia fall under Communist sway, presumably subject in the end to Peking's persuasion, the political and psychological consequences, Washington believed in 1954, would be serious to neighboring countries like Japan, India, and Australia and to other allies or friends of America. These indirect effects on the United States might well surpass the direct effects. As for the people themselves in Southeast Asia, the denial of freedom of choice and the victory of communism would represent an ideological victory of Peking that could not quickly be erased.

The value of Southeast Asia to the United States in 1954 thus reflected various interests—particularly military, economic, and political.[74] Cultural interests, apart from the Philippines and to a less extent Thailand, it might be noted, were very limited. American diplomatic initiative, of course, would increase as interests grew. It was one consideration for the United States to limit its security commitments in Southeast Asia to an alliance with the island republic of the Philippines; it was another to assume the mainland commitments under SEATO.

The American official pressure in Southeast Asia as of late 1954 was relatively modest. Embassies were maintained in Manila, Djakarta, Saigon, Phnom Penh, Bangkok, and Rangoon; a legation existed in Vientiane; a consulate general in Singapore; and consulates in Surabaya, Medan, Penang, Kuala Lumpur, Chiang Mai, and Hanoi. The economic, military, cultural, and information components of various missions would expand at a faster rate than the relatively small number of private Americans who went to Southeast Asia as businessmen, missionaries, scholars, and tourists.

The area in 1954 was handled in the Department of State by the Office of Philippine and Southeast Asian Affairs embracing the Philippines, Thailand, Indochina, British Malaya, Burma, Indonesia, British Borneo, and the South Pacific Islands. The director of the office ranked with the directors of the offices of Northeast Asian Affairs and Chinese Affairs under a deputy assistant secretary and an assistant secretary of state for Far Eastern Affairs. Other branches of government, of course, had their own organizations.

United States Objectives in 1954. American objectives in Southeast Asia both short-range and long-range had become fairly well formulated before the fall of 1954. They focused on the promotion of the security of the various states of the area and on support for their stability at home. Expressed in other words America sought to help maintain the political independence and territorial integrity of the states of Southeast Asia under hopefully stable governments which were adequately responsive to the needs of the people. Washington wanted in 1954 the states of the region to be responsible members of an orderly world community.

Through the promotion of various economic programs in Southeast

Asia it was hoped that the people's standard of living would be raised, their rising expectations for a fuller life would be met, and the peasants and city dwellers would have a larger stake in defending their country against subversion and aggression. Although the U.S. objective of stability in Southeast Asia was difficult to support in societies involved in nation-building during a transitional era of great economic and social change, Washington believed it must relate itself to the dynamics of change, associate with orderly transition, and encourage democratic processes.

American support for security, it was maintained in 1954, was essentially a holding operation until the states of the area gained in internal strength and external posture and worked together in broader patterns of regional cooperation. The internal and external aspects of security and cooperation could not be arbitrarily separated, especially if a sanctuary existed across a national border for the use and support of dissidents from a neighbor. The promotion of good-neighbor relations, of regional consciousness, and of regionalism was a broad goal supported by U.S. policy.

Another major American objective was to stop the spread of communism in Southeast Asia. By encouraging stability and security in the area, the United States believed one of the important results would be the failure of international communism in the region. This objective was constant in Washington but the Eisenhower administration with Secretary Dulles was more inclined to state it flatly than the subsequent Kennedy administration.

Apart from general objectives the United States had specific policy goals in Southeast Asia which varied from country to country and from time to time. Priority in U.S. efforts, of course, depended upon the general international situation in the world at a point in time, upon the various pressures being exerted, and upon the needed countermeasures.

IV THE AFTERMATH

The stream of American involvement in Southeast Asia after the watershed of 1954 grew into a river during the rest of the Eisenhower presidency and the Kennedy administration, and then emerged as a torrent during many of the Johnson years. After cresting in 1968 it was gradually allowed to subside under the Nixon administration despite occasional increments and become a river—some would hope a stream or less—of involvement.

There are inherent dangers in relating the 1954 watershed directly to the Second Indochinese War which emerged in early 1965 and indirectly to the emphasis in U.S. policy on development, with Indonesia as the key example, after the failure of the attempted Communist coup in the early fall of 1965. Yet it is certain that the American course was set in 1954 and had relevance to subsequent events. In the case of mainland Southeast Asia, the Pentagon Papers, for instance, establish a significant causal relationship in American policy in Indochina leading to the Second Indochinese War. As regards insular Southeast Asia, Washington was prepared when the time came to take advantage of unexpected opportunities in Indonesia. The relationship of these opportunities to the war in Indochina can be debated. Lyndon B. Johnson, Richard M. Nixon, and Ferdinand E. Marcos, for instance, have argued that American policy in Vietnam worked to the advantage of General Suharto during the struggle for power in Indonesia that lasted for some time after the failure of the coup. One point is clear: The contours of the future, however blurred, cannot be divorced from the experience of the past.

The purpose of Part Four is to focus on various aspects of two major themes in U.S. policy that followed the watershed of commitment in 1954: the Second Indochinese War and the emphasis on development. The former towered in the United States like a colossus and produced an impact more discernible in short-range than long-range terms. The evolution of the conflict after 1954, the dimensions of the war from 1965 with its patterns of escalation and de-escalation, and the association of the experience with the Nixon Doctrine will be examined. Although the emphasis on development was almost dwarfed in the headlines of the Second Indochinese War and was not conducive anyway to widespread attention, the role of development was important, clearly long-range, and promised to gain increasing momentum in Southeast Asia. Its dimensions with particular reference to Indonesia and to the United States, Japan, and regional initiatives will be examined.

Part Four will conclude with some perspectives arising from American experience in Southeast Asia.

6 WAR AND DEVELOPMENT THEMES IN AMERICAN POLICY

THE SECOND INDOCHINESE WAR: THE PRIMARY THEME

By the pricking of my thumbs,
Something wicked this way comes.

MACBETH

When Communism has long ebbed away into the past, my people will still be here, a free united nation growing from the deep roots of our Vietnamese heritage. They will remember your help in our time of need. This struggle will then be a part of our common history. And your help, your friendship, and the strong bonds between our two peoples will be a part of Viet-Nam, then as now.

President Ngo Dinh Diem to President John F. Kennedy
December 7, 1961[1]

The date of Diem's letter was twenty years to the day after Pearl Harbor. The letter, and Kennedy's response, were a significant link in the chain of events that led to the Second Indochinese War, ending after the 1960s. There was no Pearl Harbor—no dramatic event, no international traumatic experience—providing an occasion for U.S. entry into the Second Indochinese War. But there were direct and indirect causes contributing to the answer of the question, why Vietnam?

The Second Indochinese War had broad dimensions and presented a complicated pattern. It almost defied systematic analysis. Its military, political, and diplomatic fronts under Presidents Johnson and Nixon were not separate compartments but were profoundly interrelated. A major military decision in Washington had to be considered in terms of its effects on the war in Indochina, on the domestic situation in the United States, and in the world of diplomacy. These three considerations continued as the Second Indochinese War dragged from year to year. Despite the fact that a dialogue began in Paris in the spring of 1968 between the United States and North Vietnam, the settlement of the conflict long proved illusive. Victory and defeat were relative terms—not absolute terms—from the 1960s into the 1970s.

The Road to War. There were many constant patterns of viewpoint and deed in Washington from 1954 to 1965.[2] Presidents Eisenhower, Kennedy, and Johnson like Truman before them had difficulties in defining the problem of Vietnam. But define it they did in dimensions that reflected continuity in presidential outlook. In making their policies the chief executives with their sets of advisers afforded an excellent example of presidential management in a growing crisis with relatively little interference from outside government for many years. Each President in fact inherited commitments in Indochina and extended them, leaving to his successor a worse situation than what he found. Eisenhower, Kennedy, and Johnson in the years from 1954 to 1965 did what they thought was minimal to prevent South Vietnam from falling into the hands of the Communists. They believed they had done only what was essential at each stage being limited by restraints at home and by the desire not to provoke Peking and/or Moscow into a major war with possible nuclear weapons. As it was, every big step up the ladder of involvement in Indochina caused hesitation in the White House lest it trigger a grave Chinese and/or Russian response. The United States did not stumble like a blind man into the Second Indochinese War.

Each President from 1954 to 1965 concluded that disengagement would cost him more than carefully controlled further engagement. He was aware of a right wing at home which liked to cite the fall of China to Mao Tse-tung and the maintenance or establishment of Communist regimes in North Korea and North Vietnam. Influenced by the experience of the Cold War, Eisenhower, Kennedy, and Johnson also believed the world would be less dangerous if communism did not succeed in Indochina. At the same time each was frustrated by the results of his efforts there though he realized his major steps in deeper involvement and commitment between 1954 and 1965 did not promise and were not expected to be sufficient to bring success. In other words he probably could not win in a situation of excessive goals in terms of inadequate means but he still could not afford to lose and was prepared to stake limited resources and take limited risks. Eisenhower, Kennedy, and Johnson expressed optimism over their policies—it has been called controlled optimism—since public statements and private viewpoints in Washington were certainly not identical.

Indeed, the intelligence estimates and analyses in the 1950s and to a somewhat lesser extent in the 1960s were pessimistic about the future of a non-Communist Vietnam. Most major decisions were made against the advice of the intelligence community which was usually accurate about attainable goals and enemy responses. At the same time policy analyses and recommendations were realistic in stressing only the possibility that certain proposals might work and in indicating that they were the best among the alternatives.

In the internal decision making of the bureaucracy the same principal themes occurred in the discussion over the years even in crucial periods, regardless of the degree of commitment or escalation. From 1950 to mid-1967 the thrust was almost entirely on how to attain the stated basic goal in Vietnam rather than on the overall directions of U.S. policy. As the rhetoric of Presidents increasingly engaged the credibility of the United States in the "vital" stakes there, the effect on the bureaucracy was to try and do things better within the fixed course. In scenarios or in problem-solving exercises the emphasis was on the pragmatic approach to solutions. Pressure for decisive action did come at times from within the government and the President, of course, made compromises arising from conflicting viewpoints in his official family. There was, however, very little questioning of the moral basis for American policy in Indochina during the years 1954–65.

The basic American objective under Presidents Eisenhower, Kennedy, and Johnson remained constant in South Vietnam: denying to communism the control of the area. This goal also meant U.S. opposition to a coalition government with Communists in Saigon. Inherent was the prevention of defeat and humiliation for the United States. Although South Vietnam remained in existence due to American policy after the Geneva settlement of 1954 Washington often found itself at the mercy of weak and inefficient Saigon regimes. One of the most serious continuing problems for the United States related to the need of responsible leadership responsive to the people in South Vietnam.

Also constant in the Eisenhower, Kennedy, and Johnson years was the domino theory or a variation of it. (Nixon once remarked that critics had not talked to the dominoes.) The theory persisted despite the emergence of the rift between Moscow and Peking and despite the subsequent failure of the Communist coup in Indonesia and the Cultural Revolution in China. Indeed, when Vietnam was viewed from Washington in terms of global strategic considerations, there was a certain static aspect in outlook, a carry-over from an earlier period. After China fell to Mao Tsetung and American policy toward communism hardened at home the value of Indochina/Vietnam to U.S. security was taken for granted. Washington's "vital interests" in Vietnam were frozen for many years. But the reasons for priority, it should be stressed, were not found in Vietnam per se; its leaders were related to greater American concerns. The reasons in the Eisenhower, Kennedy, and Johnson years from 1954–65 were found in the complex of U.S. relations with allies and Communist states, the intricacies of domestic considerations, and even theories of peacekeeping formulated in American think tanks.

All three Presidents made far-reaching decisions on Indochina policy about which the American public knew or understood little. The announcement of piecemeal ad hoc decisions, often seemingly marginal or even contingent in nature, was sometimes the cover-up for fully planned major moves in involvement. In retrospect this approach led to widespread conviction that successive administrations deceived the American Congress and people. However, the impact of the involvement on society in the United States did not cause worries in high government circles until mid–1967.

Clandestine warfare against North Vietnam under the Eisenhower, Kennedy, and Johnson administrations, as revealed in the Pentagon Papers, has opened up new perspectives on the 1954–65 period. The revelations have made more complex the issues of growing American commitment in Indochina and have contributed to an understanding of paradoxes in the area.

Finally, it should be noted, civilian leadership in making policy for Indochina was clear-cut during the Eisenhower, Kennedy, and Johnson years. Although the military approach won over the political giving the military considerable influence the civilian leadership made the decisions. Washington, furthermore, was more confident of military power in the 1960s.

The Eisenhower administration did not long delay in reaching basic policy decisions after the Geneva settlement of 1954. The National Security Council, in no uncertain words, asserted in August that the accords jeopardized U.S. security interests in East Asia, that the United States had lost prestige there, and that the Communists had secured "an advance salient" and had "increased their military and political prestige in Asia."[3] Before President Eisenhower reached a decision on what to do in Indochina a national intelligence estimate on August 3 had indicated that the French and Vietnamese were unlikely to be capable of set-ting up a strong government in Saigon even with U.S. support. The Joint Chiefs of Staff the next day objected under the circumstances to propos-als that Washington train and equip the army of South Vietnam. Secre-tary Dulles, however, argued that a military training program would help the Saigon government to become strong. On August 20 a statement of the National Security Council in effect called for the United States to build up indigenous forces for internal security and to work politically with Premier Ngo Dinh Diem. Although the Joint Chiefs continued their opposition to a training program, they had to give in as "political consid-erations" were "overriding." Meanwhile the Saigon Military Mission under Colonel Lansdale, as approved in Washington much earlier in the year, was involved in clandestine operations in North Vietnam.[4]

After considerable discussion in Washington Ambassador Heath in South Vietnam delivered a message as of October 23 from President Eisenhower to Premier Diem. It had actually been drafted by Kenneth T. Young who was head of an interdepartmental task group on the country, and delivery of the communication had been delayed. This famous mes-sage was subsequently cited by Presidents Kennedy and Johnson to sup-port their policies in South Vietnam.* Young later referred to it as the "base line for judging what we tried and how we have done in political development [there]."[5] In response to Diem's request for U.S. assis-tance, President Eisenhower instructed Ambassador Heath to examine with the Premier

> how an intelligent program of American aid given directly to your Government can serve to assist Viet-Nam in its present hour of trial, provided that your Government is prepared to give assurances as to the standards of performance it would be able to maintain in the event such aid were supplied.[6]

This proviso was extended in the succeeding paragraph—Washington "expects that this aid will be met by performance on the part of the Gov-ernment of Viet-Nam in undertaking needed reforms."[7] The American objective in Vietnam was clearly stated in the message as "a strong, viable state, capable of resisting attempted subversion or aggression through military means"[8] or "an independent Viet-Nam endowed with a strong government" which would be "so responsive to the nationalist aspirations of its people, so enlightened in purpose and effective in performance, that it will be respected at home and abroad and discourage any who might wish to impose a foreign ideology."[9]

On November 1 President Eisenhower chose General J. Lawton Col-

*Eisenhower on August 17, 1965, stressed economic aid in his offer.

lins as a special representative to go to Vietnam for a limited time. He reached an agreement the next month with the French in Saigon under which Washington would essentially take over from them Vietnamese military training. Although it did not go into effect until the first part of 1955 it signaled another retreat of the French in Indochina and was a step in the withdrawal of their armed forces from South Vietnam.

General Collins was one of the first Americans to suggest the replacement of Ngo Dinh Diem. (So did Eisenhower's last ambassador, Eldridge Durbrow, six years later.) Secretary Dulles in response to the General's recommendation in December 1954 indicated that no other choice existed. Nevertheless, there were widespread doubts in Washington about the leadership of the Premier.

Diem faced an extremely serious challenge to his rule in March and April 1955. Involved were French intrigue, American vacillation, and Diem's stubbornness. In the end the Premier's evaluation and action proved correct, a fact which he did not forget in subsequent dealings with the Americans. The French position was greatly weakened, U.S. backing was consolidated, and Diem emerged as the man of the decade.

On March 29 fighting had erupted in Saigon between the Premier's forces and the Binh Xuyen, an organization of gangsters that controlled the police. The French with American support arranged a cease-fire. Collins left in late April for consultations in Washington where he saw Eisenhower and expressed his criticism of Diem. (He must be replaced.) The President indicated to his envoy he was willing to support what recommendations the latter made, and Collins informed the Vietnam task force of Eisenhower's attitude. Young and the other members of his group sought a compromise in the dilemma. In view of the mounting doubt about Diem as an effective leader despite his importance as a symbol of nationalism the task force recommended that he be chief of state or hold a purely titular office, but that Dr. Phan Huy Quat be general manager or possibly premier. Allen Dulles and Walter S. Robertson as well as John Foster Dulles and J. Lawton Collins accepted the shift on Diem. As the General was preparing to leave for Saigon, a cablegram dated April 27 was approved by Secretary Dulles for dispatch to the U.S. embassy in Vietnam. It called in effect for a change in Vietnamese leadership but still supported a program of security and reform in the country. Under the plans the embassy would undertake preliminary steps before Collins reached Saigon.

But in one of the fateful coincidences in the history of American-Vietnamese relations—there are others like the assassinations of Presidents Kennedy and Diem within a relatively few days of each other—the issue between Diem and the Binh Xuyen was essentially resolved in a few hours of bloody fighting in the streets of Saigon on April 29 and the American cablegram of April 27 was nullified. Colonel Lansdale was vindicated in his active support of the Premier.* For many years "sink or swim with Ngo Dinh Diem" was not an empty slogan.

The question of free elections in all Vietnam in July 1956 as foreseen by the Geneva Accords was highly controversial.† It was probably mishandled by Diem who ignored American advice to put the onus for not holding them on Ho Chi Minh. Involved also was the role of France whose military disengagement in South Vietnam spurred by Diem made it impossible for Paris to carry out all its obligations as assumed under the Geneva settlement. Nor did Moscow and Peking, when the chips were down, make an extraordinary effort to support Ho Chi Minh in his call for elections to unify Vietnam. In fact, Moscow in 1957 proposed the admission of North and South Vietnam as well as the two Koreas into the United Nations, a step opposed by Washington partly because of its fear of setting a precedent for Germany.

In July 1955 when consultations between Saigon and Hanoi were scheduled to begin Ngo Dinh Diem flatly asserted that he did not object to the principle of elections to produce unity but insisted they must be

---

*The Colonel's own account of the hectic days from the end of March to early May is found in Edward Geary Lansdale, *In the Midst of Wars: An American's Mission to Southeast Asia*, Harper and Row, New York, 1972, pp. 260–311. It was Lansdale's cable sent late April 29 that caused Dulles to leave a dinner party, go to see Eisenhower at the White House, and get the President's decision to back Ngo Dinh Diem. "I hadn't believed Diem's reports from Washington that the U.S. was about to 'dump' him," Lansdale wrote, "and had thought I was being honest when I had expressed my disbelief. From the little I ever learned, I concluded eventually that my unwitting role had been that of an expendable pawn in a political game." *Ibid.*, p. 300. Two key documents on the crisis in the Pentagon Papers are the cablegram Dulles sent the U.S. embassy in Saigon as well as in Paris, April 27, and a report by Kenneth T. Young on "Collins Visit and Viet-Nam Situation," April 30, *United States-Vietnam Relations, 1945–1967*, Book 10, pp. 941–44 and pp. 945–47.

†A government analyst of the Pentagon Papers observes in the section on "The Spirit and Practical Effect of Geneva" that "the difficulty with the election provisions of the Final Declaration, as with the Accords as a whole, relates not to their spirit, but to their practicality. It remains a matter of conjecture whether the members of the Convention genuinely thought that a political solution to unification had been postponed by only two years, or whether they felt that partition, even with the resultant risk of renewed military confrontation was, in reality, the best and only solution that the conflicting aims and pressures at Geneva could provide. . . . If the Geneva Accords were subverted, the subverters were the Geneva conferees themselves, who postulated an ideal political settlement incompatible with the physical and psychological dismemberment of Vietnam they themselves undertook on July 21, 1954." *United States-Vietnam Relations, 1945–1967*, Book 1, III.D., pp. 24–26.

truly free, a condition he doubted could be met in the North. Indeed, truly free elections under valid international supervision could probably not have been held in either North or South Vietnam in July 1956.

Washington did not force Diem or connive with him in his decision not to hold the elections—but the United States did back him in his refusal. Senator John F. Kennedy on June 1, 1956, flatly condemned in a speech before the American Friends of Vietnam "an election obviously stacked and subverted in advance, urged upon us by those who have already broken their own pledges under the agreement they now seek to enforce."[10]

President Ngo Dinh Diem in marked contrast to the travels of his North Vietnamese rival made a state visit to America in May 1957 at a time when his popularity in South Vietnam was still noticeable and Communist activity still at a low key. It was a triumphal tour, President Eisenhower himself going to the airport to greet him. While Diem was in Washington, May 8–11, he was given the honor of addressing a joint meeting of Congress. A statement of the American and Vietnamese Presidents on May 11 confirmed the will of both governments to cooperate toward a peaceful unification of divided Vietnam "in freedom in accordance with the purposes and principles of the United Nations Charter."[11] The two leaders pointedly noted that the Republic of Vietnam was covered by Article IV of the Manila Treaty and "agreed that aggression or subversion threatening the political independence of the Republic of Viet-Nam would be considered as endangering peace and stability."[12]

By the time of his American visit Ngo Dinh Diem had seen his best days. From 1956 to 1958 dissident Communist cadres in South Vietnam initiated an insurgency. Prior to then, from 1954 to 1956, they had stressed "political struggle" in view of the coming elections on unification. In 1959 Hanoi decided to assume the leadership of the insurgency and a full-scale conflict resulted. The Communists were able to capitalize on the weaknesses of Diem's leadership—he was authoritarian, rigid, suspicious, remote, and bureaucratic—and of his government—it became more and more an incompetent family oligarchy in a police state. Opposition to Diem's policies mounted in both the urban and rural population of the country and in both Communist and non-Communist circles.

President Eisenhower in his last greetings to Ngo Dinh Diem commemorating an anniversary of the Republic of Vietnam, October 26, 1960, stressed Hanoi's use of "increasing violence" in South Vietnam and assured him that "so long as our strength can be useful, the United States will continue to assist Viet-Nam in the difficult yet hopeful strug-

gle ahead."[13] At the same time Eisenhower observed that the Vietnamese people and their government had the "main responsibility" for guard-
ing the independence of the country. There was a commitment though
conditional and a liability though limited.

It was not Vietnam, however, that most concerned President Eisenhower in Southeast Asia during the last months of his presidency. It was
the situation in Laos which in Washington's viewpoint had gone from
bad to worse. The efforts of Secretary Dulles to build up a strong, pro-
Western, anti-Communist though technically neutral Laos after the
Geneva settlement of 1954 had failed. Yet U.S. military and economic
aid was very large. Washington had not favored the coalition government
in Vientiane with the Pathet Lao, backed by Hanoi, under Prime Minister Souvanna Phouma, that lasted from November 1957 into the summer
of 1958. It successfully parried, partly due to the cooperation of the
United Nations, a Pathet Lao offensive supported by North Vietnam in
the summer of 1959, but it was deeply upset over the coup of Captain
Kong Le in August 1960 which overthrew a staunchly pro-Western government. Another one sympathetic to the United States was established
in Vientiane after considerable American aid when the capital was captured in December 1960. However, a full-scale civil war developed in
Laos with Moscow actively supporting in an airlift Captain Kong Le, the
Pathet Lao, and North Vietnamese forces, and with Washington providing increased military and other assistance to the government of Prince
Boun Oum.

When President-elect Kennedy was briefed by President Eisenhower
on January 19, 1961, the latter asserted, according to Clark M. Clifford
who took notes on the briefing, that the key to Southeast Asia was Laos.

> He said that if we permitted Laos to fall, then we would have to
> write off all the area. He stated we must not permit a Communist
> take-over. He reiterated that we should make every effort to per-
> suade member nations of SEATO or the International Control
> Commission to accept the burden with us to defend the freedom of
> Laos.
> As he concluded these remarks, President Eisenhower stated it
> was imperative that Laos be defended. He said that the United
> States should accept this task with our allies, if we could persuade
> them, and alone if we could not.[14]

Looking back over the years, President Eisenhower, like President
Truman before him, in response to a query, indicated his belief that
during his period in the White House American policy in Southeast Asia
was bipartisan.

John F. Kennedy in the short term of his presidency greatly broadened the commitment of Eisenhower in South Vietnam. His policy toward the crisis in Laos affected his attitude toward commitments in both Thailand and South Vietnam as well as his relationship with Cambodia. It became much more clear under Kennedy than under Eisenhower that American involvement in mainland Southeast Asia—the two Vietnams, Laos, Cambodia, and Thailand, all the countries but Burma which was essentially off to one side*—was pronounced and heading toward a major crisis unless diverted.

Kennedy probably spent more time on Laos than on any other problem during his first two months in the White House. He personally took a deep interest in his task force on it. In March and April of 1961 and again in May of 1962 the President had to face the specific issue of American military intervention in the country. In both cases he turned away from the brink of war, but faced a sword of Damocles. If the Communists attempted an all-out offensive throughout the kingdom, "such a blatant and dramatic assault would make our intervention almost inevitable," in the words of Roger Hilsman, former Assistant Secretary of State for Far Eastern Affairs.[16] As it was, the President's televised comments of March 23, 1961, implied war, and he found it necessary in May 1962 to send combat units to Thailand as a warning to the Communists in Laos and their supporters.

Kennedy's decisions in the Mekong kingdom, however, reflected a reassessment of U.S. policy there in the light of world developments and of domestic politics at home. For instance, he faced a decision on intervention in Laos the same week as the Bay of Pigs fiasco in Cuba, an island only 90 miles from Florida. Although the new President had a deep interest in Asia he believed the United States was overcommitted in Laos and the country was not "worthy of engaging the attention of great powers."[17] At the same time Kennedy was convinced he could not honorably forget previous obligations. He realized the strategic importance of the kingdom and the political dangers at home and abroad of a humiliation over it.

In the end the President sought a political compromise in Laos through cooperation with the Soviet Union in an effort establishing a co-

*Although the expression "essentially off to one side" is accurate the National Security Council with the approval of the President on September 5, 1956, and again on July 25, 1960, in almost identical words asserted that "should overt Communist aggression occur against Burma, [the United States should] invoke the UN Charter and, subject to Burmese request for assistance, take necessary military and any other action to assist Burma if Burma is willing to resist Communist resort to force and U.S. vital interests are involved: provided that the taking of military action shall be subject to prior submission to and approval by the Congress."[15] President Kennedy inherited this policy.

alition or troika government. It consisted of Prime Minister Souvanna Phouma; his half brother Souphanouvong, the leader of the Pathet Lao, as one deputy prime minister; and the leader of the rightists, General Phoumi Nosavan, as the other. At the international level a long conference on Laos at Geneva of fourteen powers including the United States, the Soviet Union, Communist China, Great Britain, and France began on May 16, 1961, and ended on July 23, 1962, with a Declaration on the Neutrality of Laos signed by the outside powers and a protocol to it signed by all participants with the inclusion of Laos. Vientiane was in effect disassociated from SEATO.[18]

Yet, even before Kennedy's assassination in November 1963, his approach to a solution in the Mekong kingdom had failed on both the domestic and international levels and the United States was becoming deeply involved in an effort to prevent a Communist take-over in the country.

President Kennedy's policy in Laos led to deeper U.S. involvement in Thailand. Bangkok had long been greatly concerned over developments in its weak Mekong neighbor. The steps toward a coalition government and toward the neutralization of Laos against a background of the evident weakness of SEATO caused Thailand to seek stronger assurances from the United States. President Eisenhower for his part had sought over the years to reassure Bangkok, and the American role and presence under him had markedly increased in the kingdom.

At the end of February 1962 Thanat Khoman, Thai foreign minister, was invited to Washington to discuss ways to ensure the security of Thailand in the framework of SEATO. The Foreign Minister spent five days in the capital in consultation on subjects which had been thoroughly discussed in Bangkok between American and Thai officials. On March 6 he saw the President for forty minutes. Kennedy "assured Thailand of full United States support for its independence and territorial integrity, and . . . pledged American determination to meet any Communist attack on Thailand without requiring the prior agreement of other SEATO countries."[19]

On the same day a joint statement was issued by Secretary of State Dean Rusk and Foreign Minister Thanat Khoman which formalized the assurance. In addition to reaffirming the "vital" interests of the United States in Thailand the joint statement asserted that the obligations under the Manila Treaty were both individual and collective in case of Communist armed attack. The stress on the individual in addition to the collective aspect was the point. Former Ambassador Young carefully wrote in 1965 that "Bangkok and Washington were able in March 1962 to negotiate a significant interpretation of the SEATO treaty which finessed

Thailand's vigorous drive to modify the Treaty in ways which the United States could not have accepted without creating serious constitutional difficulties."[20] He asserted the interpretation "amounts to a *de facto* bilateral defense alliance within the constitutional framework of the United States."[21] Washington, it should be stressed, was not limited to the restriction of collective determination of an armed attack or of collective decision on how to meet it.

A test of Kennedy's resolution soon came. In early May Pathet Lao troops with North Vietnamese support launched an attack on Nam Tha in northwestern Laos, defeated the forces of General Phoumi Nosavan, and approached the Mekong border with Thailand. The U.S. reaction was quick and effective. In mid-May Bangkok responded to an abrupt American initiative and in an unprecedented peacetime step welcomed U.S. air and ground combat forces on its soil. The way was paved for a much greater American military role in the kingdom. In fact, a United States Military Assistance Command, Thailand, was created in 1962.

President Kennedy was concerned lest his policy in Laos and in the Bay of Pigs fiasco during the spring of 1961 drastically weaken his credibility with Nikita Khrushchev, Mao Tse-tung, and other Communist leaders. A stormy meeting June with the Russian Premier in Vienna and a new Berlin crisis provided fuel for the President's apprehension. American firmness in South Vietnam in the face of a so-called "war of national liberation" approved by Khrushchev, Mao, and Ho afforded Kennedy a chance to prove his credibility. Paradoxically the Geneva settlement on Laos had given Hanoi a better opportunity to develop the Ho Chi Minh trails through Laos into South Vietnam and later Cambodia.

Against an extended background of discussion President Kennedy on May 11, 1961, approved sending approximately 400 Special Forces soldiers to South Vietnam, the initiation of a campaign of clandestine warfare in North Vietnam and Laos by South Vietnamese with U.S. aid, and the start of negotiations with President Diem for a "new bilateral arrangement." Kennedy was well aware that the additional soldiers further violated the Geneva Accords—he had already authorized an increase of approximately 100 military advisers on April 29—but he believed the Communists were to blame for the mounting crisis and that Special Forces soldiers were a key to one of his major concerns, counter-insurgency. The program of covert warfare in North Vietnam and Laos was a step on the ladder of clandestine operations there.

Two days before at Kennedy's request Vice-President Lyndon B. Johnson had departed for Asia with Saigon and Bangkok key capitals on his itinerary. His chief purpose was to assure America's allies and friends of Washington's credibility, and he reported on May 23 to Kennedy that the choice was to help Vietnam and Thailand "to the best of our ability" or "pull back our defenses to San Francisco and a 'Fortress America' concept."[22] At the time President Diem and Prime Minister Sarit did not ask Johnson for combat forces and the latter did not recommend that Kennedy send them.

In connection with the Vice-President's visit a mission of economic and fiscal experts under Eugene A. Staley was later sent to Saigon to work with Vietnamese counterparts on planning a joint program which came to embrace military-internal security action, emergency economic and social action, and longer-range development looking toward a self-sustaining economy in Vietnam. Actually the Staley mission became deeply involved in assessing the economic and fiscal implications of increasing Saigon's armed forces to 200,000.[23] On August 4 President Kennedy approved the Staley recommendations.

As the security situation further deteriorated in South Vietnam and Diem asked for a bilateral defense treaty in late September, Kennedy decided on October 11 to send General Maxwell D. Taylor along with White House adviser Walt W. Rostow, General Lansdale, and a few others on a special mission to Saigon to recommend what the United States should do in the mounting crisis. After the survey was made in Vietnam, Taylor on November 1 sent two key telegrams from Baguio "eyes only" for Kennedy in Washington. The first telegram summarized the "fundamental conclusions" of the mission and gave the General's personal recommendations. Taylor called for a "massive joint effort" to cope with the Viet Cong and with a flood in the delta. The key provision, as he had earlier indicated, called for the United States to "offer to introduce into South Vietnam a military Task Force to operate under U.S. control" for a number of purposes one of which was to "provide an emergency reserve to back up the Armed Forces of the GVN [Government of Vietnam] in the case of a heightened military crisis."[24] In the second telegram Taylor stressed the reasons for urging that an American military force be introduced into South Vietnam. He believed the initial number should not exceed around 8,000 men, the majority of them being in logistical-type units. Taylor thought there were "considerable advantages in playing up" the role of the task force in flood relief activities. The General pointedly asserted that he did "not believe that our program to save SVN [South Vietnam] will succeed without it."[25] The formal report of the mission in the form of a loose-leaf notebook was submitted on November 3.

The subject of the military task force dominated the discussions in Washington. Involved were grave issues of American policy in Vietnam, Southeast Asia, and the world. In the end, President Kennedy did not implement the recommendation for a military task force, but he did assent to many other suggestions for a sharply increased effort along the lines of a limited Vietnamese-American partnership. He personally approved the key cablegram giving his decisions which was sent to the American Ambassador in Saigon on November 15.[26] After some delay in Saigon due to Diem's concern over the extent of the U.S. role—Washington retreated in its approach to reforms—a formal exchange of letters between Kennedy and Diem in December marked in highly general terms the accord.*

What John F. Kennedy essentially did was to greatly expand the number of U.S. military advisers and to put Americans in uniform in combat-support roles along with providing more and better military equipment. Under his administration the number of advisers rose from 685 to around 16,000. In 1962 an eightfold increase in U.S. combat casualties occurred. (In the field, support troops and combat troops are hard to separate.) But Kennedy continued to resist pressures to commit ground combat units to South Vietnam or to mount a bombing offensive in North Vietnam. At the same time he allowed the military aspect of the struggle against the Communists to override needed political reforms by the Diem regime. Optimism in the spring and summer of 1962 over military operations and over the development of strategic hamlets contributed to plans for the early phase-out of U.S. military personnel.†

In May 1963 the crisis in relations between Ngo Dinh Diem and the Buddhists erupted. Its consequences led to the overthrow of the Diem regime in early November. President Kennedy, as the Pentagon Papers

---

*Kennedy's decisions of 1961 in Vietnam have led to a literature of dissection. The government analyst in the Pentagon Papers in his "Kennedy Program and Commitments: 1961," *United States–Vietnam Relations, 1945–1967*, Book 2, has written a comprehensive account utilizing available classified sources and published works. Donald E. Nuechterlein has related the decisions to American interests in his article "U.S. National Interests in Southeast Asia: A Reappraisal," *Asian Survey*, November 1971, pp. 1054–70. General Taylor's own account of his mission to Saigon in 1961 is found in his *Swords and Plowshares*, Norton, New York, 1972, pp. 221–49.

†An analysis of the "Strategic Hamlet Program: 1961–1963" is found in *United States–Vietnam Relations, 1945–1967*, Book 3. In effect, the program died with Ngo Dinh Diem and Ngo Dinh Nhu. The account of the "Phased Withdrawal of U.S. Forces [in Vietnam]: 1962–1964," *ibid.*, is particularly interesting in the light of subsequent developments. Secretary of Defense Robert S. McNamara and General Taylor after their mission to Vietnam for President Kennedy in the early fall of 1963 called on October 2, *inter alia*, for the announcement of prepared plans to withdraw 1,000 American military personnel by the end of the year. For text of their report, see *ibid.*, Book 12, pp. 554–73.

clearly reveal, was aware of the plans at various stages that led to the coup and approved of them.* His chief concern in late August, as in October when plotting was well advanced by the Vietnamese generals, was that the coup might fail and that the appearance of U.S. complicity would have bad consequences for his government. He was shocked when he learned of the murders of Ngo Dinh Diem and Ngo Dinh Nhu.

The United States, however, did not originate the coup and did not participate in its actual execution although Washington kept in close, secret contact with the plotters. The restriction of aid to Diem in October gave them a go-ahead signal, and they knew their successor government would have full American support. Ambassador Henry Cabot Lodge in Saigon and Lieutenant Colonel Lucien Conein of CIA emerge as key U.S. figures in the overthrow of Diem. On the other hand, Vice-President Johnson, General Taylor, Frederick E. Nolting, Lodge's predecessor, and General Paul D. Harkins, ranking U.S. military officer in Vietnam, were not sympathetic to it.

The complicity of the United States in the coup of November 1963 further involved Washington in South Vietnam. Against the continued determination of the United States to prevent an increasingly possible Communist victory the pronounced instability in South Vietnam for some time inadvertently increased U.S. responsibilities and commitments.

American policy in Laos, Thailand, and Vietnam during the Kennedy years contributed to the deterioration of U.S. relations with Cambodia. Here Prince Norodom Sihanouk was the towering figure regardless of the title he had at various times. His driving objective was to maintain the independence of his kingdom. During the administration of President Eisenhower Sihanouk had moved from neutralism of the right to that of the center and during the White House years of Kennedy, from neutralism of the center to that of the left.[27] The developments in Laos and

---

*For an account by Hedrick Smith on the overthrow of Ngo Dinh Diem based largely upon the Pentagon Papers and a few others supplied *The New York Times*, see Pentagon Papers, *The New York Times*, July 1, 1971, pp. 1, 12–14, and pp. 9–12 (narrative with documents). The account of the government analyst is best found in The Senator Gravel Edition, *The Pentagon Papers*, Vol. II, pp. 224–76, with documents from *The New York Times* and the Pentagon Papers, pp. 727–93. The version published by the Government Printing Office contains omissions in both the narrative and documentation. The summary, presumably written by Leslie H. Gelb, of the account by the government analyst concludes: "For the military coup d'etat against Ngo Dinh Diem, the U.S. must accept its full share of responsibility. Beginning in August of 1963 we variously authorized, sanctioned and encouraged the coup efforts of the Vietnamese generals and offered full support for a successor government." *United States-Vietnam Relations, 1945–1967*, Book 3, IV.B.5., p. VIII. The author of this book considers the revelations of the U.S. role in the coup that overthrew Diem the most startling of the Pentagon Papers.

Thailand and the assassination of Ngo Dinh Diem coupled with a growing conviction that Peking was the morning star in Southeast Asia and
Washington the evening star caused him to terminate American military
and economic aid in November 1963. In fact, Kennedy discussed the
subject with his Assistant Secretary of State for Far Eastern Affairs the
evening before he left for his fateful appointment in Texas.

Lyndon B. Johnson inherited the Vietnamese albatross and found it
increasingly heavy during his presidency. He significantly kept Kennedy's
key advisers on Indochina. Under the new President the U.S. commitment and involvement grew to massive proportions in the Second Indochinese War.[28] After assuming office in late 1963 Johnson quickly reaffirmed Kennedy's policies in Vietnam. But they were not adequate to
cope with the Communists who were preparing for the kill or with the
continuing political instability in Saigon.

The President approved a program—more significant than previous
efforts—of clandestine warfare against North Vietnam. It began on February 1, 1964, as Operation Plan 34A under General Harkins, chief of
the United States Military Assistance Command. Hesitant and reluctant
as he always was to take decisions toward further involvement in Indochina, Johnson at least hoped Operation Plan 34A would influence
Hanoi toward stopping the insurgencies by the Viet Cong and the Pathet
Lao.

The covert war had three major components, separate though related,
which bore on the Gulf of Tonkin crisis in August: patrolling by U.S.
destroyers in the Gulf to show the flag and to gather intelligence (the
DeSoto Patrols); bombardment of coastal facilities in North Vietnam by
Saigon's PT boats and commando raids from the sea by the South Vietnamese, along with other covert 34A activities; and air operations in
Laos by T-28 fighter-bombers with Laotian Air Force markings but with
some American civilian and some Thai pilots.

President Johnson like Kennedy and Eisenhower before him realized
the close interrelationship of events in Vietnam and Laos as well as
Cambodia. United States Air Force and Navy jet planes provided the
photographic intelligence for the bombing raids of the T-28s. High-alti-
tude flights for reconnaissance at the beginning moved to low-level flights
in May. A Pathet Lao–North Vietnamese offensive, it should be noted,
aroused grave concern in Washington especially in May and June. After
two American planes were shot down early in June the others were
quickly given armed escort jets. The escorts bombed and strafed when
U.S. planes came under fire, and armed aerial reconnaissance with frequent strikes developed. In mid-October a clandestine step-up in air
operations began having been ordered by President Johnson. Two

months later a campaign of U.S. strikes by Air Force and Navy jets started in the panhandle of Laos. Substantial American military aid was given Prime Minister Souvanna Phouma—training, logistical support, and other assistance—especially in 1964 and thereafter.

As for Cambodia, Ambassador Adlai E. Stevenson observed on May 21 during a controversy at the United Nations involving the United States and South Vietnam against Norodom Sihanouk that Hanoi with the support of Peking was violating the Khmer kingdom by using it as a "passageway, a source of supply, and a sanctuary."[29]

In January 1964 General Taylor and the Joint Chiefs called for "bolder actions" against North Vietnam, and in March Secretary of Defense Robert S. McNamara suggested new plans right up to "graduated overt military pressure" involving air strikes against the North. President Johnson later in the month stressed the contingency basis of U.S. planning against North Vietnam and the need to develop a strong base in the South for possible future action. He clearly opposed neutralization and negotiation from weakness. In early June Secretary McNamara indicated seven American divisions might have to be deployed to South Vietnam. In an interesting development J. Blair Seaborn, the Canadian member of the International Control Commission, at U.S. request passed on a warning to Premier Pham Van Dong on June 18 about "the greatest devastation" for Hanoi an escalation of the war could bring. The warning was coupled with a peace proposal and a suggestion relating to U.S. economic aid to North Vietnam.

The Gulf of Tonkin episode in the light of Operation Plan 34A (as later revealed) loses at least some of its mystery.[30] At midnight July 30 two North Vietnamese islands in the Gulf were raided by Saigon's naval commandos. The American destroyer "Maddox" on an intelligence-gathering patrol was attacked in daylight on August 2 by North Vietnamese torpedo boats who apparently thought it was a South Vietnamese escort ship. President Johnson ordered the destroyer "C. Turner Joy" to join the "Maddox" in the Gulf of Tonkin patrol. Saigon's PT boats the night of August 3 went on to stage two covert bombardments against North Vietnam. The American destroyers were attacked the following night by Hanoi's torpedo boats. (The reality of the second attack was a subject of controversy.) The afternoon of the next day (August 4, Washington time) Johnson at a meeting of the National Security Council ordered reprisal air strikes by American forces against North Vietnam. The targets were chosen by the Joint Chiefs from a list of ninety-four, a version of which was prepared at the end of the previous May. The President also decided to ask for a congressional resolution of support.

The famous Gulf of Tonkin or Southeast Asia Resolution, a basic draft of which was drawn up the previous May, was passed on August 7 by a vote of 88 to 2 in the Senate and 416 to 0 in the House of Representatives. Under it the United States was "prepared, as the President determines, to take all necessary steps, including the use of armed force, to assist any member or protocol state of the Southeast Asia Collective Defense Treaty requesting assistance in defense of its freedom."[31]

Perhaps the greatest significance of the resolution was the blank check which Congress essentially gave the President in the SEATO-covered areas of Southeast Asia. It was a case of advance authority. At the same time it can be debated, as Undersecretary of State Nicholas deB. Katzenbach later tried to argue, that the Gulf of Tonkin Resolution in conjunction with the Manila Treaty was the "functional equivalent" of a declaration of war. Most congressmen probably thought they were voting in an effort to deter a war, not to sanction one then or later. The credibility gap in many circles inside and outside Congress against the President's policy in Vietnam stemmed from the Gulf of Tonkin episode and the Southeast Asia Resolution. Acts of Congress have legislative histories.

The crisis provided the occasion for the United States to take "additional precautionary measures" in Southeast Asia, essentially measures of pre-position which strengthened American capacity in the event of "any eventuality." For instance, fighter-bomber airplanes were sent to Thailand, indicative of the growing U.S. buildup in the kingdom, and interceptor and fighter-bomber aircraft were dispatched to the Republic of Vietnam. Seaborn at U.S. request delivered a sharp warning in Hanoi about its role in South Vietnam and Laos.

By early September there was a widespread conviction in many high government circles in Washington that a sustained campaign of bombing North Vietnam would quite likely have to be undertaken since the efforts to prevent a Communist victory in the South were clearly not enough. Nevertheless, despite all the planning and preparations for readiness, no decision was taken the last months of 1964 to bomb the North. President Johnson on December 1 was reportedly cautious as well as equivocal on the matter, stressing the need for allies.

During the presidential campaign Johnson had criticized his opponent, Senator Barry M. Goldwater, for urging full-scale bombing of North Vietnam and had assured the American people that he himself opposed widening the war. American boys, he indicated several times, would not be sent to fight where Asian boys should do the fighting. Although there were some qualifications in Johnson's remarks and some signals to Ho Chi Minh not to miscalculate, Hanoi may well have thought his landslide victory at the polls on November 3 meant that he would not escalate the conflict. So did many American voters. In fact, two days before, Johnson had not ordered reprisals despite strong recommendations when U.S. planes and facilities at Bien Hoa air base had been struck by a Viet Cong mortar barrage and Americans had been killed.

Dimensions of the War. The Second Indochinese War is unique in the history of the United States. It had wide ramifications whose significance will be debated for many years. The issues engendered by the conflict will long endure.

Although the naming of a war is subject to controversy the Second Indochinese War best describes the conflict in Vietnam, Laos, and Cambodia. In major respects the same area as in the First Indochinese War (1946–54) was fought over. True, the conflict centered in Vietnam in both wars but Laos and Cambodia were deeply involved. In the eyes of Ho Chi Minh the Americans replaced the French in the second struggle for Indochina. Although the colonial aspect was not valid, Hanoi's basic substitution of Washington for Paris in terms of attrition on the battle front and particularly the home front was not insignificant.

Dating the beginning of the Second Indochinese War is also controversial. American casualties are officially listed from January 1, 1961, but it would be difficult to maintain the United States was engaged in a war that year. (Only 267 Americans lost their lives in battle deaths prior to 1965.) A preferable date for the beginning is the early months of 1965 when Washington began the bombing of North Vietnam in February and introduced small numbers of combat troops in March. From then the conflict escalated to dimensions in 1969 of over 540,000 American servicemen in the Republic of Vietnam, more than 1,000,000 South Vietnamese under arms in various categories, and about 71,000 other allied forces (with late arrivals). Chart 1 is indicative of the build-up. As of 1969, over 300,000 regular and irregular Viet Cong and North Vietnamese (with political cadres) at one time may have been involved in the fighting. In the spring of 1972, twelve of Hanoi's thirteen combat divisions were engaged outside North Vietnam. These dimensions clearly indicate a war, a struggle of major proportions.

In terms of duration the Second Indochinese War is the longest conflict in U.S. history. Even if early 1965 is taken as the beginning date it outlasted the Civil War, the Korean War, and American participation in the two world wars of the twentieth century.

The absence of a formal declaration of war has further complicated the "periodization" of the conflict. President Johnson, however, observed on July 28, 1965, that "this is really war," guided by Hanoi and spurred by Peking, with objectives to conquer South Vietnam, "defeat American power," and expand the "Asiatic dominion of communism."[32] Although

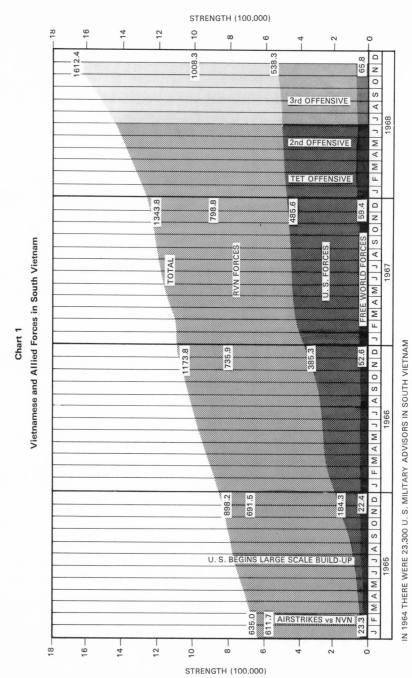

Chart 1

Vietnamese and Allied Forces in South Vietnam

STRENGTH (100,000)

IN 1964 THERE WERE 23,300 U. S. MILITARY ADVISORS IN SOUTH VIETNAM

Admiral U.S.G. Sharp and General W.C. Westmoreland. *Report on the War in Vietnam (As of 30 June 1968).* Government Printing Office, Washington. Released 1969. pp. 197 and III.

some congressmen have argued that Johnson deliberately bypassed them in the sole right of Congress to declare war, he maintained that the disadvantages of a formal declaration against North Vietnam would far outweigh the advantages. For instance, it would certainly not be in the spirit of the United Nations and would be a psychological victory for Hanoi; it would serve to question the American concept of a limited war and render more difficult the task of peacemaking; it might bring Peking and Moscow into war; and finally it was not needed for the President to prosecute the conflict and Congress to support it.[33] After all, the argument was made, he had behind him Article II of the constitution of the United States, the Manila Treaty, and the Gulf of Tonkin Resolution. President Nixon would later stress his constitutional powers as commander in chief to protect U.S. forces. In January 1971 he signed legislation that repealed the Gulf of Tonkin Resolution.

The American concept of a limited war in Southeast Asia was particularly noteworthy. Washington sought to limit the conflict in objectives, area, and choice of weapons. Although no American effort was made to overthrow the Communist regime in North Vietnam the other side of the coin was to persuade Hanoi to let South Vietnam alone. It was widely realized in Washington from the beginning of the Second Indochinese War that the Republic of Vietnam would be central in the American war effort. At the same time the United States sought by word and deed to prevent Communist China and the Soviet Union from entering the conflict in defense of Hanoi. During the American bombing of North Vietnam under President Johnson Peking's open intervention was more of a possibility than probably at any other time. But it was only a possibility. The United States, furthermore, voluntarily restricted itself in choice of arms by not employing nuclear or thermonuclear weapons in the fighting. The disadvantages of their use outweighed the advantages, and Washington did not want to be the first power to use them after the surrender of Japan in 1945.

Notwithstanding this concept of a limited war, the conflict assumed many of the aspects of a war for mainland Southeast Asia. Communist China and for a long time Cambodia were sanctuaries for North Vietnam while Thailand and the Philippines were sanctuaries for the United States. Laos was in effect partitioned more than ever before with the Pathet Lao and the North Vietnamese fighting the American-backed Royal Lao Government and the Thai. Hanoi's substantial military aid from the Soviet Union and Communist China did not take the form of combat troops. But combat forces not only from the United States, but also from South Korea, Thailand, Australia, New Zealand, and to a degree the Philippines came to Saigon's defense.

Chart 2

Department of Defense

Number of Casualties Incurred By U.S. Military Personnel
in Connection with the Conflict in Vietnam

January 1, 1961 through March 18, 1972

	1961/1962	1963	1964	1965	1966	1967	1968	1969	1970	1971	1972 to Date	Total
A. Casualties Resulting From Actions by Hostile Forces												
1. Killed	20	53	112	1,130	4,179	7,482	12,588	8,119	3,467	1,089	26	38,265
2. Wounded or Injured												
a. Died of wounds	1	5	6	87	517	981	1,636	1,170	578	153	7	5,141
b. Nonfatal wounds												
Hospital care required	43	218	522	3,308	16,526	32,371	46,799	32,940	15,211	4,817	170	152,925
Hospital care not required	38	193	517	2,806	13,567	29,654	46,021	37,276	15,432	4,180	165	149,849
3. Missing												
a. Died while missing	20	20	28	150	307	904	368	118	184	137	3	2,239
b. Returned to control	2	2	2	11	22	11	23	7	1	8	2	91
c. Current missing	xx	xx	xx	xx	xx	xx	xx	xx	xx	xx	xx	1,010
4. Captured or Interned												
a. Died while captured or interned	1	-	1	1	3	4	1	6	2	1	-	20
b. Returned to control	6	1	-	3	-	8	34	17	1	1	-	71
c. Current captured or interned	xx	xx	xx	xx	xx	xx	xx	xx	xx	xx	xx	491
5. Deaths												
a. From aircraft accidents/incidents												
Fixed Wing	24	23	39	111	168	173	250	165	88	32	3	1,091
Helicopter	7	35	38	88	185	287	631	638	610	228	20	2,853
b. From ground action	11	20	70	1,170	4,655	8,918	13,711	8,611	3,523	1,019	13	41,721
Total Deaths*	42	78	147	1,369	5,008	9,378	14,592	9,414	4,221	1,380	36	45,665
B. Casualties Not the Result of Actions by Hostile Forces												
6. Current Missing	xx	xx	xx	xx	xx	xx	xx	xx	xx	xx	xx	136
7. Deaths												
a. From aircraft accidents/incidents												
Fixed Wing	5	3	11	41	140	178	120	106	118	32	9	763
Helicopter	5	5	11	50	177	384	360	461	426	228	16	2,123
b. From other causes	13	28	26	268	728	1,118	1,439	1,546	1,300	708	41	7,215
Total Deaths	23	36	48	359	1,045	1,680	1,919	2,113	1,844	968	66	10,101

*Sum of lines 1, 2a, 3a, and 4a.

Department of Defense OASD (Comptroller)
Directorate for Information Operations March 22, 1972

The casualty figures in the Second Indochinese War mounted on both sides. With January 1, 1961, as the beginning date, American battle deaths came to 45,665 and American wounded numbered 302,774 through March 18, 1972. (See Chart 2.) In the Korean War, by way of comparison, 33,629 Americans were killed in action; in World War I, 53,402; the Civil War, 214,938; and World War II, 291,557. Figures for North Vietnam and the Viet Cong from 1960 through February 1972, almost the same duration as those for the United States, were estimated to be—in terms of deaths—803,720. (Next of kin are not notified.) The wounded numbered higher, possibly in an American estimate, "a factor of 1.5 x enemy KIA [killed in action]." South Vietnam's battle deaths for the same period came to around 157,900 and the seriously wounded to around 392,940. Vietnamese military casualties rose very sharply with Hanoi's offensive in the spring of 1972. Nor should the civilian casualties in the course of the war, largely through bombing in the North and bombing and ground fighting in the South, be discounted.

In treasure the cost of the Second Indochinese War was enormous. In 1968 it was estimated the United States was spending around $22 billion a year. Exact figures are debatable but no doubt existed about the huge sum spent to kill each of the enemy. In early 1971 President Nixon claimed the figure of $22 billion had been reduced to approximately half under his administration. But it was still huge, and reflected the vicissitudes of the war. For instance, Secretary of Defense Melvin R. Laird warned on June 5, 1972, that the offensive by North Vietnam could cost Washington an extra $5 billion if it had to keep up its current military response through the rest of 1972. Economic assistance to South Vietnam over the years also was costly. (See Chart 3.) The heavy burden of the war contributed to a rise in federal taxes, and to a threat to the dollar; it facilitated inflation. At the same time Washington sought to run the war without major economic disruption. It is even more difficult to estimate the financial cost of the Second Indochinese War to the Vietnamese living north and south of the seventeenth parallel. The ground fighting along with related bombing was concentrated in the Republic of Vietnam but systematic and sustained American bombing was severe in the Democratic Republic. Nor should the cost of the war be forgotten to Laos and Cambodia, to the Communist allies of North Vietnam, and to the various supporters, apart from the United States, of South Vietnam.

In military dimensions Washington has never fought a war like that in mainland Southeast Asia. Admiral U. S. Grant Sharp pointedly observed as of 1968: "The Vietnam War has had the most intense press coverage and has been the most thoroughly documented, most centrally controlled, most computerized, and most statistically analyzed in history.

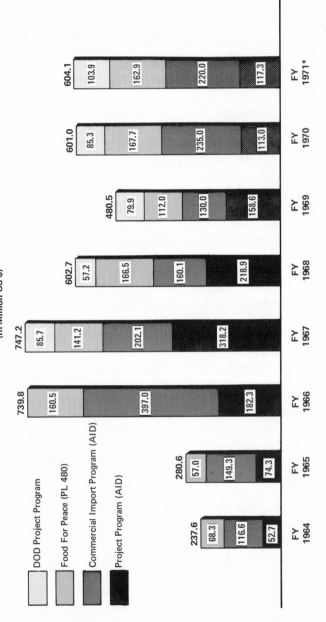

Chart 3

Direct Gross Economic Assistance Program - Vietnam
(In Million US $)

DOD Project Program

Food For Peace (PL 480)

Commercial Import Program (AID)

Project Program (AID)

	FY 1964	FY 1965	FY 1966	FY 1967	FY 1968	FY 1969	FY 1970	FY 1971*
Total	237.6	280.6	739.8	747.2	602.7	480.5	601.0	604.1
DOD	68.3	57.0	160.5	85.7	57.2	79.9	85.3	103.9
Food For Peace	116.6	149.3	397.0	141.2	166.5	112.0	167.7	162.9
Commercial	52.7	74.3	182.3	202.1	160.1	130.0	235.0	220.0
Project				318.2	218.9	158.6	113.0	117.3

*FY 1971: Congressional presentation figures, may change during legislative process.

Report to the Ambassador from the Director of the United States Agency for International Development, Vietnam, 1970. Submitted January 1, 1971, p. 4.

This was due in part to the necessity to measure the progress of a war in which there were no clearly drawn battle lines—no front, no safe rear."[34] As Commander in Chief Pacific (CINCPAC), Admiral Sharp was responsible for all U.S. military operations in the Pacific Command then extending from the Bering Sea to the eastern Indian Ocean including Vietnam. The table of organization of the Command (Chart 4) is revealing of the far-flung activities of CINCPAC in 1968.

In the Second Indochinese War there was no Dien Bien Phu of the First Indochinese War, no D-Day of World War II, no Western Front of World War I. Victory was not usually considered the progressive winning and holding of territory until the enemy surrendered or collapsed, for in most of the war he was here and there and almost everywhere. This explains why as a general rule no established battle lines existed and no great decisive battles were fought. (The North Vietnamese invasion of 1972 has necessitated the qualifications.) Essentially Saigon held the cities and part of the countryside although the Tet offensive in early 1968 proved the former could be vulnerable beyond acts of terrorism. South Vietnam like Caesar's Gaul was divided in three parts. In the countryside some territory was under effective control by the Communists, some by the government, and some by both—the former at night and the latter by day. Moreover, apart from certain areas of each contestant, the pattern in the countryside changed with time and circumstance, and in 1965, 1966, and 1967, only three years, more than two million refugees came into more secure areas controlled by Saigon.

The best feasible American military technology, under the rules of engagement, could not achieve victory for South Vietnam and the United States. The Communists bounced back and infiltration by land and sea continued, though increasingly less in the latter category. At the same time the application of General Vo Nguyen Giap's principles of warfare could not bring victory to the Viet Cong and to North Vietnam against the American and South Vietnamese opposition. Guerrilla hit-and-run combat and even conventional warfare did not succeed in the creation of a safe liberated area where the National Liberation Front (NLF) could set up a government, nor did they succeed in splitting the country in two. In many respects the United States sought a quick and cheap end of the war through frequent innovation and through modern military technology. The Communists adjusted in their own way, sometimes with primitive arms, sometimes with sophisticated weapons, to the new challenges in the mountains, jungles, and swamps of Vietnam. A well-known American military commentator, S. L. A. Marshall, once pointedly observed that "the bullet is the big killer [of Americans] by a ratio of about 4 to 1. That is true of the enemy side, too."[35]

The escalation of the conflict was quantitative and qualitative on both

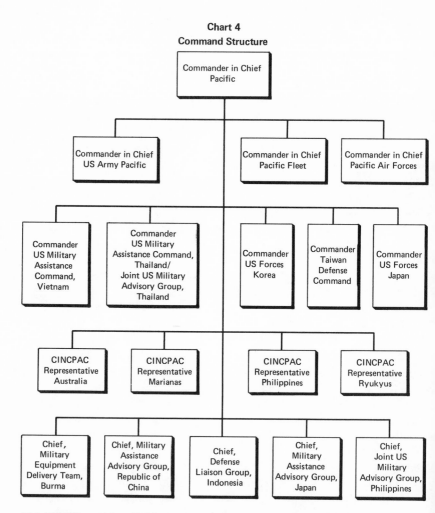

Chart 4
Command Structure

Commander in Chief
Pacific

Commander in Chief
US Army Pacific

Commander in Chief
Pacific Fleet

Commander in Chief
Pacific Air Forces

Commander
US Military
Assistance
Command,
Vietnam

Commander
US Military
Assistance Command,
Thailand/
Joint US Military
Advisory Group,
Thailand

Commander
US Forces
Korea

Commander
Taiwan
Defense
Command

Commander
US Forces
Japan

CINCPAC
Representative
Australia

CINCPAC
Representative
Marianas

CINCPAC
Representative
Philippines

CINCPAC
Representative
Ryukyus

Chief,
Military
Equipment
Delivery Team,
Burma

Chief, Military
Assistance
Advisory Group,
Republic of
China

Chief,
Defense
Liaison Group,
Indonesia

Chief,
Military
Assistance
Advisory Group,
Japan

Chief,
Joint US
Military
Advisory Group,
Philippines

Admiral U.S.G. Sharp and General W.C. Westmoreland, *Report on the War in Vietnam (As of 30 June 1968),* Government Printing Office, Washington, Released 1969, pp. 197 and III.

sides, from lower-level limits to higher-level limits. President Johnson in 1965 took the greatest steps in the American escalation by starting the sustained bombing of the North and introducing combat troops in large numbers in the South. President Ho Chi Minh infiltrated regular North Vietnamese troops and units into South Vietnam; the Viet Cong expanded, successfully for a while, their recruitment, voluntary and involuntary; and the Communist forces north and south of the seventeenth parallel were equipped with better and more sophisticated weapons furnished by the Soviet Union, mainland China, and other Communist countries. Both sides altered the ground rules of the war as it escalated. Moreover, the massive American logistical buildup in South Vietnam as well as the significant buildup of Communist facilities there and in neighboring Cambodia and Laos indicated that the two sides expected a long struggle. Indeed, the orderly military withdrawal of the United States from South Vietnam, once determined, would take considerable time.

The Second Indochinese War in large part was a complex political-military struggle for the support of the South Vietnamese—it could be stated unscientifically for their minds and hearts. The struggle like the First Indochinese War was rooted in the history, sociology, politics, and economy of the Vietnamese people. No foreigner can be certain of what they really want but in all probability it is security for themselves, their families, and their villages or cities; it is a better standard of living than what they grew up in; and it is to be left alone, when everything is said and done, by all foreigners. The nature of the struggle in South Vietnam during the Second Indochinese War determined the solution for victory. Clearly military means alone by the United States would not suffice, no matter how sophisticated the equipment, how abundant the supplies, how superior the mobility, and how extensive the firepower (B-52s of the Strategic Air Command on Guam were committed to the war in June 1965 and the battleship "New Jersey" was sent to the South China Sea in 1968). But the exact mix of military, political, economic, and social measures was debatable and would long challenge the best minds of America. In fact, this challenge was one of the most baffling of the 1960s and early 1970s. If there was a magic formula in counterinsurgency, it was elusive.

One of the basic questions in the Second Indochinese War was the identification of the foe before the open invasion by Hanoi in 1972. Was the struggle before then essentially a civil war in South Vietnam, a rebellion against the Saigon government, or was it essentially "armed aggression from the North," a "campaign to conquer South Viet-Nam," as Washington officially maintained? The evaluation of the roles of Hanoi, Peking, and Moscow would vary with the answer. Also the strategies and tactics of the American response—an emphasis on counterinsurgency or on repelling an invader in the South and discouraging him in the North. The war, it does seem, included both elements of a civil conflict in South Vietnam and of aggression from the North. As the conflict escalated, the latter became more pronounced and the support of Peking and Moscow more significant. It became necessary, Washington thought, to counter insurgency as well as to make Hanoi pay a heavy price for its role. But once more the mix was important, and priorities were a major consideration.

In a struggle as complex as the Second Indochinese War before Hanoi's open invasion of the South, valid indicators of progress or despair were baffling and hard to determine. Reports from the field were not always like those that reached the White House. Various measurements were used, such as enemy and government killed, enemy and government desertions (whether or not the former were through the Chieu Hoi or Open Arms program), actions initiated by the enemy and by the government, and enemy weapons lost and allied weapons lost (this ratio being particularly significant). Hilsman, however, frankly asserted that "the question of statistics, their accuracy, reliability, and meaning, was troublesome throughout the Vietnam struggle."[36] And, moreover, they were often revised. Although certain quantitative measurements are helpful it is beyond the confines of cold realism to quantify the Second Indochinese War. The interpretation of the indicators can also sometimes lead to false assumptions. They were, for instance, highly favorable to the Saigon government and its allies in late 1967. But the Tet offensive in early 1968 indicated that the Vietnamese Communists were pulling their punches for a big punch directed at the cities of South Vietnam. And later, at least some of the progress reports on Vietnamization in 1971 were due to Hanoi's preparations for the invasion the next year.

Victory in a war like that in Indochina prevailing before the North Vietnamese open invasion can also be theoretically measured by indicators, but human beings will probably never devise foolproof ones. Admiral Harry D. Felt once defined victory as control by the government over at least 90 per cent of South Vietnam's rural population.[37] Senator Mansfield and his colleagues in a study mission asserted in 1963 that "success" there "would mean, at the least, reduction of the guerrillas to the point where they would no longer be a serious threat to the stability of the Republic."* And Hilsman speaks of winning in terms of "whether

*They went on to specify that "if that point is reached, road and rail communications would once again become reasonably safe. Local officials would no longer live in constant fear of assassination. Rice and other major commodities would again move in volume to the cities. Development throughout the nation would be feasible."[38]

or not the government can effectively protect the people and minor government officials from acts of terrorism."[39]

The military course of the Second Indochinese War after early 1965 was not one to catch the headlines week by week for dramatic developments. Occasionally they occurred, lasted for some time, and produced world reactions. There was a certain cyclical aspect of Communist infiltration and of Communist battlefield action and there were plateaus. Hanoi obviously had its own viewpoints on what was important in the development of the conflict, and it clearly had its own ways of publicizing favorable events and trends. Each side signaled the other on escalation and de-escalation, signals not always understood and often ignored.

As the counterinsurgency efforts of the Kennedy administration and of Johnson's first months in office, with their emphasis on strategic hamlets, and as the accompanying shooting war with Americans technically as military advisers failed to produce the desired objectives, President Johnson's decisions in early 1965 on U.S. bombing and on U.S. ground combat troops drastically changed the Vietnamese military climate. The struggle was Americanized with U.S. servicemen combatants in theory as well as in fact. American military strategy (as Admiral Sharp defined it while still CINCPAC) consisted of three elements from 1965 well into 1968, all interdependent: the air and naval offensive against Hanoi, the ground and air campaign in the Republic of Vietnam, and the effort toward nation-building.

General William C. Westmoreland, Commander of the U.S. Military Assistance Command, Vietnam, and his successor General Creighton W. Abrams were not free agents. They were technically subordinate to the American Ambassador and technically only advised and assisted the armed forces of the Republic of Vietnam. The two generals with their American field commanders were subject to controlled limitations on their military activities—even from the President himself—limitations often not based as much on U.S. military capabilities as on factors of world politics. Johnson's bombing of North Vietnam was under CINCPAC and reflected White House judgments; it was the most precise bombing to date in the annals of warfare. Its value and purpose, its targets and gradualness were controversial.[40] The Commander, U.S. Military Assistance Command, Vietnam, although subject to military and political as well as economic and psychological considerations, did have considerable discretion in his ground strategy in the South. Westmoreland's own stress was on attrition of enemy forces with a search-and-destroy strategy; Abrams in his efforts had to cope with the phased reduction of U.S. ground forces.

In 1968 two major changes occurred in the course of the Second Indochinese War—the Tet offensive against the cities by the Communists in late January and February (so named because it began during Tet) and the American termination of the bombing of the North in two steps of de-escalation. In mid-1967 the Vietnamese Communists had altered their strategy, an alteration leading to the Tet offensive and to the Paris talks. The Double 31 consisted of Johnson's announcement on March 31 that he had stopped the bombing of most of North Vietnam and on October 31 that he was ending it the next morning over the remaining southern part. By late 1968, despite the Tet offensive of Ho Chi Minh, a second in May, and a third in the summer, the war was once more basically restricted to South Vietnam with Laos and Cambodia still deeply involved and hostages of its outcome.

In 1969 early in the Nixon administration the Communists clearly violated the agreement associated with the U.S. ending of all bombing in the North. The extensive shelling of various cities was protested by the new American chief executive who warned of its consequences, but he did not then resume the U.S. bombing of Hanoi's territory. The offensive of the Communists launched in late February, however, was frustrated before the middle of May when Nixon made his first major address on Vietnam.

The third big step in the American de-escalation of the war came in June as President Nixon revealed plans to withdraw about 25,000 U.S. forces from Vietnam before the end of August. A so-called lull in the fighting began in the middle of June and continued during Nixon's visit to Southeast Asia in late July, though Hanoi warned fierce fighting lay ahead. The United States had contributed to the lull by lowering the level of fighting, but B-52 attacks and search-and-destroy missions were not ended. Stressing "Vietnamization," President Nixon announced successive reductions in U.S. forces in Vietnam with a goal of "total American withdrawal" (whatever that might mean). On October 7, 1970, he called for a cease-fire-in-place in Indochina.

The Communist use of sanctuaries in the Second Indochinese War in Laos and Cambodia led to retaliation. (The Laotian border is only twenty-five miles from Hué and the Cambodian thirty-five from Saigon.) President Johnson had resisted pressures from the Joint Chiefs to move into the sanctuaries but President Nixon took a different position. On April 30, 1970, he announced that U.S. forces in Vietnam had been ordered to help Saigon's forces in attacking the Cambodian sanctuaries. The American action was limited in objective, area, and time. The last U.S. ground troops left Cambodia on June 30 but the war had clearly spread to the kingdom. In early February 1971 South Vietnamese forces openly crossed into the panhandle of Laos to cut the Ho Chi Minh trail system with American air, artillery, and logistical support but not with U.S. ground combat forces. The operation ended in late March with the

South Vietnamese in the face of fierce Communist opposition leaving earlier than planned. Hanoi's invasion of the Republic of Vietnam in the spring of 1972 opened a new phase of the Second Indochinese War. Conventional in nature, clearly facilitated by Soviet sophisticated weapons, and aimed at ending the war through victory, the military effort of the Democratic Republic of Vietnam seriously threatened the future of the Republic of Vietnam. As the forces of Saigon attempted to withstand the onslaught with varying degrees of success, President Nixon's response in early May to mount an accelerated air offensive against North Vietnam *and* to impose a semi-blockade of its ports marked to some the crossing of a firebreak and to others a reasoned response to a direct challenge from Hanoi and an indirect one from Moscow.

The Second Indochinese War had many intangible dimensions. It raised questions of national priorities and international priorities in America. Significant public opposition to the war surfaced in 1966 and the conflict became a major source of contention in the United States. Fortunately this contention cut across race, region, and party and did not, for instance, set North against South or Democrats solidly against Republicans. The intangible dimensions of the conflict accompanied each step of political, diplomatic, and military escalation and de-escalation, adding to the complexity of the struggle.

Escalation and De-escalation. Presidents Johnson and Nixon in their decision making in the Second Indochinese War qualified their approaches to escalation and de-escalation. Johnson's not mobilizing the reserves to any large extent, not putting the American economy on a wartime footing, and not bombing targets in North Vietnam that might bring retaliation from Peking cr Moscow stood in contrast to his sending over half a million servicemen to South Vietnam, his spending around $22 billion in a year to wage the war, and his extensive bombing of the North. Nixon's progressive withdrawals of American forces from South Vietnam and lowering of the cost of the war to the taxpayer was accompanied by his "protective reaction" air strikes of North Vietnam at different periods, by his dramatic incursion into the Cambodian sanctuaries in 1970, by his active support of Saigon's well-publicized incursion into the panhandle of Laos in 1971, and by his semi-blockade of North Vietnamese ports and renewal of sustained air warfare of the Democratic Republic in 1972. It was argued that while Nixon de-escalated in the deployment of American manpower with the drastic decline of casualties and with the eventual end of draftees (unless they volunteered for Vietnam), he escalated in the use of Cambodian and Laotian soil and in the more intensive application of air power and naval power against Hanoi by professional servicemen.

Both Johnson and Nixon sought to maintain public support for their policies between the most militant hawks and the most conciliatory doves.[41] LBJ found it difficult as the war dragged on to strike a balance between demands for a quick military solution and for a rapid disengagement. His valued consensus floundered as the pressures for military escalation (with no end in sight) and for peace negotiations (often at any price) increasingly eroded the core of his supporters. Richard Nixon after a review of American policy in Vietnam announced in May 1969 that he had ruled out a "one-sided withdrawal" from the country, a "disguised defeat" at the Paris talks, and a "purely military solution" in the fighting. In his appeal to "the great silent majority" in November he opposed "an immediate, precipitate withdrawal." What he essentially advocated was a withdrawal of American forces through Vietnamization or through a negotiated settlement at Paris that would leave a South Vietnam reasonably strong enough to defend its freedom.

During most of Johnson's years in the White House the question was intervention and the degree of intervention in Vietnam but under Richard Nixon it was withdrawal and the pace of withdrawal. LBJ's minimum was for a long time gradual escalation; RN's minimum was essentially gradual withdrawal. Under the two Presidents national interests in Southeast Asia were reflected in personal and organizational interests. The stakes were high in both escalation and de-escalation.

In the pattern of events key decisions should be highlighted against the international background. Johnson's decisions to bomb North Vietnam and to commit ground combat troops to South Vietnam in 1965 came at a time when there were no international crises involving U.S. interests and risks elsewhere. A confrontation over Cuba, Berlin, or the Middle East at the time might well have altered the course of American history in Southeast Asia. Under the circumstances the impending fall of Vietnam to communism assumed greater importance and American prevention of it a higher priority. Furthermore, many military measures short of open war had not succeeded in Vietnam and the United States by 1965 had built up a strong military capability of conventional forces that could be used to intervene.

Sharp attacks by the Communists on U.S. installations in South Vietnam early in February made a basic decision in Washington all the more necessary. On February 7 Americans were killed and wounded at Pleiku when the Communists attacked installations there. A quick but long-contemplated response came from the President. Within fourteen hours an American retaliatory bombing raid under the code name *Flaming Dart* occurred at Dong Hoi in North Vietnam. On February 7 Johnson asserted he had ordered American dependents out of the South—a significant move to clear the decks. He also revealed he had ordered a

Hawk air defense battalion to Da Nang, a step contemplated for some time.

Three days later the Communists attacked American barracks at Qui Nhon, once more killing and wounding U.S. servicemen. Johnson launched another reprisal raid in cooperation with South Vietnamese planes on February 11. But two days later he decided to take a more drastic step, to start sustained warfare (*Rolling Thunder*) against the North. The first strike came on March 2. Meanwhile Washington began bombing with jet aircraft, on February 19, Communist concentrations inside South Vietnam. Johnson had stated two days earlier that America's "continuing actions" in defense of Saigon would be "measured and fitting and adequate."[42]

The reasons for the U.S. air strikes on North Vietnam are complex. In retrospect Pleiku was far more of an occasion than a cause. The strikes were directed at strengthening the morale of the antineutralist army in South Vietnam and the government factions in Saigon who opposed a neutralist solution. The political situation in the republic was fragile, drastic steps being needed if only to prevent further deterioration. And the morale of the army was very low, with disaster threatening. Washington also hoped in the words of McNamara to "reduce the flow and/or to increase the cost of the continued infiltration of men and supplies from North Vietnam to South Vietnam."[43] Another American objective was to point out to Hanoi that it must "pay a price" for its continued aggression in the South. As General Taylor expressed it, the price would be "ever-increasing" or in other words "little by little through the progressive, restrained application of force by bombing."[44] The sanctuary was over. Still another reason for the strikes was to convince North Vietnam, Communist China, and the Soviet Union that Washington would honor its commitments to Saigon and elsewhere. Khrushchev had lost power in October 1964 and Johnson was facing the new leadership of Alexei Kosygin and Leonid I. Brezhnev. Peking had exploded its first nuclear device in the same October and was jubilant over its achievement. Johnson also faced what he believed was a rapidly taking shape "Djakarta-Hanoi-Peking-Pyongyang axis, with Cambodia probably to be brought in as a junior partner and Laos to be merely absorbed by the North Vietnamese and Chinese."[45] Also very important in America's decision was the desire to increase its bargaining position with North Vietnam and change the overall situation to Washington's favor. Nor should the protection of U.S. forces in the South, a sine qua non, be minimized.

It soon became clear that the American bombing of North Vietnam would not prevent the collapse of the South and would not deter Hanoi there. What should Washington do? On March 6 two Marine battalions with 3,500 men had been ordered to Da Nang to protect the airfield under a static-defense strategy. They landed two days later. On April 1 President Johnson in a secret decision—to avoid "premature publicity" —approved a change in the mission of the Marine battalions and of those arriving from defensive to limited offensive action.[46] Furthermore, General Westmoreland on June 26 was allowed to commit U.S. forces whenever they were required in his judgment to "strengthen the relative position" of those under Saigon. Viet Cong victories in May and June had caused Westmoreland to ask for more U.S. troops. By early June over 50,000 servicemen were in the country, and at the end of the month a major ground action of American forces occurred. The General was rapidly moving from a less costly enclave strategy to a much more costly search-and-destroy one.

President Johnson's decision announced in late July to commit combat troops in large numbers to the Republic of Vietnam was viewed by Ambassador Lodge in 1966 as the "turning point" in U.S. military commitment there.[47] General Earle G. Wheeler, Chairman of the Joint Chiefs of Staff, shared this opinion.* In retrospect, the step stands as Johnson's second major decision in 1965 not to let South Vietnam go Communist by American default. General Westmoreland later asserted he had called for a quick buildup of American combat forces, for the "enemy hoped to deliver the *coup de grâce* by launching a major summer offensive to cut the Republic of Vietnam in two with a drive across the central highlands to the sea."[49]

What Johnson had done was to leave open-ended the American commitment in Vietnam through approving in July the increase in U.S. forces with no absolute ceiling and through supporting Westmoreland's search-and-destroy strategy. At the same time LBJ was well aware he had a "bear by the tail." Although he saw political safety in stressing continuity his policy of gradualism and of not fully alerting Congress and the American people along the way cost him an opportunity to rally the nation. Significantly no step Johnson took was irreversible or decisive, and taken in isolation each was harder to fault. But to sustain his policy he needed quick and substantial results.

After the most serious consideration by high-ranking officials in Washington and after congressional leaders of both parties had been called to the White House President Johnson announced on July 28 that American forces in South Vietnam would be increased to meet Westmoreland's needs from the 75,000 there to 125,000 "almost immediately." And

*He said on January 17, 1967: "I doubt that any decision by any President has been more difficult or more honorable."[48]

more, he said, would follow.* The setting of this televised announcement was only a news conference with questions asked the chief executive after his statement on Vietnam, the appointment of John Chancellor to head the Voice of America, and the nomination of Abe Fortas to the Supreme Court. In response to one of the questions he noted that no "change in policy whatever" of relying chiefly on South Vietnamese for offensive operations and of relying on Americans to guard installations and be an emergency backup was implied. Nevertheless, the tone of the President's opening statement on Vietnam was reminiscent of Woodrow Wilson's war message to a joint session of Congress on the evening of April 2, 1917. Perhaps no other President has committed major American forces to combat in such prosaic surroundings as a news conference and yet in such heartfelt words. In the emotional stress of a Pearl Harbor and of a consequent White House request for a declaration of war Lyndon B. Johnson's words of July 28, 1965, would have been better remembered:

> Let me also add now a personal note. I do not find it easy to send the flower of our youth, our finest young men, into battle. I have spoken to you today of the divisions and the forces and the battalions and the units, but I know them all, every one. I have seen them in a thousand streets, of a hundred towns, in every State in this Union—working and laughing and building, and filled with hope and life. I think I know, too, how their mothers weep and how their families sorrow.
>
> This is the most agonizing and the most painful duty of your President.[50]†

For the rest of 1965 and for the next two years, the overall pattern of politics, war, and diplomacy was punctuated by few basic alterations.[51] It was essentially more of the same. In South Vietnam major steps were taken in establishing constitutional government and holding elections. But a severe setback to pacification and progress in the war would occur early in 1968. The United States continued its military buildup in South Vietnam and the American bombing of North Vietnam continued to rise in tempo. The U.S. search for peace under favorable conditions went on but with no breakthrough. In the United States opposition increased to the Second Indochinese War in Congress, in the news media, on university campuses, and elsewhere. Frustration mounted and the country was

---

*Two days later the Joint Chiefs forwarded a document that indicated the deployment of U.S. troops in South Vietnam was currently planned under Phase I for 1965 as 193,887 men.

†In his memoirs Johnson called the decision "by far the hardest" he made on Vietnam.

more and more divided—but the conflict was essentially tolerated and accepted. Television brought the struggle into the American home with consequences hard to determine.

As Washington escalated the war, it sought allies in the effort. President Johnson in early April 1965 approved "urgent" attempts to attain Australian, New Zealand, and South Korean combat forces. In early January 2,000 military advisers from the Republic of Korea had arrived. A "more flags" policy to get various allies in Asia and Europe to contribute armed support, however, was not very successful. No friends in Europe, not even Great Britain, were willing to send armed forces. The Second Indochinese War was never placed under United Nations auspices as was the Korean War, or under official SEATO sanction. In fact, the United Nations played no significant role in the conflict while SEATO as an organization proved ineffective. The Geneva machinery—the cochairmen and the international control commissions—remained paralyzed.

Nevertheless, the escalation phase of the Second Indochinese War under President Johnson saw Communist countries, especially the People's Republic of China and the Soviet Union, markedly increasing their military and economic assistance to Hanoi and the Viet Cong. Ironically, the aid policies of the two major Communist powers toward the Democratic Republic of Vietnam helped to drive them further apart.

The sending of armed forces from Australia, New Zealand, South Korea, Thailand, and to a degree the Philippines to South Vietnam was a major aspect of relations between the United States and those "troop contributing countries." Each ally had its own national interests and its own priorities. In the case of the three Asian participants the United States underwrote a considerable amount of the cost. The total military personnel of the five allies sent to Vietnam rose from over 60,000 in early 1968 to around 71,000 the next year. All but the Philippines increased their force commitments from the original figure.

Thailand and the Philippines, the only two countries in Southeast Asia to send forces to South Vietnam, also contributed to the war effort through the American use of bases on their soil. Although Thai-American relations were central, Bangkok's military support of Saigon in the Second Indochinese War was a reflection of its forward strategy at the time. The Thai decision to commit ground troops in addition to previous military assistance was made in December 1966 against a background of American assurances.

As an active participant in the war, Thailand found itself involved in a plethora of diplomatic and military activity. Even apart from its actual military role in Vietnam, its home territory reflected several dimensions of the conflict. American use of Thai bases for bombing in Laos (as well as other major activities) and in Cambodia (after the war spread there) and for bombing in Vietnam as well as stepped-up Communist insurgency in separated areas of the kingdom were evidence of Thai involvement. Bangkok was concerned over the success of the fighting in South Vietnam and the outcome of the talks in Paris. It was eager for and glad to receive renewed U.S. assurances during President Johnson's visit to Thailand in October 1966 and Prime Minister Thanom Kittikachorn's trip to the United States in May 1968. And it wanted reassurances during President Nixon's visit to Bangkok in July 1969. Criticism by Senator J. William Fulbright and others during the Johnson and Nixon administrations over the U.S. commitment to Thailand worried the Thai and they overreacted to adverse articles in the American press. Bangkok was concerned as Congress barred the commitment of U.S. ground combat troops to Thailand and Laos.

The U.S. use of bases in the kingdom during the Second Indochinese War—installations often put in place much earlier—was indicative of the very close ties between Washington and Bangkok. The bases were Thai, not American; Thailand provided the security guard; Bangkok permitted their use in carrying out obligations Thailand and the United States had undertaken under the Manila Pact of 1954. The absence of a formal treaty on the bases and of a status-of-forces agreement despite long intermittent negotiations in the latter case was significant. Thailand, it should be stressed, could restrict the use of the base facilities as it saw fit. For some time official information was scarce from both Thai and American sources.

The bases for the U.S. Air Force in the allied war effort for a long time were located at U-Tapao, Udorn, Korat, Nakom Phanon, Takhli, and Ubon. (Nam Phong was added in 1972 for the Marines.) Sattahip, a seaport on the Gulf of Siam, was made into a modern deep-water port and naval base with extensive U.S. aid. American B-52s significantly began operations from U-Tapao in April 1967.

Almost 50,000 Americans in uniform were stationed in early 1969 in Thailand, by far the greatest number being in the Air Force. Military personnel was also involved in the maintenance of port facilities, military supply depots, communications networks, strategic roads, and related facilities. Other American servicemen in small numbers were engaged in the long-standing program of helping train and equip Thai armed forces. The figures had jumped from none the first half of 1950 to around 25,-000 in 1965 to over 35,000 in early 1967 and to almost 50,000 in early 1969.

Communist-inspired insurgency in the northeast of Thailand beginning as early as 1962 was well defined before the United States escalated the Vietnamese war in 1965 and Thailand became deeply involved. Both Hanoi and Peking worked in a concerted effort through direction and support to subvert Thailand, largely via Laos. Actually the number of Communist insurgents was not high, an estimated total of 5,000 in late 1970. In addition to the northeast they were particularly active in the south near Malaysia in 1970 and even more so in the north. In 1971 their number increased and their equipment and organization improved. Both Thailand and the United States opposed the use of American servicemen to fight the insurgents. But Washington under Presidents Kennedy, Johnson, and Nixon has helped Thailand in many other ways through training, advice, and material support in its counterinsurgency effort.

After Richard M. Nixon went to the White House Bangkok was eager to get his full support. An early subject of consideration was a reaffirmation of the Rusk-Thanat joint statement of March 1962. Secretary of State William P. Rogers pointedly asserted in an address at the SEATO Council of Ministers on May 20, 1969, that the Rusk-Thanat communiqué was a "valid restatement of the responsibilities set forth in article IV(1) of the [Manila] treaty."[52] He thus reaffirmed, much to the satisfaction of Thailand, a statement made by the previous Democratic administration. The American Congress was also aware of the position, and the new President himself told Senator Fulbright he would make no secret commitments.

Nixon's visit to Bangkok in late July occasioned further opportunities for pledges of American fidelity. On July 28 he spoke extemporaneously shortly after his arrival. "We will honor our obligations," he said, "under that [SEATO] treaty. . . . We have been together in the past. We are together at the present. And the United States will stand proudly with Thailand against those who might threaten it from abroad or from within."[53]

Although the participation of the Philippines in the Second Indochinese War was comparable in many respects to that of its SEATO ally, Thailand, President Ferdinand E. Marcos faced more opposition at home than Prime Minister Thanom. Both leaders, however, found the United States the most influential outside power in their foreign policy. And the war in Vietnam focused attention on their attitudes toward Southeast Asia and Asia as a whole, toward the Communist powers, and, of course, toward the American role in regional and world affairs.

The Second Indochinese War affected Philippine politics in various ways. In 1965 President Diosdado Macapagal urged the sending of a small military unit of Filipinos to South Vietnam but the Congress in Manila postponed a decision on the matter. Early the next year President

Marcos, contrary to his attitude during his campaign for Malacañang, called for comparable action. Despite the debate in Congress the Vietnam aid bill passed in July. The Philippine military contribution to South Vietnam was next to the smallest of the Asian and Pacific allies. It was a Civic Action team. Even so, its army engineer unit of 2,000 men with security support personnel (later reduced) was not insignificant in terms of the size of the Philippine army. Manila also furnished medical and other aid to the South Vietnamese. Although the dispatch of Philippine forces aroused considerable controversy at home their presence in South Vietnam was in line at the time with Manila's basic foreign policy since independence and its special relationship with the United States.[54] Also, the role of American bases on Philippine soil in the Second Indochinese War should not be minimized. Over 30,000 U.S. servicemen were for some time in the islands, and more than 100,000 Filipino and American civilians were employees on the military installations. The Subic Bay Naval Base was a forward repair base and storehouse for the warships of the Seventh Fleet off Vietnam, and Clark Air Base was a primary staging area for airmen and supplies to Vietnam, Thailand, and Taiwan and a key aircraft maintenance and supply center.

President Marcos made a state visit to the United States in September 1966 and President Johnson traveled to Manila in connection with the Summit Conference in October. In the unusually long joint communiqué on September 15 the two chief executives agreed that the Philippines should help meet "on a full and equitable basis" American offshore procurement needs in South Vietnam, that U.S. equipment would be forthcoming not only this fiscal year for five army engineer construction battalions for civic action in internal security but also possibly in the next one for five more battalions, and that the "principal threat to peace and security" in Southeast Asia was the "Communist war of aggression and subversion being waged against the government and people of South Vietnam."[55] Johnson, of course, was pleased with the Philippine military participation in the war despite the considerable financial cost to the United States.

After the Republic of Vietnam launched a special appeal for aid on July 14, 1964, the "Free World Assistance Program" assumed significant proportions over the course of years. In addition to the help from the outside troop-contributing states, substantial continuing programs of economic, technical, and humanitarian assistance in various combinations were provided by Japan, Great Britain, Canada, the Federal Republic of Germany, and the Netherlands. Smaller continuing contributions were made by other countries such as Nationalist China and Malaysia. More than thirty states at one time were considered as contributors to the Free

World Assistance Program to Vietnam. (Some aid was token like 10,000 cans of sardines from Morocco.) Civilians in technical activities were sent from over twelve countries.

American procurement policy in the Second Indochinese War was significant in international relationships. Several less developed states were selected as eligible sources for Vietnam under the Commodity Import Program. A number of cities from Tokyo to Sydney benefited from being chosen for rest and recuperation (R&R) for American servicemen in Vietnam. The war brought significant earnings to more than one nation. In Japan, for instance, it was estimated in September 1968 that the war was responsible for perhaps $1 billion in additional earnings.

During the years of escalation from 1965 into 1968 American overtures for peace were more than once followed by a military step-up after bombing pauses, or were accompanied by it. Although the United States appeared reasonable it was quite tough in its position on negotiations. A "political solution" in the South did not include meeting Hanoi's terms. Johnson was not prepared to negotiate a settlement that produced a Communist South Vietnam. The search for peace in its political-military context had "soul-searing phases of euphoric hope and deep despair."[56] The Manila Conference of October 24–25, 1966, where the seven allies in the war were represented by their top leaders did produce a formula, strongly urged by Johnson, under which it was agreed the forces of the six outside powers would leave South Vietnam not later than six months after the other side removed its forces to North Vietnam, stopped infiltration, and the violence level thus subsided.* President Johnson took the occasion of the summit meeting to visit the allied countries and Malaysia where he presented the American viewpoint on the questions of war and peace.

A climax of the Second Indochinese War came in March 1968 when the United States began to de-escalate the conflict. For some time a stalemate in military escalation existed in Vietnam. Under the prevailing conditions it was evident that neither side could achieve a victory. But the road from war would prove long, difficult, and costly and there would be many twists and turns for both sides along the way.[58] No Appomattox or V-J Day would mark the end of the bloodshed.

The Tet offensive in late January and February directed at the cities of South Vietnam had profound consequences.[59] The main offensive, beginning January 30 and 31, surprised Washington and Saigon in terms

*This pledge appeared in the communiqué of the conference. Another statement was called "Goals of Freedom." A third was the "Declaration of Peace and Progress in Asia and the Pacific." Johnson wrote in his memoirs that "if there was a Johnson Doctrine" the cornerstones were found in this declaration.[57]

of its exact timing and scope despite knowledge of an extensive buildup. It was launched against thirty-six provincial capitals and five cities, along with some sixty district towns and various airfields of South Vietnam; Saigon, Hué, and certain other cities were particularly hard hit. Associated with Tet was the seventy-day ordeal of the U.S. Marines at Khesanh. The intensity of the offensive was indicated by the actual penetration of the American embassy compound in Saigon and by the capturing and holding against fierce opposition of the palace grounds of the citadel in historic Hué for twenty-six days.

The Communists were motivated by a desire to bring about the quick collapse of the Saigon government, to cripple the economy, to destroy the relative security of the cities, and to create a vacuum in the countryside. They sought to isolate the urban areas from the rural ones and even bypassed certain military targets in this objective.

The seriousness of the offensive was evidenced in the American and South Vietnamese response. The allied lunar new year cease-fire, partially cancelled on January 29, was totally ended shortly thereafter. President Nguyen Van Thieu declared martial law in the republic on January 31, and Secretary Rusk asserted on February 10 that the war might be reaching the "climactic period." In addition to the bombing of the Haiphong area by American planes on February 10 for the first time in a month, the Pentagon announced three days later that the United States would airlift to Vietnam 10,500 additional combat troops as requested by General Westmoreland. President Johnson on February 16 asserted that the General should stay as commander in Vietnam at this time and that the Joint Chiefs had made no recommendations for the employment of nuclear weapons in the country. On February 23, General Wheeler following Johnson's request arrived in Saigon for a review of the military situation and of manpower needs. The capture of the U.S.S. "Pueblo" on January 23 by North Korean forces had also raised questions of Communist cooperation.

What was the significance of the Tet offensive? The Communists did not collapse the Saigon government; they did not shatter the army of the republic; they could not keep control of any one of the cities they assaulted; they did not incite the "general uprising" in the urban areas they at least predicted; they suffered very heavy casualties. Johnson considered the Tet offensive a major Communist disaster, creating an opportunity for an American peace gesture. But, and this is a most important but, the Communists proved that American optimism on the course of the war was not well founded. The "coonskin" would not quickly be brought back. Under the circumstances Johnson would find it harder than ever to escalate the war, if such a decision were made. In

South Vietnam, it should be stressed, the Communists severely set back the progress in pacification (certain allied forces, for instance, had to be moved to the cities); they seriously impaired the economy and created half a million refugees; and they caused an atmosphere of crisis and doubt about the future. Saigon was faced with the immediate need to get back the degree of control and momentum it enjoyed before the Tet offensive.

An assessment of U.S. policy in Vietnam formally began on February 29 and lasted almost all the month of March. President Johnson set up a top-level task force under the chairmanship of Clifford who became Secretary of Defense on March 1 succeeding McNamara, long disillusioned about the war. The task force was to make a thorough review of American policy in Vietnam considering alternatives and making recommendations against the background of the general situation.[60] Generals Wheeler and Westmoreland had recommended on February 27 the deployment to Vietnam in three increments of 206,756 additional men by the end of the year. The Joint Chiefs were pressing for an extensive call-up of reserves. They were thinking both of a more offensive strategy in Indochina and of building up the "strategic reserves" at home.[61]

The viewpoints brought out in the day and evening sessions of the task force ultimately convinced Clifford that the current U.S. military course was both "endless" and "hopeless." Opposing further Americanization of the war, he recommended a leveling off of involvement and a movement toward gradual disengagement. The United States, the Secretary of Defense argued, had succeeded in preventing North Vietnam from subjugating the South, and now South Vietnam should carry an increasing share of responsibility.

The President himself later stressed that Secretary Rusk had informally suggested to him on March 4 an unconditional bombing halt north of the twentieth parallel and that he had urged the Secretary to present a proposal, which he did the next day. Arthur J. Goldberg, U.S. envoy to the United Nations, recommended to the President a halt in the bombing of all North Vietnam. Both proposals were sent for evaluation to Ambassador Ellsworth Bunker in Saigon. The latter strongly opposed the second but revealed he could live with the first. LBJ later indicated the Rusk proposal essentially became the basis of his decision to halt bombing most of the North. The President also stressed his fear of a "damaging press leak" before announcing his decision.

The conclusions of the task force in a brief unsigned memorandum which Clifford forwarded to Johnson early in March essentially confirmed current policy and went a long way to meet the request of the military. Yet several high-ranking but not top-ranking civilians in the Penta-

gon, including Deputy Secretary of Defense Paul H. Nitze, and Townsend Hoopes, Paul C. Warnke, and Phil G. Goulding, despite the viewpoints of more key men like Messrs. Rusk, Wheeler, Taylor, Rostow,
and Treasury Secretary Henry H. Fowler, thought they could influence
Clifford and through him the President. If the President had not been
influenced, a number of resignations would have ensued.

Dean Acheson also began to play an important role in the President's
thinking in late February. At Johnson's request he undertook a reappraisal of U.S. policy in Vietnam, and on March 15 candidly told the
President the current policy was unrealistic. Nevertheless, Johnson in
comments to his advisers the next day and in addresses March 18 and 19
indicated a continuation of his stand. Clifford under the circumstances
suggested that the President might find helpful a meeting of the Senior
Advisory Group on Vietnam or the "Wise Men." This informal gathering
since 1965 of Messrs. Dean Acheson, George W. Ball, McGeorge
Bundy, C. Douglas Dillon, Henry Cabot Lodge, Abe Fortas, Cyrus R.
Vance, Arthur H. Dean, John J. McCloy, Robert D. Murphy, and Generals Maxwell D. Taylor, Matthew B. Ridgway, and Omar N. Bradley,
with Goldberg as an addition, met March 25 and 26. It became evident
that the very widespread support for U.S. policy prior to Tet had disappeared. When the advisory group met the President March 26, he was
concerned but not shocked after questioning each participant by the
degree of change. The belief was widespread that time was limited, that
the burden of the war should be shifted to the Vietnamese just as soon as
possible, and that a negotiating stance should be found even if it did not
bring peace.[62]

Plans for a speech by Johnson on Vietnam, finally scheduled for
March 31, had occasioned the preparation of a draft by Harry C.
McPherson, one modified several times before March 28. At first tough,
as of March 22 when Johnson and his advisers discussed it, the speech
was substantially modified at Clifford's insistence six days later at a
meeting of Rusk, Rostow, William P. Bundy, McPherson, and Clifford.
Early that evening Johnson had two basic drafts before him—one militant, the alternative a "peace speech" reflecting certain ideas of
McPherson himself as approved by Rusk and Bunker. Clifford,
McPherson, and others worked with the President, even into the late
afternoon of March 31, polishing the peace speech.

Meanwhile Johnson had announced on March 22 that General Westmoreland would become Army Chief of Staff on July 2 (subject to
Senate confirmation). The step was interpreted in some circles to mean
that the President would not step up the war.

In a dramatic televised speech on the evening of March 31, one which will long live in memory, Lyndon B. Johnson not only announced the halting of American attacks by air and sea against North Vietnam, except in an area north of the Demilitarized Zone where an enemy buildup directly threatened the forward positions of the allies, but also revealed his decision not to run for reelection in November. The President hoped his unilateral and immediate step in the de-escalation of the conflict would lead to "early talks" on the substance of peace, and he assumed that during them North Vietnam would not take advantage of U.S. restraint. He asserted that even the remaining "very limited bombing of the North [south of the twentieth parallel] could come to an early end if our restraint is matched by restraint in Hanoi."[63]

Johnson called upon Great Britain and the Soviet Union as cochairmen of the Geneva conferences and as permanent members of the Security Council of the United Nations to do everything they could for "genuine peace in Southeast Asia." He designated W. Averell Harriman as his personal representative for talks in Geneva or some other suitable location when Hanoi agreed to a conference. At the same time he asserted his country would "never accept a fake solution" to the conflict and "call it peace."[64]

Against the background of the long reassessment of U.S. policy the President revealed what actually became a ceiling of 549,500 American servicemen in Vietnam. Support troops previously promised—only about 13,500—would be the new ones going there. He pointedly noted that Washington would speed up assistance to the armed forces of South Vietnam—reequipment was stressed—so that they could progressively take over more of the combat operations. (He did not use the word *Vietnamization.*)

LBJ's words toward the end of his address most surprised and startled his television audience. After directing attention to "division in the American house now" and "America's sons in the fields far away," he declared "I shall not seek, and I will not accept, the nomination of my party for another term as your President."[65]*

The effects of Johnson's speech at home and on the war were significant. By removing himself as a candidate, he left the political arena even more open for the contests of Republican, Democratic, and other political gladiators. The President of the United States was a political casualty of the Second Indochinese War; in fact, it was very uncertain if he could have been reelected. (Johnson firmly believed he would have won.) He joined a number of other prominent Americans, military and civilian, whose futures had been impaired by developments in Vietnam. At the

---

*It has been argued that Johnson was seeking a much better base for securing a favorable settlement of the war in the light of American opinion.

same time his decision announced on March 31 served to remove some of the bitterness at home directed against his administration's war policy.

Much to Washington's surprise Hanoi indicated its readiness on April 3 to meet with the United States. LBJ believed his decision not to run for the presidency and the impact of his speech abroad along with the partial bombing halt brought Hanoi to the negotiating table. After various proposals between April 6 and May 3 were exchanged on the site for the initial talks—Washington held out against Phnom Penh and Warsaw—Johnson announced on May 3 that Paris was the agreed site and an acceptable date for meeting was May 10 or shortly thereafter.

With the background of the official conversations between Hanoi and Washington in Paris, the question of a complete U.S. bombing halt of North Vietnam mounted in intensity in the summer and fall. President Johnson in a speech on September 10 insisted that the bombing would not cease "until we are confident that it [the halt] will not lead to an increase in American casualties. That is why we have placed such emphasis on reestablishing the DMZ."[66] But once more he de-escalated the war, this time by ending "all air, naval, and artillery bombardment" of the North as of 8 A.M. November 1. Since he announced his decision on the night of October 31—the presidential election falling on November 5—some of his critics believed he took the step to influence the election of Vice-President Hubert H. Humphrey as his successor. But the final decision was reached against an extended background of a shift in Hanoi's attitude and of widespread consultations. The President on August 19 had publicly asserted he would not move further until he believed the other side "seriously" intended to join in de-escalation and to move "seriously" toward peace. He consulted the Joint Chiefs of Staff on October 14 and later General Abrams (whom he called back from Vietnam) about the new developments in the Paris talks. They assured him, he said, that in their military judgment a complete bombing halt "should be taken now and this action would not result in any increase in American casualties."[67] Johnson informed the presidential candidates, Messrs. Hubert H. Humphrey, Richard M. Nixon, and George C. Wallace, and congressional leaders of both parties of the reasons for his decision. South Vietnam and other allies in the war had been involved in the discussions prior to the announcement on the end of the bombing. The President asserted that "what we now expect—what we have a right to expect—are prompt, productive, serious, and intensive negotiations in an atmosphere that is conducive to progress."[68] At the same time he made it a point to observe that the government of South Vietnam had "grown steadily stronger" and the effectiveness of its substantially increased armed forces had "steadily improved."

The decision of President Johnson to halt the bombing of the North was part of a package arrangement with Hanoi. Secretary Clifford on November 12 used the expression "general area of understanding."[69] Subsequent events were expected to reveal its scope and significance. Along with a U.S. bombing halt the DMZ was not to be violated and major cities of South Vietnam were not to be bombarded. At the same time the war would go on in the South. General Abrams followed his long-standing instructions of keeping intensive and continual pressure on enemy forces, and the Communists continued to fight. Reconnaissance operations of the United States over North Vietnam were maintained.

The problem of the representation of Saigon and the NLF was carefully handled by Washington and Hanoi in the package arrangement. The United States emphasized it was not a four-party or four-sided conference but one of only two sides. As a spokesman of the Department of State asserted on November 13: "On our side there would be the Republic of Viet-Nam and the United States. In making this proposal we said that the North Vietnamese could include on their side whomever they wished. For their part, the North Vietnamese said that representatives of the NLF would be present. It was understood that both sides would organize themselves as they chose."[70] Washington in no way recognized the NLF, still considered an "organization controlled by Hanoi." Nor in fact did it recognize North Vietnam. And the NLF as well as Hanoi recognized neither Saigon nor Washington. A rather bizarre situation.

It was Saigon, however, which delayed for a while the opening of the expanded talks at Paris. The Republic of Vietnam refused to participate until satisfactory assurances on its role and future were given by the United States. The confrontation began several days before Johnson's announcement of October 31—actually delayed it for two days—and did not end until late November. LBJ believed that Saigon's obstinacy contributed to Nixon's victory. Anyway Johnson had faced his last big crisis with the Vietnamese albatross. The expanded talks in Paris were still delayed, however, when the Republic of Vietnam and the United States became involved in a long dispute with the Communists on procedural questions or modalities like the shape of the conference table.

Vietnam in the end was not a clear-cut issue for the voters in the national election of November 5. Richard M. Nixon would find it difficult to discover a solution to the war expressed by the people in choosing their elected officials. True, the United States was divided on policy in Vietnam—the voters wanted an end to the war—but few responsible leaders sought to escalate the conflict with the goal of a military victory through nuclear arms if needed or to disengage forthwith from Vietnam lock, stock, and barrel.

Like President Eisenhower before him in 1953 President Nixon inherited from his Democratic predecessor on January 20, 1969, a land war on the mainland of Asia. Instead of being waged on a peninsula in Northeast Asia, Korea, it was being fought on a peninsula in Southeast Asia. Instead of truce negotiations in Panmunjom, expanded talks were about to begin in Paris. But American lives were being lost and American treasure expended. An honorable end of the war in Indochina was Nixon's number one priority.

As President-elect, Nixon had undertaken a thorough examination of the war, an examination of premises, statistics, and alternatives. He was assisted by Henry A. Kissinger who became a top aide in the White House. On January 21 the new President authorized through Kissinger a comprehensive review of the Vietnam problem—answers to specific questions—by government officials. In early 1969 the review was completed.[71] As President, Nixon had to cope with four major variables, namely, the developments in the fighting, the frustrating course of the expanded talks in Paris, the difficult relations with the Saigon government, and the fluid state of American public opinion.[72]

The decade of the 1970s, of course, would not be that of the 1960s. Voices were increasingly raised late in the 1960s to the effect that the United States had already accomplished its major goal in the Second Indochinese War—to prevent defeat in South Vietnam and to keep Southeast Asia from falling into the hands of the Communists. In other words the original cause for U.S. entrance in the war no longer existed. The nature of the international Communist threat, it was argued, had changed in Southeast Asia and the countries of the region had made real progress toward stability.[73]

In a major address on Vietnam, May 14, 1969, Nixon asserted that the "basic terms" of the settlement the United States wanted at Paris were "very simple," namely, "mutual withdrawal of non-South Vietnamese forces from South Viet-Nam and free choice for the people of South Viet-Nam."[74] He specifically included a request for Hanoi to withdraw its forces as well from Cambodia and Laos to ensure they would not be utilized as "bases for a renewed war." Above all the President did not want to leave the seeds of another Vietnam in the settlement.

"Vietnamization" became a key word in the Nixon administration, reportedly coined by Secretary of Defense Laird. Its two main components were strengthening the armed forces of South Vietnam to take over the U.S. military role and extending the pacification program. The concept was not new: For instance, the French under the Navarre Plan in 1953, President Kennedy in late 1963 (it can be argued), and President Johnson late in his administration were essentially moving toward "Vietnamizing" the conflict. For the rate of American troop withdrawals, Nixon gave as his criteria progress in the training and equipping of Saigon's forces, progress in the peace talks in Paris, and the level of activity of the enemy. Criteria for success in pacification centered around a hamlet's having sufficient defense and a fully functioning official of the government living there day and night.

On June 8 President Nixon took a major step in the de-escalation of the Second Indochinese War. After meeting with President Nguyen Van Thieu at Midway Nixon announced that about 25,000 American forces out of the authorized total of 549,500 would be withdrawn from Vietnam before the end of August. The cutback was small—there were 540,000 Americans in uniform in Vietnam in late January and 3,400 more came—but the cutback ranked in significance with Johnson's two major steps in de-escalation ending the bombing of the North. It set the stage for subsequent withdrawals.

These cutbacks, it should be stressed, were carefully planned in terms of international and domestic considerations. As the President announced the successive troop withdrawals, the consequences at home and abroad were weighed. In September 1969 the withdrawal figure was 40,500, in December, 50,000, in April 1970, 150,000, and in April 1971, 100,000. Under the cutback, announced on April 7, 1971, the number withdrawn would total 365,500 by December 1. On November 12, the cutback figure was 45,000, in January 1972, 70,000, in April, 20,000, in June, 10,000, and in August, 12,000, leaving by December 1, a projected 27,000. Along with the American pullout of men was a massive withdrawal of military equipment. Never before in the history of the United States had such a huge, phased, orderly withdrawal of American military forces occurred before the conclusion of the war to which they had been committed. Left essentially in Vietnam were military advisers and support forces.

President Nixon's visit to Southeast Asia and particularly South Vietnam in late July 1969 underlined the new administration's policy. He flew to Saigon on July 30 (not to Cam Ranh Bay as his predecessor had done) and he visited some American combat troops in a nearby, heavily protected base. His very presence in South Vietnam committed American prestige and was resented by North Vietnam. Moreover, it gave a boost to President Thieu and his government. Although Nixon did not make the fighting statements of Johnson in Vietnam he did tell the soldiers that the war in time might be regarded as "one of America's finest hours." He did not visit Cambodia or Laos which within a year would require much of his attention.

United States policy in Cambodia during the Second Indochinese War centered for several years around Prince Norodom Sihanouk. His downfall in 1970 had important repercussions in the United States and on the international scene. The involvement of Phnom Penh for some time in the war was less direct and less extensive than that of Hanoi, Saigon, and Vientiane. Nevertheless, it was real and Cambodians, Vietnamese, and Americans lost their lives in the border areas of the Khmer kingdom and South Vietnam. Prince Norodom Sihanouk's formal facade of neutrality was conditioned by his inability to exercise effective control along Cambodia's frontier reaches like the northeast and along waterways to South Vietnam. Although exact figures are difficult to present it is estimated that from 1965 to early 1968 some 12,000 Communist supporters had infiltrated into South Vietnam through the territory of the Khmer kingdom. More than 20,000 Viet Cong and North Vietnamese soldiers were located by early 1968 in several sanctuaries in the border areas of Cambodia facing South Vietnam, sanctuaries systematically set up since 1965. Representatives of Hanoi were successful in getting rice and other necessities in the kingdom for their forces in the Laos corridor and South Vietnam and supplies for their friends in northwest Cambodia in the province of Battambang. Sihanoukville was being used successfully for getting Chinese and Russian arms and ammunition across Cambodia to Communist forces in an effort to supplement the Ho Chi Minh network. For over five years most of the war material came through this port for southern South Vietnam. Phnom Penh in a gesture toward Hanoi even sent in 1965 a token gift of pharmaceuticals to North Vietnam to help victims of U.S. air raids. Some token rice was also presented to the NLF.

It added up to an intensified use of Cambodian territory as sanctuaries for Communist forces—for storing or transiting supplies, for training purposes, and for rest and recuperation. The sanctuaries also increasingly served as springboards for infiltration and for attacks on allied forces in South Vietnam. The province of Svay Rieng jutting into the latter's territory toward Saigon like a "Duckbill" or "Parrot's Beak" was of special use to the Viet Cong and North Vietnamese. "Fishhook" was another particularly significant sanctuary. Saigon and Washington had to divert military personnel to the border provinces of South Vietnam tying down valuable resources.

Sihanouk broke diplomatic relations with the United States in May 1965. Another bombing incident along the Cambodian–South Vietnamese frontier and an article in *Newsweek* about the Queen Mother provided the occasion. But between the rupture and the reestablishment of formal ties in July 1969 relations between Phnom Penh and Washington were paradoxical. True, there was no official U.S. representation in the kingdom for several years (Australia handled American interests) but there were frequent contacts. American tourists continued to visit the ruins at Angkor, and journalists arrived on occasion. Various high-ranking Americans were well received in Phnom Penh, sometimes by Sihanouk himself—Senator Mansfield in 1965, Mrs. John F. Kennedy in 1967, and Eugene R. Black in 1968. The war in Vietnam overshadowed Khmer-U.S. relations and brought in its wake the aggravated complex of Cambodian-Thai-American relations and Cambodian-Vietnamese (North and South, both NLF and Saigon)-American relations. Even Minos of Crete would have envied this labyrinth.

In 1969 the Nixon administration took steps that restored diplomatic ties between Cambodia and the United States. Late the previous year Sihanouk had indicated such an interest. Washington stated on April 16 that it recognized and respected in conformity with the Charter of the United Nations the independence, sovereignty, neutrality, and territorial integrity of Cambodia "within its present frontiers." The key words, desired by Sihanouk, related to recognition and respect, territorial integrity and present frontiers. Similar statements despite unpleasantness in a few cases had been made by Australia, Great Britain, West Germany, India, France, Japan, the Soviet Union, Communist China, and others. The American step was not appreciated in Saigon and Bangkok; nor, of course, was Cambodia's reaction appreciated in Hanoi and Peking. Phnom Penh considered ties with the United States particularly desirable in view of Communist insurgency in the kingdom. They served as a pointed warning to Hanoi.

On March 18, 1970, much to the surprise of the United States, Prince Norodom Sihanouk was deposed as Chief of State by the National Assembly and Council of the Kingdom. General Lon Nol who was prime minister emerged as the key figure in Cambodia. A Khmer Republic was proclaimed on October 9. When Sihanouk was deposed he was on a visit to Moscow and Peking in an effort to get the removal of North Vietnamese and Viet Cong troops from their sanctuaries in the kingdom. He had been fighting his own Khmer Rouge insurgents since 1967. In fact, Sihanouk tried in the late 1960s to get the Vietnamese Communists to reduce their presence and to lower the scale of their activities in Cambodia, and he tacitly permitted the use of U.S. artillery and air strikes against their positions in unpopulated areas. Protests routinely continued to America.

Efforts by the new Cambodian regime to negotiate a Vietnamese troop withdrawal were rejected by Hanoi. In the face of strong opposition from

Phnom Penh to the presence of the Communists, North Vietnamese troops in early April started to expand their control over southern and eastern areas of the country and establish a huge contiguous base area.

President Nixon's announcement on April 30 that he had ordered U.S. forces in Vietnam to help those of Saigon in attacking the Cambodian sanctuaries aroused severe criticism at home.[75] His statements that the American action was taken not to broaden the war but to forestall an increased threat to U.S. forces in Vietnam and to Vietnamization just were not believed in many circles like college campuses. Nevertheless, the extent of penetration—only twenty-one miles—and the withdrawal of the last American ground troops on June 30 testified to the limited action in terms of area and duration. The Communists lost the use of Sihanoukville, renamed Kompong Som, and their sanctuaries in Cambodia were disrupted while their capabilities in the southern part of South Vietnam were significantly reduced and pacification was enhanced.

Washington stressed that it was not making a military commitment to defend the Cambodian government. On June 29 Secretary of State Rogers asserted that the United States was not in favor of Cambodia's becoming reassociated with the Southeast Asia Treaty Organization. Although Washington backed Phnom Penh in its announced policy of remaining neutral the United States became deeply involved in supporting the Khmers. American air operations continued after the U.S. troop withdrawal against enemy forces, lines of communication, and supplies. Indeed, over 50,000 North Vietnamese and Viet Cong troops were in the country at the end of 1970. South Vietnamese forces operating in Cambodia were given limited American air combat and logistic support. Congress barred U.S. ground combat troops or advisers in Cambodia. A significant American military assistance program including training and arming Khmer troops airlifted to South Vietnam was provided Phnom Penh in its efforts to cope with widespread North Vietnamese attacks. Thailand and South Vietnam helped furnish military training with limited American financial aid. Substantial U.S. economic help was also provided as the Cambodian economy was disrupted by the war and the aid could be put to good use. On the diplomatic front, the United States staunchly backed the Khmer Republic in its international posture. It welcomed in May 1970 the efforts of eleven Asian and Pacific nations at Djakarta to find a solution to the Khmer crisis. The active roles of Indonesia and Japan were particularly noteworthy. Washington later joined several nations in an Exchange Support Fund for Phnom Penh.

Several months after American ground troops left Cambodia President Nixon made a significant move on October 7 when he proposed an immediate cease-fire-in-place in Indochina, a peace conference on the area, and a political settlement. He also called for the full withdrawal of all external forces and the release at once of all prisoners of war. Hanoi was not responsive.

Laos like Cambodia was so deeply involved in the Second Indochinese War that any realistic Vietnamese peace settlement could not bypass the landlocked kingdom. There were, for instance, around 90,000 North Vietnamese troops in the country at the end of 1970. Actually two wars were being waged in Laos—one in the north by the Pathet Lao and the North Vietnamese against the forces of Prime Minister Souvanna Phouma and the other in the south by the Americans and Laotians against the entrenched North Vietnamese in the broad Ho Chi Minh trail complex. In the north the pattern was usually Communist attacks in the dry season and government counterattacks in the wet. In the south the pattern was an intensification of effort by both sides with a climax coming in February and March 1971. The overt and covert activities of the Americans and North Vietnamese, not to mention the U.S.-supported Thai, in Laos will probably never be fully chronicled. In addition, it was estimated in 1969 that some 7,000 Chinese construction troops were building roads in northwest Laos toward North Vietnam and Thailand, adding to the complexity of the international scene.

American military and economic aid to the Mekong kingdom was of such significance that Secretary Rusk asserted on May 2, 1968, that "it is no overstatement to say that the survival of Laos as an independent nation depends on United States help."[76] He called attention to the financing of much of the military effort of the Laotians through an economic stabilization program. Economic aid alone, it should be pointed out, came to $643 million in the years 1955–69. American assistance ranged from supporting air transportation in Laos like the flights of Air America and Continental Air Services giving Vientiane's troops and irregulars considerable mobility to helping the many refugees from the fighting, the civil police, and village "clusters" or "manageable areas of operation" in community development. The clandestine army of Meo and other hill tribesmen under Major General Vang Pao in the so-called twilight war was paid and fed, equipped and armed, tactically helped, and often moved to and from battle by the United States, Americans from CIA and U.S. military advisers being very important in the operations.[77] Although there were no American ground combat troops in Laos, a key U.S. task was military training. (Since the beginning of 1966 American servicemen in the country received hostile-fire pay.) The United States Ambassador presided over an extensive American presence, civilian and military, embassy, CIA, AID, USIA, and other personnel during the Second Indochinese War. It was somewhat like the old days.

On March 6, 1970, President Nixon released a comprehensive statement entitled "Scope of the U.S. Involvement in Laos."[78] He noted that when he went to the White House, American air operations had been increasing for four years and an American military assistance program had been in existence for six years. Nixon in the north stepped up as needed air operations and military assistance in support of the government of Prime Minister Souvanna Phouma, and in the south expanded air strikes and other operations in the Ho Chi Minh trail network in an effort to assist Vietnamization.

During Hanoi's dry season offensive, February–May 1970, the Communists pushed beyond the Plain of Jars and occupied a large area traditionally held by government troops. American support missions for Laotian forces were augmented at the time amid apprehension in Congress about the extent of U.S. involvement. But the war resumed its cyclical aspect. And once more early in 1971 the North Vietnamese and Pathet Lao were at the height of a dry season campaign, occupying new areas, and again the government forces later returned to the Plain of Jars.*

After the shutoff of the Communist route from the Gulf of Siam across Cambodia to South Vietnam in the spring and early summer of 1970 Hanoi undertook in the fall a rapid buildup of forces and supplies in southern Laos. When Saigon's forces crossed into the panhandle to cut the Ho Chi Minh trails in early February 1971 and when they were provided U.S. air, artillery, and logistical support apprehension arose in the United States that President Nixon was broadening the war. The ending of the operation in late March relieved this apprehension but left a number of questions about the effectiveness of Saigon's forces. Nixon on April 7 insisted that the record of the South Vietnamese in both Laos and Cambodia proved the success of Vietnamization. He claimed that they had fought well without U.S. advisers in Laos, had inflicted heavy casualties on the foe, and had badly disrupted enemy supply lines. Other observers were not so optimistic in their evaluation of the operation in the Laotian panhandle. President Nixon like a number of his predecessors learned that trying to preserve a neutral and independent Laos in the framework of the Geneva settlement of 1962 and trying to contain Hanoi's aggression were not easy.

As the United States moved along the road of de-escalation with the

---

*On December 17, 1971, the North Vietnamese and Pathet Lao launched their dry season offensive in north-central Laos. They drove government forces from the Plain of Jars and besieged the key base of General Vang Pao at Long Tieng northeast of Vientiane.

withdrawal of troops in Vietnam, other allies began to move their forces out of the country. First to go were the Filipinos. Marcos had been re-elected president in November 1969 and he decided to bring home the Philippine Civic Action Group by the end of the next month. His step was taken in the wake of congressional criticism in Washington about the financing of the Civic Action Group and in the wake of rising Philippine nationalism and concern over U.S. policy. During the previous July Nixon had visited Manila; his opening remarks at the airport mentioned the special relationship between Americans and Filipinos in the past tense though at his departure he referred to it in the present tense. The U.S. military presence in the Philippines began to be reduced in 1969 and Sangley Point Naval Air Station was turned over to Manila in 1971.

Thailand also started to remove its forces from South Vietnam but in stages. Plans were made to withdraw half of the Thai division of around 12,000 men by the end of July 1971 and the rest later. In time only a liaison group remained. Also a reduction of American forces in Thailand began in 1969. The Thai were aroused at the time over congressional criticism of the secret military contingency plan of the Johnson adminis-tration to defend the Mekong valley. Bangkok and Washington agreed on September 30 that 6,000 U.S. military personnel would be withdrawn by July 1, 1970. The goal was reached, and another agreement called for 9,800 more to leave by June 30, 1971. Australia and New Zealand like-wise took steps to withdraw their forces from Vietnam. Having already made reductions, they announced on August 18, 1971, that all their combat forces would leave in a few months but small training units would remain. The former objective was met in December. Korea was the last to take serious steps toward calling home its military personnel.

Moscow and Peking reduced their military aid to Hanoi from the amount given during the zenith of military escalation.

Near the end of March 1972 the North Vietnamese began their big-gest offensive since Tet in 1968—the so-called Easter weekend offensive. It was an all-out conventional effort directed toward military victory in the South. With Russian-made heavy tanks, long-range artillery, and massed antiaircraft weapons, Hanoi's forces moved into Quang Tri prov-ince in Military Region I from across the Demilitarized Zone. A few days later they launched an attack from Cambodia with comparable sophisticated equipment into Binh Long province in Military Region III, took Loc Ninh, and besieged, in a costly struggle, the provincial capital of An Loc only sixty miles from Saigon. In the Central Highlands Hanoi's forces attacked from Laotian territory threatening Kontum in Military Region II and trying to divide South Vietnam. Meanwhile various villages in the important Mekong delta were seized or taken over by Communist guerrillas, seriously setting back pacification. Hanoi was able to take control of the northern part of Binh Dinh province on the central coast with its rice supplies. The dimensions of the war effort of the North Vietnamese were reflected in their initial commitment of all but one of their thirteen combat divisions to fight outside home territory, most of them in South Vietnam. Hanoi was prepared to take heavy battle losses and pay the price of U.S. bombing at home.

The United States soon called North Vietnam's offensive "naked aggression" and a "massive invasion." In Washington's viewpoint it should destroy any lingering interpretation of the conflict as a "civil war" and prove beyond doubt the weakness of the Viet Cong. The offensive also violated the understanding reached with Hanoi in 1968 whereby the United States ended the systematic bombing of the North. But despite the use of the terms "aggression" and "invasion" Saigon and Washington did not involve SEATO. An excellent legal case could have been made, but what could SEATO have done?

The North Vietnamese invasion was a direct challenge to President Nixon's Vietnamization program. Would Saigon despite severe battle losses, heavy civilian casualties, a new torrent of refugees, and wide-spread destruction be able to stand up to the invaders? In an effort to influence the outcome Nixon authorized air and sea attacks on North Vietnam and on enemy targets in South Vietnam. Retaliatory bombing of the North began on April 6; B-52s joined the assault over Hanoi's southern territory four days later; and the President ordered the bombing of targets in Hanoi and Haiphong, deeper in the North, on April 16. Although apparently caught offguard, the United States began a huge buildup of air and sea power involving B-52s and other planes as well as aircraft carriers and other ships for use in the war zone. Directly involved in various aspects of the buildup were bases in Thailand and Guam with South Vietnam less significant. Various support forces were increased at U.S. installations in the Philippines, Okinawa, and Japan. Indeed, by the end of June around 45,000 American servicemen were in Thailand and 42,000 in naval forces off Vietnam.

In an April 26 address, Nixon was generally optimistic about the course of the fighting. He asserted that the American air and naval attacks on the North would continue until Hanoi stopped its offensive in the South. But he coupled this policy with an announcement that 20,000 more American troops would be withdrawn by July 1, thus reducing the authorized ceiling to 49,000. Most ground combat troops had already left Vietnam, and remaining land forces had an essentially defensive and base security role. On April 30 the President pointedly warned Hanoi that it was assuming "a very great risk" if it continued the offensive in the South.

The military and diplomatic situation as regards Vietnam took a turn for the worse. On May 1 the provincial capital of Quang Tri fell to Hanoi's forces and the old imperial capital of Hué appeared the next major target. Henry Kissinger had gone to Moscow on April 20 to confer with Communist General Secretary Brezhnev; the former, encouraged by the Russians, then met privately with Hanoi's Le Duc Tho on May 2 in Paris. But despite everything North Vietnam still proved adamant and inflexible.

Against this background President Nixon on the evening of May 8 announced one of his major decisions of the Second Indochinese War. Although he discussed his policy with the National Security Council that day and informed congressional leaders of it before his speech, he—and no one else—bore full responsibility. In no uncertain words Nixon asserted:

> I therefore concluded that Hanoi must be denied the weapons and supplies it needs to continue the aggression. In full coordination with the Republic of Viet-Nam I have ordered the following measures, which are being implemented as I am speaking to you:
> All entrances to North Vietnamese ports will be mined to prevent access to these ports and North Vietnamese naval operations from these ports.
> United States forces have been directed to take appropriate measures within the internal and claimed territorial waters of North Viet-Nam to interdict the delivery of any supplies.
> Rail and all other communications will be cut off to the maximum extent possible.
> Air and naval strikes against military targets in North Viet-Nam will continue.[79]

At the same time he offered a peace proposal in which the United States would "stop all acts of force" in Indochina once American prisoners of war were released and once an internationally supervised cease-fire had started there. Moreover, at that time Washington would proceed to a complete withdrawal of all U.S. forces from Vietnam within a period of four months. The President indicated very clearly that the United States would not join North Vietnam in installing a Communist government in the South.

Operation *Linebacker* and Operation *Pocket Money,* the code names for the American air and sea effort to choke off Hanoi's military pipeline and to destroy systematically its ability to sustain a war, involved an accelerated bombing campaign and a semi-blockade of North Vietnam's ports. The United States pointedly barred the use of its nuclear weapons and the introduction of its ground combat troops. The air-sea war against North Vietnam proved to be more intensive than ever mounted there. The air campaign varied from the effort under the Johnson administration in being not at all so gradualistic, in having less restricted targets, and in giving more control to the military. A new generation of weapons facilitated pinpoint attacks with devastating effect. Despite some spectacular Communist gains on the ground in South Vietnam, the military situation there by the end of spring was a stalemate. American air power was critical in stopping the offensive. In late June, however, Saigon launched a counteroffensive to retake Quang Tri and seize the initiative in the north. The provincial capital was finally captured in September.

The reaction at home and abroad to Nixon's military steps was influenced by the role played by Hanoi in launching the invasion. In general the criticism and support in Congress were predictable, but the public appeared less disturbed and the demonstrations were less popular than at the time of the Cambodian invasion in 1970. Vietnam was brought for a while to the forefront in American politics. Overseas the reaction in the Soviet Union and in Communist China was bitter but relatively restrained partly due to Nixon's summit diplomacy. Among allies of the United States and neutrals, praise or criticism, more often the latter, was somewhat muted. Greatly feared was an armed confrontation between Moscow and Washington especially after May 8, though this apprehension soon subsided.

Despite the direct challenge to the Kremlin of the American semi-blockade of North Vietnam's ports—Haiphong, for instance, was the major port for Soviet military aid—Moscow did not cancel the visit of President Nixon scheduled to begin May 22. In fact, the summit produced a number of accords, the most notable being the agreements relating to nuclear arms.

As for the expanded peace talks in Paris, they remained long stalemated with both sides invoking pauses at various times. The fighting went on as the dialogue in Paris went on. On January 16, 1969, Hanoi and Washington with the support of their respective associates had announced an agreement on certain basic procedural matters that would enable the broader new talks to begin. On January 18, two days before Nixon's inauguration, the two sides (or four parties) met and formally agreed on procedures. The longstanding dispute over the shape of the conference table was resolved. It would be round with no division; there would be no nameplates or flags; and two small rectangular tables for secretaries would flank the round table on opposite sides but not touch it. The United States maintained that its stance of two sides was revealed in the arrangement, and the Communists claimed their viewpoint of four parties was supported in it. President Johnson, backed by President-elect Nixon, worked for the compromise. Moscow helped in a quiet way in both the October 1968 and January 1969 accords.

President Johnson on January 16 welcomed the agreement and told his countrymen that three lessons had emerged from the experience since March 31. First, the United States must be "clear and firm" in the pursuit with its allies of the "limited but vital objectives" it seeks in Southeast Asia; second, it must be "patient and face the hard fact" of probably having to fight while negotiations go forward; and third, it should be "confident that an honorable peace is possible" if Americans "remain steady" at home.[80] After twenty-eight formal bilateral meetings between May 13 and October 30 with secret talks away from the conference site between Hanoi and Washington and after three crises—where to meet before Paris was chosen, the terms for halting the U.S. bombing of the North, and the procedures for the new expanded talks—the stage was set for the first plenary face-to-face meeting of the ranking delegates of Washington, Saigon, Hanoi, and the NLF. It came on January 25, 1969, a date that ushered in another long, agonizing experience for the United States. Exactly three years later, President Nixon on January 25, 1972, gave a public accounting of his secret efforts, outside the formal framework of the Paris talks, to reach a negotiated settlement with Hanoi. He revealed the long negotiations of Kissinger with the North Vietnamese in Paris. On May 8 Nixon observed in a speech that Hanoi had met his various offers "with insolence and insult." But renewed efforts involving Moscow and Peking were made.

The Nixon Doctrine. The Second Indochinese War provided much of the background for the formulation and evolution of the Nixon Doctrine. Vietnamization has been called a major application of it. But there were broader horizons and broader considerations behind the Doctrine than the conflict in Indochina.

The postwar period of World War II was over. The polarization of power was less pronounced, for it was being weakened by polycentrism in each grouping of allies. True, Washington and Moscow remained the two superpowers of the world but the differences between Washington and Paris, on the one hand, and at a far more serious level Moscow and Peking, on the other, had weakened their influence among their formal allies and in the world. At the same time the Federal Republic of Germany and Japan had risen from the ashes of defeat to power positions and potentials of great significance while Communist China and France had joined the United States, the Soviet Union, and Great Britain in the ranks of nuclear countries. Moreover, Moscow shared with Washington a thermonuclear balance of power. In another development the overall impact of the so-called Third World of newly independent, underdeveloped nations declined, for their leaders were not able to present a unified front in the continuing political and security problems of the day. India, for instance, lost its early leadership through the split with Communist China and the death of Prime Minister Nehru. Neocolonialism, once a subject of concern, faded and decolonization in its formal aspects became more and more a page in history. The Cold War was not ended but its intensity generally declined. The old "isms" lost their punch. Finally the United Nations failed to live up to the expectations of many of its founders though it remained a world forum with great potential.

In Asia, specifically, the evolution of the Nixon Doctrine reflected major developments in relationships in 1971 and 1972.[81] President Nixon asserted in early 1970 that negotiation along with partnership and strength constituted the three pillars of the "structure of a durable peace." His call for an "era of negotiation" bore fruit in his visit to Peking in February 1972 and to Moscow in May. On the other side of the coin, he approved a "national security strategy of realistic deterrence," one fully developed in the 1972 Defense Report of Secretary Laird.

The People's Republic of China and Japan in Northeast Asia, India and Pakistan in South Asia, and the Eurasian Soviet Union dramatically figured in the events of 1971 and 1972. Communist China was seated in the United Nations in place of the Republic of China in October 1971. Nixon's visit to Peking early the next year marked the formal beginning of a détente between the United States and the People's Republic. It also meant that the ultimate role of Taiwan was weakened in American defense planning. Nixon's relations with Japan were tested in July 1971 by the announcement unexpected in Tokyo of his planned trip to Peking and in August by his sharp restrictions on Japanese imports. However, they were improved by the reversion of Okinawa and the rest of the Ryukyus to Tokyo on May 15, 1972. In South Asia and the Indian Ocean the Indo-Pakistani War in December 1971 saw Washington and Peking sympathetic to Pakistan while Moscow backed India. The dismemberment of Pakistan and the independence of Bangladesh strengthened the roles of New Delhi and Moscow in South Asia and the Indian Ocean, weakened the influence of the United States in the area, and removed Pakistan as a neighbor of Southeast Asia. Bangladesh, the former East Pakistan, renounced any connection with SEATO. Nixon's relations with the U.S.S.R. obviously were influenced by developments in his policy toward the People's Republic of China, Japan, India, and Pakistan. But the Moscow summit in May 1972 reflected an effort by both superpowers to create better relations without papering over differences on Southeast Asia, the Middle East, and other areas as well as on several topics of concern. The situation in Asia by the summer of 1972 had thus markedly·changed from that three years earlier.

President Nixon's comments on U.S. policy at an informal news conference in Guam on July 25, 1969, bloomed into the Nixon Doctrine.[82] It was enunciated in Asia as the chief executive was on his way to discussions with leaders in the Philippines, Thailand, Indonesia, and South Vietnam. The essence of future U.S. policy in Asia embodied three precepts. First, Washington would keep its treaty commitments. Second, it would provide a shield if a nuclear state menaced the freedom of an ally or of a country whose survival the United States considered vital to its security and that of the region as a whole. Third, in instances when other types of aggression were involved, Washington would provide military and economic aid when asked and as appropriate in accordance with its treaty commitments. But the United States would look to the state directly threatened to take on the primary responsibility for furnishing manpower in its defense.[83] Associated with the Nixon Doctrine as corollaries was support through partnership for rapid economic development and support for Asian initiatives in increased regional cooperation.

The Doctrine represented inputs from both the State Department and the Pentagon. At Guam the latter was more pronounced but in Manila the former very noticeable. The origins of the Doctrine go back at least in part to Nixon's visit as a private citizen to Djakarta in 1967. It has been made more difficult to understand by early differences in official terminology defining it.

Moreover, on January 20, 1972, President Nixon in his State of the Union Address to a joint session of Congress spoke of the Nixon Doctrine in very broad terms. And later on June 26 he wrote:

> What has come to be known as the Nixon Doctrine is essentially a plan for strengthening our alliances, for spreading more equitably the burdens of peacekeeping, for enlisting more nations more fully in the task of securing their own defenses, and for helping ensure that future conflicts which are peripheral to the central interests of the great powers should not directly involve the great powers themselves.[84]

What did the Doctrine mean in practice? Kissinger has pointedly observed that it is not "a cookbook" but rather "a philosophy." It did mean, however, less American capability, prominence, and involvement in Asian affairs. It also called for less presence.* At the same time it meant that the United States in view of its significant interests would continue to play a role in the defense and in the development of its Asian friends and allies. The responsibility of these friends and allies was emphasized. Also, Washington would not return to its traditional stress on Europe.

At home the Nixon Doctrine was related to the American experience in the Second Indochinese War and to the trend toward isolationism. The mood of Congress and the public called for retrenchment. The Doctrine sought to strike a balance between the widespread disillusionment over the U.S. role in the world and the need to play a responsible role as a superpower. In Asia the principles of the Nixon Doctrine were widely approved but allies were generally apprehensive about their implementation. There is a twilight zone between indirect and direct aggression. But when the final evaluation is made only events will have provided the answer.

THE EMPHASIS ON DEVELOPMENT: THE SECONDARY THEME

I have been posing an alternative to our present policy of over-involvement in the affairs of these [Southeast Asian] nations. Briefly, that alternative envisions a resurrection of the ancient art of diplomacy and a substitution of cooperation in development for involvement in counterinsurgent warfare.

Eugene R. Black[85]

Foreign assistance in the economic development of the new nations, therefore, will help determine in a crucial fashion what kind of societies will eventually emerge in the Southeast Asian area. Will they be open or closed societies, increasingly free or increasingly repressive, friendly or hostile to the West? It will be an

---

*In early 1972 the United States maintained embassies in Southeast Asia in Manila, Djakarta, Singapore, Kuala Lumpur, Rangoon, Bangkok, Phnom Penh, Vientiane, and Saigon. It had consulates in Cebu, Medan, Surabaya, Mandalay, Chiang Mai, Songkhla, Udorn, and Da Nang. The Bureau of East Asian and Pacific Affairs in the Department of State included the assistant secretary with four deputy assistant secretaries, directors for the Republic of China, Japan, Korea, Laos and Cambodia, Indonesia, Malaysia and Singapore, Philippines, Thailand and Burma, and Australia, New Zealand and Pacific Islands, a director of the Vietnam Working Group, one of regional affairs, and a director of Asian Communist affairs. Other branches of government in Washington, of course, had their own tables of organization, and some of them their own representation overseas.

important factor in determining whether nationalism in Southeast
Asia will turn towards the world its aggressive, xenophobic face or
its constructive and cooperative aspect.

Soedjatmoko[86]

The quotations from Eugene R. Black, former president of the World
Bank, and Soedjatmoko, former Indonesian ambassador to the United
States, call attention to cooperation in development. Indeed, post-Ges-
tapu Indonesia became a leading example of it although precedents
existed in Southeast Asia. It should not be forgotten that President
Truman once thought of a Marshall Plan which would embrace the area.
American assistance for relief and rehabilitation paved the way in basic
respects for U.S. aid in economic development.

President Johnson in his famous speech at Johns Hopkins University
on April 7, 1965, took a significant step forward. On "this quiet
campus" he called upon the nations of Southeast Asia with the help of U
Thant, Secretary General of the United Nations, to work together in a
"greatly expanded cooperative effort for development" and hoped North
Vietnam would join it under conditions of peaceful cooperation. He indicated he would ask Congress for a billion-dollar investment when the
effort was under way. Significantly the President hoped the Soviet Union
would join all other industrialized states in the grand endeavor. Eugene
R. Black was designated to head a team of Americans to facilitate U.S.
participation in a number of programs for cooperative effort in Southeast
Asia.

In his speech on March 31, 1968, when he announced his intention
not to run again for the presidency Johnson returned to the theme of
development in the region. The ravages of the war, he believed, made the
subject "more urgent than ever." Throughout his years in the White
House Johnson had shown genuine interest in the development of the
Mekong Basin; and he authorized David E. Lilienthal in 1966 to
undertake a study with the Vietnamese on the postwar development of
South Vietnam. President Nixon for his own part revealed on January
25, 1972, that on July 26 of the previous year the United States had privately indicated to the North Vietnamese that it remained prepared to
undertake a reconstruction program of major proportions in Indochina
that would include North Vietnam. The actual implementation of such a
program would have international dimensions.

The quiet, nonmilitary, multilateral approach to U.S. aid, the roles of
the United States and Japan as key participants in international programs, and the stress on regional initiatives were components of the
development theme under Presidents Johnson and Nixon. "Low profiles"

and "low silhouettes" found widespread usage in the vocabulary of diplomacy. The Association of Southeast Asian Nations (ASEAN), the Asian and Pacific Council (ASPAC), and many other regional organizations entered the international galaxy. But it was the startling events in Indonesia in 1965 that gave the development theme its greatest opportunity to prove itself.

The Case of Post-Gestapu Indonesia. On the night of September 30, 1965, the balance of forces in the island republic was subjected to a challenge that had momentous results in its domestic and foreign policy. The attempted coup that night of "progressive, revolutionary" military officers backed by the Communist (PKI) leadership—the so-called Gestapu affair or G.30.S. (September 30 Movement)—involved the kidnapping and murder of six generals of the Indonesian army.[87] Generals Suharto and Nasution who escaped death (the former not being on the priority list and the latter being wounded) rallied opposition forces and put down the coup. The objective of the rebels had been to purge the army general staff of critics of the PKI and of Sukarno. (It is quite possible that the Communists and Sukarno himself believed that an army plot of generals was in existence against them.) If Suharto and Nasution had been killed, the coup might have succeeded and a Communist regime might well have emerged. Indonesia in the wake of a power struggle clearly passed under the control of the army, General Suharto with widespread student support emerging as the key figure with Adam Malik and the Sultan of Jogjakarta as able associates. Sukarno's puzzling role during the attempted coup (he was privy and possibly party to it with his health a factor in its timing) and his attitudes after its failure contributed to the reduction of his influence by steps—despite his efforts to prevent it. He delegated power to Suharto in March 1966; a year later the General became acting president and in 1968 president. The PKI, the largest Communist party at the time of the Gestapu affair in a non-Communist state, was decimated and finally outlawed; its fronts were declared illegal; and leaders like D. N. Aidit, M. H. Lukman, and Njoto slain. Possibly 300,000 Communists were killed in the blood bath. In 1970 probably fewer than 5,000 Communist members were active in Indonesia, for Djakarta's security forces in 1968 had dealt another blow to the PKI by suppressing a Communist attempt to organize guerrilla warfare in East Java.

The United States was not involved in the dramatic developments in Indonesia in the early fall of 1965. Washington had been able before the abortive coup to maintain diplomatic relations with Sukarno despite the grave provocations. Ambassador Marshall Green had replaced Howard

P. Jones in the U.S. embassy. As Green was not associated in the past in any way with Sukarno, the new Ambassador was able to capitalize on the fact after the attempted coup. American policy before the fateful night late in September was to show restraint and ride out the storm. And actually there was no other meaningful alternative before or after the coup attempt. John Hughes, a Pulitzer Prize winner for his reporting, observed that, during the time when the outcome was not clear, direct intervention or involvement by the United States would have hindered and embarrassed the new leaders. It would have undercut their position and aided the PKI in its charge that they were subservient to the West.[88] American nonintervention in Indonesia paid dividends.

The failure of the Communist-supported coup the night of September 30, 1965, was one of the most significant developments in Asia since World War II and cannot be isolated from world events. William P. Bundy has noted: "A hostile and eventually Communist Indonesia could over time have undermined all that we were doing to defend Viet-Nam and to preserve the security of the rest of Southeast Asia."[89] Yet it is difficult to establish any direct connection between the U.S. stand in Vietnam as it developed in 1965 and the events of the abortive coup in Indonesia. But there is a degree of relevance to the subsequent struggle for power in Djakarta. It can be argued that the U.S. stand in Vietnam bought time for the generals in Indonesia and a contrary American position would have worked against them. Richard M. Nixon for his part wrote in October 1967:

> The U. S. presence [in Vietnam] has provided tangible and highly visible proof that communism is not necessarily the wave of Asia's future. This was a vital factor in the turnaround in Indonesia, where a tendency toward fatalism is a national characteristic. It provided a shield behind which the anti-communist forces found the courage and the capacity to stage their counter-coup and, at the final moment, to rescue their country from the Chinese orbit. . . . Indonesia constitutes by far the greatest prize in the Southeast Asian area.[90]

President Sukarno once noted that his country had its "ups and downs" and American relations with Indonesia while he was the key figure were an excellent example of diplomacy based on such a characterization. The Sukarno era provides perspective for the Suharto one. The United States had no role in the dissolution of the Netherlands-Indonesian Union nor in the Bandung Conference in the 1950s. However, President Eisenhower on December 22, 1954, approved a sweeping policy statement of the National Security Council which called for the United States to

Employ all feasible covert means, and all feasible overt means, including, in accordance with constitutional processes, the use of armed force if necessary and appropriate, to prevent Indonesia or vital parts thereof from falling under Communist control by overt armed attack, subversion, economic domination, or other means; concerting overt actions with other ANZUS nations.[91]

Under President Kennedy Washington took an active part in the settlement of the West New Guinea controversy in August 1962 but it was less active in the later confrontation crisis between Indonesia and Malaysia. (LBJ had a tougher approach to Sukarno than Kennedy.) Although the United States was implicated in the attempt—the Padang Revolt—to overthrow the regime of Sukarno in 1958 it was not implicated in the Gestapu affair. American relations with Indonesia in the Sukarno era contrasted with the special relationship between the United States and the Philippines and the relatively normal relations between the United States and Malaya/Malaysia.*

In the light of Suharto's stress on development it is interesting to note the abortive effort of President Kennedy in this direction. When he met Sukarno in Washington in April 1961 the American chief executive offered to send a high-level group of economists to Djakarta to confer with their counterparts on the best way Washington could help Indonesia achieve its Eight-Year Development Plan. The recommendations of the economic survey team led by Professor D. D. Humphrey called for American and other foreign aid over a period of five years providing Indonesia took the essential steps toward stabilization. For a while Sukarno indicated he might stress economic stabilization and development at home but the planning and final creation of Malaysia in 1963 provided an occasion for another noisy venture in regional, Asian, and even world politics. During his confrontation with Malaysia loyally backed by Great Britain, Australia, and New Zealand, Washington was involved in the contrapuntal relations of Djakarta and Kuala Lumpur while becoming more and more engaged in Vietnam.

By the summer of 1965 following a year of anti-Americanism, U.S. relations with Indonesia were at the lowest point in their history. Virtually all American aid had ended after approximately $897 million of it from 1950 through early 1965. A mission of Ellsworth Bunker to Dja-

---

*On September 5, 1956, President Eisenhower approved a policy statement of the National Security Council which included the following: "After Malaya attains full self-government and independence, [the United States should] be prepared, as appropriate and consistent with recognition of [British] Commonwealth responsibility, to assist Malaya to maintain stability and independence, and encourage it to join SEATO."[92]

karta in April had resulted in a decision to keep an American program of technical assistance to certain Indonesian universities but to withdraw the Peace Corps. After a series of attacks on USIS libraries, often encouraged by Indonesian officials, Washington ordered the closing of all of them in early 1965 and ended USIS activities in the island republic. As propaganda attacks on the United States and demonstrations against it cumulated, as Americans were harassed, a break in diplomatic relations seemed likely.

Not only was Indonesia at odds with the United States but also with the Soviet Union. A Djakarta-Peking axis was emerging, cutting across old friendships. Sukarno left the United Nations. India, Yugoslavia, and the United Arab Republic were now "arrivée" in Djakarta but ties were becoming firmer with Pakistan and Cambodia. The PKI had clearly opted for Peking, influencing the direction of Sukarno's policy. Indonesia was profusely sympathizing with Ho Chi Minh in the Second Indochinese War and condemning the role of the United States in it. At home the PKI was growing in strength, and some of the armed forces had been infiltrated. In the power equation Sukarno was clearly favoring the Indonesian Communists who seemed on the verge of triumph.

Djakarta's foreign and domestic policy drastically shifted under the new leadership of the pragmatic Suharto. He sought to follow a more traditional policy, "independent and active," in world politics while he concentrated on domestic problems. Foreign Minister Adam Malik noted in January 1968 that Indonesia's chief task was "to reestablish her position as a respectable and respected nation based on a policy described usually as nonalignment."[93] Economic stabilization and rehabilitation with subsequent development under the New Order became the center of attention at home. The country was fortunate in having some able and energetic economists, often trained in America.

It was clear that Djakarta could not start payments in the immediate future on its foreign debts of around $2.5 billion. About $1.3 billion of this was owed to the Soviet Union and East European nations and the rest to the United States, other Western countries, and Japan. In separate negotiations with Moscow and with other Communist states and at a round-table conference in Paris with Western and pro-Western creditors in late 1966 Indonesia succeeded in having its payments of the Sukarno debt rescheduled or in effect postponed. Further negotiations especially on the long-term aspects were successfully held in April and August 1970. Emergency assistance was also needed for necessary imports and help was forthcoming. A gathering of officials from non-Communist states and from international organizations interested in assisting Indonesia in long-term credits took place significantly in Amsterdam in early 1967. Active in the meeting were the Netherlands, West Germany, Japan, Great Britain, Australia, France, Italy, Belgium, Canada, and the World Bank, International Monetary Fund, and Asian Development Bank. The Inter-Governmental Group on Indonesia became an institution periodically meeting and providing assistance.[94]

In the gatherings of both creditors and donors the United States played a significant role of support and assistance for Djakarta, and in providing long-term aid Washington was willing to make and did make a major contribution to the island nation (a rule of thumb being one third U.S. and two thirds foreign). Djakarta occupied very high priority in American aid; some $700 million worth was provided between 1965 and 1970. Welcome in Washington was Indonesia's encouragement of foreign capital, and American private investments substantially rose. In 1970 Djakarta's exports to the United States amounted to $182 million and imports from it to $264 million.

The official American presence in Indonesia in 1972 was no Little America in terms of the embassy proper, AID and USIA representation, and the Defense Liaison Group. Agreements Washington has signed with the Suharto regime have related to furnishing military equipment, materials, and services (the aid ran to about $6 million a year but was later increased by $13 million), and furnishing agricultural commodities (here a "fair share" of food aid was involved). Aviation, investment guarantees, and other matters were dealt with in accords. The visit of President Nixon in July 1969, the first U.S. presidential visit, symbolized the cordial relations between Washington and Djakarta. President Suharto returned the visit the next spring during the American incursion in Cambodia. Indonesia wanted more American economic and military aid but the United States continued to emphasize the economic. Although Djakarta maintained its policy of nonalignment despite some questioning at home it welcomed an American naval and nuclear presence "over the horizon."

Indonesia, the giant of Southeast Asia, with its population of 120 million people in 1972, is the key indigenous country in the security of the region, at least of insular Southeast Asia. It was not until June 23, 1969, however, that Kissinger felt the need to commission a National Security Study Memorandum on Indonesia. Djakarta ended confrontation with Malaysia in August 1966 when an agreement was signed terminating hostile acts and restoring diplomatic relations. It also joined in August 1967 Malaysia, the Philippines, Thailand, and Singapore (which had become independent from Malaysia through being "kicked out" on

August 9, 1965) in the creation of the Association of Southeast Asian Nations. Indonesia thus began to play a significant role in regional affairs.

Cordial ties were established between Djakarta and London, Canberra, and Wellington. Indonesia watched with interest and no objection the development of the Five-Power Defense Arrangement, effective November 1, 1971, among three of its close neighbors, Malaysia, Singapore, and Australia, along with New Zealand and Great Britain. Under the arrangement London, Canberra, and Wellington would continue to station forces (ANZUS forces) in the Malaysia-Singapore area and all five powers would consult at once in the event of any type of external armed attack or threat of it against Malaysia or Singapore.[95] President Nixon had stressed in early May 1969 the importance of ANZUS and had strongly backed Australia and New Zealand in their February decision to maintain ground, air, and naval forces in the area even though Prime Minister Harold Wilson against U.S. opposition (partly motivated by the war in Indochina) had planned to withdraw the British military presence by the end of 1971. The United States was very sympathetic to the new Five-Power Defense Arrangement.

Indonesia under Suharto returned to the United Nations. It suspended relations with Communist China in October 1967 though it sought better ties with the Soviet Union. Moscow was slow but began to respond in 1970. Indonesian relations with Japan were increasingly significant, and Djakarta came to get over one third of Tokyo's bilateral aid. Japan like other maritime powers has expressed concern over the Indonesian and Malaysian attitude that the Strait of Malacca and the Singapore Strait do not constitute "international straits."

As for the future, for probable developments in Southeast Asia after the Second Indochinese War, President Suharto pointedly observed:

> I do realize that the general situation in the area after Vietnam will give the communists a bigger scope for infiltration and subversion in the countries of the region. The main threat, however, will not derive from communist military strength but rather finds its source in ideological fanaticism. This threat should not be met by military pacts or military power, but by strengthening these countries' national will and capacity to resist, through international and regional cooperation in the fields of economic development, culture and ideology.[96]

The United States in the Indonesia of Suharto has sought to maintain a "low profile," to keep the minimum presence that is feasible, and to work through international organizations and arrangements where possible. Its role in Indonesia's development was later considered in Washington an example of the Nixon Doctrine in practice.

The United States, Japan, and Regional Initiatives. The development theme put considerable stress on Asian regionalism. Many observers in Washington foresaw in the 1970s regionalism and multipolarity in Southeast Asia as two sides of the same coin. On the one hand, the Southeast Asians would increasingly cooperate in common endeavors, thus strengthening themselves and the region. On the other hand, four major outside powers, Communist China, the Soviet Union, Japan, and the United States, would be active and balance one another.

Be that as it may, the growth of regional and subregional cooperation, whatever the geographical definition in Asia and the Western Pacific, and of meaningful institutions however varied to implement it, was one of the most significant developments of the latter half of the 1960s. Mutuality of interest—the spirit is important—matched multilateral institutions. An effort was also launched to stimulate a real knowledge of one another or a regional consciousness among Southeast Asians, aided by technology through communications and transport. It was widely recognized that cooperation on a broad basis in economic, technical, and cultural activities was more realistic at the time than political and security cooperation. Regional and subregional cooperation achieved a dynamism in the late 1960s and early 1970s that could acquire under certain conditions security dimensions in the future. Economic, technical, and cultural cooperation represented in the end political decisions in the capitals of Southeast Asia, and cooperation in dealing with subversion having external support could be a first step toward collective security.

At the same time no person realistically could minimize the obstacles to effective cooperation among the countries of Southeast Asia and their neighbors. Differences among ASEAN partners could not easily be defused as evidenced by the surfacing of the dispute between the Philippines and Malaysia over Sabah and the bitterness for a while in relations between Singapore and Indonesia over the former's execution of two Indonesian terrorists (as Singapore believed) captured during confrontation but not executed until 1968. And not to be forgotten—many animosities predated the era of Western colonization especially in mainland Southeast Asia. Apart from geographic barriers and transportation problems, from the widespread lack of regional consciousness, from the pride in newly won independence (except Thailand), from the contrasts in security policy, and from the competition for markets and for external capital and skill for economic development, the basic diversity in Southeast Asia along ethnic, linguistic, religious, and cultural lines remained.

Professor Charles A. Fisher has stressed the "ethnographic and sociological immaturity of the area" considering it a "zone of passage."[97]

The United States has pointedly reiterated that it provided a shield and bought time, especially through its defense of South Vietnam, for Asian initiatives in regional and subregional cooperation. President Johnson asserted in his State of the Union Address, January 17, 1968, that "in Asia, the nations from Korea and Japan to Indonesia and Singapore worked behind America's shield to strengthen their economies and to broaden their political cooperation."[98] President Nixon in his report to Congress on American foreign policy, February 25, 1971, asserted: "We provided the security shield which made credible their [free Asian nations'] plans for their own future."[99]

By the latter half of the 1960s when regionalism received such a great impetus the Economic Commission for Asia and the Far East and the Colombo Plan for Cooperative Economic Development in South and South-East Asia were already oldsters. ECAFE which had been founded in 1947 under the auspices of the United Nations had spawned a large number of subsidiary organizations, many efficient and some inefficient. It never really became what a few people called it—the economic parliament of Asia. The Colombo Plan, suggested by Australia at a meeting of the foreign ministers of the Commonwealth at Colombo in January 1950 and getting under way the next year, had continued its work in economic and technical assistance although it lost its early appeal. Aid from donors, it should be stressed, was bilaterally given.

The record of regional and subregional cooperation in East Asia since the beginning of 1965 was evidenced in the proliferation of institutions with considerable duplication of effort. Though they represented functional attempts to cope with practical problems the institutions embraced concepts of broader cooperation with more ambitious objectives. Two new organizations only had membership from Southeast Asian countries: the Association of Southeast Asian Nations and the Southeast Asian Ministers of Education Organization (SEAMEO) with the early membership of Indonesia, Laos, Malaysia, Singapore, the Philippines, Thailand, and South Vietnam.

The Association of Southeast Asian Nations, reflecting both Maphilindo and Association of Southeast Asia concepts, came into existence on August 8, 1967, when the five charter members approved a joint declaration at a meeting in Bangkok.[100] ASEAN was directed toward cooperation in the economic, cultural, social, scientific, technical, and administrative fields and toward promoting social progress, economic advancement, and cultural development for a peaceful and prosperous Southeast

Asia. It reflected the thinking of the foreign ministers of four of its members and the deputy prime minister of the fifth when they expressed their resolve "to ensure their stability and security from external interference in any form or manifestation in order to preserve their national identities" and when they asserted that "all foreign bases are temporary and remain only with the expressed concurrence of the countries concerned and are not intended to be used directly or indirectly to subvert the national independence and freedom of states in the area."[101] Proposals in the fields of intraregional trade, shipping, fisheries, and tourism as well as in other areas of interest would be considered. Annual meetings of foreign ministers were planned. ASEAN upon its creation drew considerable attention, being generally hailed in the Western world and widely criticized in the Communist countries. It went through a period of testing with its potential preserved.*

SEAMEO has placed considerable emphasis on cooperation in higher education. It was created in 1965 but formalized three years later. Various regional centers were planned, and the two most significant early operational ones were the Regional English Language Center at Singapore and the Asian Institute of Technology (formerly the SEATO Graduate School of Engineering). The United States has helped to support some of the SEAMEO activities. For instance, it agreed in May 1969 to join Singapore in financing the construction of a building for the Regional English Language Center and in providing support for the program.

Broader in geographic scope were the Asian Development Bank (ADB) which began operations in December 1966 and the Asian and Pacific Council which was founded in June. The former became more significant than the latter. ECAFE-sponsored, the Asian Development Bank in Manila with its regional and nonregional members had an initial subscribed capital of $1,100 million of which more than 60 per cent came from Asian members. At first Washington opposed its establishment but changed policy in connection with Johnson's speech at Johns Hopkins in April 1965. Eugene R. Black was asked by the President to see U Thant about new U.S. initiatives and the latter urged the United States to support an ADB. Johnson quickly agreed and pushed it.[103] Tokyo and Washington became the major contributors although Congress long refused to provide special funds for concessional aid to sup-

---

*On November 27, 1971, the representatives of the five ASEAN powers issued the "Kuala Lumpur Declaration" which called for "efforts to secure the recognition of, and respect for, Southeast Asia as a Zone of Peace, Freedom and Neutrality, free from any form or manner of interference by outside Powers."[102]

port various and regional programs. The bank, it is clear, could be a catalyst in regional activities. Nixon while in Manila in July 1969 addressed a statement to ADB warmly praising its role.

Despite the fact that the Mekong Coordinating Committee of Thailand, Cambodia, Laos, and South Vietnam was formed in 1956 under the Economic Commission for Asia and the Far East its work achieved greater prominence in the Johnson administration. At the same time it should be noted that President Eisenhower had approved a National Security Council policy statement on September 5, 1956, that asserted, "in order to promote increased cooperation in the area [mainland Southeast Asia] and to deny the general area of the Mekong River Basin to Communist influence or domination, [the United States should] assist as feasible in the development of the Mekong River Basin as a nucleus for regional cooperation and mutual aid."[104] President Johnson was personally interested in the future of the Mekong. Before his trip as Vice-President to Southeast Asia an old friend, Arthur Goldschmidt, had told him about the Mekong project. While in Bangkok he visited ECAFE headquarters, observing he was "a river man" and had long been interested in river development.[105]

The objectives of the Mekong scheme were to develop the agricultural, irrigation, power, navigational, and other potentials of the Mekong River and Basin for the common welfare of the riparian states of Thailand, Laos, Cambodia, and South Vietnam. As of early 1968 the project was actively aided by twenty-seven countries including the four members of the Mekong Coordinating Committee and eleven agencies of the United Nations, as well as foundations and private groups. Although the contributors included no Communist states the major donors to the Mekong Development Program were the United States, Japan, West Germany, Thailand, Cambodia, Australia, Canada, France, and the Netherlands. The total resources pledged or contributed at the end of December 1967 came to $147,835,752 of which the U.S. share was the largest, $32,476,591. In addition to supporting studies and investigations Washington continued to finance a major part of the cost of the Nam Ngum dam in Laos. (It was dedicated in December 1971.) After a favorable feasibility report, the United States faced a decision about pushing ahead in the 1970s with the expensive multipurpose Pa Mong project focusing on a dam on the mainstream of the Mekong between Laos and Thailand above Vientiane.[106] Johnson in contrast to Nixon had been sympathetic to the project. While in Bangkok in July 1969, Nixon met with the Mekong Committee, expressing interest in its work and stressing its role in peace. But he was guarded on the degree of future U.S. aid.

The efforts of the Mekong Coordinating Committee with its able executive agent Dr. C. Hart Schaaf for many years continued in the midst of the Second Indochinese War. True, progress was slowed by the conflict, but it was still maintained. Local security conditions very often let much to be desired, and relations among some of the riparian states were at times bad, indeed ruptured. Cambodia did not always attend the meetings of the Mekong Coordinating Committee. But once more, the work went on.[107] The diplomacy of the Mekong project merits a treatise in itself.

Japan has evidenced a growing interest and played an increasingly significant role in overall regional activities. American and Japanese policies have converged, at least to a substantial degree, in the promotion of regionalism and modernization in Southeast Asia. There was, however, a difference of emphasis between the Americans and Japanese, Washington in the late 1960s and early 1970s firmly believing that Tokyo could and should play a fuller role in the region. But the Japanese primarily focused on their spectacular gains in trade and investment, remained essentially tough and selective in their economic dealings, and steadfastly opposed a security role for themselves in Southeast Asia. At the same time they were well aware of their economic and geopolitical stake in the region. For example, the Japanese could not forget that about 90 per cent of their oil requirements passed through the Strait of Malacca from the Middle East. Access to raw materials and freedom of movement in and through Southeast Asia were very important in Japan's security. Tokyo had every interest in encouraging economic viability in the countries of the area to help preclude a Communist take-over.[108]

The United States did not seek to push Japan into security responsibilities for which Tokyo and its neighbors were not ready. Washington realized Japan was not likely to undertake a direct role in regional security activities for several years. At the same time both countries, now the two leading economic powers of the Free World, knew that security in Southeast Asia depended on the social, economic, and political welfare of the various states as well as on military strength, and that Japan could make a large contribution through providing more capital resources and technical skills for economic development and nation-building. Washington hoped Japan—it was not at all a new hope—would "provide more assistance on better terms, both bilaterally and through such multilateral organizations as the ADB."[109]

The Japanese for their part promised to substantially increase their economic aid and improve its terms and conditions to other nations above the significant amounts already provided. In fact, Tokyo promised in April 1969 to increase its total economic assistance from $1,049 million in 1969 to $2,000 million by 1973, a period of five years. A substantial part of the aid would go to countries in Southeast Asia, especially Indonesia with all its attractive oil reserves.

In 1965 Japan took a number of steps that signaled a new interest in the region. Some related to programs under way or planned, like promising a grant of $4 million for the Mekong Committee's Nam Ngum dam and withdrawal of objection to the creation of the ADB and a pledge of $200 million to its capital fund (one third of the Asian share). In May Tokyo favored the establishment of the Pacific Basin Economic Cooperation Committee of businessmen from the United States, Japan, Canada, Australia, and New Zealand to explore ways of encouraging private investment in Southeast Asia,[110] and in December called for the creation of an "Aid to Indonesia Club" which became the consortium or Inter-Governmental Group on Indonesia.

In April 1966 Japan sponsored the Ministerial Conference on economic development in Southeast Asia in Tokyo attended by Prime Minister Eisaku Sato with representation including observers from Indonesia, the Philippines, Singapore, Malaysia, Thailand, South Vietnam, Cambodia, and Laos (but not Burma and North Vietnam). In December another high-level conference, this time on agricultural development in Southeast Asia, met in Tokyo with participation from the same countries. Japan agreed to set up a Marine Fisheries Research and Development Center in Southeast Asia; it also supported what became the Special Fund for Agricultural Development in the area within ADB. (Tokyo came to provide significant funds for it.) Both ministerial conferences have continued on an annual basis and problems of cooperation in economic development and of cooperation in increasing agricultural productivity in Southeast Asia have been discussed.

Japan has used the occasions to present its viewpoints (sometimes a little too forcefully), to promise increased economic and technical aid and take new initiatives, and to get the reactions of the Southeast Asian leaders. It took very much at times a political role. The ministerial conferences have provided a means for Japan to assert leadership in development, and they also help to preclude an economic grouping in Southeast Asia harmful to Tokyo's interests. Furthermore, its key role and dominant influence in ADB as biggest contributor in the total of capital and special funds—Nippon won the first presidency but not the permanent location of the institution—is reflected in the bank's policies. Japan also became very influential in the Mekong project.

Although the Nipponese role and presence in Southeast Asia were marked and increasing in the late 1960s and early 1970s it could not be assumed that Tokyo would fill the vacuum left by an American withdrawal. Indeed, the Japanese role was predicated to a large extent on an American presence though desirably not so pronounced as in the 1960s. At the same time Tokyo's policy was based on its evaluation of its own interests, not America's. The Southeast Asians themselves were still suspicious of Japanese activities and concerned over growing economic dependence on Tokyo but their distrust arose less from the memories of World War II than from the frequent attitudes of Japanese officials and businessmen or as some journalists taking a leaf from two American writers called them, The Ugly Japanese. However, a number of prominent people like Ambassador Soedjatmoko have already begun to talk about multipolarity in the area. Many Southeast Asians believed that when all is said and done what Japan and the United States were going to do in the region was the most important dynamic factor in the years ahead. They saw both powers at the center of the future growth and development of their countries. Tokyo was widely viewed as a partner and a problem and Washington was sometimes seen as a friend who could soften Japan's impact. Cooperation in a regional, multilateral framework can smooth many difficulties.

American viewpoints on the future of regional and subregional alignments in Asia were presented in a thought-provoking address by Eugene R. Black in Japan on September 17, 1968, in connection with his visit there and to other Asian countries. The basic U.S. position, it should be stressed, has been to encourage Asian initiatives, attempts, and momentum in regionalism and to participate only when requested and when appropriate. The American presence, it was believed, was widely welcomed but American predominance was feared. United States interest was needed but so was restraint.

Black in his Tokyo speech called for "a new and different diplomacy in Southeast Asia" which first required "mechanisms of regional cooperation through which modern technology can be more effectively planted and shared in the countries of the region," and which then required "firm commitments to provide the development capital to make these regional mechanisms work both economically and politically."[111] He went on to note that the "initiative by the countries of Southeast Asia in devising regional mechanisms for development will need be matched by the leadership of Japan and the United States in responding to these initiatives."[112] Black pointedly asserted that "capital by itself is no substitute for diplomacy."[113] In many respects President Johnson's Special Adviser on Asian Economic and Social Development was speaking of the diplomacy of modernization.

Black emphasized in his speech that development bankers believed "cooperation in development can someday become a substitute for war among nations."[114] He carefully distinguished between simple economic growth, on the one hand, and development, on the other, whose roots were deep in the society of a country. He looked to regional cooperation in Southeast Asia as a way of dealing with nationalism but indicated his conviction the former would "grow initially around common services" like a Southeast Asian Transport Authority. Much of Black's thinking was based on "the prospect of important and fairly rapid technical advance."[115]

The development theme of the United States with its stress on Asian initiatives and regionalism in the latter half of the 1960s and early 1970s cannot be properly evaluated for some time. It provided an umbrella for a large number of U.S. interests and activities including postwar reconstruction in Vietnam, the multilateral effort to lift Indonesia from its economic doldrums and to further the economic development of Malaysia, the Philippines, and Thailand, the grand dimensions of the Mekong project, the shift to support for an Asian Development Bank, encouragement of various other regional organizations, and the stress on the development role of Japan in an emerging international environment of multipolarity in Southeast Asia.

Washington believed, of course, that the development theme was in the national interest. But its many facets did not lend themselves to a tidy package for presentation to Congress and the taxpayer as recent legislation well reveals. Yet Melvin Gurtov has pointedly observed that "regionalism as a military formula has turned out to have serious limitations, which perhaps can be overcome through less ambitious economic and social cooperative arrangements in which the American role is reduced."[116] And Richard Nixon, the fourth American chief executive of the 1960s and the first of the 1970s, gave indication through his Doctrine of emphasizing the importance of the development theme.[117] Beating swords into plowshares has proved not an easy task in Southeast Asia.

PERSPECTIVES FROM AMERICAN EXPERIENCE

In the light of the traumatic experience of the Second Indochinese War and of events in post-Gestapu Indonesia what has become the value of Southeast Asia to the United States? What are American objectives against the background of these developments? Were opportunities lost in years gone by for Washington in Southeast Asia? Where was the United States headed in the summer of 1972?

The value of the region to the United States in the 1970s is not that of the 1960s or the 1950s. A major war affects national interests, and if one of the superpowers is a participant, the whole international system of relationships is influenced. War up to a point increases the stakes, and major policies generate a large family of minor ones. Attempts per se to justify a conflict increase the stakes of the decision-maker and his place in history. How the United States disengaged from the Second Indochinese War had ramifications not only for Indochina and Southeast Asia but also for Asia and the world.

The value of Southeast Asia to the United States in the light of the conflict and of post-Gestapu Indonesia cannot be easily estimated. Certainly its territory is not vital to the direct defense of the fifty states of the union. Nor does Washington require access to the resources of. Southeast Asia either human or material. American trade and investments and the presence of private U.S. citizens despite their increase do not add up to a paramount consideration. Yet the future of the people of Southeast Asia—certainly now over 250 million of them—cannot be discounted, nor can the strategic location of the area which through modern transportation is closer than ever before to the United States. And both Peking and Hanoi (the former now less than in the past) have placed emphasis on the validity of "wars of national liberation" as the correct avenue to world revolution while Washington, it has been stressed, has invested much of its credibility in an effort to discount the concept. But the value of Southeast Asia to the United States probably lies in the years ahead more in its value to Japan and Australia, two key American allies in the Pacific. If Southeast Asia should fall under the control of a hostile power or power combination, a threat would be posed to Tokyo and Canberra, one which might well impair American ties with them. This threat might involve military, political, and economic dimensions in various combinations.

The Second Indochinese War has highlighted a basic American objective in Southeast Asia, namely that no power or combination of powers hostile to U.S. interests dominate it. This objective also serves the goal of close American-Japanese and American-Australian ties, and helps preserve the goal of freedom of choice in the countries of Southeast Asia. Another U.S. objective in the area, associated with the circumstances of those above and strengthened through developments in post-Gestapu Indonesia, is the further encouragement of regional cooperation in terms of an expanding scope of activities and of broader association between the countries of Southeast Asia and its neighbors like Japan and Australia. The increased promotion of economic and social development along the road of modernization is another American objective hopefully helping to contribute to stability. The last two goals relate, of course, to the American theme of development.

Although these various objectives represent no basic departure from the earlier ones of stability and security, greater emphasis is given certain goals like regional cooperation and more attention is called to the roles of Japan and Australia. Their validity depends upon the value of Southeast Asia to the United States. The goals would have been impaired, however, if the Communists had won a victory in the Second Indochinese War and/or if Indonesia had fallen to them. The final returns are not in, but the South Vietnamese, it should be stressed, have been given time to put their house in order and the Southeast Asians, apart from the North Vietnamese, time to build regional cooperation behind an American shield.

The lost opportunities of the United States in Southeast Asia involve the ifs of history and no one can validly assert what would have happened if Washington had chosen different courses of action. The variables in international relations are so many and so complex that accurate prediction is impossible. It is unlikely that theorizing about or trying to quantify the international relations of Southeast Asia will offer any help. The lost opportunities may well have existed before late 1949—Roosevelt's trusteeship for Indochina, American policy toward military occupation in Southeast Asia in connection with the Pacific War, cooperation with Ho Chi Minh as a Communist-nationalist leader in 1945 and into 1946, and the early U.S. role in the Bao Dai experiment. After China went under Communist control and after the events of the Korean War in 1950 the thrust of American policy was shifted to mainland China and its implications for Southeast Asia. In this frame of reference the United States pursued a policy toward Vietnam of increasing involvement from 1950 to 1965 leading to the Second Indochinese War. There were, of course, many opportunities for basically altering the course of U.S. action during this period but a succession of Presidents with their advisers contributed to the mainstream.

By the summer of 1972 the United States was headed in its policy toward withdrawal from or termination of the Second Indochinese War hopefully on honorable terms and toward increasing emphasis in various ways on the development of Southeast Asia through economic and regional cooperation under Asian initiatives.

General George C. Marshall once remarked on the advantages of studying Greek and Roman history, for here the full sweep of cause and effect can be traced in the affairs of man. But Southeast Asia is not ancient Greece or Rome, and in 1972 a new system of international order was in the process of being created. In this effort the United States was following a policy of partial engagement, a compromise between complete disengagement on the one hand and full engagement on the other, one that sought to minimize liabilities and maximize opportunities, one that tried to match commitment and capability, and one that aimed toward a genuine international framework for international activities. At the same time the United States has learned it can influence but it is not able to determine the contours of the future in Southeast Asia. The people themselves will make the ultimate decision.

NOTES

CHAPTER 1

1. See Joseph Ralston Hayden, *The Philippines: A Study in National Development*, Macmillan, New York, 1942, and his "The United States and the Philippines: A Survey of Some Political Aspects of Twenty-five Years of American Sovereignty," *Annals of the American Academy of Political and Social Science*, November 1925, pp. 26–48.

2. Quoted in Theodore Friend, *Between Two Empires: The Ordeal of the Philippines, 1929–1946*, Yale, New Haven, 1965, p. 4.

3. Quoted in *ibid*.

4. A valuable account of Wilson's policy is Roy Watson Curry, "Woodrow Wilson and Philippine Policy," *Mississippi Valley Historical Review*, December 1954, pp. 435–52.

5. Margaret M. Wood, "Forerunners of the Peace Corps: Pioneer American Teachers in the Philippines" (a manuscript).

6. A careful evaluation is Robert L. Beisner, *Twelve against Empire: The Anti-Imperialists, 1898–1900*, McGraw-Hill, New York, 1968.

7. Winston Churchill, "Defense in the Pacific," *Collier's*, December 17, 1932, pp. 12–13, 30.

8. See Louis Morton, "War Plan *Orange:* Evolution of a Strategy," *World Politics*, January 1959, pp. 221–50.

9. Quoted in Friend, *Between Two Empires*, p. 71.

10. For French and Russian evaluations see Georges Fischer, *Un Cas de décolonisation: Les Etats-Unis et les Philippines*, Pichon et Durand-Anzias, Paris, 1960; and Georgi Ilyich Levinson, *Filippiny Mezhdu Pervoy i Vtoroy Mirovymi Voynami (The Philippines between the First and Second World Wars)*, Izdatel' stvo Vostochnoy Literatury Akademii Nauk USSR, Moscow, 1958, and his *Filippiny Vehera i Segodnia (The Philippines Yesterday and Today)*, Izdatel' stvo Sotsial' no-Ekonomicheskoy Literatury, Moscow, 1959.

11. See Frank C. Darling, *Thailand and the United States*, Public Affairs Press, Washington, 1965.

12. Quoted in Tyler Dennett, *Americans in Eastern Asia: A Critical Study of the Policy of the United States with Reference to China, Japan and Korea in the 19th Century*, Macmillan, New York, 1922, p. 352.

13. *Ibid.*, p. 270.

14. Quoted in Abbot Low Moffat, *Mongkut; The King of Siam*, Cornell, Ithaca, 1961, p. 95.

15. See Kenneth T. Young, "The Special Role of American Advisers in Thailand, 1902–1949," *Asia*, Spring 1969, pp. 1–31.

16. Francis Bowes Sayre, *Glad Adventure*, Macmillan, New York, 1957, pp. 106–23.

17. For a detailed proposal see *Papers Relating to the Foreign Relations of the United States, Japan: 1931–1941*, Vol. II, Government Printing Office, Washington, 1943, pp. 552–53. Hereafter cited as *Foreign Relations*.

18. A period survey is Lennox A. Mills, ed., "Southeastern Asia and the Philippines," *Annals of the American Academy of Political and Social Science*, March 1943, pp. IX, 1–150.

19. Quoted in Frank N. Trager, *Burma—From Kingdom to Republic: A Historical and Political Analysis*, Praeger, New York, 1966, pp. 278–79.

20. *Foreign Relations of the United States, Japan: 1931–1941*, Vol. II, p. 282.

21. *Ibid.*, p. 527.

22. See Bernard B. Fall, "U.S. Policies in Indochina 1940–1960," *Last Reflections on a War*, Doubleday, Garden City, 1967, pp. 118–48. The stress is on the 1940–54 period.

23. For a revealing telegram from the American Chargé in Vichy to the Secretary of State, September 19, 1940, covering the June–September 1940 period, see *Foreign Relations of the United States, 1940*, Vol. IV, *The Far East*, Government Printing Office, Washington, 1955, pp. 131–34.

24. *Foreign Relations of the United States, Japan: 1931–1941*, Vol. II, p. 529.

25. Herbert Feis, *The Road to Pearl Harbor: The Coming of the War between the United States and Japan*, Princeton, Princeton, 1950, p. 333. For contrasting views on the "Road," see Paul W. Schroeder, *The Axis Alliance and Japanese-American Relations, 1941*, Cornell for the American Historical Association, Ithaca, 1958. The bibliography on the outbreak of the Pacific War, by revisionists and nonrevisionists, is extensive. See selections from 11 authors and annotated bibliography in George M. Waller, ed., *Pearl Harbor: Roosevelt and the Coming of the War*, rev. ed., Heath, Boston, 1965. A widely acclaimed work in the 1960s was Roberta Wohlstetter, *Pearl Harbor: Warning and Decision*, Stanford, Stanford, 1962.

CHAPTER 2

1. An excellent account is found in Samuel Eliot Morison, *The Rising Sun in the Pacific: 1931–April 1942*, Little, Brown, Boston, 1955.

2. See F. C. Jones, *Japan's New Order in East Asia: Its Rise and Fall, 1937–45*, Oxford, London, 1954, for a thorough analysis of the subject.

3. For a stimulating evaluation see David J. Steinberg, *Philippine Collaboration in World War II*, Michigan, Ann Arbor, 1967.

4. James V. Martin, Jr., "Thai-American Relations in World War II," *Journal of Asian Studies*, August 1963, pp. 451–67.

5. A revealing account is U Ba Maw, *Breakthrough in Burma: Memoirs of a Revolution, 1939–1946*, Yale, New Haven, 1968.

6. The Governor General's version is found in *A la barre de l'Indochine: histoire du mon gouvernement général, 1940–1945*, Plon, Paris, 1949.

7. Claire Lee Chennault, *Way of a Fighter: The Memoirs of Claire Lee Chennault* (ed. Robert Hotz), Putnam's, New York, 1949, p. 342.

8. General Albert C. Wedemeyer, *Wedemeyer Reports!*, Holt, New York, 1958, pp. 340, 343.

9. *Foreign Relations of the United States, 1945*, Vol. VI, *The British Commonwealth; The Far East*, Government Printing Office, Washington, 1969, p. 300.

10. *Ibid.*, p. 306.

11. See Harry J. Benda, *The Crescent and the Rising Sun: Indonesian Islam under the Japanese Occupation, 1942–1945*, van Hoeve, The Hague, 1958, for a comprehensive evaluation.

12. Official documentation on the Quebec Conference is found in *Foreign Relations of the United States: The Conferences at Washington and Quebec, 1943*, Government Printing Office, Washington, 1970.

13. For a global map of theaters of operations (before the revision of SWPA), see *General Marshall's Report: The Winning of the War in Europe and the Pacific*, Simon and Schuster, New York, 1945, pp. 76–7. Maps and a valuable report on SEAC as it operated are found in Vice-Admiral The Earl Mountbatten of Burma, *Report to the Combined Chiefs of Staff by the Supreme Allied Commander, South-East Asia, 1943–1945*, His Majesty's Stationery Office, London, 1951. Section E was not published until 1969.

14. For a penetrating analysis see "The Japanese Interregnum" in John Bastin and Harry J. Benda, *A History of Modern Southeast Asia: Colonialism, Nationalism, and Decolonization*, Prentice-Hall, Englewood Cliffs, 1968, pp. 123–52. Also Josef Silverstein, ed., *Southeast Asia in World War II*, Yale, New Haven, 1966.

15. *United States-Vietnam Relations, 1945–1967*, Study Prepared by the Department of Defense, Book 8, Government Printing Office, Washington, 1971, pp. 13–14.

16. Elliott Roosevelt, *As He Saw It*, Duell, Sloan, and Pearce, New York, 1946, pp. 223–24.

17. *Ibid.*, p. 115.

18. Cordell Hull, *The Memoirs of Cordell Hull*, Vol. II, Macmillan, New York, 1948, p. 1596.

19. *Ibid.*, p. 1595.

20. *Foreign Relations of the United States: The Conferences at Cairo and Tehran, 1943*, Government Printing Office, Washington, 1961, p. 485.

21. *Ibid.*

22. Joseph W. Stilwell, *The Stilwell Papers* (ed. Theodore H. White), Sloane, New York, 1948, p. 246.

23. *Foreign Relations of the United States: The Conferences at Cairo and Tehran, 1943,* p. 485.

24. Edward R. Stettinius, Jr., *Roosevelt and the Russians: The Yalta Conference* (ed. Walter Johnson), Doubleday, Garden City, 1949, p. 238.

25. *Foreign Relations of the United States, 1944,* Vol. V, *The Near East, South Asia, and Africa; The Far East,* Government Printing Office, Washington, 1965, p. 1206.

26. *Ibid.* Across the memorandum of February 17 Roosevelt wrote: "No French help in Indochina—country on trusteeship." *United States-Vietnam Relations, 1945–1967,* Book 7, V.B.1., p. 33.

27. *Foreign Relations of the United States, 1944,* Vol. III, *The British Commonwealth and Europe,* Government Printing Office, Washington, 1965, p. 777.

28. *Ibid.*

29. *Ibid.,* p. 780.

30. Memorandum on Indochina by the Assistant to the President's Naval Aide (Lt. George M. Elsey) submitted to Admiral William D. Leahy, July 1, 1945, and then forwarded to President Truman, *Foreign Relations of the United States: The Conference of Berlin (The Potsdam Conference), 1945,* Vol. 1, Government Printing Office, Washington, 1960, pp. 915–16. This memorandum is revealing although it lacks perspective.

31. Quoted in *ibid.,* p. 916.

32. *Foreign Relations of the United States, 1944,* Vol. V, pp. 1285–86.

33. *Foreign Relations of the United States, 1945,* Vol. VI, p. 203.

34. *Foreign Relations of the United States: The Conferences at Malta and Yalta, 1945,* Government Printing Office, Washington, 1955, p. 770.

35. *Foreign Relations of the United States, 1945,* Vol. I, *General: The United Nations,* Government Printing Office, Washington, 1967, p. 121.

36. *Ibid.,* p. 124.

37. *Ibid.*

38. Chennault, *Way of a Fighter,* p. 342.

39. Wedemeyer, *Wedemeyer Reports!,* p. 340.

40. *Foreign Relations of the United States: The Conference of Berlin (The Potsdam Conference), 1945,* Vol. I, p. 917 (Elsey memorandum).

41. *Ibid.*

42. *Foreign Relations of the United States, 1944,* Vol. V, pp. 1186–89.

43. *Ibid.,* pp. 1190–94.

44. *Ibid.,* pp. 1195–98.

45. *Ibid.,* pp. 1261–62.

46. Hull, *The Memoirs of Cordell Hull*, Vol. II, p. 1601.

47. *Ibid.*, p. 1600.

48. *Ibid.*, p. 1601.

49. For documentation see *United States-Vietnam Relations, 1945–1967*, Book 8, pp. 1–25.

50. *Foreign Relations of the United States, 1945*, Vol. VI, p. 556.

51. *Ibid.*, p. 568, the policy section on Indochina.

52. *Ibid.*, p. 558 (italics added).

53. *Ibid.*, p. 580.

54. Atlantic Charter, *A Decade of American Foreign Policy: Basic Documents, 1941–49*, U.S. Senate, 81st Congress, 1st Session, Government Printing Office, Washington, 1950, p. 1.

55. Cairo Conference Statement, *ibid.*, p. 22.

56. Quoted in Elsey memorandum, *Foreign Relations of the United States: The Conference of Berlin (The Potsdam Conference), 1945*, Vol. I, p. 918.

57. Elsey memorandum, *ibid.*, p. 920.

58. *United States-Vietnam Relations, 1945–1967*, Book 8, p. 31.

59. Charles de Gaulle, *The Complete War Memoirs of Charles de Gaulle*, Simon and Schuster, New York, 1964, p. 910.

60. *Foreign Relations of the United States, 1945*, Vol. VII, *The Far East: China*, Government Printing Office, Washington, 1969, pp. 540–41.

61. *Foreign Relations of the United States: The Conference of Berlin (The Potsdam Conference), 1945*, Vol. II, p. 1319.

62. *Ibid.*, p. 377.

63. *Ibid.*, pp. 1462–73.

64. De Gaulle, *The Complete War Memoirs of Charles de Gaulle*, p. 855.

65. *Foreign Relations of the United States, 1945*, Vol. VI, pp. 308–9.

66. *Foreign Relations of the United States: The Conference of Berlin (The Potsdam Conference), 1945*, Vol. II, pp. 1471–72.

67. John Carter Vincent *et al.*, *America's Future in the Pacific*, Rutgers, New Brunswick, 1947, p. 153.

68. *Ibid.*, p. 145.

CHAPTER 3

1. For a thought-provoking article, see Zbigniew Brzezinski, "The Implications of Change for United States Foreign Policy," *Department of State Bulletin*, July 3, 1967, pp. 19–23.

2. A significant study is Rupert Emerson, *From Empire to Nation: The Rise to Self-Assertion of Asian and African Peoples*, Harvard, Cambridge, 1962. Contrast with a much earlier study, Parker Thomas Moon, *Imperialism and World Politics*, Macmillan, New York, 1926.

3. An accurate definition of decolonization still defies the scholar. John Bastin and Harry J. Benda in their *A History of Modern Southeast Asia: Colonialism, Nationalism, and Decolonization*, Prentice-Hall, Englewood Cliffs, 1968, p. vii, note: "Certainly it would be a mistake to regard decolonization as a simple matter involving the withdrawal or expulsion of the Western colonial powers from Southeast Asia in the years immediately following the War."

4. See Louis J. Halle, *The Cold War As History*, Harper and Row, New York, 1967, p. 2.

5. Paul Seabury used these words in his *The Rise and Decline of the Cold War*, Basic Books, New York, 1967.

6. For an analysis with a basic bibliography see Arthur Schlesinger, Jr., "Origins of the Cold War," *Foreign Affairs*, October 1967, pp. 22–52. Critical of Schlesinger is the article by Christopher Lasch, "The Cold War, Revisited and Re-Visioned," *The New York Times Magazine*, January 14, 1968, pp. 26 ff. See also for the revisionist viewpoint, Joyce and Gabriel Kolko, *The Limits of Power: The World and United States Foreign Policy, 1945–1954*, Harper and Row, New York, 1972.

7. W. Averell Harriman, "Our Wartime Relations with the Soviet Union Particularly As They Concern the Agreements Reached at Yalta" (Statement submitted to a Joint Senate Committee, August 17, 1951), privately printed, pp. 51 and 53.

8. Schlesinger, "Origins of the Cold War," p. 49.

9. See especially Vice-Admiral The Earl Mountbatten of Burma, *Post Surrender Tasks, Section E of the Report to the Combined Chiefs of Staff by the Supreme Allied Commander, South-East Asia, 1943–1945*, Her Majesty's Stationery Office, London, 1969.

10. An admirable analysis is William Reitzel, Morton A. Kaplan, and Constance G. Coblenz, *United States Foreign Policy: 1945–1955*, Brookings, Washington, 1956, pp. 30–46.

11. *Ibid.*, p. 83.

12. One of the most significant articles bearing on American-Soviet relations ever published in *Foreign Affairs* was written by George F. Kennan. Having official blessing, it appeared as X, "The Sources of Soviet Conduct," *Foreign Affairs*, July 1947, pp. 566–82. Kennan later asserted that he was thinking of peaceful mobilization by the West, not a military confrontation with the Soviet Union.

13. Truman Doctrine, *A Decade of American Foreign Policy: Basic Documents, 1941–49*, U.S. Senate, 81st Congress, 1st Session, Government Printing Office, Washington, 1950, p. 1256. For valuable insights on the Truman Doctrine, see Joseph M. Jones, *The Fifteen Weeks (February 21–June 5, 1947)*, Viking, New York, 1955.

14. *Foreign Relations of the United States, 1944*, Vol. V, *The Near East, South Asia, and Africa; The Far East*, Government Printing Office, Washington, 1965, p. 1232.

15. John F. Melby and Norman A. Graebner in papers entitled "The Origins of the Cold War in Asia: China" and "Genesis of Containment in Asia" for the annual convention of the American Historical Association in 1967 related the Cold War to Asia. See also Department of State, *United States Relations with China,*

with Special Reference to the Period 1944–1949, Government Printing Office, Washington, 1949.

16. *United States-Vietnam Relations, 1945–1967*, Study Prepared by the Department of Defense, Book 8, Government Printing Office, Washington, 1971, p. 15.

17. John Carter Vincent *et al., America's Future in the Pacific*, Rutgers, New Brunswick, 1947, p. 17.

18. *Ibid.*, p. 18.

19. *United States-Vietnam Relations, 1945–1967*, Book 8, p. 9.

20. *Foreign Relations of the United States, 1945*, Vol. VI, *The British Commonwealth; The Far East*, Government Printing Office, Washington, 1969, pp. 1389–90.

21. *Ibid.*, p. 1389.

22. For a revealing account of Philippine-American relations six months before July 4, 1946, and six months thereafter, see *Foreign Relations of the United States, 1946*, Vol. VIII, *The Far East*, Government Printing Office, Washington, 1971, pp. 861–943.

23. Harry S. Truman, *Memoirs by Harry S. Truman*, Vol. 1, *Year of Decisions*, Doubleday, Garden City, 1955, pp. 65–66, 275–77.

24. Carlos P. Romulo, *Crusade in Asia: Philippine Victory*, Day, New York, 1955, p. 5.

25. A critical evaluation of the U.S. role is found in George E. Taylor, *The Philippines and the United States: Problems of Partnership*, Praeger for the Council on Foreign Relations, New York, 1964, pp. 124–33.

26. For a critique see memorandum by Secretary of State Byrnes to President Truman, April 18, 1946, *Foreign Relations of the United States, 1946*, Vol. VIII, pp. 873–75.

27. *Ibid.*, p. 925.

28. *Ibid.*

29. *Ibid.*, p. 926.

30. *Ibid.*, p. 934.

31. The American Assembly (Frank H. Golay, ed.), *The United States and the Philippines*, Prentice-Hall, for The American Assembly, Englewood Cliffs, 1966, p. 31.

32. Russell H. Fifield, "The Hukbalahap Today," *Far Eastern Survey*, January 24, 1951, pp. 13–18. This article was based on field research in the summer of 1950.

33. "The Problem of Indonesia," *Major Problems of United States Foreign Policy: 1949–1950*, Brookings, Washington, 1949, p. 352.

34. For British problems in Indonesia during the early months of Mountbatten's command, as reported to the Department of State, see *Foreign Relations of the United States, 1945*, Vol. VI, pp. 1158–92. For the whole period see Mountbatten, *Post Surrender Tasks*, pp. 289 ff.

35. See *Foreign Relations of the United States, 1946*, Vol. VIII, pp. 787–89, for Washington's basic position.

36. Vincent *et al., America's Future in the Pacific*, p. 15. Note also letter relative

to Indonesia from Secretary Byrnes to Sol Bloom, Chairman of the House Committee on Foreign Affairs, May 24, 1946, in *Foreign Relations of the United States, 1946*, Vol. VIII, pp. 822–25.

37. Alastair M. Taylor, *Indonesian Independence and the United Nations*, Cornell, Ithaca, 1960, p. 398. For official American policy in connection with the first police action, see *Foreign Relations of the United States, 1947*, Vol. VI, *The Far East*, Government Printing Office, Washington, 1972, pp. 981–1101.

38. Compare, for example, Indonesian views in George McTurnan Kahin, *Nationalism and Revolution in Indonesia*, Cornell, Ithaca, 1952, with Dutch views in P. S. Gerbrandy, *Indonesia*, Hutchinson, London, 1950, and Dirk U. Stikker, *Men of Responsibility: A Memoir*, Harper and Row, New York, 1965.

39. Sir Josiah Crosby, "Observations on a Post-War Settlement in South-East Asia," *International Affairs*, July 1944, p. 362.

40. Alec Peterson, "Britain and Siam: The Latest Phase," *Pacific Affairs*, December 1946, p. 365.

41. For an official account of Anglo-American disagreement in 1944 see *Foreign Relations of the United States, 1944*, Vol. V, pp. 1311–21.

42. *Foreign Relations of the United States, 1943, China*, Government Printing Office, Washington, 1957, pp. 13–14, 23–24, 36–37.

43. An extremely revealing article, based on official sources, is Herbert A. Fine, "The Liquidation of World War II in Thailand," *Pacific Historical Review*, February 1965, pp. 65–82. In 1969 many official sources of 1945 were published. See *Foreign Relations of the United States, 1945*, Vol. VI, pp. 1240–1415.

44. *Department of State Bulletin*, January 6 and 13, 1946, p. 5.

45. *British and Foreign State Papers, 1946*, Vol. 146, Her Majesty's Stationery Office, London, 1953, pp. 455–61.

46. Fine, "The Liquidation of World War II in Thailand," p. 82.

47. Vincent *et al.*, *America's Future in the Pacific*, p. 17.

48. See the documents in *Foreign Relations of the United States, 1946*, Vol. VIII, pp. 978–1106. They were compiled by Herbert A. Fine.

49. *Ibid.*, p. 1045.

50. *Ibid.*, p. 1092.

51. For an inside account of Thai diplomacy in connection with World War II, see Direk Chayanam, *Thai kap Songkhram Lok Khrang Thi Song*, 2 vols., Prae Pittaya, Bangkok, 1966.

52. *British and Foreign State Papers, 1947*, Vol. 147, Part 1, Her Majesty's Stationery Office, London, 1955, p. 1010.

53. Frank N. Trager, *Burma—From Kingdom to Republic: A Historical and Political Analysis*, Praeger, New York, 1966, p. 282.

54. See especially Hugh Tinker, *The Union of Burma: A Study of the First Years of Independence*, 4th ed., Oxford, London, 1967, pp. 16–17.

55. *Foreign Relations of the United States, 1946*, Vol. VIII, p. 7.

56. *Ibid.*, p. 13. Quoted from telegram from Secretary Byrnes to American Consul General in Rangoon, December 24, 1946.

57. For an excellent period study on Moscow and Southeast Asia, see Charles B. McLane, *Soviet Strategies in Southeast Asia: An Exploration of Eastern Policy under Lenin and Stalin,* Princeton, Princeton, 1966.

58. Only a few good biographies of postwar leaders in Southeast Asia have been written. One is Richard Butwell, *U Nu of Burma,* rev. ed., Stanford, Stanford, 1969.

59. John Scott Everton, "The Foreign Policy of Contemporary Burma," p. 14 (a manuscript).

60. For a basic and carefully researched study on revolution in Vietnam see John T. McAlister, Jr., *Viet Nam: The Origins of Revolution,* Knopf for the Center of International Studies (Princeton University), New York, 1969. Also see John T. McAlister, Jr., and Paul Mus, *The Vietnamese and Their Revolution,* Harper and Row, New York, 1970, and Bernard B. Fall, ed., *Ho Chi Minh on Revolution: Selected Writings, 1920–66,* Praeger, New York, 1967.

61. Chester L. Cooper, *The Lost Crusade: America in Vietnam,* Dodd, Mead, New York, 1970, p. 25.

62. Quoted in Robert Shaplen, *The Lost Revolution: The U.S. in Vietnam, 1946–1966,* rev. ed., Harper and Row, New York, 1966, p. 33. For a French viewpoint on Ho's early relations with Americans see Jean Lacouture, *Ho Chi Minh: A Political Biography,* Random House, New York, 1968, pp. 261–75.

63. Quoted in Shaplen, *The Lost Revolution,* p. 41.

64. Jean Sainteny, *Histoire d'une paix manquée: Indochine, 1945–1947,* Fayard, Paris, 1967, p. 137.

65. Cooper, *The Lost Crusade,* p. 27.

66. See Bert Cooper *et al., Case Studies in Insurgency and Revolutionary Warfare: Vietnam, 1941–1954,* Special Operations Research Office, American University, Washington, 1964, p. 107.

67. Quoted in Shaplen, *The Lost Revolution,* p. 30.

68. A valuable study which reflects significant research on the U.S. role in Hanoi in 1945 after the collapse of Japan is Edward R. Drachman, *United States Policy toward Vietnam, 1940–1945,* Fairleigh Dickinson, Rutherford, 1970. General Gallagher's viewpoints on conditions in North Vietnam were well expressed in his debriefing at the Department of State on January 30, 1946, and those of Colonel Nordlinger on October 24, 1945, in a report by the American Consul in Kunming to Washington of the same date. See *United States-Vietnam Relations, 1945–1967,* Book 8, pp. 53–57, and *ibid.,* Book 1, I.C., pp. 77–78, respectively.

69. For some time Harold R. Isaacs reported from Saigon. See his *No Peace for Asia,* Macmillan, New York, 1947.

70. *United States-Vietnam Relations, 1945–1967,* Book 1, I.C., p. 70.

71. Charles de Gaulle, *The Complete War Memoirs of Charles de Gaulle,* Simon and Schuster, New York, 1964, p. 928.

72. For some texts and relevant documentation see *United States-Vietnam Relations, 1945–1967,* Book 1, I.C., pp. 71–101.

73. For an excellent analysis see "Ho Chi Minh: Asian Tito?" in *ibid.,* pp. 1–7. The analysis takes into account versions of the hypothesis by different authors,

Ho's political record, 1890–1950, and his communications with the United States, 1945–46. According to the analyst, the best time for U.S. intervention on behalf of Ho Chi Minh would have been in the fall of 1945. It would have to be assumed that his appeals were sincere.

74. *Documents Relating to British Involvement in the Indo-China Conflict, 1945–1965*, Cmnd. 2834, Her Majesty's Stationery Office, London, 1965, p. 49. Quotation taken from extract of Mountbatten's report to Combined Chiefs of Staff on June 30, 1947. This excellent collection of documents contains a bibliography of previous British official publications on the subject (pp. 267–68).

75. Donald Lancaster, *The Emancipation of French Indochina*, Oxford for the Royal Institute of International Affairs, London, 1961, p. 130.

76. Allan B. Cole, ed., *Conflict in Indo-China and International Repercussions: A Documentary History, 1945–1955*, Cornell, Ithaca, 1956, p. 40.

77. The course of the war is well covered in Bernard B. Fall, *Street without Joy: Indochina at War, 1946–54*, Stackpole, Harrisburg, 1961. In addition to Lancaster's *The Emancipation of French Indochina*, previously cited, see Ellen J. Hammer, *The Struggle for Indochina*, Stanford, Stanford, 1954, and Philippe Devillers, *Histoire du Viêt-Nam de 1940 à 1952*, Éditions du Seuil, Paris, 1952. Also, Lucien Bodard, *The Quicksand War: Prelude to Vietnam*, Little, Brown, Boston, 1967.

78. *Foreign Relations of the United States, 1945*, Vol. VI, p. 313.

79. *Ibid.*, p. 1167.

80. *Foreign Relations of the United States, 1946*, Vol. VIII, p. 800.

81. *Ibid.*, p. 58.

82. *United States-Vietnam Relations, 1945–1967*, Book 1, I.C., p. 104.

83. *Foreign Relations of the United States, 1946*, Vol. VIII, p. 67.

84. *Ibid.*, p. 73.

85. *Ibid.*, p. 74.

86. Robert Trumbull, *The Scrutable East*, McKay, New York, 1964, pp. 195–96.

87. *United States-Vietnam Relations, 1945–1967*, Book 8, p. 146.

88. *Ibid.*, pp. 98–9.

89. For full text, see *ibid.*, pp. 144–49.

90. *Ibid.*, pp. 148–49.

91. *Ibid.*, p. 150.

92. Dean Acheson, *Present at the Creation: My Years in the State Department*, Norton, New York, 1969, p. 671.

93. *United States-Vietnam Relations, 1945–1967*, Book 8, pp. 154–189.

94. *Ibid.*, pp. 201–16.

95. *Department of State Bulletin*, July 18, 1949, p. 75.

96. *United States-Vietnam Relations, 1945–1967*, Book 8, p. 277.

97. *Department of State Bulletin*, February 20, 1950, p. 291.

98. *Ibid.*, pp. 291–92.

99. *Ibid.*, p. 292.

100. Quoted in Milton Sacks, "The Strategy of Communism in Southeast Asia," *Pacific Affairs*, September 1950, p. 242.

CHAPTER 4

1. See Herbert Feis, *The China Tangle: The American Effort in China from Pearl Harbor to the Marshall Mission*, Princeton, Princeton, 1953.

2. *United States Relations with China, with Special Reference to the Period 1944–1949*, Government Printing Office, Washington, 1949, p. XVI. For a significant review describing the background of the preparation of the White Paper, see Gaddis Smith, "Last View of the Chinese Scene," *The New York Times Book Review*, February 25, 1968, pp. 3, 35.

3. *United States Relations with China, with Special Reference to the Period 1944–1949*, p. XVII.

4. Among the books on McCarthyism, see especially Robert Griffith, *The Politics of Fear: Joseph R. McCarthy and the Senate*, Kentucky, Lexington, 1970.

5. For John Foster Dulles' remarks on bipartisanship in foreign policy, see his *War or Peace*, Macmillan, New York, 1950, pp. 120–37, 178–84.

6. A penetrating analysis covering the first decade of the People's Republic is A. Doak Barnett, *Communist China and Asia: Challenge to American Policy*, Harper for the Council on Foreign Relations, New York, 1960.

7. For many insights see Kenneth T. Young, *Negotiating with the Chinese Communists: The United States Experience, 1953–1967*, McGraw-Hill for the Council on Foreign Relations, New York, 1968.

8. *The New York Times*, March 1, 1970.

9. For the Burmese case note *Kuomintang Aggression against Burma*, Ministry of Information, Rangoon, 1953.

10. U.S. Senate, *Hearings on Nomination of Philip C. Jessup to Be United States Representative to the Sixth General Assembly of the United Nations*, 82nd Congress, 1st Session, Government Printing Office, Washington, 1951, p. 603.

11. *United States-Vietnam Relations, 1945–1967*, Study Prepared by the Department of Defense, Book 8, Government Printing Office, Washington, 1971, p. 227.

12. *Ibid.*, p. 248.

13. *Ibid.*, p. 266.

14. *Ibid.*, p. 288.

15. A perceptive article by Raymond B. Fosdick is "Asia's Challenge to Us—Ideas, Not Guns," *The New York Times Magazine*, February 12, 1950, pp. 7 ff.

16. See Edwin F. Stanton, *Brief Authority: Excursions of a Common Man in an Uncommon World*, Harper, New York, 1956, pp. 233–36.

17. See *Department of State Bulletin*, April 24, 1950, pp. 627–30.

18. *United States-Vietnam Relations, 1945–1967*, Book 8, p. 281.

19. Samuel P. Hayes, ed., "The Griffin Mission Reports of 1950: The Beginning of United States Economic and Technical Aid in Southeast Asia," p. I 9 (a manu-

script). This study was subsequently revised and published in 1971. See Samuel P. Hayes, ed., *The Beginning of American Aid to Southeast Asia: The Griffin Mission of 1950*, Lexington Books, Lexington, 1971.

20. *American Foreign Policy, 1950–1955: Basic Documents*, Vol. II, Government Printing Office, Washington, 1957, p. 2318.

21. *Ibid.*

22. *Ibid.*, p. 2319.

23. *Ibid.*, p. 2318.

24. *Ibid.*

25. *Department of State Bulletin*, February 27, 1950, pp. 334 ff.

26. *Ibid.*, April 10, 1950, p. 562.

27. *Ibid.*, March 27, 1950, p. 471.

28. See Matthew B. Ridgway, *The Korean War*, Doubleday, Garden City, 1967, and David Rees, *Korea: The Limited War*, St. Martin's, New York, 1964.

29. *American Foreign Policy, 1950–1955: Basic Documents*, Vol. II, p. 2540.

30. For this decision see Allen S. Whiting, *China Crosses the Yalu: The Decision to Enter the Korean War*, Macmillan, New York, 1960.

31. Address of General Douglas MacArthur to a joint meeting of Congress, April 19, 1951, U.S. Senate, *Representative Speeches of General of the Army Douglas MacArthur*, 88th Congress, 2nd Session, Government Printing Office, Washington, 1964, p. 19.

32. Ridgway, *The Korean War*, pp. vi, vii.

33. *Ibid.*, p. 245.

34. U.S. Senate, Committee on Foreign Relations, *Background Information Relating to Southeast Asia and Vietnam*, 2nd rev. ed., 89th Congress, 2nd Session, Government Printing Office, Washington, 1966, p. 146.

35. *American Foreign Policy, 1950–1955: Basic Documents*, Vol. II, p. 2627.

36. *United States-Vietnam Relations, 1945–1967*, Book 8, p. 359.

37. *Ibid.*, p. 429.

38. *Ibid.*, p. 427.

39. *Ibid.*, p. 428.

40. *Ibid.*, Book 10, p. 734.

41. *American Foreign Policy, 1950–1955: Basic Documents*, Vol. II, p. 2611.

42. *Ibid.*, p. 2662.

43. *United States-Vietnam Relations, 1945–1967*, Book 8, p. 429.

44. *Ibid.*, p. 435.

45. *Ibid.*, p. 437.

46. For various insights see Frederick S. Dunn, *Peace-Making and the Settlement with Japan*, Princeton, Princeton, 1963. Also, Shigeru Yoshida, *The Yoshida Memoirs: The Story of Japan in Crisis*, Houghton Mifflin, Boston, 1962, and Dean Acheson, *Present at the Creation: My Years in the State Department*, Norton, New York, 1969, pp. 426–35, 539–50.

47. *American Foreign Policy, 1950–1955: Basic Documents*, Vol. I, p. 886.

48. *Treaties and Other International Acts Series* 4509.

49. *American Foreign Policy, 1950–1955: Basic Documents*, Vol. I, p. 464.

50. *Department of State Bulletin*, April 30, 1951, p. 699.

51. *American Foreign Policy, 1950–1955: Basic Documents*, Vol. I, p. 874.

52. See J. G. Starke, *The ANZUS Treaty Alliance*, Melbourne, Melbourne, 1965. Also, Sir Percy Spender, *Exercises in Diplomacy: The Anzus Treaty and the Colombo Plan*, Sydney, Sydney, 1969.

53. John Robinson Beal, *John Foster Dulles: A Biography*, Harper, New York, 1957, pp. 226–27. The Secretary read this manuscript prior to publication.

54. *American Foreign Policy, 1950–1955: Basic Documents*, Vol. I, p. 946.

55. *Ibid.*, p. 878 (ANZUS Treaty).

56. *Ibid.*, p. 911.

57. For an article based on field research, 1953–54, see Russell H. Fifield, "The Challenge to Magsaysay," *Foreign Affairs*, October 1954, pp. 149–54.

58. A fascinating account by an American adviser to Magsaysay as he rose to the presidency is Edward Geary Lansdale, *In the Midst of Wars: An American's Mission to Southeast Asia*, Harper and Row, New York, 1972, pp. 1–125.

59. Mohammad Hatta, "Indonesia's Foreign Policy," *Foreign Affairs*, April 1953, p. 445.

60. *Ibid.*

61. Quoted in John M. Allison, "United States Diplomacy in Southeast Asia: The Limits of Policy," in William Henderson, ed., *Southeast Asia: Problems of United States Policy*, M.I.T., Cambridge, 1963, p. 170.

62. For the mission's report, see Hayes, *The Beginning of American Aid to Southeast Asia*, pp. 269–319.

63. *Ibid.*, p. 270.

64. "TCA Aid to Indonesia," *Indonesian Affairs*, January 1953, p. 3.

65. *United States-Vietnam Relations, 1945–1967*, Book 8, p. 436.

66. *Ibid.*, p. 501.

67. *Ibid.*, p. 500.

68. *Ibid.*, p. 499.

69. *Ibid.*, Book 9, p. 494.

70. *Ibid.*, p. 352.

71. Frank N. Trager, *Burma—From Kingdom to Republic: A Historical and Political Analysis*, Praeger, New York, 1966, p. 328. Trager was Director of the Point Four Program in Burma, 1951–53.

72. For an account by the Chairman of the Burma Economic Aid Committee, written in 1968, see Hla Maung, "Beginning of American Aid to Burma," in Hayes, *The Beginning of American Aid to Southeast Asia*, pp. 201–22.

73. *Treaties and Other International Acts Series* 2602.

74. Trager, *Burma—From Kingdom to Republic*, p. 321.

75. *United States-Vietnam Relations, 1945–1967*, Book 9, p. 494.

76. A helpful collection of documents including coverage of events in this period of time is Allan W. Cameron, ed., *Viet-Nam Crisis: A Documentary History*, Vol. I, *1940–1956*, Cornell, Ithaca, 1971.

77. For a relevant study see King C. Chen, *Vietnam and China, 1938–1954*, Princeton, Princeton, 1969.

78. George McTurnan Kahin and John W. Lewis, *The United States in Vietnam,* Dell, New York, 1967, p. 31. (A revised ed., 1969, adds a section covering the period from November 1966 to mid-1969.)

79. Bundy, "The Path to Viet-Nam," p. 2.

80. Acheson, *Present at the Creation*, pp. 672–73.

81. *United States-Vietnam Relations, 1945–1967*, Book 1, IV.A.2., p. 8.

82. *American Foreign Policy, 1950–1955: Basic Documents*, Vol. II, p. 2366.

83. Hayes, *The Beginning of American Aid to Southeast Asia*, p. 62.

84. *United States-Vietnam Relations, 1945–1967*, Book 8, p. 401.

85. *Ibid.*, p. 436.

86. *American Foreign Policy, 1950–1955: Basic Documents*, Vol. II, pp. 2366–67.

87. Senator John F. Kennedy, *The Strategy of Peace*, Harper, New York, 1960, p. 60.

88. Quoted in Robert Shaplen, *The Lost Revolution: The U.S. in Vietnam, 1946–1966*, rev. ed., Harper and Row, New York, 1966, p. 86.

89. Quoted in *ibid.*, p. 87.

90. *American Foreign Policy, 1950–1955: Basic Documents*, Vol. II, p. 2367.

91. The available documentation on the different positions is found in *United States-Vietnam Relations, 1945–1967*, Book 8, pp. 468–76, 485-507.

92. *Ibid.*, p. 522.

93. *Ibid.*, p. 527.

94. *American Foreign Policy, 1950–1955: Basic Documents*, Vol. II, p. 2369.

95. Acheson, *Present at the Creation*, p. 673.

96. *Ibid.*

97. *American Foreign Policy, 1950–1955: Basic Documents*, Vol. II, p. 2386.

98. Harry S. Truman, *Memoirs by Harry S. Truman, Years of Trial and Hope,* Vol. II, Doubleday, Garden City, 1956, p. 519.

99. *The New York Times*, January 28, 1953.

100. U.S. House of Representatives, *Report of the Special Study Mission to Pakistan, India, Thailand, and Indochina, Pursuant to H. Res. 113*, 83rd Congress, 1st Session, Government Printing Office, Washington, 1953, p. 53.

101. Dulles, *War or Peace*, p. 231.

102. Quoted in Melvin Gurtov, *The First Vietnam Crisis: Chinese Communist Strategy and United States Involvement, 1953–1954*, Columbia, New York, 1967, p. 28.

103. *American Foreign Policy, 1950–1955: Basic Documents*, Vol. I, p. 1673.

104. Quoted in Shaplen, *The Lost Revolution*, p. 93.

105. *Congressional Record*, Senate, June 30, 1953, p. 7623.

106. Kennedy, *The Strategy of Peace*, p. 60. Kennedy quoted from his speech in the Senate on April 6, 1954.

107. *Indochina*, Report of Senator Mike Mansfield on a Study Mission to the Associated States of Indochina, Vietnam, Cambodia, Laos, October 27, 1953, Committee Print, Senate Committee on Foreign Relations, 83rd Congress, 1st Session, Government Printing Office, Washington, 1953, p. 3.

108. Eisenhower, *The White House Years: Mandate for Change*, p. 336.

109. *Ibid.*, pp. 337–38.

110. *Department of State Bulletin*, July 27, 1953, p. 105.

111. *Ibid.*, September 28, 1953, p. 415.

112. *American Foreign Policy, 1950–1955: Basic Documents*, Vol. II, p. 2371.

113. *Ibid.*

114. In this respect, see a memorandum for the National Security Council, September 11, 1953, in *United States-Vietnam Relations, 1945–1967*, Book 9, pp. 153–55.

115. Sherman Adams, *Firsthand Report: The Story of the Eisenhower Administration*, Harper, New York, 1961, p. 121.

116. *The New York Times*, November 5, 1953.

117. *United States-Vietnam Relations, 1945–1967*, Book 9, p. 178.

118. *Ibid.*, p. 182.

119. For Navarre's map as reproduced, see Kahin and Lewis, *The United States in Vietnam*, p. 34.

120. *Department of State Bulletin*, January 25, 1954, p. 108 (all quotations).

121. *United States-Vietnam Relations, 1945–1967*, Book 9, pp. 219–35.

122. *Public Papers of the Presidents of the United States, Dwight D. Eisenhower, 1954*, Government Printing Office, Washington, 1960, p. 253.

123. Eisenhower, *The White House Years: Mandate for Change*, p. 344.

124. *Congressional Record*, Senate, April 6, 1954, p. 4672.

125. *The New York Times*, March 6, 1954.

126. For the analysis of the Joint Chiefs, some aspects of which were relevant to Korean participation in the Second Indochinese War, see their memorandum for the Secretary of Defense, March 1, 1954, *United States-Vietnam Relations, 1945–1967*, Book 9, pp. 259–63.

127. *Congressional Record*, Senate, March 9, 1954, p. 2904.

128. *United States-Vietnam Relations, 1945–1967*, Book 9, p. 268.

129. Général d'Armée Paul Ély, *Mémoires: L'Indochine dans la tourmente*, Plon, Paris, 1964, p. 64.

130. *Ibid.*, pp. 76–77.

131. Gurtov, *The First Vietnam Crisis*, p. 80. Based on Gurtov's interview with Radford.

132. Ély, *Mémoires: L'Indochine dans la tourmente*, pp. 83–84.

133. *United States-Vietnam Relations, 1945–1967*, Book 9, pp. 277–90.

134. *Public Papers of the Presidents of the United States, Dwight D. Eisenhower, 1954*, p. 366.

135. *American Foreign Policy, 1950–1955: Basic Documents*, Vol. II, p. 2375.

136. *Ibid.*, p. 2376.

137. See Bernard B. Fall, *Hell in a Very Small Place: The Siege of Dien Bien Phu*, Lippincott, Philadelphia, 1966. For General Vo Nguyen Giap's account, see his *People's War, People's Army*, Praeger, New York, 1962, pp. 133–62.

138. The best article on the subject is probably Chalmers M. Roberts, "The Day We Didn't Go to War," *Reporter*, September 14, 1954, pp. 31–35. See also his "Blocked by British 'No'—U.S. Twice Proposed Indochina Air Strike," *Washington Post and Times Herald*, June 7, 1954. Another source is James Shepley, "How Dulles Averted War," *Life*, January 16, 1956, pp. 70–80. Beal, *John Foster Dulles: A Biography*, is less specific than Roberts. See comments of Congressman John McCormack, *The New York Times*, January 23, 1956.

139. Roberts, "The Day We Didn't Go to War," pp. 31–32.

140. Eisenhower, *The White House Years: Mandate for Change*, p. 347.

141. *Ibid.*

142. Anthony Eden, *The Memoirs of Anthony Eden: Full Circle*, Houghton Mifflin, Boston, 1960, p. 117.

143. *Public Papers of the Presidents of the United States, Dwight D. Eisenhower, 1954*, p. 383.

144. *Congressional Record*, Senate, April 6, 1954, p. 4673.

145. *Ibid.*, p. 4679.

146. *Official Gazette*, Republic of the Philippines, April 1954, pp. 1539–40.

147. *Public Papers of the Presidents of the United States, Dwight D. Eisenhower, 1954*, p. 421.

148. Adams, *Firsthand Report*, p. 123.

149. *Public Papers of the Presidents of the United States, Dwight D. Eisenhower, 1954*, p. 428.

150. *American Foreign Policy, 1950–1955: Basic Documents*, Vol. II, p. 2383.

151. *Ibid.*, p. 2389.

152. Speech of Lyndon B. Johnson, Jefferson-Jackson Day Dinner, Washington, D.C., May 6, 1954.

153. Gurtov, *The First Vietnam Crisis*, p. 145.

154. General Matthew B. Ridgway, *Soldier: The Memoirs of Matthew B. Ridgway*, Harper, New York, 1956, p. 278.

155. Eisenhower, *The White House Years: Mandate for Change*, p. 372.

CHAPTER 5

1. Although Korea was first on the conference agenda Indochina was soon discussed, although there were separate participants for each area. The Korean phase of the Geneva Conference ended on June 15 with no achievement. For the earlier part of the conference, see *Documents Relating to the Discussion of Korea and Indo-China at the Geneva Conference, 27 April–15 June, 1954*, Cmd. 9186, Her Majesty's Stationery Office, London, 1954.

2. *United States-Vietnam Relations, 1945–1967*, Book 9, p. 448.

3. *Ibid.*, p. 451.

4. *Ibid.*, p. 487.

5. *Ibid.*, p. 491.

6. *Ibid.*, pp. 559–60.

7. *Department of State Bulletin*, May 24, 1954, p. 782.

8. *United States-Vietnam Relations, 1945–1967*, Book 9, p. 458.

9. *American Foreign Policy, 1950–1955: Basic Documents*, Vol. II, Government Printing Office, Washington, 1957, p. 2394.

10. *Ibid.*, p. 2395.

11. *Ibid.*

12. Eden, *The Memoirs of Anthony Eden: Full Circle*, p. 149.

13. *American Foreign Policy, 1950–1955: Basic Documents*, Vol. I, p. 1707.

14. *Public Papers of the Presidents of the United States, Dwight D. Eisenhower, 1954*, Government Printing Office, Washington, 1960, p. 604.

15. See letter from Nehru to author, Russell H. Fifield, *The Diplomacy of Southeast Asia: 1945–1958*, Harper, New York, 1958, pp. 510–11.

16. *Documents on International Affairs, 1954*, Oxford for the Royal Institute of International Affairs, London, 1957, p. 127.

17. For a specific discussion of the Viet Minh and Sino-Soviet objectives and strategy at Geneva, see *United States-Vietnam Relations, 1945–1967*, Book 1, III.C., pp. 1–26.

18. Cooper, *The Lost Crusade*, p. 101.

19. *Journal Officiel de la République Française, Débats parlementaires, Assemblée Nationale*, vendredi 23 juillet 1954, p. 3534.

20. For text see *American Foreign Policy, 1950–1955: Basic Documents*, Vol. I, pp. 750–67.

21. For text see *ibid.*, pp. 775–85.

22. For text see *ibid.*, pp. 767–75.

23. For texts see *Further Documents Relating to the Discussion of Indo-China at the Geneva Conference, 16 June–21 July, 1954*, Cmd. 9239, Her Majesty's Stationery Office, London, 1954.

24. *Ibid.*

25. *Ibid.*

26. *Ibid.*

27. *Ibid.*

28. *Ibid.*

29. *American Foreign Policy, 1950–1955: Basic Documents*, Vol. I, pp. 785–87 (all quotations).

30. *Ibid.*, p. 788.

31. For an analysis of the background of the declaration, see *United States-Vietnam Relations, 1945–1967*, Book 10, pp. 676–78.

32. *American Foreign Policy, 1950–1955: Basic Documents*, Vol. II, p. 2397.

33. *Ibid.*

34. *Ibid.*, p. 2398.

35. *Department of State Bulletin*, August 2, 1954, p. 163.

36. According to Emmet John Hughes, *The Ordeal of Power: A Political Memoir of the Eisenhower Years*, Atheneum, New York, 1963, p. 208.

37. Quoted in *The United States in World Affairs, 1954*, Harper for the Council on Foreign Relations, New York, 1956, p. 255.

38. *U.S. News & World Report*, July 30, 1954, p. 92.

39. *Ibid.*, pp. 87–88.

40. See J. G. Starke, *The ANZUS Treaty Alliance*, Melbourne, Melbourne, 1965, pp. 4–36.

41. *United States-Vietnam Relations, 1945–1967*, Book 10, p. 722.

42. *Ibid.*, p. 723.

43. *Ibid.*, p. 736.

44. *Ibid.*, Book 1, IV.A.1., p. 2A.

45. *The Signing of the Southeast Asia Collective Defense Treaty, the Protocol to the Southeast Asia Collective Treaty and the Pacific Charter: Proceedings*, Conference Secretariat, Manila, September 8, 1954, p. 41.

46. *Ibid.*, p. 42.

47. *Ibid.*, p. 37.

48. *Ibid.*, p. 45.

49. *Ibid.*, p. 46.

50. *Ibid.*, p. 34.

51. *American Foreign Policy, 1950–1955: Basic Documents*, Vol. I, p. 913.

52. *Ibid.*, p. 916.

53. *Ibid.*, p. 913.

54. *Ibid.*, p. 916.

55. *Ibid.*

56. Robert Aura Smith, *Philippine Freedom: 1946–1958*, Columbia, New York, 1958, p. 211.

57. *American Foreign Policy, 1950–1955: Basic Documents*, Vol. I, p. 945.

58. William P. Bundy, "The Path to Viet-Nam," Department of State Publication 8295, Released September 1967, p. 5.

59. *Parliamentary Debates (Hansard)*, 5th Series, Vol. 532, *House of Commons Official Report*, November 1–12, 1954, col. 929.

60. Devillers and Lacouture, *End of a War: Indochina, 1954*, p. 327.

61. Kenneth T. Young, "The Foreign Policies of Thailand," p. 60 (a manuscript).

62. Kahin and Lewis, *The United States in Vietnam*, p. 63.

63. *The New York Times*, October 29, 1954.

64. *American Foreign Policy, 1950–1955: Basic Documents*, Vol. I, p. 932.

65. *Ibid.*, p. 926.

66. *Ibid.*, p. 943.

67. See George Modelski, "International Relations and Area Studies," *International Relations*, April 1961, pp. 143–55, and Michael Brecher, "International Relations and Asian Studies: The Subordinate State System of Southern Asia," *World Politics*, January 1963, pp. 213–35.

68. The geographer of the Department of State has issued a series of valuable international boundary studies. A number of these relate to Southeast Asia. See, for instance, *Malaysia-Thailand Boundary*, Department of State, No. 57, November 15, 1965. A most stimulating article is Robert L. Solomon, "Boundary Concepts and Practices in Southeast Asia," *World Politics*, October 1970, pp. 1–23. See also Alastair Lamb, *Asian Frontiers: Studies in a Continuing Problem*, Pall Mall, London, 1968.

69. For minorities see Virginia Thompson and Richard Adloff, *Minority Problems in Southeast Asia*, Stanford, Stanford, 1955, and Peter Kunstadter, ed., *Southeast Asian Tribes, Minorities, and Nations,* 2 vols., Princeton, Princeton, 1967.

70. *Asian Relations, Being Report of the Proceedings and Documentation of the First Asian Relations Conference, New Delhi, March–April, 1947*, Asian Relations Organization, New Delhi, 1948, p. 23.

71. For one aspect see Rupert Emerson, "Post-Independence Nationalism in South and Southeast Asia: A Reconsideration," *Pacific Affairs*, Summer 1971, pp. 173–92.

72. For a thought-provoking consideration of the subject of "value," see Charles Wolf, Jr., "Some Aspects of the 'Value' of Southeast Asia to the United States," in William Henderson, ed., *Southeast Asia: Problems of United States Policy*, M.I.T., Cambridge, 1963, pp. 27–44.

73. *Ibid.*, p. 34.

74. See Bundy, "The Path to Viet-Nam," p. 5, already cited, for how Washington viewed Southeast Asia at the time of the watershed in terms of the Communist threat and its possible consequences.

CHAPTER 6

1. *American Foreign Policy: Current Documents, 1961*, Government Printing Office, Washington, 1965, p. 1054.

354 NOTES

2. See the Pentagon Papers in *The New York Times*, June 13, 14, and 15, and July 1, 2, 3, 4, and 5, 1971. (Also *The Pentagon Papers*, Bantam, New York, 1971.) Four volumes of papers appeared in The Senator Gravel Edition, *The Pentagon Papers: The Defense Department History of United States Decisionmaking on Vietnam*, Beacon, Boston, 1971, and twelve books in *United States-Vietnam Relations, 1945–1967*, Study Prepared by the Department of Defense, Government Printing Office, Washington, 1971. A review comparing the three editions was written by Gaddis Smith in *The New York Times Book Review*, November 28, 1971, pp. 3, 5. Involved in the Pentagon Papers are the documents themselves and the contributions of the Pentagon and *The New York Times'* analysts. A valuable assessment of *The New York Times* version is Max Frankel, "The Lessons of Vietnam: Pentagon's Study Uniquely Portrays the 'Greek Tragedy' of the U.S. Role," *The New York Times*, July 6, 1971. Leslie H. Gelb, who was the director of the research project in the Pentagon, prepared a paper for the convention of the American Political Science Association in September 1970 entitled "Vietnam: Some Hypotheses about Why and How" and Daniel Ellsberg, one entitled "Escalating in a Quagmire." The papers did not attract unusual attention at the time but they subsequently grew in importance.

3. *United States-Vietnam Relations, 1945–1967*, Book 10, p. 731–32.

4. For excerpts of the team's report, mainly covering August 1954 to August 1955, see Pentagon Papers, *The New York Times*, July 5, 1971, pp. 11–12.

5. Kenneth T. Young, "United States Policy and Vietnamese Political Viability, 1954–1967," *Asian Survey*, August 1967, p. 510.

6. *Department of State Bulletin*, November 15, 1954, p. 735.

7. *Ibid.*

8. *Ibid.* The word democracy was not used.

9. *Ibid.*, p. 736.

10. Quoted in Frank N. Trager, *Why Viet Nam?*, Praeger, New York, 1966, pp. 114–15. Kennedy did not include this statement in his *The Strategy of Peace*.

11. *Department of State Bulletin*, May 27, 1957, p. 851.

12. *Ibid.*, p. 852.

13. *Ibid.*, November 14, 1960, p. 758.

14. Clark M. Clifford, "A Viet Nam Reappraisal: The Personal History of One Man's View and How It Evolved," *Foreign Affairs*, July 1969, p. 604.

15. *United States-Vietnam Relations, 1945–1967*, Book 10, p. 1091.

16. Roger Hilsman, *To Move a Nation: The Politics of Foreign Policy in the Administration of John F. Kennedy*, Doubleday, Garden City, 1967, pp. 140–41.

17. Quoted in Arthur M. Schlesinger, Jr., *A Thousand Days: John F. Kennedy in the White House*, Fawcett, Greenwich, 1967, p. 307.

18. For insights on this period see Stuart Simmonds, "The Development of Foreign Policy in Laos" (a manuscript), Arthur J. Dommen, *Conflict in Laos: The Politics of Neutralization*, rev. ed., Praeger, New York, 1971, and Hugh Toye, *Laos: Buffer State or Battleground*, Oxford, London, 1968.

19. According to Donald E. Nuechterlein, *Thailand and the Struggle for Southeast Asia*, Cornell, Ithaca, 1965, p. 230.

20. Kenneth T. Young, "The Foreign Policies of Thailand" (a manuscript), p. 66.

21. *Ibid.*

22. *United States-Vietnam Relations, 1945–1967*, Book 11, p. 164.

23. For text of the Staley Report, see *ibid.*, pp. 182–209.

24. *Ibid.*, pp. 335–36.

25. *Ibid.*, p. 341.

26. *Ibid.*, pp. 400–05.

27. For an analysis of Sihanouk's policies from different viewpoints, see Philippe Devillers, "The Foreign Policy of Cambodia" (a manuscript), Roger M. Smith, *Cambodia's Foreign Policy*, Cornell, Ithaca, 1965, and Michael Leifer, *Cambodia: The Search for Security*, Praeger, New York, 1967.

28. For his own account see Lyndon Baines Johnson, *The Vantage Point: Perspectives of the Presidency, 1963–1969*, Holt, Rinehart and Winston, New York, 1971. In The Senator Gravel Edition of the Pentagon Papers, Volume III has 212 pages of documents and Volume IV twenty pages from the Johnson administration. One or more of these documents was published in *The New York Times*. The Government Printing Office edition does not contain "internal documents" of the Johnson presidency apart from those found in the narratives of the analysts.

29. United Nations, Security Council, *Official Records*, Nineteenth Year, 1119th Meeting, May 21, 1964, p. 12.

30. For a narrative by Neil Sheehan based partly on the Pentagon Papers but more on a classified summary of a command and control study by the Defense Department in 1965, see the Pentagon Papers, *The New York Times*, June 13, 1971, p. 40. The account by the government analyst is found in *United States-Vietnam Relations, 1945–1967*, Book 4, IV.C. 2.b., pp. 1–24. Two significant studies relating to the episode are Eugene G. Windchy, *Tonkin Gulf*, Doubleday, Garden City, 1971, and Anthony Austin, *The President's War: The Story of the Tonkin Gulf Resolution and How the Nation Was Trapped in Vietnam*, Lippincott, Philadelphia, 1971.

31. *Department of State Bulletin*, August 24, 1964, p. 268. For the draft resolution of May 25, 1964, see the Pentagon Papers, *The New York Times*, June 13, 1971, p. 36.

32. *Public Papers of the Presidents of the United States, Lyndon B. Johnson, 1965*, Book II, Government Printing Office, Washington, 1966, p 794.

33. For a position paper of the Department of State as of November 19, 1965, on the question of a formal declaration of war, see U.S. Senate, Committee on Foreign Relations, *Background Information Relating to Southeast Asia and Vietnam*, 2nd rev. ed., 89th Congress, 2nd Session, Government Printing Office, Washington, 1966, pp. 253–55. The bibliography on the legal aspects of the American engagement in Vietnam is extensive. For various viewpoints see Richard A. Falk, ed., *The Vietnam War and International Law*, American Society of International Law, Vol. I, Princeton, Princeton, 1968, and Vol. II, Princeton, Princeton, 1969.

The official viewpoint is well expressed by Leonard C. Meeker, "The Legality of United States Participation in the Defense of Viet-Nam," *Department of State Bulletin,* March 28, 1966, pp. 474–89. For a bibliography see Wesley R. Fishel, ed., *Vietnam: Anatomy of a Conflict,* Peacock, Itasca, 1968, p. 99.

34. Admiral U. S. G. Sharp and General W. C. Westmoreland, *Report on the War in Vietnam (As of 30 June 1968),* Government Printing Office, Washington, Released 1969, p. 1. This report is valuable although it has various omissions.

35. Brigadier General (Ret.) S. L. A. Marshall, "Big Guns Not Answer," in Fishel, *Vietnam: Anatomy of a Conflict,* p. 465.

36. Hilsman, *To Move a Nation,* p. 445.

37. *Viet Nam and Southeast Asia,* Report of Senator Mike Mansfield *et al.* to the Committee on Foreign Relations, Committee Print, Senate Committee on Foreign Relations, 88th Congress, 1st Session, Government Printing Office, Washington, 1963, p. 6.

38. *Ibid.*

39. Hilsman, *To Move a Nation,* p. 524.

40. Compare, for instance, Sir Robert Thompson's viewpoints in his *No Exit from Vietnam,* McKay, New York, 1969, with those of Admiral U.S. Grant Sharp (Ret.) in "We Could Have Won in Vietnam Long Ago," *Reader's Digest,* May 1969, pp. 118–23.

41. For an article stressing the importance of American public opinion, see Leslie H. Gelb, "The Essential Domino: American Politics and Vietnam," *Foreign Affairs,* April 1972, pp. 459–75.

42. *Public Papers of the Presidents of the United States, Lyndon B. Johnson, 1965,* Book I, p. 205.

43. Testimony of McNamara, August 25, 1967, *Air War Against North Vietnam,* Hearings before the Preparedness Investigating Subcommittee, Senate Committee on Armed Services, 90th Congress, 1st Session, Government Printing Office, Washington, 1967, p. 275.

44. Maxwell D. Taylor, *Responsibility and Response,* Harper and Row, New York, 1967, p. 27.

45. Johnson, *The Vantage Point,* p. 136.

46. For text of National Security Action Memorandum No. 328, April 6, 1965, see *United States-Vietnam Relations, 1945–1967,* Book 4, IV.C.5., pp. 124–26.

47. Interview with Ambassador Henry Cabot Lodge:
Q. Mr. Ambassador, do you feel that some sort of turning point has been reached here in Vietnam?
A. Yes, we have reached a turning point. We did so in the President's far-sighted decision formally announced on July 28, 1965, to commit U.S. troops on a large scale here—which, as time goes by, appears more and more as a big turning point of history.
U.S. News and World Report, November 21, 1966, p. 67.

48. *Department of State Bulletin,* February 6, 1967, p. 187.

49. Interview with General Westmoreland:
Q. It has been said you were in trouble logistically a year or so ago. Do you still have logistical problems?

A. Early in 1965 we knew that the enemy hoped to deliver the *coup de grâce* by launching a major summer offensive to cut the Republic of Vietnam in two with a drive across the central highlands to the sea. I had to make a decision, and did. I chose a rapid build-up of combat forces, in the full knowledge that we would not have a fully developed logistic base to support those forces. We lived with austerity, and used backed-up ships as floating warehouses. *U.S. News and World Report*, November 28, 1966, p. 49.

50. *Public Papers of the Presidents of the United States, Lyndon B. Johnson, 1965*, Book II, p. 797. See also Johnson, *The Vantage Point*, pp. 137–53, for details behind the announcement.

51. The Government Printing Office version of the Pentagon Papers has three subdivisions on the American buildup in South Vietnam, 1965–67 (Book 4—Marine Combat Units Go to Da Nang, March 1965, Phase I in the Build-Up of U.S. Forces: March–July 1965, and Book 5—U.S. Ground Strategy and Force Deployments: 1965–1967). The first two subdivisions retain footnotes at the end but the third has omissions in places. The American bombing of the North, 1965–68, has two subdivisions (Book 4—Rolling Thunder Program Begins: January–June 1965 and Book 6—Air War in the North: 1965–1968). Footnotes are omitted in the latter reference. Book 7 includes in twenty-four pages a Statistical Survey of the War, North and South: 1965–1967. The open record on negotiations toward a settlement of the conflict, 1965–67, is covered in Book 12, VI.A., pp. 1–78, and VI.B., pp. 1–271.

52. *Department of State Bulletin*, June 9, 1969, pp. 477–78.

53. *Ibid.*, August 25, 1969, p. 153. The subject of U.S. commitments to Thailand is thoroughly examined in *United States Security Agreements and Commitments Abroad: Kingdom of Thailand*, Hearings before the Subcommittee on United States Security Agreements and Commitments Abroad, Senate Committee on Foreign Relations, 91st Congress, 1st Session, Part 3, November 10–14, 17, 1969, Government Printing Office, Washington, 1970, pp. 607–917. Also helpful is David A. Wilson, *The United States and the Future of Thailand*, Praeger, New York, 1970.

54. A key reference, a gold mine of information, is *United States Security Agreements and Commitments Abroad: The Republic of the Philippines*, Hearings before the Subcommittee on United States Security Agreements and Commitments Abroad, Senate Committee on Foreign Relations, 91st Congress, 1st Session, Part 1, September 30–October 3, 1969, Government Printing Office, Washington, 1969, p. 1–363.

55. *Department of State Bulletin*, October 10, 1966, p. 534.

56. Chester L. Cooper, *The Lost Crusade: America in Vietnam*, Dodd, Mead, New York, 1970, p. 324. Cooper was officially involved for the United States in many of the peace leads.

57. Johnson, *The Vantage Point*, p. 249.

58. See the perceptive reporting in Robert Shaplen, *The Road from War: Vietnam 1965–1971*, rev. ed., Harper and Row, New York, 1971.

59. For an excellent analysis of the offensive and its consequences, see Don Oberdorfer, *Tet!*, Doubleday, Garden City, 1971.

60. A revealing account of the task force is Clifford, "A Viet Nam Reappraisal," pp. 609–14. Subsequent accounts of the clashes among the President's advisers

point up the intensity of the debate both inside and outside the Ad Hoc Task Force on Vietnam. A significant study focusing on the six months leading to the President's March decisions is Townsend Hoopes, *The Limits of Intervention (an inside account of how the Johnson policy of escalation in Vietnam was reversed),* McKay, New York, 1969. Hoopes was deputy assistant secretary of defense for international security affairs, 1965–67, and undersecretary of the Air Force, 1967–69. Johnson's own account of the "decision to halt the bombing" was given in a CBS news special on February 6, 1970. Chapter 17 of his memoirs "The Making of a Decision: Vietnam 1967–1968" presents in considerable detail his viewpoints. Johnson, *The Vantage Point,* pp. 365–424. The events of March 1968 will long be debated.

61. An article strengthened by extensive high-level interviewing is John B. Henry, II, "February, 1968," *Foreign Policy,* Fall 1971, pp. 3–33.

62. For the contrasting views on Vietnam of two generals present, see General Matthew B. Ridgway, "Indochina: Disengaging," *Foreign Affairs,* July 1971, pp. 583–92, and Taylor, *Swords and Plowshares,* pp. 381–92.

63. *Department of State Bulletin,* April 15, 1968, p. 482.

64. *Ibid.,* p. 484.

65. *Ibid.,* p. 486.

66. *Ibid.,* September 30, 1968, p. 328.

67. *Ibid.,* November 18, 1968, p. 518.

68. *Ibid.*

69. *Ibid.,* December 2, 1968, p. 569.

70. *Ibid.,* p. 563.

71. For text of National Security Study Memorandum No. 1, see *Congressional Record,* House of Representatives, May 10, 1972, pp. E4976–E5005, and *ibid.,* May 11, 1972, pp. E5009–66. The topics of National Security Study Memoranda from January 21, 1969, to October 2, 1971—138 in all—are found as an appendix to a revealing article by John P. Leacacos, "Kissinger's Apparat," *Foreign Policy,* Winter 1971–72, pp. 3–27.

72. The changing events in Indochina during the first part of the Nixon administration are reflected in the literature of the period. See especially Joseph J. Zasloff and Allan E. Goodman, *Indochina in Conflict: A Political Assessment,* Heath, Lexington, 1972, which contains timely articles by twelve different authors. A comprehensive survey is found in "Vietnam and After: What Lessons Have We Learned?," *Great Decisions 1972,* Foreign Policy Association, New York, 1972. See also for insights N. Khac Huyen, *Vision Accomplished? The Enigma of Ho Chi Minh,* Macmillan, New York, 1971, and Jon M. Van Dyke, *North Vietnam's Strategy for Survival,* Pacific Books, Palo Alto, 1972.

73. For an interpretation of developments see William P. Bundy, "New Tides in Southeast Asia," *Foreign Affairs,* January 1971, pp. 187–200.

74. *Department of State Bulletin,* June 2, 1969, p. 460.

75. The American incursion in Cambodia has produced a bibliography on the controversy. The President's address of April 30, 1970, his interim report on June 3,

and his statement at the conclusion of U.S. ground operations on June 30 are conveniently found in *United States Foreign Policy, 1969–1970: A Report of the Secretary of State*, Government Printing Office, Washington, 1971, pp. 380–84, 384–87, and 441–50. For some highly critical comments see Clark Clifford, "Set a Date in Vietnam. Stick to It. Get Out.", *Life*, May 22, 1970, pp. 34–48. A comprehensive monograph is Douglas Pike, "Cambodia's War," *Southeast Asian Perspectives*, March 1971, pp. 1–48.

76. *Department of State Bulletin*, June 3, 1968, p. 727.

77. See especially articles by Henry Kamm, *The New York Times*, October 26 and 28, 1969.

78. *Department of State Bulletin*, March 30, 1970, pp. 405–09. Another valuable source of information is *United States Security Agreements and Commitments Abroad: Kingdom of Laos*, Hearings before the Subcommittee on United States Security Agreements and Commitments Abroad, Senate Committee on Foreign Relations, 91st Congress, 1st Session, Part 2, October 20–22, 28, 1969, Government Printing Office, Washington, 1970, pp. 365–606. Also see Roland A. Paul, "Laos: Anatomy of an American Involvement," *Foreign Affairs*, April 1971, pp. 533–47, and Robert Shaplen, "Our Involvement in Laos," *ibid.*, April 1970, pp. 478–93. Paul was counsel to the Senate subcommittee.

79. *Department of State Bulletin*, May 29, 1972, p. 749.

80. *Ibid.*, February 3, 1969, p. 91.

81. The literature on these relationships reveals evaluations and interpretations. See, for instance, Edwin O. Reischauer, "Fateful Triangle—The United States, Japan and China," *The New York Times Magazine*, September 19, 1971, pp. 12 ff., Hedley Bull, "The New Balance of Power in Asia and the Pacific," *Foreign Affairs*, July 1971, pp. 669–81, and Ronald I. Spiers, "U.S. National Security Policy and the Indian Ocean Area," *Department of State Bulletin*, August 23, 1971, pp. 199–203.

82. *The New York Times*, July 26, 1969.

83. The "three precepts" are formally set forth in *United States Foreign Policy, 1969–1970: A Report of the Secretary of State*, pp. 36–37. (In the third precept the reference to treaty commitments appears in the President's speech of November 3, 1969.) Secretary Rogers in his next report observed that "in 1971, the implementation of the Nixon Doctrine continued as the principal focus of U.S. policy in East Asia." *United States Foreign Policy, 1971: A Report of the Secretary of State*, Government Printing Office, Washington, 1972, p. 50. For a critique, see Earl C. Ravenal, "The Nixon Doctrine and Our Asian Commitments," *Foreign Affairs*, January 1971, pp. 201–17.

84. *U.S. News & World Report*, June 26, 1972, p. 36.

85. Eugene R. Black, *Alternative in Southeast Asia*, Praeger, New York, 1969, p. 177.

86. *Indonesian News & Views*, Special Issue, May 12, 1969.

87. For an authoritative account of the Gestapu affair see Howard Palfrey Jones, *Indonesia: The Possible Dream*, Harcourt Brace Jovanovich, New York, 1971, pp. 371–93. John Hughes, *Indonesian Upheavel,* McKay, New York, 1967, and Robert

Shaplen, *Time out of Hand: Revolution and Reaction in Southeast Asia*, Harper and Row, New York, 1969, have valuable accounts of developments. Arnold C. Brackman in *The Communist Collapse in Indonesia*, Norton, New York, 1969, has extensive notes and a comprehensive bibliography representing various viewpoints.

88. Hughes, *Indonesian Upheaval*, p. 289.

89. William P. Bundy, Statement of May 2, 1967, before the House Foreign Affairs Committee, p. 26 (separate press release).

90. Richard M. Nixon, "Asia after Viet Nam," *Foreign Affairs*, October 1967, p. 111. This article should be compared with the author's statements on Guam in July 1969.

91. *United States-Vietnam Relations, 1945–1967*, Book 10, p. 841–42.

92. *Ibid.*, p. 1094.

93. Adam Malik, "Promise in Indonesia," *Foreign Affairs*, January 1968, p. 301.

94. For a helpful perspective on the new economic outlook in Djakarta involving foreign aid, see "Indonesia: Plans and Prospects," eight talks, in *Asia*, Autumn 1970, pp. 1–138. Also see David B. H. Denoon, "Indonesia: Transition to Stability?," *Current History*, December 1971, pp. 332–38, 367–68.

95. A significant article on a complex subject is T. B. Millar, "The Five-Power Defence Agreement and Southeast Asian Security," *Pacific Community*, January 1972, pp. 341–51.

96. Quoted in *Indonesian News & Views*, Special Issue, May 14, 1969.

97. Charles A. Fisher, "Southeast Asia" in W. Gordon East and O. H. K. Spate, eds., *The Changing Map of Asia: A Political Geography*, 4th ed., Methuen, London, 1961, p. 248.

98. *Department of State Bulletin*, February 5, 1968, p. 162.

99. *U.S. Foreign Policy for the 1970's: Building for Peace, A Report to the Congress by Richard Nixon, President of the United States, February 25, 1971*, Government Printing Office, Washington, 1971, p. 93.

100. For the origins of ASEAN and its potential see Bernard K. Gordon, *Toward Disengagement in Asia: A Strategy for American Foreign Policy*, Prentice-Hall, Englewood Cliffs, 1969, pp. 111–30.

101. The ASEAN Declaration, *Current Notes on International Affairs*, August 1967, pp. 327–28. A specific objective was "to promote South-East Asian studies." *Ibid.*, p. 328.

102. *Malaysian Digest*, November 30, 1971, p. 4.

103. Black, *Alternative in Southeast Asia*, pp. 97–98.

104. *United States-Vietnam Relations, 1945–1967*, Book 10, p. 1090.

105. Schlesinger, *A Thousand Days*, p. 500.

106. See *To Tame a River*, Government Printing Office, Washington, 1968.

107. See Virginia Morsey Wheeler, "Co-Operation for Development in the Lower Mekong Basin," *American Journal of International Law*, July 1970, pp. 594–609.

108. The bibliography on Japan's postwar role in Southeast Asia is increasing. Among the recent references Walter C. Lenahan has written two unpublished mono-

graphs: "Japan's Expanding Role in Asian International Organizations," December 1969, and "Japan and Southeast Asia," April 1970. Both have extensive bibliographies. A very timely article is John M. Allison, "Japan's Relations with Southeast Asia," *Asia*, Winter 1969–70, pp. 34–59. Another former U.S. ambassador to Japan, Edwin O. Reischauer, provides some valuable perspectives in *Beyond Vietnam: The United States and Asia*, Random House, New York, 1967. Last but not least is an able study by Lawrence Olson, *Japan in Postwar Asia*, Praeger for the Council on Foreign Relations, New York, 1970.

109. U. Alexis Johnson, "The Role of Japan and the Future of American Relations with the Far East," *Department of State Bulletin*, April 27, 1970, p. 540.

110. It was formally set up in Tokyo in 1967. See U. Alexis Johnson, address at a meeting in May 1969, "The Pacific Basin," *Pacific Community*, October 1969, pp. 11–19.

111. Eugene R. Black, "Towards a New Diplomacy in East Asia," p. 7 (address of September 17, 1968).

112. *Ibid.*

113. *Ibid.*

114. *Ibid.*, p. 3.

115. *Ibid.*, p. 10.

116. Melvin Gurtov, *Southeast Asia Tomorrow: Problems and Prospects for U.S. Policy*, Johns Hopkins, Baltimore, 1970, p. 5.

117. See *U.S. Foreign Policy for the 1970's: A New Strategy for Peace, A Report to the Congress by Richard Nixon, President of the United States, February 18, 1970*, Government Printing Office, Washington, 1970, p. 56. Also see *U.S. Foreign Policy for the 1970's: The Emerging Structure of Peace, A Report to the Congress by Richard Nixon, President of the United States, February 9, 1972*, Government Printing Office, Washington, 1972, pp. 73–78.

ACKNOWLEDGMENTS

Permission to quote or utilize certain specified material in this book has been kindly given by the following publishers and others:

Allan B. Cole (Editor), *Conflict in Indo-China and International Repercussions: A Documentary History, 1945–1955,* © 1956 by The Fletcher School of Law and Diplomacy. Used by permission of Cornell University Press.

Abbot Low Moffat, *Mongkut, The King of Siam,* © 1961 by Cornell University. Used by permission of Cornell University Press.

Donald E. Nuechterlein, *Thailand and the Struggle for Southeast Asia,* Copyright © 1965 by Cornell University. Used by permission of Cornell University Press.

Alastair M. Taylor, *Indonesian Independence and the United Nations,* © Stevens & Sons Limited, London 1960. Used by permission of Cornell University Press.

Kenneth T. Young, "United States Policy and Vietnamese Political Viability, 1954–1967," *Asian Survey,* August 1967, p. 510. © 1967 by The Regents of the University of California. Reprinted from *Asian Survey, Volume VII, Number 8,* p. 510, by permission of The Regents.

Herbert A. Fine, "The Liquidation of World War II in Thailand," *Pacific Historical Review,* February 1965, p. 82. © 1965 by the Pacific Coast Branch, American Historical Association. Reprinted from *Pacific Historical Review, Volume XXXIV, Number 1,* p. 82, by permission of the Branch.

The Road to Pearl Harbor: The Coming of the War Between the United States and Japan, by Herbert Feis (copyright © 1950 by Princeton University Press, Princeton Paperback, 1971): a brief quote on p. 333.

The New York Times, Short quotes as submitted from: January 28, 1953, November 5, 1953, March 6, 1954, and October 29, 1954. © 1953-54 by The New York Times Company. Reprinted by permission.

Samuel P. Hayes (Editor), *The Beginning of American Aid to Southeast Asia: The Griffin Mission of 1950* (Lexington, Mass.: Lexington Books, D. C. Heath and Company, 1971), pp. 62, 131–32, 270. Reprinted by permission of the publisher.

The American Assembly (Frank H. Golay, ed.), *The United States and the Philippines*, Prentice-Hall, Inc., Englewood Cliffs, New Jersey, 1966. Copyright © 1966 by The American Assembly, Columbia University.

John Bastin and Harry J. Benda, *A History of Modern Southeast Asia: Colonialism, Nationalism, and Decolonization*, Prentice-Hall, Inc., Englewood Cliffs, New Jersey, 1968.

Brigadier General (Ret.) S.L.A. Marshall, "Big Guns Not Answer," in Wesley R. Fishel, ed., *Vietnam: Anatomy of a Conflict*, F. E. Peacock, Publishers, Inc., Itasca, Illinois, 1968. Copyright for the article by *The Washington Post*. Quotation reprinted by permission.

John Carter Vincent et al., *America's Future in the Pacific*, Rutgers University Press, New Brunswick, 1947. Copyright 1947 by The Trustees of Rutgers College in New Jersey.

Charles de Gaulle, *The Complete War Memoirs of Charles de Gaulle*, Simon & Schuster, Inc., New York, 1964. Copyright 1955 by Simon & Schuster, Inc. Reprinted by permission of the publisher.

Alec Peterson, "Britain and Siam: The Latest Phase," *Pacific Affairs*, December 1946. Copyright by *Pacific Affairs*, University of British Columbia.

Milton Sacks, "The Strategy of Communism in Southeast Asia," *Pacific Affairs*, September 1950. Copyright by *Pacific Affairs*, University of British Columbia.

Dean Acheson, *Present at the Creation: My Years in the State Department*, W. W. Norton & Company, Inc., New York, 1969. Copyright © 1969 by Dean Acheson.

Melvin Gurtov, *Southeast Asia Tomorrow: Problems and Prospects for U. S. Policy*, The Johns Hopkins University Press, Baltimore, 1970. Copyright © 1970 by The Rand Corporation.

Anthony Eden, *The Memoirs of Anthony Eden: Full Circle*, Houghton Mifflin Company, Boston, 1960.

Arthur M. Schlesinger, Jr., *A Thousand Days: John F. Kennedy in the White House*, Houghton Mifflin Company, Boston, 1965. Copyright © 1965 by Arthur M. Schlesinger, Jr. Reprinted with permission of Houghton Mifflin Company.

Carlos P. Romulo, *Crusade in Asia: Philippine Victory*, The John Day Company, Inc., New York, 1955.

Emmet John Hughes, *The Ordeal of Power: A Political Memoir of the Eisenhower Years*, Atheneum Publishers, New York, 1963. Copyright © 1962, 1963 by Emmet John Hughes, Atheneum Publishers, New York, p. 208.

Général d'Armée Paul Ély, *Mémoires: L'Indochine dans la tourmente*, Librairie Plon, Paris, 1964. Copyright 1964 by Librairie Plon.

Charles A. Fisher, "Southeast Asia" in W. Gordon East and O.H.K. Spate, eds., *The Changing Map of Asia: A Political Geography*, 4th ed., Methuen & Co. Ltd., London, 1961.

Donald Lancaster, *The Emancipation of French Indochina*. Oxford University Press for the Royal Institute of International Affairs, London, 1961.

Documents on International Affairs, 1954, Oxford University Press for the Royal Institute of International Affairs, London, 1957.

Sir Josiah Crosby, "Observations on a Post-War Settlement in South-East Asia," *International Affairs*, July 1944.

Jean Sainteny, *Histoire d'une paix manquée: Indochine, 1945–1947*, Librairie Arthème Fayard, Paris, 1967. Copyright 1967 by Librairie Arthème Fayard, Jean Sainteny, *Histoire d'une paix manquée: Indochine, 1945–1947*, p. 137.

Claire Lee Chennault, *Way of a Fighter: The Memoirs of Claire Lee Chennault* (edited by Robert Hotz), Putnam's, New York, 1949. Copyright © 1949 by Claire Lee Chennault. Reprinted by permission of G. P. Putnam's Sons from *Way of a Fighter* by Claire Lee Chennault.

General Albert C. Wedemeyer, *Wedemeyer Reports!*, The Devin-Adair Company, Old Greenwich, Connecticut, 1958. With the permission of General Albert C. Wedemeyer.

William Reitzel, Morton A. Kaplan, and Constance G. Coblenz, *United States Foreign Policy: 1945–1955*, The Brookings Institution, Washington, 1956. Copyright 1956 The Brookings Institution, Washington, D. C.

Lyndon Baines Johnson, *The Vantage Point: Perspectives of the Presidency, 1963–1969*, Holt, Rinehart and Winston, Inc., New York, 1971.

George McTurnan Kahin and John W. Lewis, *The United States in Vietnam*, The Dial Press, New York, 1967.

Richard P. Stebbins, *The United States in World Affairs, 1954*, Harper & Row Publishers, Inc., for the Council on Foreign Relations, New York, 1956.

Alternative in Southeast Asia, by Eugene R. Black, © 1969 by Praeger Publishers, Inc. Reprinted by permission of Praeger Publishers.

Why Viet Nam? by Frank N. Trager, © 1966 by Praeger Publishers, Inc. Reprinted by permission of Praeger Publishers.

Burma—From Kingdom to Republic: A Historical and Political Analysis, by Frank N. Trager, © 1966 by Praeger Publishers, Inc. Reprinted by permission of Praeger Publishers.

Melvin Gurtov, *The First Vietnam Crisis: Chinese Communist Strategy and United States Involvement, 1953–1954*, Columbia University Press, New York, 1967. Copyright © 1967 by Columbia University Press.

Cordell Hull, *The Memoirs of Cordell Hull*, Vol. II, The Macmillan Company, New York, 1948. Copyright 1948 by Cordell Hull.

John M. Allison, "United States Diplomacy in Southeast Asia: The Limits of Policy," in William Henderson, ed., *Southeast Asia: Problems of United States Policy*, The M.I.T. Press, Cambridge, 1963. Copyright 1963 by The

Massachusetts Institute of Technology.

Chester L. Cooper, *The Lost Crusade: America in Vietnam*, Dodd, Mead & Company, Inc., New York, 1970. Copyright © 1970 by Chester L. Cooper. Reprinted by permission of Dodd, Mead & Company, Inc.

"Outlook Now For War In Vietnam," *U. S. News & World Report*, November 21, 1966, p. 67. Quotation from a copyrighted article in *U. S. News & World Report*, November 21, 1966.

"Westmoreland Reports On Vietnam War," *U. S. News & World Report*, November 28, 1966, p. 49. Quotation from a copyrighted article in *U. S. News & World Report*, November 28, 1966.

"The Real Road To Peace," *U. S. News & World Report*, June 26, 1972, p. 36. Quotation from a copyrighted article in *U. S. News & World Report*, June 26, 1972.

Clark M. Clifford, "A Viet Nam Reappraisal: The Personal History of One Man's View and How It Evolved," *Foreign Affairs*, July 1969.

Adam Malik, "Promise in Indonesia," *Foreign Affairs*, January 1968.

Mohammad Hatta, "Indonesia's Foreign Policy," *Foreign Affairs*, April 1953.

Arthur Schlesinger, Jr., "Origins of the Cold War," *Foreign Affairs*, October 1967.

John . K. Fairbank, "China's Foreign Policy in Historical Perspective," *Foreign Affairs*, April 1969.

Richard M. Nixon, "Asia after Viet Nam," *Foreign Affairs*, October 1967.

Maxwell D. Taylor, *Responsibility and Response*, Harper & Row Publishers, Inc., New York, 1967.

Robert Shaplen, *The Lost Revolution: The U. S. in Vietnam, 1946–1966*, rev. ed., Harper & Row Publishers, Inc., New York, 1966.

Louis J. Halle, *The Cold War As History*, Harper & Row Publishers, Inc., New York, 1967.

Edward Geary Lansdale, *In the Midst of Wars: An American's Mission to Southeast Asia*, Harper & Row Publishers, Inc., New York, 1972.

Edwin F. Stanton, *Brief Authority: Excursions of a Common Man in an Uncommon World*, Harper & Brothers, Publishers, New York, 1956.

Sherman Adams, *Firsthand Report: The Story of the Eisenhower Administration*, Harper & Brothers, Publishers, New York, 1961.

Senator John F. Kennedy, *The Strategy of Peace*, Harper & Brothers, Publishers, New York, 1960.

General Matthew B. Ridgway, *Soldier: The Memoirs of Matthew B. Ridgway*, Harper & Brothers, Publishers, New York, 1956.

Elliott Roosevelt, *As He Saw It*, Duell, Sloan, and Pearce, New York, 1946. Reprinted by permission of Hawthorn Books, Inc.

U.S. Policy and the Security of Asia, by Fred Greene, Copyright © 1968 by the Council on Foreign Relations, Inc. Used with permission of McGraw-Hill Book Company.

Dwight D. Eisenhower, *The White House Years: Mandate for Change, 1953–1956*, Doubleday, Garden City, New York, 1963. Copyright © 1963

BIBLIOGRAPHY

Publications on American policy in Southeast Asia for the administrations of Presidents Roosevelt, Truman, and Eisenhower represent a contrast from the output for the Kennedy, Johnson, and Nixon administrations. In the first category there was a relative paucity of publications, both official and unofficial, but in the second there was a genuine plethora of them. Consequently, the discriminating student is faced with two different problems in locating and selecting bibliography. Furthermore, the publications on U.S. policy in Southeast Asia for most of the 1960s and into the early 1970s have become widely polarized between the "I accuse" and the "I defend" schools of thought. Official publications support American policy but many unofficial ones censure it. One of the consequences is that objective research in the field of the international relations of Southeast Asia has been outdistanced by that on the governments and politics or political systems of the region. The Second Indochinese War provoked from the very beginning a strong revisionist school in bibliography and sired a controversy which only another generation may be able to resolve.

The Pentagon Papers have brought to the forefront the question of restrictions on archival material. Secretary of State Dean Rusk in 1966 pointedly observed:

> We in Government share with the media of information the broadest common interest in informing the public. . . . It is also true that there is an inevitable tension between officials and reporters about that tiny fraction of our business—some 1 or 2 percent—which is or ought to be secret, at least temporarily. . . . Actually, secrets are not secret for very long—at least in the United States. And I can

tell you quite honestly that I do not know of any secrets which could have a significant effect upon the judgments which citizens or commentators are able to make upon matters of policy or public interest.[1]

Nevertheless, archival material, as the Pentagon Papers reveal, provides deeper dimensions to the study of U.S. policy in Southeast Asia. Obstacles to the timely and full availability of the material are well expressed by Herbert Feis, "Speaking of Books: Unpublic Public Papers," *New York Times Book Review*, April 21, 1968, pp. 2, 58, and William M. Franklin, "The Future of the 'Foreign Relations' Series," *Department of State Bulletin*, September 15, 1969, pp. 247–51. Published after the Supreme Court decision on the Pentagon Papers is Carol M. Barker and Matthew H. Fox, *Classified Files: The Yellowing Pages: A Report on Scholars' Access to Government Documents,* Twentieth Century Fund, New York, 1972.

Considerable stress has been placed in this study on public documents. It was very important to know who said what, at what time, and under what circumstances. Too often authors depend upon the testimony of other writers without checking and rechecking the original statements. I have read over a period of more than five years in connection with this work almost every statement coming from a high-ranking official of the U.S. government or prominent member of Congress on American policy in Southeast Asia since 1945. At the same time I have systematically tried to read the writings of the best authors outside government circles, authors both pro and con U.S. policy.

Special attention should be called to a number of bibliographies. My previous work is found in *The Diplomacy of Southeast Asia: 1945–1958*, Harper and Brothers, New York, 1958, pp. 520–66, and *Southeast Asia in United States Policy,* Praeger for the Council on Foreign Relations, New York, 1963, pp. 441–72. Mention should be made of the excellent bibliographical essays in Robert O. Tilman, ed., *Man, State, and Society in Contemporary Southeast Asia,* Praeger, New York, 1969, pp. 599–617, and David Joel Steinberg *et al., In Search of Southeast Asia: A Modern History*, Praeger, New York, 1971, pp. 439–98. The carefully organized and very inclusive annual bibliography associated with the *Journal of Asian Studies* (formerly the *Far Eastern Quarterly*) is a key listing of publications primary and secondary, both books and articles. Noteworthy are the bibliographies of the Southeast Asia Studies Program of Yale University and the *Behavior Sciences Bibliographies* of the Human Relations Area Files, Inc., dealing with various Southeast Asian countries.

1. *Department of State Bulletin*, April 4, 1966, pp. 514–15.

The American Universities Field Staff issued *A Select Bibliography: Asia, Africa, Eastern Europe, Latin America* (Vance Weaver Composition, Inc., New York, 1960) and several supplements have followed it. Cecil Hobbs of the Orientalia Division of the Library of Congress compiled *Southeast Asia: An Annotated Bibliography of Selected Reference Sources in Western Languages,* rev. and enl. (Government Printing Office, Distributor, Washington, 1964). Another valuable bibliography is K. G. Tregonning, *Southeast Asia: A Critical Bibliography* (Arizona, Tucson, 1968). Henry L. Roberts edited *Foreign Affairs Bibliography, 1942–1952* (Harper for the Council on Foreign Relations, New York, 1955) and *Foreign Affairs Bibliography, 1952–1962* (Bowker for the Council on Foreign Relations, New York, 1964). Byron Dexter is the editor of *The Foreign Affairs 50-Year Bibliography: New Evaluations of Significant Books on International Relations, 1920–1970* (Bowker for the Council on Foreign Relations, New York, 1972).

The quarterly issues of the influential journal *Foreign Affairs* have a current selected listing of books on Southeast Asia with brief annotations. *International Affairs,* published quarterly under the auspices of the Royal Institute of International Affairs in London, has extensive book reviews that include the area. Some issues of *Intercom* under the auspices of the Foreign Policy Association focused on South and Southeast Asia (November-December 1963 and January-February 1967) with careful bibliographical references. *International Organization,* a quarterly journal, offers a bibliography which includes some references to Southeast Asia in various organizations.

The proliferation of books focusing on Vietnam in the 1960s and early 1970s has led to a number of bibliographies. I have selected three of particular value bearing on the subject which have appeared in three different periods of time. They are John F. Embree and Lillian Ota Dotson, *Bibliography of the Peoples and Cultures of Mainland Southeast Asia* (Southeast Asia Studies, Yale, New Haven, 1950); Vietnam Project, Michigan State University, *What to Read on Vietnam: A Selected Annotated Bibliography,* 2nd ed. (Institute of Pacific Relations, New York, 1960); and Engineer Agency for Resources Inventories, *Vietnam Subject Index Catalog* (Research Files of the Engineer Agency for Resources Inventories and Vietnam Research and Evaluation Information Center, Bureau for Vietnam, Agency for International Development, January 1970).

In my research I have particularly utilized the *Congressional Record,* the *Department of State Bulletin, Official Records* of the United Nations, and *The New York Times.*

SELECTED PUBLIC DOCUMENTS

U.S. Executive

Department of Defense. *United States–Vietnam Relations, 1945–1967.* 12 Books. Washington: Government Printing Office, 1971.

Department of State. *Papers Relating to the Foreign Relations of the United States, Japan: 1931–1941.* Vol. II. Washington: Government Printing Office, 1943.

————. *Foreign Relations of the United States, 1940,* Vol. IV, *The Far East.* Washington: Government Printing Office, 1955.

————. *Foreign Relations of the United States, 1943, China.* Washington: Government Printing Office, 1957.

————. *Foreign Relations of the United States, 1944,* Vol. III, *The British Commonwealth and Europe.* Washington: Government Printing Office, 1965.

————. *Foreign Relations of the United States, 1944,* Vol. V, *The Near East, South Asia, and Africa; The Far East.* Washington: Government Printing Office, 1965.

————. *Foreign Relations of the United States, 1945,* Vol. I, *General: The United Nations.* Washington: Government Printing Office, 1967.

————. *Foreign Relations of the United States, 1945,* Vol. VI, *The British Commonwealth; The Far East.* Washington: Government Printing Office, 1969.

————. *Foreign Relations of the United States, 1945,* Vol. VII, *The Far East: China.* Washington: Government Printing Office, 1969.

————. *Foreign Relations of the United States, 1946,* Vol. VIII, *The Far East.* Washington: Government Printing Office, 1971.

————. *Foreign Relations of the United States, 1947,* Vol. VI, *The Far East.* Washington: Government Printing Office, 1972.

————. *Foreign Relations of the United States: The Conferences at Washington and Quebec, 1943.* Washington: Government Printing Office, 1970.

————. *Foreign Relations of the United States: The Conferences at Cairo and Tehran, 1943.* Washington: Government Printing Office, 1961.

————. *Foreign Relations of the United States: The Conferences at Malta and Yalta, 1945.* Washington: Government Printing Office, 1955.

————. *Foreign Relations of the United States: The Conference of Berlin (The Potsdam Conference), 1945.* 2 Vols. Washington: Government Printing Office, 1960.

————. *United States Relations with China, with Special Reference to the Period 1944–1949.* Washington: Government Printing Office, 1949.

————. *American Foreign Policy, 1950–1955: Basic Documents.* 2 Vols. Washington: Government Printing Office, 1957.

―――. *American Foreign Policy: Current Documents, 1956.* Washington: Government Printing Office, 1959.

―――. *American Foreign Policy: Current Documents, 1958.* Washington: Government Printing Office, 1962.

―――. *American Foreign Policy: Current Documents, 1959.* Washington: Government Printing Office, 1963.

―――. *American Foreign Policy: Current Documents, 1960.* Washington: Government Printing Office, 1964.

―――. *American Foreign Policy: Current Documents, 1961.* Washington: Government Printing Office, 1965.

―――. *American Foreign Policy: Current Documents, 1962.* Washington: Government Printing Office, 1966.

―――. *American Foreign Policy: Current Documents, 1963.* Washington: Government Printing Office, 1967.

―――. *American Foreign Policy: Current Documents, 1964.* Washington: Government Printing Office, 1967.

―――. *American Foreign Policy: Current Documents, 1965.* Washington: Government Printing Office, 1968.

―――. *American Foreign Policy: Current Documents, 1967.* Washington: Government Printing Office, 1969.

―――. *United States Foreign Policy, 1969–1970: A Report of the Secretary of State.* Washington: Government Printing Office, 1971.

―――. *United States Foreign Policy, 1971: A Report of the Secretary of State.* Washington: Government Printing Office, 1972.

―――. *A Threat to the Peace: North Viet-Nam's Effort to Conquer South Viet-Nam.* 2 Parts. Department of State Publication 7308, Released December 1961. Washington: Government Printing Office, 1961.

―――. *Aggression from the North: The Record of North Viet-Nam's Campaign to Conquer South Viet-Nam.* Department of State Publication 7839, Released February 1965. Washington: Government Printing Office, 1965.

―――. Bundy, William P. "The Path to Viet-Nam: A Lesson in Involvement." Department of State Publication 8295, Released September 1967. Washington: Government Printing Office, 1967. This article is the substance of an address on August 15, 1967.

―――. Meeker, Leonard C. "The Legality of United States Participation in the Defense of Viet-Nam," *Department of State Bulletin*, March 28, 1966, pp. 479–89.

―――. "Scope of the U.S. Involvement in Laos," Statement by President Nixon, March 6, 1970, *Department of State Bulletin*, March 30, 1970, pp. 405-9.

―――. "A Report on the Conclusion of the Cambodian Operation," Statement by President Nixon, June 30, 1970, *Department of State Bulletin*, July 20, 1970, pp. 65-75.

Public Papers of the Presidents of the United States, Dwight D. Eisenhower, 1954. Washington: Government Printing Office, 1960.

Public Papers of the Presidents of the United States, John F. Kennedy, 1961. Washington: Government Printing Office, 1962.

Public Papers of the Presidents of the United States, John F. Kennedy, 1962. Washington: Government Printing Office, 1963.

Public Papers of the Presidents of the United States, John F. Kennedy, 1963. Washington: Government Printing Office, 1964.

Public Papers of the Presidents of the United States, Lyndon B. Johnson, 1963–64. Book II. Washington: Government Printing Office, 1965.

Public Papers of the Presidents of the United States, Lyndon B. Johnson, 1965. Book II. Washington: Government Printing Office, 1966.

Public Papers of the Presidents of the United States, Lyndon B. Johnson, 1966. Book I. Washington: Government Printing Office, 1967.

Public Papers of the Presidents of the United States, Lyndon B. Johnson, 1967. Book II. Washington: Government Printing Office, 1968.

U.S. Foreign Policy for the 1970's: A New Strategy for Peace, A Report to the Congress by Richard Nixon, President of the United States, February 18, 1970. Washington: Government Printing Office, 1970.

U.S. Foreign Policy for the 1970's: Building for Peace, A Report to the Congress by Richard Nixon, President of the United States, February 25, 1971. Washington: Government Printing Office, 1971.

U.S. Foreign Policy for the 1970's: The Emerging Structure of Peace, A Report to the Congress by Richard Nixon, President of the United States, February 9, 1972. Washington: Government Printing Office, 1972.

Sharp, Admiral U. S. G. and General W. C. Westmoreland. *Report on the War in Vietnam (As of 30 June 1968).* Washington: Government Printing Office, Released 1969.

To Tame a River. Washington: Government Printing Office, 1968.

U.S. Congress

U.S. Congress. Senate. Committee on Armed Services and Committee on Foreign Relations. Hearings, 82nd Congress, 1st Session, June 1951. *Military Situation in the Far East.* Washington: Government Printing Office, 1951.

———. Committee on Foreign Relations. Hearings, 82nd Congress, 1st Session, 1951. *Nomination of Philip C. Jessup to Be United States Representative to the Sixth General Assembly of the United Nations.* Washington: Government Printing Office, 1951.

———. Hearings, 83rd Congress, 2nd Session, November 11, 1954. *The Southeast Asia Collective Defense Treaty.* Washington: Government Printing Office, 1954.

————. Hearings, 88th Congress, 2nd Session, August 6, 1964. *The Southeast Asia Resolution.* Washington: Government Printing Office, 1966.

————. Hearings, 89th Congress, 2nd Session, January—February, 1966. *Supplemental Foreign Assistance Fiscal Year 1966—Vietnam.* Washington: Government Printing Office, 1966.

————. 89th Congress, 2nd Session, 1966. *Background Information Relating to Southeast Asia and Vietnam.* 2nd rev. ed. Washington: Government Printing Office, 1966.

————. Hearings, 90th Congress, 2nd Session, February 20, 1968. *The Gulf of Tonkin, The 1964 Incidents.* Washington: Government Printing Office, 1968.

————. 90th Congress, 2nd Session, 1968. *The Gulf of Tonkin, The 1964 Incidents.* Part II, Supplemetary Documents. Washington: Government Printing Office, 1968.

————. 90th Congress, 2nd Session, 1968. *Background Information Relating to Southeast Asia and Vietnam.* 4th rev. ed. Washington: Government Printing Office, 1968.

————. Subcommittee on United States Security Agreements and Commitments Abroad. Hearings, 91st Congress, 1st Session, September 30–October 3, 1969. Part 1. *United States Security Agreements and Commitments Abroad: The Republic of the Philippines.* Washington: Government Printing Office, 1969.

————. Hearings, 91st Congress, 1st Session, October 20-22, 28, 1969. Part 2. *United States Security Agreements and Commitments Abroad: Kingdom of Laos.* Washington: Government Printing Office, 1970.

————. Hearings, 91st Congress, 1st Session, November 10-14, 17, 1969. Part 3. *United States Security Agreements and Commitments Abroad: Kingdom of Thailand.* Washington: Government Printing Office, 1970.

————. Committee on Armed Services. Preparedness Investigating Subcommittee. Hearings, 90th Congress, 1st Session, August 25, 1967 (Testimony of Secretary of Defense Robert S. McNamara). *Air War against North Vietnam.* Washington: Government Printing Office, 1967.

U.S. Senate. 81st Congress, 1st Session, 1950. *A Decade of American Foreign Policy: Basic Documents, 1941-49.* Washington: Government Printing Office, 1950.

————. 88th Congress, 2nd Session, 1964. *Representative Speeches of General of the Army Douglas MacArthur.* Washington: Government Printing Office, 1964.

The United States and Vietnam: 1944–1947. A Staff Study Based on the Pentagon Papers, April 3, 1972, Committee Print, Senate Committee on Foreign Relations, 92nd Congress, 2nd Session, 1972. Washington: Government Printing Office, 1972. Includes in the appendices a series of letters

1946 by Abbot Low Moffat written when he was in Indochina in December

by Abbot Low Moffat written when he was in Indochina in December 1946.

Report of the Special Study Mission to Pakistan, India, Thailand, and Indo-china, Pursuant to H. Res. 113, 83rd Congress, 1st Session, 1953. Washington: Government Printing Office, 1953.

Indochina. Report of Senator Mike Mansfield on a Study Mission to the Associated States of Indochina, Vietnam, Cambodia, Laos, October 27, 1953, Committee Print, Senate Committee on Foreign Relations, 83rd Congress, 1st Session, 1953. Washington: Government Printing Office, 1953.

Report on Indochina, Report of Senator Mike Mansfield on a Study Mission to Vietnam, Cambodia, Laos, October 15, 1954, Committee Print, Senate Committee on Foreign Relations, 83rd Congress, 2nd Session, 1954. Washington: Government Printing Office, 1954.

Viet Nam, Cambodia, and Laos. Report by Senator Mike Mansfield, October 6, 1955, Committee Print, Senate Committee on Foreign Relations, 84th Congress, 1st Session, 1955. Washington: Government Printing Office, 1955.

Viet Nam and Southeast Asia. Report of Senator Mike Mansfield, Senator J. Caleb Boggs, Senator Claiborne Pell, Senator Benjamin A. Smith to the Committee on Foreign Relations, Committee Print, Senate Committee on Foreign Relations, 88th Congress, 1st Session, 1963. Washington: Government Printing Office, 1963.

The Vietnam Conflict: The Substance and the Shadow. Report of Senator Mike Mansfield, Senator Edmund S. Muskie, Senator Daniel K. Inouye, Senator George D. Aiken, Senator J. Caleb Boggs to the Committee on Foreign Relations, Committee Print, Senate Committee on Foreign Relations, 89th Congress, 2nd Session, 1966. Washington: Government Printing Office, 1966.

The Rim of Asia. Report of Senator Mike Mansfield to the Committee on Foreign Relations, Committee Print, Senate Committee on Foreign Relations, 90th Congress, 1st Session, 1967. Washington: Government Printing Office, 1967.

National Security Study Memorandum No. 1, *Congressional Record*, House of Representatives, May 10 and 11, 1972, pp. E 4976–E 5005 and E 5009–5066.

Others

Vice-Admiral The Earl Mountbatten of Burma. *Report to the Combined Chiefs of Staff by the Supreme Allied Commander, South-East Asia, 1943–1945.* London: His Majesty's Stationery Office, 1951.

————. *Post Surrender Tasks, Section E of the Report to the Combined Chiefs of Staff by the Supreme Allied Commander, South-East Asia, 1943–1945.* London: Her Majesty's Stationery Office, 1969.

Documents Relating to British Involvement in the Indo-China Conflict, 1945–1965. Cmnd. 2834. London: Her Majesty's Stationery Office, 1965.

Documents Relating to the Discussion of Korea and Indo-China at the Geneva Conference, 27 April–15 June, 1954. Cmd. 9186. London: Her Majesty's Stationery Office, 1954.

Further Documents Relating to the Discussion of Indo-China at the Geneva Conference, 16 June–21 July, 1954. Cmd. 9239. London: Her Majesty's Stationery Office, 1954.

British and Foreign State Papers, 1946. Vol. 146. London: Her Majesty's Stationery Office, 1953.

British and Foreign State Papers, 1947. Vol. 147, Part 1. London: Her Majesty's Stationery Office, 1955.

Parliamentary Debates (Hansard), 5th Series, Vol. 532, *House of Commons Official Report,* November 1-12, 1954.

Journal Officiel de la République Française, Débats parlementaires, Assemblée Nationale, juillet 1954.

Kuomintang Aggression against Burma. Rangoon: Ministry of Information, 1953.

The Signing of the Southeast Asia Collective Defense Treaty, the Protocol to the Southeast Asia Collective Defense Treaty and the Pacific Charter: Proceedings. Manila: Conference Secretariat, September 8, 1954.

Yearbook of the United Nations, 1950. New York: Columbia, 1951.

United Nations, General Assembly, Sixth Session, *Official Records,* First Committee, 503rd Meeting, January 28, 1952.

United Nations, Security Council, *Official Records,* Nineteenth Year, 1119th Meeting, May 21, 1964.

The ASEAN Declaration, *Current Notes on International Affairs,* August 1967, pp. 327–28.

SELECTED BOOKS AND ARTICLES

Acheson, Dean. *Present at the Creation: My Years in the State Department.* New York: Norton, 1969.

Adams, Sherman. *Firsthand Report: The Story of the Eisenhower Administration.* New York: Harper, 1961.

Allison, John M. "Japan's Relations with Southeast Asia," *Asia,* Winter 1969/70, pp. 34–59.

Asian Development Bank. *Southeast Asia's Economy in the 1970's.* New York: Praeger, 1971.

Asian Relations, Being Report of the Proceedings and Documentation of the First Asian Relations Conference, New Delhi, March-April, 1947. New Delhi: Asian Relations Organization, 1948.

Austin, Anthony. *The President's War: The Story of the Tonkin Gulf Resolution and How the Nation Was Trapped in Vietnam.* Philadelphia: Lippincott, 1971.

Ball, George W. "We Should De-escalate the Importance of Vietnam," *The New York Times Magazine,* December 21, 1969, pp. 6 ff.

Ba Maw, U. *Breakthrough in Burma: Memoirs of a Revolution, 1939–1946.* New Haven: Yale, 1968.

Barnett, A. Doak. *Communist China and Asia: Challenge to American Policy.* New York: Harper for the Council on Foreign Relations, 1960.

Bastin, John and Harry J. Benda. *A History of Modern Southeast Asia: Colonialism, Nationalism, and Decolonization.* Englewood Cliffs: Prentice-Hall, 1968.

Bator, Victor. *Vietnam, A Diplomatic Tragedy: The Origins of the United States Involvement.* Dobbs Ferry, N.Y.: Oceana, 1965.

Beal, John Robinson. *John Foster Dulles: A Biography.* New York: Harper, 1957.

Beisner, Robert L. *Twelve against Empire: The Anti-Imperialists, 1898–1900.* New York: McGraw-Hill, 1968.

Benda, Harry J. *The Crescent and the Rising Sun: Indonesian Islam under the Japanese Occupation, 1942–1945.* The Hague: van Hoeve, 1958.

Black, Eugene R. *Alternative in Southeast Asia.* New York: Praeger, 1969.

Bloodworth, Dennis. *An Eye for the Dragon: Southeast Asia Observed, 1954–1970.* New York: Farrar, Straus and Giroux, 1970.

Bodard, Lucien. *The Quicksand War: Prelude to Vietnam.* Boston: Little, Brown, 1967.

Brackman, Arnold C. *The Communist Collapse in Indonesia.* New York: Norton, 1969.

Brandon, Henry. *Anatomy of Error: The Inside Story of the Asian War on the Potomac, 1954–1969.* Boston: Gambit, 1969.

Brecher, Michael. "International Relations and Asian Studies: The Subordinate State System of Southern Asia," *World Politics,* January 1963, pp. 213–35.

Brzezinski, Zbigniew. "The Implications of Change for United States Foreign Policy," *Department of State Bulletin,* July 3, 1967, pp. 19–23.

Bull, Hedley. "The New Balance of Power in Asia and the Pacific," *Foreign Affairs,* July 1971, pp. 669–81.

Bullitt, William C. "The Saddest War," *Life,* December 29, 1947, pp. 64–69.

Bundy, William P. "New Tides in Southeast Asia," *Foreign Affairs,* January 1971, pp. 187–200.

Buttinger, Joseph. *Vietnam: A Political History.* New York: Praeger, 1968.

Butwell, Richard. *U Nu of Burma*, rev. ed. Stanford: Stanford, 1969.

Cameron, Allan W., ed. *Viet-Nam Crisis: A Documentary History*, Vol. I, *1940–1956*. Ithaca: Cornell, 1971.

Carver, George A., Jr. "The Faceless Viet Cong," *Foreign Affairs*, April 1966, pp. 347–72.

Chen, King C. *Vietnam and China, 1938–1954*. Princeton: Princeton, 1969.

Chennault, Claire Lee. *Way of a Fighter: The Memoirs of Claire Lee Chennault*, ed. Robert Hotz. New York: Putnam's, 1949.

Churchill, Winston. "Defense in the Pacific," *Collier's*, December 17, 1932, pp. 12–13, 30.

Clifford, Clark M. "A Viet Nam Reappraisal: The Personal History of One Man's View and How It Evolved," *Foreign Affairs*, July 1969, pp. 601–22.

———. "Set a Date in Vietnam. Stick to It. Get Out," *Life*, May 22, 1970, pp. 34–38.

Cole, Allen B., ed. *Conflict in Indo-China and International Repercussions: A Documentary History, 1945–1955*. Ithaca: Cornell, 1956.

Collective Defence in South East Asia. London: Oxford for the Royal Institute of International Affairs, 1956.

Cooper, Bert *et al. Case Studies in Insurgency and Revolutionary Warfare: Vietnam, 1941–1954*. Washington: Special Operations Research Office (American University), 1964.

Cooper, Chester L. *The Lost Crusade: America in Vietnam*. New York: Dodd, Mead, 1970.

Crosby, Sir Josiah. "Observations on a Post-War Settlement in South-East Asia," *International Affairs*, July 1944, pp. 357–68.

Curry, Roy Watson. "Woodrow Wilson and Philippine Policy," *The Mississippi Valley Historical Review*, December 1954, pp. 435–52.

Darling, Frank C. *Thailand and the United States*. Washington: Public Affairs Press, 1965.

Decoux, Jean. *A la barre de l'Indochine: histoire du mon gouvernement général, 1940–1945*. Paris: Plon, 1949.

De Gaulle, Charles. *The Complete War Memoirs of Charles de Gaulle*. New York: Simon and Schuster, 1964.

Dennett, Tyler. *Americans in Eastern Asia: A Critical Study of the Policy of the United States with Reference to China, Japan and Korea in the 19th Century*. New York: Macmillan, 1922.

Denoon, David B. H. "Indonesia: Transition to Stability?" *Current History*, December 1971, pp. 332–38, 367–68.

Devillers, Philippe. *Histoire du Viêt-Nam de 1940 à 1952*. Paris: Editions du Seuil, 1952.

―――― and Jean Lacouture. *End of a War: Indochina, 1954.* New York: Praeger, 1969.

Direk, Chayanam. *Thai kap Songkhram Lok Khrang Thi Song.* 2 Vols. Bangkok: Prae Pittaya, 1966.

Documents on International Affairs, 1954. London: Oxford for the Royal Institute of International Affairs, 1957.

Dommen, Arthur J. *Conflict in Laos: The Politics of Neutralization.* rev. ed. New York: Praeger, 1971.

Donovan, Major General William J. "Our Stake in Thailand," *Fortune,* July 1955, pp. 94–95.

Drachman, Edward R. *United States Policy toward Vietnam, 1940–1945.* Rutherford: Fairleigh Dickinson, 1970.

Draper, Theodore. *Abuse of Power.* New York: Viking, 1967.

Dulles, John Foster. *War or Peace.* New York: Macmillan, 1950.

Duncanson, Dennis J. *Government and Revolution in Vietnam.* New York: Oxford for the Royal Institute of International Affairs, 1968.

Dunn, Frederick S. *Peace-Making and the Settlement with Japan.* Princeton: Princeton, 1963.

East, W. Gordon and O. H. K. Spate, eds. *The Changing Map of Asia: A Political Geography.* 4th ed. London: Methuen, 1961.

Eden, Anthony. *The Memoirs of Anthony Eden: Full Circle.* Boston: Houghton Mifflin, 1960.

―――― *Toward Peace in Indochina.* Boston: Houghton Mifflin, 1966.

Eisenhower, Dwight D. *The White House Years: Mandate for Change, 1953–1956.* Garden City: Doubleday, 1963.

Ellsberg, Daniel. *Papers on the War.* New York: Simon and Schuster, 1972. See especially "The Quagmire Myth and the Stalemate Machine," pp. 42–135.

Ely, Général d'Armée Paul. *Mémoires: L'Indochine dans la tourmente.* Paris: Plon, 1964.

Emerson, Rupert. *From Empire to Nation: The Rise to Self-Assertion of Asian and African Peoples.* Cambridge: Harvard, 1962.

――――. "Post-Independence Nationalism in South and Southeast Asia: A Reconsideration," *Pacific Affairs,* Summer 1971, pp. 173–92.

Fairbank, John K. "China's Foreign Policy in Historical Perspective," *Foreign Affairs,* April 1969, pp. 449–63.

Falk, Richard A., ed. *The Vietnam War and International Law.* American Society of International Law. 2 Vols. Princeton: Princeton, 1968 and 1969.

Fall, Bernard B. *Hell in a Very Small Place: The Siege of Dien Bien Phu.* Philadelphia: Lippincott, 1966.

————. *Street without Joy: Indochina at War, 1946–54.* Harrisburg: Stack-pole, 1961.

————. *The Two Viet-Nams: A Political and Military Analysis.* 2nd rev. ed. New York: Praeger, 1967.

————. "U. S. Policies in Indochina 1940–1960," *Last Reflections on a War.* Garden City: Doubleday, 1967.

————, ed. *Ho Chi Minh on Revolution: Selected Writings, 1920–66.* New York: Praeger, 1967.

Feis, Herbert. *The Road to Pearl Harbor: The Coming of the War between the United States and Japan.* Princeton: Princeton, 1950.

————. *The China Tangle: The American Effort in China from Pearl Harbor to the Marshall Mission.* Princeton: Princeton, 1953.

Fifield, Russell H. "The Challenge to Magsaysay," *Foreign Affairs,* October 1954, pp. 149–54.

————. *The Diplomacy of Southeast Asia: 1945–1958.* New York: Harper, 1958.

————. "The Hukbalahap Today," *Far Eastern Survey,* January 24, 1951, pp. 13–18.

————. *Southeast Asia in United States Policy.* New York: Praeger for the Council on Foreign Relations, 1963.

Fine, Herbert A. "The Liquidation of World War II in Thailand," *Pacific Historical Review,* February 1965, pp. 65–82.

Fischer, Georges. *Un Cas de décolonisation: Les Etats-Unis et les Philippines.* Paris: Pichon et Durand-Anzias, 1960.

Fishel, Wesley R., ed. *Vietnam: Anatomy of a Conflict.* Itasca: Peacock, 1968.

Fitzgerald, Charles Patrick. *The Third China: The Chinese Communities in South-East Asia.* Melbourne: Cheshire, 1965.

FitzGerald, Frances. *Fire in the Lake: The Vietnamese and the Americans in Vietnam.* Boston: Atlantic–Little, Brown, 1972.

Fosdick, Raymond B. "Asia's Challenge to Us—Ideas, Not Guns," *The New York Times Magazine,* February 12, 1950, pp. 7 ff.

Frankel, Max. "The Lessons of Vietnam: Pentagon's Study Uniquely Portrays the 'Greek Tragedy' of the U.S. Role," *The New York Times,* July 6, 1971, pp. 1, 14.

Friend, Theodore. *Between Two Empires: The Ordeal of the Philippines, 1929–1946.* New Haven: Yale, 1965.

Gelb, Leslie H. "The Essential Domino: American Politics and Vietnam," *Foreign Affairs,* April 1972, pp. 459–75.

General Marshall's Report: The Winning of the War in Europe and the Pacific. New York: Simon and Schuster, 1945.

Gerbrandy, P. S. *Indonesia.* London: Hutchinson, 1950.

Geyelin, Philip. *Lyndon B. Johnson and the World.* New York: Praeger, 1966.

Giap, Vo Nguyen. *People's War, People's Army.* New York: Praeger, 1962.

Golay, Frank H., ed. *The United States and the Philippines.* Englewood Cliffs: Prentice-Hall for The American Assembly, 1966.

Gordon, Bernard K. *The Dimensions of Conflict in Southeast Asia.* Englewood Cliffs: Prentice-Hall, 1966.

————. *Toward Disengagement in Asia: A Strategy for American Foreign Policy.* Englewood Cliffs: Prentice-Hall, 1969.

Gould, James W. *The United States and Malaysia.* Cambridge: Harvard, 1969.

Goulden, Joseph C. *Truth Is the First Casualty: The Gulf of Tonkin Affair —Illusion and Reality.* Chicago: Rand McNally, 1969.

Goulding, Phil G. *Confirm or Deny: Informing the People on National Security.* New York: Harper and Row, 1970.

Greene, Fred. *U. S. Policy and the Security of Asia.* New York: McGraw-Hill for the Council on Foreign Relations, 1968.

Griffith, Robert. *The Politics of Fear: Joseph R. McCarthy and the Senate.* Lexington: Kentucky, 1970.

Guhin, Michael A. *John Foster Dulles: A Statesman and His Times.* New York: Columbia, 1972.

Gurtov, Melvin. *The First Vietnam Crisis: Chinese Communist Strategy and United States Involvement, 1953–1954.* New York: Columbia, 1967.

————. *Southeast Asia Tomorrow: Problems and Prospects for U. S. Policy.* Baltimore: Johns Hopkins, 1970.

Halberstam, David. *The Best and the Brightest.* New York: Random House, 1972.

Halle, Louis J. *The Cold War As History.* New York: Harper and Row, 1967.

Hammer, Ellen J. *The Struggle for Indochina.* Stanford: Stanford, 1954.

Harriman, W. Averell. *Our Wartime Relations with the Soviet Union Particularly As They Concern the Agreements Reached at Yalta* (Statement submitted to a Joint Senate Committee, August 17, 1951), privately printed.

————. "What We Are Doing in Southeast Asia," *The New York Times Magazine,* May 27, 1962, pp. 7 ff.

Hatta, Mohammad. "Indonesia's Foreign Policy," *Foreign Affairs,* April 1953, pp. 441–52.

Haviland, H. Field, Jr. *et al. Vietnam after the War: Peacekeeping and Rehabilitation.* Washington: Brookings, 1968.

Hayden, Joseph Ralston. *The Philippines: A Study in National Development.* New York: Macmillan, 1942.

————. "The United States and the Philippines: A Survey of Some Political Aspects of Twenty-five Years of American Sovereignty," *The Annals of the American Academy of Political and Social Science,* November 1925, pp. 26–48.

Hayes, Samuel P., ed. *The Beginning of American Aid to Southeast Asia: The Griffin Mission of 1950.* Lexington, Mass.: Lexington Books, Heath, 1971.

Henderson, William, ed. *Southeast Asia: Problems of United States Policy.* Cambridge: M.I.T., 1963.

Henry, John B., II. "February, 1968," *Foreign Policy,* Fall 1971, pp. 3–33.

Hilsman, Roger. *To Move a Nation: The Politics of Foreign Policy in the Administration of John F. Kennedy.* Garden City: Doubleday, 1967.

Hohenberg, John. *Between Two Worlds: Policy, Press, and Public Opinion in Asian-American Relations.* New York: Praeger for the Council on Foreign Relations, 1967.

Hoopes, Townsend. *The Limits of Intervention (an inside account of how the Johnson policy of escalation in Vietnam was reversed).* New York: McKay, 1969.

Hughes, Emmet John. *The Ordeal of Power: A Political Memoir of the Eisenhower Years.* New York: Atheneum, 1963.

Hughes, John. *Indonesian Upheaval.* New York: McKay, 1967.

Hull, Cordell. *The Memoirs of Cordell Hull.* Vol. II. New York: Macmillan, 1948.

Huyen, N. Khac. *Vision Accomplished? The Enigma of Ho Chi Minh.* New York: Macmillan, 1971.

"Indonesia: Plans and Prospects," Eight Talks on Indonesia's New Economic Outlook, *Asia,* Autumn 1970, pp. 1–138.

Isaacs, Harold R. *No Peace for Asia.* New York: Macmillan, 1947.

Johnson, Lyndon Baines. *The Vantage Point: Perspectives of the Presidency, 1963–1969.* New York: Holt, Rinehart and Winston, 1971.

Johnson, U. Alexis. "The Pacific Basin," *Pacific Community,* October 1969, pp. 11–19.

————. "The Role of Japan and the Future of American Relations with the Far East," *Department of State Bulletin,* April 27, 1970, pp. 537–42.

Joint Development Group. *The Postwar Development of the Republic of Vietnam: Policies and Programs.* New York: Praeger, 1970.

Jones, F. C. *Japan's New Order in East Asia: Its Rise and Fall, 1937–45.* London: Oxford, 1954.

Jones, Howard Palfrey. *Indonesia: The Possible Dream.* New York: Harcourt Brace Jovanovich, 1971.

Jones, Joseph M. *The Fifteen Weeks (February 21–June 5, 1947).* New York: Viking, 1955.

Jordan, Amos A., Jr. *Foreign Aid and the Defense of Southeast Asia.* New York: Praeger, 1962.

Kahin, George McTurnan. *Nationalism and Revolution in Indonesia.* Ithaca: Cornell, 1952.

———— and John W. Lewis. *The United States in Vietnam.* rev. ed. New York: Dell, 1969.

Kalb, Marvin and Elie Abel. *Roots of Involvement: The U.S. in Asia, 1784–1971.* New York: Norton, 1971.

Kamm, Henry. Articles on Laos, *The New York Times,* October 26 and 28, 1969.

Kennedy, Senator John F. *The Strategy of Peace.* New York: Harper, 1960.

Kissinger, Henry A. "The Viet Nam Negotiations," *Foreign Affairs,* January 1969, pp. 211–34.

Kolko, Joyce and Gabriel. *The Limits of Power: The World and United States Foreign Policy, 1945–1954.* New York: Harper and Row, 1972.

Kunstadter, Peter, ed. *Southeast Asian Tribes, Minorities, and Nations.* 2 Vols. Princeton: Princeton, 1967.

Lacouture, Jean. *Ho Chi Minh: A Political Biography.* New York: Random House, 1968.

————. *Vietnam: Between Two Truces.* New York: Random House, 1966.

———— and Philippe Devillers, *La Fin d'une guerre: Indochine, 1954.* Paris: Editions du Seuil, 1960.

Lake, Anthony. "Lying around Washington," *Foreign Policy,* Spring 1971, pp. 91–113.

Lamb, Alastair. *Asian Frontiers: Studies in a Continuing Problem.* London: Pall Mall, 1968.

Lancaster, Donald. *The Emancipation of French Indochina.* London: Oxford for the Royal Institute of International Affairs, 1961.

Langer, Paul F. and Joseph J. Zasloff. *North Vietnam and the Pathet Lao: Partners in the Struggle for Laos.* Cambridge: Harvard, 1970.

Lansdale, Edward G. "Viet Nam: Still the Search for Goals," *Foreign Affairs,* October 1968, pp. 92–98.

————. *In the Midst of Wars: An American's Mission to Southeast Asia.* New York: Harper and Row, 1972.

Lasch, Christopher. "The Cold War, Revisited and Re-Visioned," *The New York Times Magazine,* January 14, 1968, pp. 26 ff.

Leacacos, John P. "Kissinger's Apparat," *Foreign Policy*, Winter 1971–72, pp. 3–27.

Leifer, Michael. *Cambodia: The Search for Security.* New York: Praeger, 1967.

Levinson, Georgi Ilyich. *Filippiny Mezhdu Pervoy i Vtoroy Mirovymi Voynami* (The Philippines between the First and Second World Wars). Moscow: Izdatel' stvo Vostochnoy Literatury Akademii Nauk USSR, 1958.

―――. *Filippiny Vehera i Segodnia* (The Philippines Yesterday and Today). Moscow: Izdatel' stvo Sotsial' no-Ekonomicheskoy Literatury, 1959.

Malik, Adam. "Promise in Indonesia," *Foreign Affairs*, January 1968, pp. 292–303.

Martin, James V., Jr. "Thai-American Relations in World War II," *The Journal of Asian Studies*, August 1963, pp. 451–67.

McAlister, John T., Jr. *Viet Nam: The Origins of Revolution.* New York: Knopf for the Center of International Studies (Princeton University), 1969.

――― and Paul Mus. *The Vietnamese and Their Revolution.* New York: Harper and Row, 1970.

McLane, Charles B. *Soviet Strategies in Southeast Asia: An Exploration of Eastern Policy under Lenin and Stalin.* Princeton: Princeton, 1966.

Mecklin, John. *Mission in Torment: An Intimate Account of the U.S. Role in Vietnam.* Garden City: Doubleday, 1965.

Millar, T.B. "The Five-Power Defence Agreement and Southeast Asian Security," *Pacific Community*, January 1972, pp. 341–51.

Mills, Lennox A., ed. "Southeastern Asia and the Philippines," *The Annals of the American Academy of Political and Social Science*, March 1943, pp. 1–150.

Modelski, George. "International Relations and Area Studies," *International Relations*, April 1961, pp. 143–55.

―――, ed. *SEATO: Six Studies.* Melbourne: Cheshire, 1962.

Moffat, Abbot Low. *Mongkut: The King of Siam.* Ithaca: Cornell, 1961.

Moon, Parker Thomas. *Imperialism and World Politics.* New York: Macmillan, 1926.

Morison, Samuel Eliot. *The Rising Sun in the Pacific: 1931–April 1942.* Boston: Little, Brown, 1955.

Morton, Louis. "War Plan Orange: Evolution of a Strategy," *World Politics*, January 1959, pp. 221–50.

The New York Times, July 26, 1969, p. 8. Excerpts from President Nixon's informal news conference in Guam on July 25, 1969.

Nixon, Richard M. "Asia after Viet Nam," *Foreign Affairs,* October 1967, pp. 111–25.

———. "The Real Road to Peace," *U.S. News & World Report,* June 26, 1972, pp. 32–41.

Nuechterlein, Donald E. *Thailand and the Struggle for Southeast Asia.* Ithaca: Cornell, 1965.

———. "U.S. National Interests in Southeast Asia: A Reappraisal," *Asian Survey,* November 1971, pp. 1054–70.

Oberdorfer, Don. *Tet!* Garden City: Doubleday, 1971.

Olson, Lawrence. *Japan in Postwar Asia.* New York: Praeger for the Council on Foreign Relations, 1970.

Paul, Roland A. "Laos: Anatomy of an American Involvement," *Foreign Affairs,* April 1971, pp. 533–47.

The Pentagon Papers. New York: Bantam, 1971. See also *The New York Times,* June 13–15, July 1–5, 1971.

The Senator Gravel Edition. *The Pentagon Papers: The Defense Department History of United States Decisionmaking on Vietnam.* 4 Vols. Boston: Beacon, 1971.

Peterson, Alec. "Britain and Siam: The Latest Phase," *Pacific Affairs,* December 1946, pp. 364–72.

Pfeffer, Richard M., ed. *No More Vietnams? The War and the Future of American Foreign Policy.* New York: Harper and Row for the Adlai Stevenson Institute of International Affairs, 1968.

Pike, Douglas. "Cambodia's War," *Southeast Asian Perspectives,* March 1971, pp. 1–48.

———. *Viet Cong: The Organization and Techniques of the National Liberation Front of South Vietnam.* Cambridge: M.I.T., 1966.

———. *War, Peace, and the Viet Cong.* Cambridge: M.I.T., 1969.

"The Problem of Indonesia," *Major Problems of United States Foreign Policy: 1949–1950.* Washington: Brookings, 1949.

Randle, Robert F. *Geneva 1954: The Settlement of the Indochinese War.* Princeton: Princeton, 1969.

Ravenal, Earl C. "The Nixon Doctrine and Our Asian Commitments," *Foreign Affairs,* January 1971, pp. 201–17.

Rees, David. *Korea: The Limited War.* New York: St. Martin's, 1964.

Reischauer, Edwin O. *Beyond Vietnam: The United States and Asia.* New York: Random House, 1967.

———. "Fateful Triangle—The United States, Japan and China," *The New York Times Magazine,* September 19, 1971, pp. 12ff.

Reitzel, William, Morton A. Kaplan, and Constance G. Coblenz, *United States Foreign Policy: 1945–1955.* Washington: Brookings, 1956.

Ridgway, General Matthew B. *The Korean War.* Garden City: Doubleday, 1967.

————. "Indochina: Disengaging," *Foreign Affairs*, July 1971, pp. 583–92.

————. *Soldier: The Memoirs of Matthew B. Ridgway.* New York: Harper, 1956.

Roberts, Chalmers M. "The Day We Didn't Go to War," *The Reporter*, September 14, 1954, pp. 31–35.

Romulo, Carlos P. *Crusade in Asia: Philippine Victory.* New York: Day, 1955.

Roosevelt, Elliott. *As He Saw It.* New York: Duell, Sloan and Pearce, 1946.

Sacks, Milton. "The Strategy of Communism in Southeast Asia," *Pacific Affairs*, September 1950, pp. 227–47.

Sainteny, Jean. *Histoire d'une paix manquée: Indochine, 1945–1947.* Paris: Fayard, 1967.

Sayre, Francis Bowes. *Glad Adventure.* New York: Macmillan, 1957.

Schlesinger, Arthur M., Jr. "Origins of the Cold War," *Foreign Affairs*, October 1967, pp. 22–52.

————. *A Thousand Days: John F. Kennedy in the White House.* Greenwich: Fawcett, 1967.

Schroeder, Paul W. *The Axis Alliance and Japanese-American Relations, 1941.* Ithaca: Cornell for the American Historical Association, 1958.

Scigliano, Robert. *South Vietnam: Nation under Stress.* Boston: Houghton Mifflin, 1963.

Seabury, Paul. *The Rise and Decline of the Cold War.* New York: Basic Books, 1967.

Shaplen, Robert. "The Enigma of Ho Chi Minh," *The Reporter*, January 27, 1955, pp. 11–19.

————. *The Lost Revolution: The U.S. in Vietnam, 1946–1966.* rev. ed. New York: Harper and Row, 1966.

————. "Our Involvement in Laos," *Foreign Affairs*, April 1970, pp. 478–93.

————. *The Road from War: Vietnam 1965–1971.* rev. ed. New York: Harper and Row, 1971.

————. *Time Out of Hand: Revolution and Reaction in Southeast Asia.* New York: Harper and Row, 1969.

Sharp, Lauriston. "Paradoxes in the Indochinese Dilemma," *The Annals of the American Academy of Political and Social Science*, July 1954, pp. 89–98.

Shepley, James. "How Dulles Averted War," *Life*, January 16, 1956, pp. 70–80.

Silverstein, Josef, ed. *Southeast Asia in World War II*. New Haven: Yale, 1966.

Simon, Sheldon W. *The Broken Triangle: Peking, Djakarta, and the PKI*. Baltimore: Johns Hopkins, 1969.

Smith, Gaddis. *Dean Acheson*. New York: Cooper Square Publishers, 1972.

————. "Last View of the Chinese Scene," *The New York Times Book Review*, February 25, 1958, pp. 3, 35.

————. No specific title but a review of three versions of Pentagon Papers. *The New York Times Book Review*, November 28, 1971, pp. 3, 30.

Smith, Robert Aura. *Philippine Freedom: 1946–1958*. New York: Columbia, 1958.

Smith, R. Harris. *OSS: The Secret History of America's First Central Intelligence Agency*. Berkeley: California, 1972.

Smith, Roger M. *Cambodia's Foreign Policy*. Ithaca: Cornell, 1965.

Solomon, Robert L. "Boundary Concepts and Practices in Southeast Asia," *World Politics*, October 1970, pp. 1–23.

Sorensen, Theodore C. *Kennedy*. New York: Harper and Row, 1965.

Spender, Sir Percy. *Exercises in Diplomacy: The Anzus Treaty and the Colombo Plan*. Sydney: Sydney, 1969.

Spiers, Ronald I. "U.S. National Security Policy and the Indian Ocean Area," *Department of State Bulletin*, August 23, 1971, pp. 199–203.

Stanton, Edwin F. *Brief Authority: Excursions of a Common Man in an Uncommon World*. New York: Harper, 1956.

————. "Spotlight on Thailand," *Foreign Affairs*, October 1954, pp. 72–85.

Starke, J. G. *The ANZUS Treaty Alliance*. Melbourne: Melbourne, 1965.

Steinberg, David J. *Philippine Collaboration in World War II*. Ann Arbor: Michigan, 1967.

Stettinius, Edward R., Jr. *Roosevelt and the Russians: The Yalta Conference,* ed. Walter Johnson. Garden City: Doubleday, 1949.

Stikker, Dirk U. *Men of Responsibility: A Memoir*. New York: Harper and Row, 1965.

Stilwell, Joseph W. *The Stilwell Papers,* ed. Theodore H. White. New York: Sloane, 1948.

Taylor, Alastair M. *Indonesian Independence and the United Nations*. Ithaca: Cornell, 1960.

Taylor, George E. *The Philippines and the United States: Problems of Partnership*. New York: Praeger for the Council on Foreign Relations, 1964.

Taylor, Maxwell D. *Responsibility and Response*. New York: Harper and Row, 1967.

————. *Swords and Plowshares*. New York: Norton, 1972.

Taylor, Telford. *Nuremberg and Vietnam: An American Tragedy*. Chicago: Quadrangle, 1970.

Thompson, Sir Robert. *No Exit from Vietnam*. New York: McKay, 1969.

Thompson, Virginia and Richard Adloff, *Minority Problems in Southeast Asia*. Stanford: Stanford, 1955.

Thomson, James C., Jr. "How Could Vietnam Happen? An Autopsy," *The Atlantic Monthly*, April 1968, pp. 47–53.

Tinker, Hugh. *The Union of Burma: A Study of the First Years of Independence*. 4th ed. London: Oxford, 1967.

Toye, Hugh. *Laos: Buffer State or Battleground*. London: Oxford, 1968.
Trager, Frank N. *Burma—From Kingdom to Republic: A Historical and Political Analysis*. New York: Praeger, 1966.

———. *Why Viet Nam?* New York: Praeger, 1966.

Truman, Harry S. *Memoirs by Harry S. Truman*, Vol. I, *Years of Decisions*. Garden City: Doubleday, 1955.

———. *Memoirs by Harry S. Truman*, Vol. II, *Years of Trial and Hope*. Garden City: Doubleday, 1956.

Trumbull, Robert. *The Scrutable East*. New York: McKay, 1964.

Tuchman, Barbara W. *Stilwell and the American Experience in China, 1911–1945*. New York: Macmillan, 1970.

United States Economic Survey Team to Indonesia. *Indonesia: Perspective and Proposals for United States Economic Aid: A Report to the President of the United States*. New Haven: Yale, Southeast Asia Studies, 1963.

The United States in World Affairs, 1954. New York: Harper for the Council on Foreign Relations, 1956.

Van Dyke, Jon M. *North Vietnam's Strategy for Survival*. Palo Alto: Pacific Books, 1972.

"Vietnam and After: What Lessons Have We Learned?" *Great Decisions 1972*. New York: Foreign Policy Association, 1972.

Vincent, John Carter *et al*. *America's Future in the Pacific*. New Brunswick: Rutgers, 1947.

Waller, George M., ed. *Pearl Harbor: Roosevelt and the Coming of the War*. rev. ed. Boston: Heath, 1965.

Wedemeyer, General Albert C. *Wedemeyer Reports!* New York: Holt, 1958.

Wheeler, Virginia Morsey. "Co-Operation for Development in the Lower Mekong Basin," *American Journal of International Law*, July 1970, pp. 594–609.

White, William S. *The Professional: Lyndon B. Johnson*. Boston: Houghton Mifflin, 1964.

Whiting, Allen S. *China Crosses the Yalu: The Decision to Enter the Korean War.* New York: Macmillan, 1960.

―――. "How We Almost Went to War with China," *Look,* April 29, 1969, pp. 76 ff.

Wicker, Tom. *JFK and LBJ: The Influence of Personality upon Politics.* New York: Morrow, 1968.

―――― et al. Articles on CIA, *The New York Times,* April 25–29, 1966.

Wightman, David. *Toward Economic Cooperation in Asia.* New Haven: Yale for the Carnegie Endowment for International Peace, 1963.

Williams, Lea E. *The Future of the Overseas Chinese in Southeast Asia.* New York: McGraw-Hill for the Council on Foreign Relations, 1966.

Wilson, David A. *The United States and the Future of Thailand.* New York: Praeger, 1970.

Windchy, Eugene G. *Tonkin Gulf.* Garden City: Doubleday, 1971.

Wise, David. "The Twilight of a President," *The New York Times Magazine,* November 3, 1968, pp. 27 ff.

―――― and Thomas B. Ross. *The Invisible Government.* New York: Random House, 1964.

Wit, Daniel. *Thailand: Another Vietnam?* New York: Scribner's, 1968.

Wohlstetter, Roberta. *Pearl Harbor: Warning and Decision.* Stanford: Stanford, 1962.

Wolf, Charles, Jr. *Foreign Aid: Theory and Practice in Southern Asia.* Princeton: Princeton, 1960.

X, "The Sources of Soviet Conduct," *Foreign Affairs,* July 1947, pp. 566–82.

Yoshida, Shigeru. *The Yoshida Memoirs: The Story of Japan in Crisis.* Boston: Houghton Mifflin, 1962.

Young, Kenneth T. *Negotiating with the Chinese Communists: The United States Experience, 1953–1967.* New York: McGraw-Hill for the Council on Foreign Relations, 1968.

―――. "The Special Role of American Advisers in Thailand, 1902–1949," *Asia,* Spring 1969, pp. 1–31.

―――. "United States Policy and Vietnamese Political Viability, 1954–1967," *Asian Survey,* August 1967, pp. 507–14.

Zasloff, Joseph J. and Allan E. Goodman. *Indochina in Conflict: A Political Assessment.* Lexington: Heath, 1972.

Unpublished Manuscripts
(copies in the possession of the author of this book)*

Black, Eugene R. "Towards a New Diplomacy in East Asia." 1968.

Devillers, Philippe. "The Foreign Policy of Cambodia." 1965.

*Some of the manuscripts were revised and later published or awaiting publication.

Ellsberg, Daniel. "Escalating in a Quagmire." 1970.

Everton, John Scott. "The Foreign Policy of Contemporary Burma." 1965.

Gelb, Leslie H. "Vietnam: Some Hypotheses about Why and How." 1970.

Hayes, Samuel P., ed. "The Griffin Mission Reports of 1950: The Beginning of United States Economic and Technical Aid in Southeast Asia." 1970.

Henderson, William and Wesley R. Fishel. "The Foreign Policy of Ngo Dinh Diem." 1965.

Honey, P. J. "The Foreign Policy of North Vietnam." 1965.

Johnson, Lyndon B. "LBJ: 'Why I Chose Not to Run,' " CBS News Special, December 27, 1969. (A transcript)

———. "LBJ: The Decision to Halt the Bombing," CBS News Special, February 6, 1970. (A transcript)

Lenahan, Walter C. "Japan's Expanding Role in Asian International Organizations." 1969.

———. "Japan and Southeast Asia." 1970.

Moffat, Abbot Low, Statement before the Senate Committee on Foreign Relations, May 11, 1972.

Nolting, Frederick E. "The Origin and Development of United States Commitment in Vietnam." 1968.

Simmonds, Stuart. "The Development of Foreign Policy in Laos." 1965.

Wood, Margaret M. "Forerunners of the Peace Corps: Pioneer American Teachers in the Philippines." 1961.

Young, Kenneth T. "The Foreign Policies of Thailand." 1965.

INDEX